The Nature of Socialist Economies

PETER MURRELL

The Nature of Socialist Economies

Lessons from Eastern European

Foreign Trade

PRINCETON UNIVERSITY PRESS

PRINCETON, NEW JERSEY

Library of Congress Cataloging-in-Publication Data

Murrell, Peter, 1950–
The nature of socialist economies : lessons from Eastern European
foreign trade / Peter Murrell.
p.   cm.   Bibliography: p.   Includes index.
ISBN 0–691–04246–2
1. Europe, Eastern—Commerce—Econometric models.
2. International trade—Econometric models.   3. Neoclassical school of
economics.   4. Capitalism.   I. Title.
HF3500.7.Z5E8525   1989   382′.0947—dc20   89–34333

This book has been composed in Linotron Times Roman and Helvetica

Princeton University Press books are printed on acid-free paper, and meet the guidelines
for permanence and durability of the Committee on Production Guidelines for Book
Longevity of the Council on Library Resources

Printed in the United States of America by Princeton University Press,
Princeton, New Jersey

10 9 8 7 6 5 4 3 2 1

Designed by Laury A. Egan

Contents

CHAPTER 4

Qualitative Information on Nonstandard Trade Determinants: Summary Statistics from Trade Data

CHAPTER 5

The Econometrics of Estimating Endowments Implicit in Trade Decisions and Measuring Country Conformity to Trade Models

CHAPTER 6

The Levels of Resource Endowments Implicit in Eastern European Trade Patterns: Estimates for Eleven Endowments

List of Figures

List of Tables

Acknowledgments

Of the many scholars who have given generous advice while I was writing this book, I would especially like to thank Josef Brada for detailed and encouraging criticism. Clopper Almon, Christopher Clague, Donald Green, Irena Grosfeld, Ed Hewett, Norbert Hornstein, Ioannis Kessides, Deborah Milenkovitch, Dennis Mueller, and Arvind Panagariya provided valuable comments and help with locating important data. For fine and patient research assistance on this book and related projects, I thank Cindy Clement, Barbara Hopkins, Barbara Robles, Lynn Rodgers, and Randi Ryterman. Financial assistance was provided by the National Council for Soviet and East European Research, the Pew Charitable Trusts, the General Research Board of the University of Maryland, the Computing Science Center of the University of Maryland, and the Scholarship Incentive Fund of the College of Behavioral and Social Sciences of the University of Maryland.

The Nature of Socialist Economies

CHAPTER 1

An Overview of the Research,

the Theories Underlying the Interpretation

of the Results, and the Conclusions

The stationary condition is that point of equilibrium to which we conceive all forms of economic activity to be tending and which would actually be obtained if new factors did not, in the meantime, create a new equilibrium. In the imaginary state of equilibrium all the units of the factors of production are employed in the most economic way, and there is no reason to contemplate any changes in their number or their disposition. . . . It is quite easy to postulate a socialist economic order under stationary conditions.
—von Mises, *Socialism* (1932)

The bourgeoisie cannot exist without constantly revolutionising the instruments of production, and thereby the relations of production, and with them the whole relations of society. . . . All fixed, fast-frozen relations, with their train of ancient and venerable prejudices and opinions, are swept away, all new-formed ones become antiquated before they can ossify.

. . . [The bourgeoisie] has drawn from under the feet of industry the national ground on which it stood. . . . In place of the local and national seclusion and self-sufficiency, we have intercourse in every direction, universal interdependence of nations. And as in material, so also in intellectual production.
—Marx and Engels, *The Communist Manifesto* (1848)

In the closing paragraphs of *The General Theory*, Keynes remarks on the powerful influence of the ideas of economists, both when they are right and when they are wrong. This remark comes easily to mind at present, on reading the extended analyses of the problems of the Eastern European economies and their possibilities for economic reform. Much of the discussion of the properties of the socialist economies, both academic and popular, is cast in terms that are directly derived from the standard paradigm of Western economics—the set of ideas that economists call neoclassical economics. The present book examines whether that paradigm is truly an adequate tool for analyzing the nature of socialist economies. In answering this question, the book develops new methods for analyzing the comparative behavior of economic systems and presents new evidence on the nature of the differences between capitalist and socialist economies.

This book originated in an attempt to view the basic differences between socialism and capitalism through the lens of neoclassical theory. By applying neoclassical theory in an empirical framework, I sought to discover the characteristic features of socialist economic behavior, but as the analysis proceeded it became clear that marked differences between the two types of economic systems were not a significant element of the results derived from the traditional economic models. Once the empirical analysis stepped outside the confines of these models, however, distinctive features in the behavior of the socialist economies became readily apparent. Hence, it seems that the most important determinants of the contrasting behavior of capitalism and socialism lie outside the scope of neoclassical theory. To understand the comparative behavior of the two systems, one must seek an alternative analytical framework.

In explaining the results of the empirical analysis, I have sought refuge in a Schumpeterian theory of economic behavior.[1] The Schumpeterian view point does not attach great significance to the claim that price systems achieve static efficiency in the allocation of resources, which is the focus of neoclassical economics. To Schumpeterians, the decisive factors in economic performance are the generation of institutional and technological change and adaptation to this change. In the Schumpeterian view, change can be best accomplished in a process akin to Darwinian evolution, in which new ideas come disproportionately from new competitors and in which adjustment occurs through the increasing dominance of the successful.

The ensuing chapters examine the neoclassical and Schumpeterian paradigms as rivals in interpreting the behavioral regularities of socialist systems. I use a particularly rich data source—foreign trade statistics —to discover those regularities. The approach is unabashedly empirical: the data analysis is descriptive, rather than centering on formal tests of theories. Nevertheless, this study does present new analytical techniques for dissecting the behavior of socialist economies, techniques that constitute a contribution to the empirical methods of comparative economics.

The present chapter guides the reader through the thickets of the analysis and foreshadows the most important conclusions. The orientation is provided in two ways. Sections 1.1–1.3 outline the theoretical framework by contrasting the Schumpeterian and neoclassical perspectives. These sections summarize the main sets of economic ideas that are used when interpreting the

---

[1] For the most complete exposition of the set of ideas on which I loosely draw, see Nelson and Winter (1982), who use the term "evolutionary" to describe their approach. Because I do not follow their exposition closely, and because the term "Schumpeterian" is more common, I use the latter term.

empirical results. Section 1.1 reviews the principal features of neoclassical theory and examines the role of that theory in the analysis of socialist economies. Section 1.2 considers some of the central limitations of that theory. Section 1.3 outlines the alternative theoretical viewpoint—the Schumpeterian perspective.

The second element of this chapter's orientation to the book briefly explains the methods used in the study and summarizes the main results that are derived from those methods. Because the interpretation of the results depends upon an understanding of the methods by which they are derived, the summaries of methods and results are presented simultaneously in Section 1.4.

The countries examined in this study are Albania, Bulgaria, Czechoslovakia, the German Democratic Republic (GDR), Hungary, Poland, Romania, the U.S.S.R., and Yugoslavia. I have been unable to settle on a single term for this group of countries that would satisfy all readers. The terms "socialist economies," "centrally planned economies" (CPEs), and "Eastern Europe" are each preferred by a different group of interested scholars. Therefore, I use all these expressions interchangeably to refer to these nine countries.

1.1. The Neoclassical Model and the Analysis
of Socialist Economies

The overwhelming majority of readers of this book, whether from the West or not, will readily agree that the socialist economies have much to learn from the experience of capitalism. Nothing in the pages that follow is likely to change anybody's mind on this score, and nothing is intended to have that effect. But I do hope to influence the way readers interpret socialist economic experience compared to that of capitalism.

The notion that socialist societies can learn organizational principles from capitalism has existed at least since the market-socialist debates of the interwar period. As those debates show, what precisely can be learned is largely dependent on the way capitalism is viewed, because economists' understanding of socialist economies, in the West at least, is very much a product of the way capitalism is analyzed. This could be no other way, because Western students of the socialist economies are trained in the same economics departments, learn the same economic theory, as students with more domestic concerns.

An important conclusion of later chapters is that emphases within neoclassical theory might lead analysts in the wrong direction when seeking to understand the comparative behavior of capitalist and socialist economies. It is not my intention to impugn neoclassical theory in general. The imposing edifice of modern microeconomic theory, especially the systematization of general equilibrium and welfare economics within the Arrow-Debreu framework, is a great intellectual achievement. Nevertheless, all theories shed greater light on some aspects of reality than on others. In this book I argue that the strengths of neoclassical theory do not lie in analyzing the features of economic behavior in which socialism and capitalism most differ.

The next paragraphs identify the key features of neoclassical theory and argue that these features are present in contemporary economic analyses of the socialist economies. In subsequent sections I discuss the limitations of neoclassical theory for such analyses and examine the central characteristics of an alternative: the Schumpeterian view.

The core of neoclassical microeconomic theory is the "competitive paradigm"—the image of an economy as a set of equally well informed agents engaging in arm's-length equilibrium transactions. Models of imperfect competition, oligopoly, and monopoly are elements of that paradigm, whose name derives from the jewel in the crown—the theory of perfect competition (analytically formulated in its Arrow-Debreu variant, applied intuitively in its Marshallian form). In characterizing the key elements of neoclassical economics, the following discussion focuses on this competitive paradigm.

The characterization below applies to standard economics as presented in textbooks of advanced economic theory.[2] It is at that level of analysis that the central characteristics of a discipline are most correctly identified.[3] Current research represents scholars' attempts to plug the holes in the paradigm, or even to bring about changes. (Indeed, in the next section, I use some of that research to show that economic theorists are also questioning important aspects of the competitive paradigm.) Thus, a summarization of the current, unfinished, research agenda cannot adequately depict the set of ideas applied economists are using in everyday practice. It is such ideas with which I am presently concerned, because applied economists, and not economic theorists, provide the accepted analysis of the socialist economies.

The competitive model views an economy as comprising a set of independent economic agents each making decisions on the basis of clearly known objectives and constraints. The objectives and constraints are invariably expressed as functions of tangible goods and monetary variables. The acquisition of information is usually examined only to the extent that this process can be placed on a par with the procurement of tangible goods: the competitive model concentrates its attention on the decisions made after the acquisition of information. A central focus of the analysis is on the adjustment in decisions that occurs in the wake of some exogenous change in objectives or constraints. In the study of the socialist economies, this focus translates most directly into the detailed examination of how producers' decisions change when the reward system for managers is changed. For example, there has been much delib-

---

[2] The best of this species, and the best exemplar, is Varian 1984.

[3] Nelson and Winter (1982, pp. 6–9) make this argument, focusing on an even lower level of analysis, the undergraduate textbook.

eration on whether one can design managerial incentive structures that produce results equivalent to those occurring under profit maximization.[4]

A central element in the competitive paradigm is the characterization of agents as interacting at arm's length through the price system. Prices completely describe the alternatives offered an agent by the rest of society. The passing of information between agents, and the exchanges they undertake, are always mediated by this price system. Moreover, it is assumed that all information transfer (in the form of prices) and exchanges occur when the economy is in equilibrium.

A central goal of neoclassical analysis is evaluation, invariably using the criterion of Pareto efficiency—whether there are opportunities to better the lot of one person without making another worse off. There seems to be nothing objectionable about this criterion as a necessary condition for good economic organization. However, as discussed in the next section, the domain of easy application of the criterion is limited. Consistently, the notion of Pareto efficiency is applied to situations in which information is constant and the focus is on the ability to allocate physical resources alone.

The reader might notice that in the previous paragraph, I used the words "economic organization" in a situation where that phrase might seem misapplied. The system of competitive markets hardly seems to conform to what one might usually call an organization. However, the "invisible hand" theorems—the results showing that the price system leads to efficiency —are consistently interpreted as implying that the best way to organize economic activity is the competitive marketplace. Here, of course, is the emotive power of the phrase "invisible hand"—the notion that one can enjoy the fruits of optimal organization without suffering the strong arm of bureaucracy.

Thus, one can distinguish three central elements of economic systems upon which the neoclassical model focuses. First, there is the characterization of the objectives and constraints of individual economic agents and the analysis of the changes in decisions when these objectives and constraints change exogenously. Because of the role that price-taking profit-maximizing behavior plays in the "invisible hand" theorems, the analysis especially focuses upon the effect of deviations from this behavior. Second, there is the notion that the price system is an informational mechanism that is sufficient to convey all necessary information between agents. Third, there is the claim that competitive markets are the most efficient form of economic organization.[5]

---

[4] For a summary of the literature on this subject and for conclusions about the nonequivalence of organizational bonus schemes and profit maximization, see Miller and Murrell 1981.

[5] Some readers might object that the foregoing paragraphs omit essential details of the neoclassical paradigm. (Those with such views might find it instructive to compare the above discussion with Varian's "Description of Microeconomics" (1984, p. 1), which is intended to summarize the content of his textbook.) However, I have tried to present only the very essence

I have proceeded to this juncture on the assumption that the competitive paradigm underlies much of the analysis of socialist economies. The remaining paragraphs of this section justify this claim.

One of the most profound and subtle ways in which a paradigm can influence analysis is in dictating the very categories of discourse. The analysis of the socialist economies is heavily influenced in this way by neoclassical economics. This point can be exhibited by reference to two important works on the Soviet economy: Hewett's *Reforming the Soviet Economy* (1988) and Berliner's *Innovation Decision in Soviet Industry* (1976). These two books are chosen for discussion here both because they represent the best examples of works in the field and because they deal with topics that are central in any analysis of the socialist economies—reform and innovation.

Hewett (1988, p. 14) states that any economic system can be classified according to three characteristics of its institutions: the incentive mechanism, the information system, and the decision-making hierarchy that defines rights and responsibilities. Each of these corresponds in a straightforward manner to one of the three central elements of the competitive paradigm identified above. The focus on incentives follows from the neoclassical concern with the profit motive, the association of profit-maximizing behavior with efficiency, and the concern with the effects on behavior of deviations from price-taking profit maximization. The emphasis on the information system is a consequence of the informational properties of the price system that are intrinsic to the competitive model.

The focus on hierarchy as defining rights and responsibilities follows from the organizational implications of the efficiency results of the competitive model. It is usual to interpret those results as implying that competitive markets define the optimal organizational form. If this is the case, then one can characterize economic systems by noting the extent to which they deviate from these decentralized markets—that is, to examine inefficiencies, one examines the degree of hierarchy. Hence, reform discussions usually center on "how much decentralization" instead of "optimal organizational structure," as if the two were equivalent.[6]

---

of the knowledge imparted to those primarily concerned with application rather than with research on fundamentals. In such a presentation, one should not be concerned with the nuances and caveats that are the daily life of research theorists. In applying theory, only the broad sweep of the discipline's lessons and the best known of its tools are relevant. The problems that occupy research theorists are largely forgotten, and this seems especially so in applying the results that establish the superiority of the competitive market. As Nelson and Winter (1982, pp. 7–8) observe, "There seems a remarkable tendency for discussion of [the efficiency properties of market systems] to throw off the encumbrances of the advanced learning and revert to a more primitive and vigorous form."

[6] Portes (1972, p. 629) writes that the most common way of describing economic reforms is in terms of the amount of decentralization they introduce. Nove (1980, p. 315) believes that

One might ask what alternatives can be used to define the central characteristics of an economic system. The focus would be on innovation, which here refers both to the creation of new institutions and to the use of new technologies. One might say that the three central features of an economic system are the process for generating innovations, the mechanisms that society employs to identify the most useful innovations, and the procedures by which society commits its resources to the most useful innovations. I have intentionally formulated this list of features in a challenging manner. After a more deliberative analysis, one might add components from the neoclassical paradigm, because societies really do engage in the allocation of resources as well as innovate. The point here, however, is that analysis focusing only on resource allocation might obscure identification of the characteristics that are most salient to innovation.

In fact, in examining innovation, Berliner (1976, p. 5) centers his attention on the "working arrangements for resource use," a reflection of the competitive model's focus on the allocation of resources. The elements of the working arrangements Berliner discusses (pp. 5–19) are prices, incentives, decision rules, and bureaucratic organization. As in the case of Hewett's categories, it is easy to see how this list of features corresponds to those dictated by the competitive paradigm.[7]

In introducing each characteristic of the economic system, Berliner uses as the point of departure the theoretical framework of Lange's (1938) seminal essay. Indeed, this use of Lange is consistent with much of the literature on the socialist economies, which explicitly or implicitly uses the market-socialist model to identify the possibilities for improvement in the working arrangements of socialism. The use of the Lange model is symbolic, because that model is an almost perfect embodiment of the emphases and concerns that lie at the heart of the neoclassical tradition. That model presents a vision of a socialist economy as comprising profit-maximizing agents, interacting at arm's length using equilibrium prices determined by the forces of supply and demand. Indeed, given that the Lange model was created when modern microeconomics was in its formative stages, and that Lange was one of the main contributors, one could claim that the market-socialist model was an integral part in the synthesis of the neoclassical paradigm (Murrell 1983).

So far, only the emphases within Western analyses of socialist economies have been noted here. Although neoclassical economics is not dominant in Eastern European countries, one can easily find similar emphases among economists who are at the forefront of reform discussions in those countries.

Soviet scholars might be ahead of Western scholars in understanding that optimal choice of institutions is a much more complex issue.

[7] The extra category—decision rules—is simply another aspect of incentives, because in general, the purpose of incentives is to encourage certain types of behavior. When using rules, the behavior is encouraged by stipulating conduct and enforcing it with incentives.

For example, on reading the essay by the Polish economist Winiecki (1986), which diagnoses the ills of the Eastern European economies, the similarity of the analysis to that of standard Western works is clear. In the characterization of Hungary's reform by Csikos-Nagy (1972), a highly placed Hungarian economist, the resonances from neoclassical theory are particularly strong. Csikos-Nagy's use of the expression "rational allocation of resources," his focus on the price system as an informational mechanism, his mention of the concept of Pareto efficiency, and his linking of efficiency to the price system are all redolent of neoclassical economics.

Kornai (1986 p. 1728) identifies some common elements in the ideas behind reforms and reform attempts in Hungary, China, Czechoslovakia, Poland, and the Soviet Union. These common themes were the need for the autonomy of firms (decentralization), the elimination of shortages, the focus on the profit incentive guided by appropriate price signals, and the use of the market. Again, it is easy to see how the emphases of neoclassical economics are directly reflected in this list of priorities. Moreover, ideas with similar origins are still alive. As Kornai (1986, p. 1727) observes, hopes for decentralizing reforms based on the Lange model still abound in Eastern Europe.

I do not claim that the neoclassical paradigm is central to the thoughts of economists in Eastern Europe, in the way that it is in the West. A simpler claim is sufficient for this work. Elements of that paradigm have come to play a part in Eastern European thinking, and indeed could have a significant effect on the direction of economic reforms. That is certainly not the case for the alternative paradigm considered in this work, the Schumpeterian paradigm.[8]

1.2. Some Limitations of the Competitive Model Pertinent to the Study of Socialist Economies

In the 1970s, theorists began to recognize the problems of the informational assumptions of the competitive model. This recognition has resulted in research that questions much of conventional economic wisdom (Holmstrom 1985, p. 200). Indeed, such research reopens debate on the relative informational properties of markets and central planning (Arrow 1987, p. 210; Holmstrom 1985, p. 207; Grossman and Stiglitz 1976, p. 252). But this new focus in the research of neoclassical theorists is only in its infancy, and the competitive model has not yet been dislodged from its dominant position in the set of ideas used by economists.[9] Although the limitations of the com-

---

[8] The work of Kornai (1980, 1986, 1987) might be an exception to this statement. Many of his ideas can be interpreted from a Schumpeterian standpoint, although Kornai himself does not give center stage to the "evolutionary" aspects of economic progress.

[9] For an example, consider again Varian's (1984) textbook. The new approaches are still

petitive model are widely recognized, it is still the ideas of that model which lie at the center of applied economics and policy recommendations.

I now turn to some limitations of the competitive model that seem to be particularly pertinent when using theory to examine the differences between capitalist economic behavior and socialist economic behavior. The following statements cannot be said to be literally true of all analyses conducted within that tradition, but they are certainly reflective of the basic theory used by applied economists, among them those who study the socialist economies.

1. The competitive model focuses on the examination of economies in equilibrium in which individual markets attain a balance of supply and demand. As Nelson (1981, p. 1059) has remarked, in a different context, "If equilibrium meant only a tendency for the better economic technique, the more effective organization, the more profitable firm to drive out competitors or to force their reform, there would be no particular difficulty with this concept as a tool for analyzing long-run economic change. The equilibrium concept, however, as it is conventionally employed in economics, does not depict such an economic process; it presumes the process is (always) complete." Hence, the competitive model excludes consideration of the processes by which economic change comes about (Arrow 1987, p. 203). This emphasis is consistent with the model's informational assumptions, because it is new knowledge—new institutional forms, new products, new technologies—which promotes change.

Given the focus on equilibrium, there is also a tendency to adopt the normative view that imbalance in any market is harmful per se. Hence, it is assumed that underemployment of resources cannot have a functional aspect. Moreover, shortages are often viewed as a problem completely independently of their consequences.[10]

2. The normative criterion of Pareto efficiency is ideally suited to analyzing the allocation of physical resources between alternative uses. However, this criterion has not proven as useful in evaluating informational activities, such as the design of internal organization or the generation and spread of new technologies. Indeed, Hirshleifer and Riley (1979, p. 1441) remark: "Information generation is in large part a disequilibrium-creating process [Schumpeter 1936], and information dissemination a disequilibrium-repairing process. . . . It does not yet seem that we are very close to having an efficiency concept that can be usefully employed to measure the dynamically optimal level of such activities." A subtle bias then ensues. Theory focuses on situations in which the normative criterion is applicable, and the policy recom-

---

treated as peripheral, within a final chapter. What I have called the "competitive model" is the subject of the first seven chapters.

[10] This statement, of course, does not apply to the works of Kornai, who has carefully focused on the consequences of shortage.

mendations of the applied economist center on facets of economic activity illuminated by that criterion.

3. The emphasis on equilibrium and Pareto efficiency interact to give a particularly narrow view of the economic role of entry and exit of firms. In the competitive model, entry changes the behavior of existing firms, forcing them to act like perfect competitors (Novshek and Sonnenschein 1987). McNulty (1968) points out how limited this notion of competition is, especially when one is trying to explain the sources of economic progress. Nowhere is there consideration of the possibility that new entrants might possess something that existing firms do not have, or of the fact that new entrants might destroy existing firms. The competitive model of economic progress then is Lamarckian rather than Darwinian.

4. The competitive model focuses on transactions between firms (and between firms and consumers), not on relations within firms. In the literature analyzing socialism, this focus translates into an assumption of the superiority of arm's-length transactions and the notion that bureaucratic interactions are inherently inefficient. This view seems to be stubbornly held even though *ex post* inefficiencies are the natural result of *ex ante* efficient decisions in the presence of informational constraints (Holmstrom 1985, p. 204). Hence, if the competitive model is applied without taking its limitations into consideration, there can be too much emphasis on prices as conveyors of information, and on profit maximization as the rational decision-making criterion. But there are situations where price information is not available—new products, for example—and where profit maximization simply cannot be implemented (Nelson 1981, p. 1059). In comparative analysis, the largest danger in this market bias might lie not in misdiagnosis of the problems of socialism but in overlooking important properties of capitalism—for example, the fact that a large part of the international transmission of technological information occurs within bureaucracies (Mansfield et al. 1982, p. 14).

The competitive model provides a compelling vision—all agents acting independently, gathering information that comes free in the form of prices, and behaving rationally by maximizing a simple criterion. Then, society attains an optimum—no slack, no shortage, no waste. Political ideologies and religious creeds can only aspire to such beauty of rigor, such promise of harmony. Nevertheless, vision is gained at some cost. If one applies this model to situations where information is private, where markets are incomplete, where there is imperfect competition, one must assume that every single agent uses a model of the whole economic system. "Indeed, under these knowledge conditions, the superiority of market over centralized planning disappears. Each individual agent is in effect using as much information as would be required for a central planner" (Arrow 1987, p. 208). This is a chilling insight for those who have used the competitive model, and its descendant market socialism, to analyze the problems of the socialist economies and their prospects for economic reform.

1.3. Alternative Views

Turning away from the competitive model, one must be content with a more eclectic style of inquiry. Because no single rival offers such a consistent, rigorous system, I borrow elements from a variety of sources in order to suggest an alternative approach to analyzing the differences between capitalism and socialism. Since major elements of the following arise from a Schumpeterian perspective, I attach Schumpeter's name to this alternative approach.[11] However, the following summarizes a hybrid of ideas, some of which are inconsistent with hypotheses often associated with Schumpeter.[12]

The alternative, Schumpeterian view begins with the premise that efficiency in static resource allocation is not important in comparisons between capitalist and socialist societies. There are several reasons why this might be the case. First, the perspective of von Mises, contained in the quotation that opens this chapter, is that static allocation is not difficult and could be accomplished by a socialist bureaucracy. Second, one might claim that the whole orientation of the apparatus of central planning focuses on resource allocation and that bureaucracies are not as inept as the folklore of capitalism portrays them. Moreover, there are in capitalist society, myriad static inefficiencies that might rival those of a socialist bureaucracy. Evidence consistent with these viewpoints is presented in Chapter 7.

The third perspective on resource allocation, which is explicitly Schumpeterian, is that the emphasis on efficiency and competition within a static framework is misplaced:

[I]t is . . . competition within a rigid pattern of invariant conditions, methods of production and forms of organization in particular, that practically monopolizes attention. But in capitalist reality as distinguished from its textbook picture, it is not that kind of competition that counts but the competition from the new commodity, the new technology, the

[11] I explicitly reject the use of the term "Austrian" to describe this alternative approach. Although much credence can be given to the Austrian assault on Lange (Murrell 1983), many features of the Austrian paradigm are unsatisfactory. For example, the Austrian emphasis on the informational properties of free-market prices seems excessive and Panglossian. There has been no attempt to take into account the neoclassical lessons on the informational properties of the price system under conditions of advancing knowledge. Moreover, in Austrian theory there seems to be no willingness to ask searching questions about the efficiency properties of free markets.

[12] I especially reject the hypothesis that large corporations are the most efficient means of undertaking all necessary innovation. This hypothesis seems to have been rejected by modern Schumpeterians. For the relevant evidence, see Baldwin and Scott 1987, especially the conclusion on p. 111.

new source of supply, the new type of organization. . . . This kind of
competition is much more effective than the other as a bombardment is
in comparison with forcing a door, and so much more important that it
becomes a matter of comparative indifference whether competition in
the ordinary sense functions more or less promptly. (Schumpeter 1950,
pp. 84–85)

Thus, the Schumpeterian view does not say that the neoclassical theory of
competition and static efficiency is incorrect, but rather that it describes features of capitalism that are of only secondary importance. Moreover, full
employment of resources could even be detrimental to economic progress:

A system—any system, economic or other—that at *every* given point
of time fully utilizes its possibilities to the best advantage may yet in
the long run be inferior to a system that does so at *no* point of time,
because the latter's failure to do so may be a condition for the level or
speed of long-run performance. (Schumpeter 1950, p. 83)

Consistent with such a view, one might mention Mansfield's (1968b, p. 117)
evidence that excess capacity is necessary for the introduction of innovations.

If one follows a Schumpeterian view, then, one explains the successes of
capitalism by innovation and mechanisms for change, not by any presumed
efficiency in static resource allocation. It is therefore natural to look toward
the same explanation for the differences between capitalism and socialism.

Studies identifying causes of the slowness of innovation in socialist economies usually emphasize two sets of factors.[13] First, there are the myriad
dysfunctions of bureaucracy—for example, the remoteness of R & D workers
from users of innovations. Second, it is usually assumed that the incentives
of enterprise managers to adopt technological change are diminished by features of the structure of prices, of bonus schemes, and of the motives implicit
in traditional career patterns. The conclusion follows that the most important
steps in speeding up productivity growth would be the decentralization of
decision-making and the creation of optimal incentives. Consider, for example, the following statement of Wiles (1977, p. 404): "The [socialist econo-
mies] are not catching up any more. What are they to do? To most Western
economists and to many Communist revisionists, the answer is simple: de-
centralize and revivify the price mechanism." This conclusion is completely
consistent with the notion that the competitive model provides a blueprint for
the ideal economy.

I do not intend to dispute here the view that bureaucratic structure or
incentives play a role in technological change, but I do question whether these
explanations are sufficient to explain the differences in innovation under capitalism and socialism. An alternative but not inconsistent explanation would

[13] See, e.g., Amann 1982, pp. 11–18, and Bergson 1978, pp. 43, 169.

focus not only on divergences between the socialist economies and the competitive model, but on the process of economic change.

The alternative explanation notes that the supposed dysfunctions of bureaucracy exist everywhere. The literature on innovation under capitalism contains many references to rigidities and to the gulfs between R & D, production, and marketing personnel.[14] Indeed, for organizations that must produce balance between routine and adaptability, such features might be optimal. The direct consequence of these features, however, is that a large share of capitalist innovative activity is produced by organizations and individuals outside the sector that is primarily affected by the innovation.[15] Innovation is usually followed by entry of new firms and firms from other sectors.[16] And these new firms are so important precisely because they are different from the established ones. As Arrow (1974, pp. 56–59) emphasizes, new organizations are often essential for change, because established ones are likely to have an irreversible capital commitment to existing arrangements. The contribution of the new firms is not competition per se, but rather the fact that they bring something that existing firms do not, and perhaps cannot, have.

The alternative explanation proceeds with the observation that uncertainty is inherent in innovation. Indeed, the range of possibilities and consequences simply cannot be specified (Nelson 1981, p. 1046). A new technology is a venture into the unknown, and consumer reactions to a new product are unpredictable.[17] Moreover, a significant part of technological change lies in learning-by-doing, the lessons of which take many years to assimilate and are not easily transferred.

Given the uncertainties in the development and use of new technologies, there can be no consensus on the optimal way to proceed. In fact, the optimum is revealed only after a long process of learning. Therefore, society needs a mechanism to generate experience with a diverse set of alternatives and a mechanism to use that experience in choosing between options. Moreover, there must be a means of shifting resources to the chosen alternative despite the difficulties of transferring the lessons of experience between organizations.

How do capitalist societies accomplish the process of generating alternatives, selecting among them, and executing the required changes? The process of free entry—new firms, firms from other sectors, foreign firms —implies that many innovations are undertaken and a variety of experience is generated.[18] The more successful innovators grow much faster (Mansfield 1968a,

[14] See, e.g., Mansfield 1968a, pp. 88–89; Utterback 1979, p. 54; and Scherer 1980, pp. 437–38.

[15] See, e.g., Mansfield et al. 1971, p. 16; Gort and Konakayama 1982, p. 1115; and Baldwin and Scott 1987, pp. 111–12.

[16] See Gort and Klepper 1982 and Kaplinsky 1983 for examples.

[17] Witness Akio Morita's (1986, p. 82) comment that no amount of marketing expertise could have predicted the success of the Sony Walkman.

[18] See, e.g., Scherer 1980, pp. 437–48; Utterback 1979, p. 48; Mansfield et al. 1971, p. 14.

p. 106), and firms that made the wrong bet exit (Gort and Klepper 1982). The process of growth of the successful and demise of the unsuccessful is fundamental because the lessons of experience are costly to transfer outside an organization. Growth and change is accomplished not so much by the effect of competition on the behavior of existing units, but by the changing balance of firms through growth and selection. This, then, is not the competition of Arrow-Debreu or of Marshall, but rather that of Darwin or Schumpeter.

The above discussion emphasizes that some economic activities must be undertaken within organizations. The competitive model cannot produce such conclusions because it does not analyze the way transactions are divided between bureaucracies and the market. Moreover, by treating bureaucracies as black boxes and focusing on the efficiency of arm's-length transactions, there is a tendency for the model to be interpreted as showing the efficiency of the market compared with bureaucracy. But such interpretation is inappropriate, and especially inconsistent with theory on the nature and causes of internal organization (Williamson 1975). Focusing on informational difficulties, this theory shows that some transactions are accomplished most efficiently within bureaucracies. Examples of such transactions are the transfer of technological information and the exchange of goods for which quality is difficult to ascertain.

The observations on the advantages of internal organization apply equally to transactions across borders. Therefore, one can expect that multinational corporations (MNCs) play a large role in the transfer of technology. Three-quarters of direct technology transfer by U.S. corporations is adjudged to flow to MNC affiliates rather than at arm's-length to licensees.[19] Indeed, it has been claimed that technology transfer is exactly the activity in which multinationals excel (Dunning 1983, p. 348). For example, Mansfield et al. (1982, p. 36) estimate that it takes six years to transfer a technology overseas to an MNC subsidiary in a developed economy, but the lag is thirteen years if licensing is the method of transfer.

Multinational corporations can also be instrumental in technology transfer through the exchange of new products. Presently 75% of R & D activity is directed at creating new products, as opposed to new processes (Scherer 1984, p. 448). New products are costly to exchange at arm's length because the value of new technology is difficult for a buyer to estimate, especially in view of the fact that learning-by-doing is important in using the item. For some new products, internal transactions might be the only feasible mechanism of exchange.

---

[19] "Direct" technology transfer is taken to mean that which is the direct object of an exchange, rather than transfer that is implicit in the exchange of a good. The estimate is from Vernon 1980, p. 737. Of course, such estimates, obtained from data on payments for technology, are highly imprecise.

Countries refusing to countenance the internal operations of MNCs lose two sources of technology: direct transfers occurring within organizations, and technology embodied in new goods that cannot be easily exchanged on the market. The centrally planned economies (CPEs) are such countries. Even joint ventures between Western corporations and CPE enterprises are rather rare (Zaleski and Wienert 1980). And joint ventures, in which a contract must be negotiated between two separate entities, are no real substitute for internal organization.

I have emphasized two features of capitalist society that might at first seem unconnected: the generation of and adaptation to new technologies, and information transmission within multinationals. But in fact the connection is direct. The above analysis simply emphasizes that price competition and static efficiency are only a small part of the story when examining economic success. Two other features of economic organization are more important. First, society must widen the bounds of possible sources of new institutional forms and new technologies, so both free entry and foreign firms are important. Second, the new institutional forms and technologies can best be spread by the expansion of successful early users and the contraction of the unsuccessful, rather than by information transfer between institutions. Hence, one emphasizes both freedom for domestic enterprises to expand (and to fail) and the importance of cross-border internal organization, the multinationals.

If the above views are correct, they have unique implications for comparisons of capitalism and socialism.[20] These implications are developed in the forthcoming chapters. The evidence relevant to them constitutes the core of this book. The next section briefly describes the methods used to obtain that evidence and the results derived therefrom.

1.4. An Overview of the Book and a Foretaste of the Results

In examining empirically the implications of rival theoretical views, the first task is to decide upon the type of data to use. In such a decision, one consideration becomes paramount. The most critical test of alternative theories in the present context is to examine which theory best explains the differences between capitalist economic performance and that of socialism. Therefore,

---

[20] I use the word "unique" after some consideration. I have reviewed the Western literature on socialism for mention of Schumpeter and use of Schumpeterian ideas and have found little. It is significant that, in contrast to the use of Schumpeter in the present work, Berliner 1976, pp. 3, 323, cites Schumpeter only to establish the connection between innovation and profit. Hanson (1982, p. 429) does use Schumpeter's ideas in exactly the way they could make their most profound influence. His remarks hint at the idea that "natural selection" could be efficient in choosing the technologies to be imported. However, the mention of Schumpeter is relegated to a footnote rather than given center stage.

one must obtain data that have a high degree of comparability across a wide range of countries, both capitalist and socialist.

There is one type of data for which there are fewer than usual problems of cross-country comparability. Because all foreign trade interactions involve two countries, any given foreign trade transaction is more likely than an analogous domestic activity to be reported. If one uses reports from many countries, therefore, trade data have fewer country-specific gaps and idiosyncrasies than do domestic data. Moreover, the transactions undertaken by one country are usually reported in the same way for all partner countries: the foreign trade data reported by one country are comparable across partner countries.[21] Consequently, one can use trade statistics to construct a rather complete and comparable data set. This is the set of so-called mirror statistics. The details of the construction of these statistics are given in Chapter 2, where I also examine some of the problems in the mirror data that have been necessarily glossed over above.

One point must be emphasized at this juncture. In focusing on international trade, the aim has been to employ information that sheds light on the fundamental properties of Eastern European socialism, especially compared with Western capitalism. The interest is not in international trade per se, but in what international trade interactions reveal about the more fundamental features of socialist economies. However, in order to use international trade data to reflect features of domestic organization, one must be guided by theories relating trade to the features of the domestic economy. Chapter 3 provides an overview of such theories.

There are two central elements in the review of theories. First, neoclassical trade theories are employed to generate formal multiequation models of trade. These models take the form of relationships between trade patterns and a country's stock of physical endowments (capital, skilled labor, oil, etc.). Because the neoclassical theories do not take into account any of the special institutional characteristics of the socialist economies, an important use of these models is to examine whether one can characterize the trade of all economies with the same set of relationships.

Two principal neoclassical theories are examined. The Heckscher-Ohlin (HO) model embodies the standard lessons of the neoclassical theory of resource allocation. The second formal model is of more recent vintage, being based on theories of imperfect competition in markets with *product* differentiation and *economies* of scale. This second model will also be referred to as the PE model.[22] The importance of the PE model is that some of the motivation underlying it can be derived from the Schumpeterian perspective (although the analytics are resoundingly neoclassical). Given the absence of a formal model of trade squarely in the Schumpeterian tradition, differences

---

[21] There are exceptions to this statement. See Chapter 3 for discussions of this point.

[22] See, e.g., Helpman and Krugman 1985.

between the results for the HO model and the PE model are used to indicate the effect of Schumpeterian forces.

The second element of Chapter 3 is an examination of how the peculiarities of socialist institutions affect trade patterns. As an example, one can cite Rosefielde's (1973) hypothesis that the socialist economies overexport capital-intensive goods because interest rates have been set too low. Such a theory could be called neoclassical in nature because it pinpoints failures in the informational role of the price system. Chapter 3 also uses the Schumpeterian perspective to formulate hypotheses on trade behavior. For example, that perspective leads to the prediction that socialist economies have a comparative disadvantage in markets in which entry of new firms is easy in capitalist societies, because such entry is one of the main forces of dynamism under capitalism.

Chapter 3 presents a detailed review of the trade theory of socialist economies. The result is a large number of hypotheses—some new, some borrowed—formulated so that they highlight the information about domestic economies that is implicit in trade patterns. Though some of these hypotheses are of interest in their own right, they are offered primarily to guide the process of using trade data to obtain insights on the fundamental nature of socialist economies.

The remainder of the book is devoted to empirical analysis, focusing on the hypotheses generated in Chapter 3. Two basic methods of analyzing trade data are employed. The difference between the two methods is dictated by the availability of the information required in testing the different hypotheses. For some hypotheses (for example, those bearing on the capital intensivity or the energy content of trade), one can obtain all relevant data —trade figures, capital and energy endowments—for a large number of countries. Hence, it is possible to examine these hypotheses within formal multiequation econometric models. This examination is the subject of Chapters 5, 6, and 7 and is outlined in some detail in the closing paragraphs of this section.

The results presented in Chapter 4 are derived in a less formal manner than through the application of multiequation econometric models. To see why some hypotheses cannot be tested within such models, consider an example: the prediction that socialist economies perform poorly in areas of economic activity that require salesmanship. No cross-country comparable data on salesmanship endowments exist, and in fact it is not even clear how one would exactly measure such an endowment. Nevertheless, the absence of precise measurement should not bar the examination of an hypothesis, especially because some of the most critical hypotheses about socialist economies have characteristics similar to those of the salesmanship example.

To examine hypotheses bearing on country characteristics that cannot be measured, I use trade statistics for goods whose production or sale is particularly dependent on the abundance of a specific characteristic. For example, data on the cross-sectoral importance of marketing activities allow one to identify goods that require much salesmanship. Then, to detect a country's prowess at salesmanship one examines the country's relative trade performance for those particular goods. By carefully constructing the pertinent product groups, by comparing matched groups of countries, and by creating informative summary statistics from trade data, one can derive results that bear directly on many hypotheses that could not be tested in a more formal econometric setting. Chapters 2 and 4 discuss in detail the methods by which such results are derived and the implications that can be reliably drawn from those results.[23]

The results in Chapter 4 show trade performance for a wide variety of product groups—commodities that are disproportionately traded within multinational corporations, goods whose production entails a large amount of pollution, and a host of others. The most important message from these results is the consistent picture that is revealed. These results show a pattern of differences between capitalist and socialist economies that is particularly conducive to interpretation using the Schumpeterian perspective. Here, only a sampling of the results to justify this conclusion can be given, because explaining the meaning and significance of many of the results requires too much space for a summary. Of the results that can be easily summarized, the following show the strength of the Schumpeterian perspective:

1. The centrally planned economies have a striking comparative disadvantage in industries in which free entry is common in capitalist societies. This supports a fundamental Schumpeterian prediction.

2. The socialist economies have a low level of imports in sectors in which the multinational corporations are important, even though these are high-technology sectors in which the socialist countries are known to be weak. This is consistent with the Schumpeterian perspective, which emphasizes that technology cannot be easily bought at arm's length by existing firms, but instead must be spread by the expansion of existing firms.

3. The socialist countries are successful in the sectors in which business concentration is high in the West. Hence, the socialist countries seem to be taking advantage of static inefficiencies in capitalist economies by selling in markets in which competition is less strong under capitalism. This could imply that the ability of the socialist economies in the static allocation of resources might rival that of the market economies.

4. Hungary and Yugoslavia can be viewed as typical of socialist economies.[24] From the neoclassical viewpoint, this is inconsistent with the fact that

---

[23] Among the issues discussed are the nature of the descriptive statistics that should be created from trade data, the properties of these statistics, the problems created by ignoring the effects of extraneous endowments, the appropriate groupings of countries against which one should compare the socialist economies, and the precise data used to create the categories of goods.

[24] These results on Hungary are consistent with the observations of Kornai 1986, which emphasizes that the consequences of the reform are largely to be found outside the state sector.

these two economies are much more decentralized than the rest of Eastern Europe. From the Schumpeterian perspective, it is consistent with the fact that the essence of the capitalist marketplace is a process akin to natural selection, not simply decentralization of authority within a given set of institutions.

The second major set of empirical results in this book is derived from formal multiequation models that link trade to resource endowments. The econometrics underlying these results are developed in Chapter 5, and the results, with their economic interpretation, are presented in Chapters 6 and 7. To understand the techniques used in these chapters, one must realize that more data are available for Western economies than for CPEs. In particular, for a wide variety of Western economies, Leamer (1984) presents data on the values for 1975 of eleven resource endowments—capital, three grades of labor, four types of land, and three minerals. The statistical procedures use these Western endowment data plus trade statistics for both socialist and capitalist economies to obtain estimates of the values of the eleven resource endowments that are implicit in the trade patterns of socialist countries.

The econometric procedures begin with the relationships derived from Heckscher-Ohlin theory, which postulates that trade performance is determined by a country's resource endowments. Using Western data, one can estimate the relationships between trade performance and resource endowments. At the most basic level of understanding, the estimates of resource endowments implicit in trade are found by entering the Eastern trade data into an inverted form of these relationships. (There is much econometric nuance behind this process of "inversion," but details are omitted here.) These estimates show, for example, the capital endowments consistent with the trade behavior of a country if that country's behavior had conformed to that implicit in the estimated trade model. (In the following, these estimates are called either "endowments implicit in trade" or "the implicit factor content of trade.")

The results derived from the econometric procedures provide a wealth of new information on the behavior of the Eastern European countries. For the nine countries, Chapter 6 presents figures on the levels of eleven resource endowments implicit in the trade patterns of 1975. Moreover, the econometric procedures also allow one to develop a picture of the temporal progression of the factor content of trade by using trade data spanning a number of years (1975–83).[25] It is hardly an exaggeration to say that no previous studies of the centrally planned economies have presented information approaching the content and scope of that in Chapter 6.

The results on factor contents of trade cannot be easily and succinctly summarized because of their great detail. In fact, the most important contri-

---

[25] Because the relationships between trade and endowments are estimated for one year only, the time-series estimates of endowments implicit in trade are much less reliable than the estimates for 1975. More detailed comments on this point are presented in Chapter 6.

bution of this element of the present book to the understanding of the nature
of the CPEs lies in the details of the results, details that provide much information both for country specialists and for scholars of comparative economic
behavior.

One central message does emanate from the results on endowments. This
is the reasonableness of the estimates, given currently available information
on the CPEs. Especially for the more orthodox CPEs, the estimated factor
contents present a coherent picture, and one that is largely consistent with
objective economic circumstances. The results certainly do not lead to the
characterization of the CPEs as having a structure of trade that is fundamentally
at odds with the neoclassical view. To be sure, there are some signs in the
estimates of behavioral causes of inefficiencies. A particularly strong example
is the relatively slow adjustment to the changing world energy prices of the
1970s. However, this inefficiency seems as easy to explain using the Schumpeterian emphasis on lack of entry as by employing the usual neoclassical
emphasis on the slowness of bureaucracy.

A central conclusion emanating from the results on the implicit factor
content of trade is that the basic neoclassical model—the Heckscher-Ohlin
model—seems to be eminently applicable to the socialist economies. This
conclusion suggests that one should develop formal measures of the closeness
with which each country's trade data fits the trade models. Chapter 5 presents
the econometric theory behind such measures, and Chapter 7 presents the
results, with their economic interpretation.

The results of Chapter 7 show that the trade of the Eastern European countries, on average, fits the Heckscher-Ohlin model more closely than does that
of corresponding market economies. Only two Eastern European countries
stand out as having poor performance: Poland and Yugoslavia. The poor
performance of these two countries on the econometric tests is absolutely
consistent with what one would expect on the basis of economic performance
in the years following 1975. Moreover, Yugoslavia's results force one to
doubt whether decentralization improves the allocation of resources in socialist
societies. These doubts are reinforced by the observation that Hungary's results are worse than those of all its neighbors, except Poland and Yugoslavia.

Chapter 7 also presents measures on the degree to which trade patterns fit
the product-differentiation and economies-of-scale model. The results for this
model present a striking contrast to those for the Heckscher-Ohlin model. The
relative performance of the CPEs is reversed. The Eastern European economies
fit the product-differentiation and economies-of-scale model—the PE model—
less well than any matched grouping of market economies.

The interpretation of the contrasting results for the two models arises naturally from the intuition underlying them. The HO model focuses on the ability
of a country to allocate physical endowments. That model does not reflect
upon the nature of product development, the role of marketing, the importance

of quality control, and so on. In contrast, the PE model focuses on the types of behavior that are characteristic of industries subject to product differentiation. In such industries, the rapid creation of new products is important, as well as the ability to promote these new products on world markets. As we shall see, the ability to produce and market new products is very much dependent upon those elements stressed by the Schumpeterian perspective. Hence, the contrast in the results for the two models can be seen as buttressing the claim that the Schumpeterian view is more powerful than neoclassical theory in explaining the basic differences between socialist and capitalist economies.

1.5. A Note for Skeptics

The data analysis summarized in this book was not driven by any desire to test a particular theory. Rather the process of sifting, manipulating, and pondering on the data has led me to a new theoretical outlook—the Schumpeterian view. The book presents the set of facts that led me to reinterpret the lessons of socialist economic experience. When each fact is considered in the context of different theoretical viewpoints, the sheer weight of evidence argues persuasively for the Schumpeterian perspective. No other broad theoretical perspective of which I am aware can explain the range of results presented in this book.

The theoretical interpretation I propose will seem unobjectionable to anyone accepting the empirical evidence at face value. Consequently, I do not expect the primary criticism of this book to come from those who accept the empirical evidence but disagree with the implications drawn therefrom. The main objections to the analysis will come from those who think that the assumptions underlying the empirical work strain credibility too much, or that the data have too many omissions or inaccuracies to show anything resembling my claims.

The following analyses do employ strong assumptions, and the data are less than perfect—the former being partially a result of the latter. There is no way to escape this predicament. The incompleteness of economic theory, the imperfection of available data, and the limits of computational capacity are enduring features of all research. This book offers a consistent set of results based on a reasonable set of theoretical assumptions, which do not simplify reality more than is traditional and necessary and which will be defended in later chapters. Thus, compelling objections to the results of later chapters would in all probability need to present alternative empirical evidence based on different assumptions. For the subject examined here, such a challenge would certainly require new empirical work, because many of the ensuing results bear on topics that have been investigated little in the past.

The feature of the data that will be most troubling to readers is the omission of trade between the member countries of the Council for Mutual Economic Assistance (CMEA). (This omission was not a matter of choice, but a consequence of data availability.) Because such trade has a very different pattern from that of East-West trade, one might be tempted to conclude immediately that the results are therefore necessarily flawed. I do not think this is the case, for reasons that can be adequately explained only in the body of the text. In particular, the methodology of Chapters 4, 6, and 7 does make allowance for data omissions. Moreover, Section 6.5 provides a detailed discussion of the biases that might result from those omissions and argues that the substance of the results would not be altered if intra-CMEA data were available and included in the analysis. Therefore, I ask readers to suspend their judgment on the effects of data imperfections until they have encountered the relevant arguments.

C H A P T E R 2

The Variables Used in the Analysis:
Their Properties and Sources of Data

Economics studies facts, and seeks to arrange the facts in such ways as to make it possible to draw conclusions from them. As always, it is the arrangement which is the delicate operation. Facts arranged in the right way speak for themselves; unarranged they are as dead as mutton.
—**J. R. Hicks (1971)**

The methods of many empirical studies in economics are constrained by the absence of appropriate data. This is especially the case for cross-national studies, for which one must negotiate the Babel created by differing procedures of data collection across countries. To understand the techniques of analysis used in subsequent chapters, it is therefore necessary to have a basic overview of the types of data that were available for this study.

The present chapter has a dual purpose. First, for those interested only in absorbing the basic results of this book, there is a brief description of all data used. The description aims to be as succinct as possible, given the requirement that readers should find sufficient detail to enable them to follow the material presented in subsequent chapters. This overview of the data is contained in Sections 2.1 and 2.3. Section 2.4 lists the regional groupings of countries that are used in the presentation of results in Chapters 4, 6, and 7.

Another group of readers might want to follow the procedures closely enough so that they could use the methods later. Thus, a second aim is to give information sufficient for any reader to understand the detailed properties of the study's methods. The material included to accomplish the second aim is embodied in Sections 2.2, 2.5, and 2.6. Most readers could skip those sections without any loss of continuity.

As the ensuing section makes clear, it was necessary to transform the trade data before it could be used in the analysis. This study uses the transformation that produces the "revealed comparative advantages" (RCAs) of Balassa (1967). These measures have been used frequently in empirical studies of trade, so the rationale underlying their construction is familiar to many readers. However, there is still much discussion on the appropriateness of their use and on the nature of their properties. I examine those properties in Section 2.2. The results in that section are new. The theorems show the conditions under which one can safely use the RCAs in empirical studies. Because these conditions are weak, the theorems justify the use of RCAs in ensuing chapters.

2.1. The Trade Data: An Overview

The present section focuses on the trade data. The source of information is described, and the transformations producing the ''revealed comparative advantages'' are defined.

This study uses trade data at both the two-digit and the three-digit levels of the U.N. Standard International Trade Classification, Revision 1 (SITC). The three-digit data, which contain 182 commodity groups, were employed primarily in creating the summary trade statistics presented in Chapter 4. For reasons best examined in Chapter 5, fewer than 182 commodity groups could be employed when estimating the multiendowment regression model. Therefore, the results presented in Chapters 6 and 7 use data on sixty-one trade aggregates defined at the two-digit level.[1] The raw trade data were all expressed in U.S. dollars, using the exchange rates employed by the United Nations.

The method of creating a country's trade statistics was determined partially by data availability and partially by a methodological consideration regarded as central to the present work. The present research aims to be truly comparative—that is, the results are derived using methods that treat all countries in an identical manner. Only by using such methods can one be sure that those results are the product of real differences between countries, not caused by some artifact of the data collection process.

If one insists on exact comparability of trade measures across countries, difficulties arise when a nation's report of its own foreign trade is used. The trade reports of most CMEA countries cannot be easily made comparable with those of Western nations. The U.N. and CMEA classification systems are so different that they make reconciliation at the required level of aggregation impossible. Prices within the Council for Mutual Economic Assistance are so far removed from world-market prices that the meaning of value measures is unclear. Moreover, because intra-CMEA trade is effectively done on a barter basis, one would need to create a whole system of product-specific exchange rates to convert intra-CMEA data to true dollar values (Murrell 1986). For these reasons, Vanous (1981a, p. 714) concludes that the official trade data of the CMEA countries cannot be compared with those of the market economies.

---

[1] In fact, even these sixty-one groups had to be further aggregated, in the manner to be discussed in Chapter 5.

For those reasons, I decided to use in this study only data reported to the United Nations. Hence, the trade measures for each country were assembled from the reports of their trading partners—the so-called mirror statistics, whose construction is described in much greater detail in Section 2.5. Thus, for example, Hungary's exports of wine were found by adding British imports of Hungarian wine, Swedish imports of Hungarian wine, and so on.

The mirror statistics do not cover the whole of a country's trade behavior. Because some countries, most particularly the Eastern European countries, do not provide trade statistics to the United Nations,[2] and because obtaining data from all reporting countries[3] would have consumed a prohibitive amount of research resources, only a subset of a country's trading partners is used.[4] Of course, in order to ensure comparability, the same trading partners are employed to construct each country's trade statistics. The subset chosen comprises forty countries, listed in Table 2.1, that together undertake approximately 80% of world trade and virtually all of non-CPE, non-OPEC trade.[5]

There are two possible issues of concern when evaluating the accuracy and usefulness of these mirror data. First, there is the problem of the omission of intra-CMEA trade. The exports of the smaller Eastern European socialist countries to their neighbors are much more concentrated in manufactures than their exports to the West. Of course, to a large extent this difference must be a result of the forces described in later chapters. Therefore, the important issue is not whether the mirror statistics reflect reality, for they do, but whether one can deduce important facts about the behavior of the Eastern European countries from these statistics, which reflect only part of their economic behavior. To answer this question, many more facts and much more theory are needed. I therefore postpone the relevant discussion until later in the book— in Section 6.5.—where the usefulness of results based on these mirror statistics is made clear.

The second issue of concern is that the mirror statistics often do not match up well with a nation's own report of its trade. This is true not only for the socialist countries but also for much Western trade. The problem seems to arise because different countries treat middleman trade in different ways (Marer 1978). Given Marer's extended discussion of this mirror-statistics problem, it seems that the main problem is in estimating the volume of trade and the trade balance. There is little evidence that one should be concerned when one uses such statistics to examine the structure of trade, as this book does.

From the reports of the forty trading partners, mirror trade statistics were

---

[2] At least not at the level of disaggregation required by this study.

[3] Upward of 150 nations.

[4] One country's trade reports at the three-digit level for one year consists of 40,000 items of information.

[5] For the relevant information on shares of world trade, see Kelly 1982.

Table 2.1
Countries Whose Trade Reports Were Used to Construct the Data for
the Dependent Variables

Argentina[a]	India[c]	Philippines[b]
Australia[b]	Indonesia[a]	Portugal[a]
Austria[a]	Ireland[c]	Sinapore[b]
Belgium-Lux[a]	Israel[a]	Spain[a]
Brazil[d]	Italy[a]	Sweden[b]
Canada[b]	Japan[b]	Switzerland[a]
Colombia[a]	Korea, South[a]	Thailand[c]
Denmark[b]	Malaysia[b]	Turkey[a]
Egypt[a]	Mexico[b]	U.K.[c]
Finland[b]	Netherlands[a]	U.S.[c]
France[a]	New Zealand[c]	Venezuela[a]
Germany, West[a]	Norway[b]	Yugoslavia[a]
Greece[a]	Pakistan[a]	
Hong Kong[b]	Peru[a]	

Note: Key to trade accounting systems:
[a] A country that reports special exports and special imports.
[b] A country that reports general exports and general imports.
[c] A country that reports national exports and general imports.
[d] A country that reports national exports and special imports.

found for seventy-seven countries, at the two-digit and three-digit levels, for a number of years spanning the period 1966 to 1983. These seventy-seven countries, listed in Table 2.2, were chosen by the author on the basis of size (idiosyncratic country features would have too large an effect on the trade patterns of small countries) and level of development (the poorest countries are unlikely to be informative in the present analysis).

The basic trade data comprises three measures. X_{ij} is the gross exports of good i by country j to the countries listed in Table 2.1. Similarly, M_{ij} is gross imports, and W_{ij} ($= X_{ij} - M_{ij}$) is net exports. The i subscript is taken to vary either over the 61 two-digit categories of the SITC, or over the 182 three-digit categories, depending on context.[6] The j subscript varies over the seventy-seven countries of Table 2.2, or a subset of these countries, as appropriate. Although in the construction of the mirror statistics only a subset of trading partners is used it is convenient to use the term "exports" instead of the more verbose "exports to the forty countries listed in Table 2.1." Also, an analogous meaning is attached to "imports" and "net exports."

[6] Or, indeed, over a smaller number of aggregates, which are used in the econometric analysis detailed in Chapter 5.

It is important to emphasize that Western and Eastern countries are treated identically when the trade measures are created. Even though it would be possible to obtain the measures X_{ij}, M_{ij}, and W_{ij} for a Western country, j, from its own trade reports, these reports are not used in constructing j's data. The trade data for Western countries are found the same way trade data for Eastern countries are found. Thus, for example, France's X_{ij} is estimated using the reported imports of all the countries listed in Table 2.1. No French data is used in obtaining this figure. Thus, Western and Eastern countries are treated identically when the trade variables are constructed.

X_{ij}, M_{ij}, and W_{ij} are summaries of only part of a country's trade behavior— that element conducted with the countries listed in Table 2.1. These countries undertake a larger share of trade within the West than in Eastern Europe. Therefore, for the nations that are of central interest in this study—the members of the CMEA—X_{ij}, M_{ij}, and W_{ij} cover a much smaller proportion of total trade activity than they do for Western countries. One would not want to use these mirror trade statistics in an analysis that focuses on the *level* of trade.

To avoid problems that might arise when using data on the absolute size of trade flows, one can transform those data to obtain measures of the *structure*

Table 2.2.
Countries Whose Trade Performance Measures Were Used in the Analysis

Algeria	Egypt	Jordan	Romania
Albania	Finland	Kenya	Singapore
Argentina	France	Korea, North	Sri Lanka
Australia	Germany, West	Korea, South	Spain
Austria	GDR	Malawi	Sweden
Bangladesh	Greece	Malaysia	Switzerland
Belgium	Guatemala	Mexico	Syria
Bolivia	Hong Kong	Morocco	Thailand
Brazil	Hungary	Netherlands	Trinidad
Bulgaria	Iceland	New Zealand	Tunisia
Canada	India	Nicaragua	Turkey
Chile	Indonesia	Nigeria	USSR
China	Iran	Norway	U.K.
Colombia	Iraq	Pakistan	U.S.
Costa Rica	Ireland	Panama	Uruguay
Cuba	Israel	Paraguay	Venezuela
Czechoslovakia	Italy	Peru	Yugoslavia
Denmark	Ivory Coast	Philippines	Zambia
Ecuador	Jamaica	Portugal	
	Japan	Poland	

of trade. Therefore, for exports and imports, one creates variables, $\tilde{x}_{ij}$ and $\tilde{m}_{ij}$, which give the proportion of country j's trade conducted in good i:

$$\tilde{x}_{ij} = \left[\frac{X_{ij}}{\sum_{n=1}^{N} X_{nj}} \right]. \tag{2.1}$$

$$\tilde{m}_{ij} = \left[\frac{M_{ij}}{\sum_{n=1}^{N} M_{nj}} \right]. \tag{2.2}$$

For net exports, one must use a different procedure for deriving a measure of trade structure. One should not, as in (2.1) and (2.2), make the denominator equal to the country total for the numerator, because that total for net exports represents the trade balance, rather than the level of trade. One should compare net exports to total trade flows in order to obtain a measure that shows the significance of net flows in any commodity category. Because trade can be unbalanced, total flows are measured by the average of imports and exports:

$$\tilde{w}_{ij} = \left[\frac{W_{ij}}{\sum_{n=1}^{N} (X_{nj} + M_{nj})/2} \right]. \tag{2.3}$$

Notice that the denominators of (2.1), (2.2), and (2.3) are identical if trade is balanced.

For the analysis that follows, it is important to notice a basic difference in the properties of the measures, X_{ij}, M_{ij}, and W_{ij}, on the one hand, and $\tilde{x}_{ij}$, $\tilde{m}_{ij}$, and $\tilde{w}_{ij}$, on the other. It could never be argued that the former variables are a plausible estimate of *total* trade flows, because a share of world trade is missing from the data used to construct them. However, one can reasonably claim that $\tilde{x}_{ij}$, $\tilde{m}_{ij}$, and $\tilde{w}_{ij}$ are estimates of the *structure* of a country's trade. Whether one thinks that this claim is plausible depends on one's view of the effect of the omission of intra-CMEA trade flows on the data. This matter is addressed in Section 6.5.

The $\tilde{x}_{ij}$, $\tilde{m}_{ij}$, and $\tilde{w}_{ij}$ are used in Chapters 6 and 7, in the multiendowment regression models. For the summary trade statistics used in Chapter 4, it is helpful to normalize these measures further, in order to obtain data that have a natural scale. Because $\tilde{x}_{ij}$ gives the share of country j's trade that is in commodity i, one naturally compares $\tilde{x}_{ij}$ with the analogous measure for the world as a whole. The resultant measures have an average value across all countries of unity. Thus, define the following:

$$x_{ij} = \frac{\left[X_{ij} \middle/ \sum_{n=1}^{N} X_{nj} \right]}{\left[\sum_{t=1}^{T} X_{it} \middle/ \sum_{n=1}^{N} \sum_{t=1}^{T} X_{nt} \right]} = \frac{\bar{x}_{ij}}{\left[\sum_{t=1}^{T} X_{it} \middle/ \sum_{n=1}^{N} \sum_{t=1}^{T} X_{nt} \right]} . \quad (2.4)$$

$$m_{ij} = \frac{\left[M_{ij} \middle/ \sum_{n=1}^{N} M_{nj} \right]}{\left[\sum_{t=1}^{T} M_{it} \middle/ \sum_{n=1}^{N} \sum_{t=1}^{T} M_{nt} \right]} = \frac{\bar{m}_{ij}}{\left[\sum_{t=1}^{T} M_{it} \middle/ \sum_{n=1}^{N} \sum_{t=1}^{T} M_{nt} \right]} . \quad (2.5)$$

All the analysis in this book compares trade performance in a specific good across countries. I make no comparisons, either explicit or implicit, of the numerical values of the trade statistics for different goods. Hence, $\bar{x}_{ij}$ and $\bar{m}_{ij}$. will give exactly the same results as x_{ij} and m_{ij}: the only difference between them is division by a factor that is constant across countries. The reason for creating x_{ij} and m_{ij} is solely that the results of Chapter 4 are more easily interpretable, when the data have a natural scale.

For obvious reasons, a statistic exactly analogous to (2.4) or (2.5) cannot be defined for net exports.[7] However, when examining "net" trade performance in a commodity, it is still useful to have a descriptive measure with a natural scale. Thus, define:

$$w_{ij} = x_{ij}/m_{ij} . \quad (2.6)$$

It is easy to see that if trade is balanced (2.6) becomes:

$$w_{ij} = X_{ij}/M_{ij} . \quad (2.7)$$

That is, w_{ij} is the ratio of exports to imports, with adjustments made for any trade imbalance.

The variables defined at (2.4), (2.5), and (2.6) are usually referred to by the name coined by Balassa (1967): "revealed comparative advantages" (RCAs). These measures are referred to here as "export" (x_{ij}), "import" (m_{ij}), and "export-import" (w_{ij}) RCAs. The meaning behind these measures is easy to summarize. For example, x_{ij} measures the share of j's exports that are in good i relative to the share of world exports that are in good i. Therefore, x_{ij} shows the export success in good i of country j relative to the rest of the world. This ease of interpretation underlies the use of these measures in

[7] Because the average value of net exports will be zero.

the present study. No doubt the same reasons account for the popularity of the RCAs and similar measures in the empirical trade literature. Moreover, the information content of the measures is readily apparent. If one finds that the RCA of a country is high for goods requiring much R & D, one can probably conclude that the country has a large endowment of R & D skills. Much of the methodological discussion in this book, beginning with the next section, is devoted to examining whether such a conclusion would be reliable.

2.2 The Properties of Revealed Comparative Advantages

This section examines whether the revealed comparative advantages really do reveal the structure of comparative advantage. The focus is on whether the RCAs reflect the comparative advantage in a particular good when the best-known model of trade, the Heckscher-Ohlin model, is assumed.[8] I do not consider whether one can make judgments about the factor endowments of a country from RCAs. The analysis justifying such judgments is left for later chapters, after the relevant trade theory is presented.

Hillman (1980) provides the starting point for an examination of whether the RCAs are suitable for cross-country comparisons.[9] Hillman (p. 318) analyzes the use of RCAs when comparing two countries that have different preferences and different factor endowments. He shows that in such cases the measures reveal nothing about factor endowments. This is not surprising. Some of the most cherished theorems of international economics fall in the presence of cross-country variations in preferences. It is unreasonable to expect the RCAs to succeed where the core of trade theory collapses. However, as Hillman shows, once one accepts the assumption of identical homothetic preferences, revealed comparative advantages do in fact reveal something about a country's internal character. The following discussion adapts and extends Hillman's analysis in order to establish the properties of x_{ij}. The analyses of m_{ij}, and w_{ij} follow by analogy.

Hillman's basic argument appears in Figures 2.1 and 2.2. Those figures examine two countries, a and b, trading in a multicountry world. Information relevant to a and b is depicted in Figure 2.1, which shows the production, consumption, and exports of two goods, Q^1 and Q^2. In order to depict the exports of two goods on one diagram, all other goods must be ignored. Thus, one must assume that the production levels for importables are already fixed.

[8] The analysis does presume that readers have some basic familiarity with the assumptions and techniques of analysis used in applying that model.

[9] Bowen 1983 has also presented criticisms of the use of RCAs. Bowen's critique centers on the interpretation of precise numerical values of x_{ij}, and in particular on the conclusions that can be drawn by comparing that measure with unity. Previous authors had used the value 1 to indicate the borderline between comparative advantage and comparative disadvantage. Bowen shows convincingly that unity has no special significance, but his argument does not invalidate the use of RCAs in general.

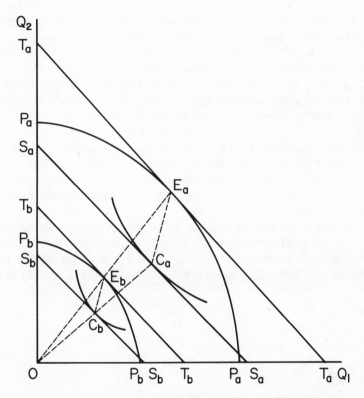

Figure 2.1. The RCAs of Two Countries Differing Only in Scale

The remaining resources are used to produce the exportables, goods 1 and 2. Also, the levels of imports are assumed to be fixed. The given levels of importables production and of imports are implicit in the positions of the production possibility curves and of indifference curves.

Initially, the two countries differ only in scale—the data for country a are a fixed multiple of the data for country b. (Remember that this is possible because a and b are just two countries in a multicountry world.) The production possibility curves are P_aP_a and P_bP_b. With the fixed world prices embodied in the slopes of the lines T_aT_a and T_bT_b, the countries produce at E_a and E_b, on the same ray from the origin. In order to pay for imports, the countries must trade down to the lines S_aS_a and S_bS_b.[10] (The distance between T_aT_a and S_aS_a and T_bT_b and S_bS_b represent the total value of imports, which is fixed.) They then consume at C_a and C_b (which are on the same ray from the origin, given identical homothetic preferences) and export both goods.

[10] Note that, because the countries differ only by a factor of proportionality, $OT_a / OT_b = OS_a / OS_b$.

The fact that the countries have identical revealed comparative advantages follows from simple geometry. Because the two countries differ only in scale, $OC_a/OC_b = OE_a/OE_b$ and $OT_a/OT_b = OS_a/OS_b$. Hence, OC_aE_a and OC_bE_b are congruent triangles, and the rays along which the countries export, C_aE_a and C_bE_b, are parallel. Therefore, the set of lines relevant to a and those relevant to b are identical except for a scale factor. Country a's data can be found by multiplying country b's data by a fixed parameter. Hence, the value of exports of each good as a proportion of total trade is the same in each country, and the numerators of the RCAs for each good are identical for each country. Given that the denominators are equal by definition, it follows that $x_{ia} = x_{ib}$ for $i = 1, 2$. The RCAs accomplish the task of appropriately adjusting for scale, in a world that satisfies the standard Heckscher-Ohlin model of trade.

Now we must consider whether the RCAs give an appropriate indication when there are differences other than scale between the countries. Consider a change in the factor endowments of country a that preserves the free-trade value of gross output. The endowment of the factor used intensively in the

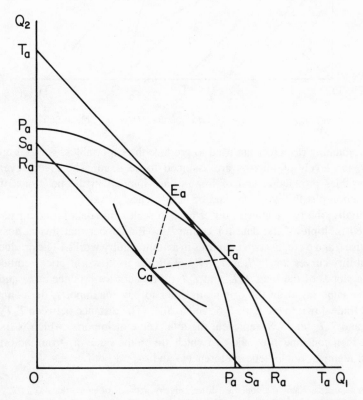

Figure 2.2. The Change in a Country's RCAs When Factor Endowments Change

production of good 1 increases. The effect of this change is depicted in Figure 2.2. The production possibility curve shifts from P_aP_a to R_aR_a and the new equilibrium production point will be F_a. Because the value of gross output and the total value of exports remain the same, the consumption point is still C_a. The exports of good 1 increase, and the exports of good 2 decline. The RCA for country b has not changed from that depicted in Figure 2.1, so it immediately follows that in the new situation $x_{1a} > x_{1b}$ and $x_{2a} < x_{2b}$. The RCAs indicate the appropriate information concerning the relative comparative advantages of the two countries.

One can extend this analysis to the case of a change in tastes of one country—a movement from the original position in which the countries have identical homothetic preferences. This change is depicted for country a in Figure 2.3. All initial information for a is identical to that in Figure 2.1. Tastes in a then shift so that more of good 2 and less of good 1 is consumed, when prices and income remain constant. The best attainable indifference curve becomes I_n, rather than I_a, with the consequent movement of the consumption point from C_a to C_n. As the RCAs for country b remain the same

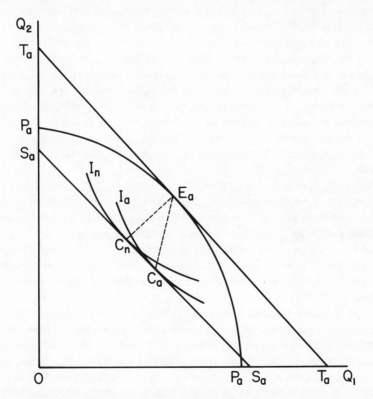

Figure 2.3. The Change in a Country's RCAs When Preferences Change

as in Figure 2.1, simple geometry then shows that $x_{1a} > x_{1b}$ and $x_{2a} < x_{2b}$: the fact that country a has relatively greater preference for good 2 means that its export performance on good 2 declines relative to that of country b.

It is easy to see that the above argument could be used to establish the properties of the m_{ij} and that these measures behave in the same way as the x_{ij}. The w_{ij}, however, cannot easily be discussed in the context of the Heckscher-Ohlin model. In that context, they are equal to either zero or infinity (that is, they trivially reflect comparative advantage). Hence, examination of the properties of the w_{ij} must await the introduction of intraindustry trade, which is discussed in Chapters 3 and 4.

Although the above arguments are intuitively convincing, one might choose to object to several assumptions made to facilitate diagrammatic analysis. It was assumed that the value of total exports of the country remained unchanged when factor endowments changed. Also, world prices were assumed constant. If one is willing to use an algebraic analysis, these assumptions can be relaxed. Hillman (1980) did begin to provide such an analysis, but he went little beyond Figure 2.2 because he assumed that all trade flows were constant except the exports of good i by country a. His assumptions were therefore unsatisfactory because they implied that no other country reacted to the change in exports of country a. For this reason trade was unbalanced in Hillman's study.

The algebraic analysis examines the effect that an increase in a country's exports of one good would have on world trade. It assumes that all countries react to the change in prices caused by the initial change in resource endowments, or tastes, of one country. Because many readers will regard the diagrammatic argument as convincing, and because there are many details with which the average reader will not be concerned, I relegate the algebraic argument to Appendix A. Here, however, it is appropriate to summarize the results.

Appendix A examines the effect of an increase in X_{ij}, the exports of good i by country j, which causes all other countries to adjust their trade flows because of price effects. It is assumed that the change in X_{ij} was caused by a change in factor endowments giving country j a greater ability to export good i. Appendix A formulates the conditions under which the change in exports results in an appropriate change in x_{ij}. (Of course, all the results of the appendix can be trivially adapted to reflect upon the relation between M_{ij} and m_{ij}.)

Appendix A contains two theorems: the first examining changes in the absolute size of a particular RCA, the second focusing on the relative changes in the RCAs of two countries. Theorem A.1 analyzes the conditions under which x_{ij} increases when X_{ij} increases. These conditions are a function of the share of good i in j's trade, of the share of j in world trade and production, and of the demand elasticity of good i. Details are in the appendix; here, an example will suffice to show that the conditions are not stringent.

Theorem 1 implies that if good i accounts for less than 20% of country j's trade, and if j accounts for less than 20% of world trade in i and for less than 20% of the world gross national product (GNP), then x_{ij} has the requisite properties if the elasticity of demand for i is greater than $1/3$. In 1975, the national income of the world's largest country, the United States, was less than 20% of world income (Kravis et al. 1982, pp. 12, 345) and U.S. exports in 1979 were less than 13% of world exports (Kelly 1982). Also, in a study using a classification with eighty commodities, Kravis, et al. (1982, pp. 360–63) found only six demand elasticities under $1/3$. It is obvious that the overwhelming majority of cases must fit within this one numerical example. Moreover, there are trade-offs between the size of the trade shares and the elasticity value. Hence, Theorem A.1 can be used to justify the use of RCAs in the vast majority of cases examined in the present work.

Theorem A.2 (in Appendix A) compares the RCA of country j in good i to that of another exporter of i, country t. It establishes the conditions under which the ratio x_{ij}/x_{it} rises as a result of the increase in X_{ij}. These conditions are much weaker than those of Theorem A.1. The ratio will rise if good i accounts for less than 50% of j's total exports. Thus, one could use the RCAs in comparisons between net exporters of good i, even in situations in which one is unsure whether the absolute values of the RCAs have the required properties.

The results of this section reflect on the use of RCAs as properties of goods. These results do not consider the question of making inferences about factor endowments from knowledge of RCAs, which must be addressed in different ways according to the type of analysis conducted. Hence, answers are reserved until Chapters 4 and 6, when those analyses are conducted.

2.3. The Measurement of Factor Endowments

In the econometric analyses of later chapters, methods for estimating variables describing features of the domestic Eastern European economies are set out. These methods combine trade measures for all countries and Western data on domestic variables. In this section, those latter variables are described briefly; Section 2.6 provides more detail. The information in the present section should be sufficient for most readers.

Those who indulge themselves in comparative economic research know that it is an arduous task to obtain a consistent data set spanning a large number of countries. Therefore, this author is fortunate to be able to utilize published data on exactly those factor endowments that are most relevant to international trade patterns. Leamer (1984) gives information on eleven variables across sixty countries for both 1958 and 1975. The data for the latter year are used in this study. The intersection of the set of countries chosen by Leamer and the set in Table 2.2, for which trade measures have been constructed, comprises forty-six countries.[11] These are listed in Table 2.3 and are the ones called "Western" in the econometric studies of later chapters. Here are the factor endowments Leamer (1984) uses.

- Capital stock, in millions of current U.S.$
- Number of professional and technical workers, in thousands
- Number of nonprofessional literate workers, in thousands
- Number of illiterate workers, in thousands
- Area of tropical land, in thousands of hectares
- Area of dry land (desert and steppe), in thousands of hectares
- Area of humid mesothermal land, in thousands of hectares
- Area of humid microthermal land, in thousands of hectares
- Value of coal production, in thousands of current U.S.$
- Value of mineral production, in thousands of current U.S.$
- Value of oil and gas production, in thousands of current U.S.$

The estimating equations derived in Chapter 6 use resource endowments measured in per capita terms. The names and definitions of these per capita endowments are as follows:

Capital stock: Per capita capital stock, in thousands of current U.S.$ per person

Table 2.3.
Western Countries Used in Estimating Trade Equations

Argentina	Finland[a]	Jamaica	Philippines
Australia[a]	France[a]	Japan[a]	Portugal[a]
Austria[a]	Germany, West[a]	Korea, South	Singapore
Belgium[a]	Greece[a]	Malaysia	Sri Lanka
Brazil	Hong Kong[b]	Mexico	Spain[a]
Canada[a]	Iceland[a]	Netherlands[a]	Sweden[a]
Chile	India	New Zealand[a]	Switzerland[a]
Columbia	Indonesia	Nigeria	Thailand
Costa Rica	Ireland[a]	Norway[a]	Turkey[a]
Denmark[a]	Israel	Panama	U.K.[a]
Ecuador	Italy[a]	Paraguay	U.S.[a]
Egypt		Peru	

[a] Member of the Organization for Economic Cooperation and Development (OECD).
[b] Data on central government spending (CGS) unavailable.

[11] I chose the list in Table 2.1 before Leamer's study was published. Given the set of countries that were in Leamer's study and not included in that list (Malta, Honduras, etc.), there seemed to be no compelling reason to reverse the decisions that had led to the construction of that list. The logic underlying that decision was adumbrated in Section 2.1.

Technical labor: Proportion of population that is professional and technical
  workers
Educated labor: Proportion of population that is nonprofessional literate
  workers
Illiterate labor: Proportion of population that is illiterate workers
Tropical land: Hectares of tropical land per person
Dry land: Hectares of dry land (desert and steppe) per person
Warm land: Hectares of humid mesothermal land per person
Cold land: Hectares of humid microthermal land per person
Coal: Value of coal production per person, in current U.S.$
Ores: Value of mineral production per person, in current U.S.$
Oil and gas: Value of oil and gas production per person, in current U.S.$

Many theories of trade could be used to justify the inclusion of a measure
of the level of development in the estimating equation (see Section 3.3, below). The most obvious proxy for such a measure is income per person.
Therefore, data on GDP (gross domestic product per capita, as a percentage
of that in the United States) have been used.

In some checks on the robustness of the results of Chapter 7, I attempt to
control for the effects of government intervention in the economy. It is difficult
to measure such intervention. but given the countries that are the focus of
this study, it is useful in Chapter 7 to experiment with a proxy for the effect
of government, no matter how rudimentary the data. Thus, CGS, central
government spending as a proportion of gross domestic product, is used to
proxy the extent of government intervention in the economy.

2.4. The Country Groupings Used
in the Presentation of the Results

When the results are presented in later chapters, country aggregates are
used. The purpose of this is twofold. First, because ''irrelevant'' resource
endowments are likely to be closer to world relative levels for groups of
countries than for individual countries, conclusions made about the variable
under scrutiny are more reliable. Second, it is useful to have groups of countries against which to compare Eastern Europe. Often a theoretical question
can be best answered by placing the behavior of centrally planned economies
as a whole against the behavior of a suitably chosen control group of market
economies.

Seven country groupings are used in the results. The rationale for construction of these groups and their membership, is as follows:

1. ''All.'' This group includes the seventy-seven countries listed in Table
2.2. These countries provide a cross-section of the world's countries at all
levels of development.

2. ''Market.'' The forty-six market-capitalist economies listed in Table

2.3.[12] This grouping provides a broad cross-section of market economies, both developed and developing. In 1975 these countries had an average per capita GDP equal to 44.5% of the U.S. level.[13]

3. "OECD."This group includes the countries of the OECD (Organization for Economic Cooperation and Development), noted in Table 2.3. These countries provide results that are representative of the behavior of the most developed market economies.[14] The 1975 average per capita GDP was 66.2% of the U.S. level.

4. "Market minus OECD." After removing the OECD countries, the remaining twenty-three countries of group 2 constitute a sample of developing mixed economies. The 1975 per capita GDP was 22.5% of the U.S. level.

5. "Low-income OECD (LIO)." The results of the "market" grouping will disproportionately reflect the behavior of the OECD countries because these countries account for such a large share of world trade. Therefore, one should construct a group of market economies whose income levels lie in the same range as those of Eastern Europe. This group comprises Austria, Greece, Ireland, Italy, Portugal, Spain, and Turkey. In 1975, its per-capita GDP was 41.6% of the U.S level.

6. "Eastern European 9." Nine countries in Europe have systems that differ markedly from market capitalism. According to Summers and Heston (1984), the average per capita income of this group, excluding Albania, was 50% of the U.S. level in 1975. There is, however, substantial disagreement concerning the level of national income in Eastern Europe. Marer (1985, p. 7) gives estimates for six countries averaging 38% of the U.S. level.[15] The Summers-Heston and Marer figures probably span the range of those available.

7. "Eastern European 6." Three countries in Eastern Europe are far from typical: the Soviet Union, endowed with a huge raw material base; Yugoslavia, with its self-managed market economy; and Albania, having a rather primitive economy. This last grouping excludes those countries. Estimates of the group's average per capita income relative to the United States vary between the 52% given by Summers and Heston and the 38% of Marer.[16] Groups 5 and 7 are samples of market-capitalist economies and CPEs that are as closely matched as can be obtained.

[12] The label "market-capitalist" is certainly an approximation for many of the countries in this list, but all the countries do have a significant market element in their economic systems.

[13] The income figures for groups 2 to 5 are calculated using the data in Summers and Heston 1984.

[14] Only twenty-three countries are listed in the relevant table, because Belgium's and Luxembourg's trade data are always reported together.

[15] These figures are for GNP per capita in 1980. Bulgaria and Yugoslavia are omitted from Marer's table. The change, from the Summers-Heston study, in year, in income concept, and in countries included would make little difference in the estimates. The difference between the two sets of estimates is primarily due to methodology.

[16] Again the latter estimates omit Bulgaria and are for a later year, 1980.

2.5. Further Details on the Trade Data

The present section provides complete information on the collection of the trade data. The basic units of observation are X_{ij}^c, the report by country c of its imports from country j of good i, and M_{ij}^c, the report by country c of the amount of good i that it exported to country j. (If, at this stage, the symbols of the variables seem to be inconsistent with those in Section 2.2, the reader should remember that X_{ij}^c will be used to obtain data on j's *exports*.) The superscript c varies over the forty countries listed in Table 2.1. The subscript j varies over the seventy-seven countries listed in Table 2.2. The subscript i varies over two different ranges: the 182 categories of the U.N. three-digit SITC classification and the 61 categories of the two-digit classification. The three-digit data are used in Chapter 4, the two-digit in Chapters 6 and 7. For details of the structure of these classification systems, the reader should consult the U.N. *Standard International Trade Classification, Revised* (1961).

All trade data cover annual periods. The data came from the standard U.N. international trade statistics computer tapes. On those tapes, trade flows are denominated in U.S. dollars, having been converted from domestic currency units by the United Nations. The exchange rates used to undertake that conversion can be found in the relevant edition of the U.N. *Yearbook of International Trade Statistics*.

The accounting systems used to record trade data vary from reporting country to reporting country in some important respects. If one were to use a country's own reports to construct the trade dependent variable, these differences might be significant. In this study, however, where a country's data is constructed from the reports of its trading partners, one would not expect the data to have any bias resulting from differences in accounting procedures. Nevertheless, for completeness, these differences can be noted.[17]

The basic difference between the various accounting systems centers on the treatment of entrepôt trade. Under the "general" system, all trade is recorded, whether it is entrepôt or not. The "special" system excludes trade activity conducted within duty-free areas that does not involve substantial transformation of the commodity. Further, some countries choose to report only "national" exports—that is, commodities that have had substantial value added domestically.[18] The accounting systems used by the reporting countries are noted in Table 2.1, using information from the U.N. *Yearbook of International Trade Statistics* for 1975.

Finally, in defining the trade data, the procedure for constructing the X_{ij} and the M_{ij} from the X_{ij}^c and the M_{ij}^c should be strictly defined, for the sake of

---

[17] The following summarizes Leamer 1984, pp. 241–43. Readers interested in further details should consult that work.

[18] Thus, they might record goods bound for reexport as imports but not as exports.

completeness. Let C be the number of countries for which trade reports are available. Then:

$$X_{ij} = \sum_{c=1}^{C} X_{ij}^c \qquad M_{ij} = \sum_{c=1}^{C} M_{ij}^c .$$

2.6. Details on the Data Used for the Measures of Factor Endowments

The data on resource endowments were taken from Leamer (1984), where the reader can find the most minute details of the definitions of the those variables (see especially Leamer's "Appendix B"). However, because some readers might find it useful at this stage to know more about those variables than is presented here in Section 2.2, I shall briefly paraphrase the variable descriptions contained in Leamer's appendix. (In using these variables, I have converted them to per capita measures. The following descriptions apply to the levels variables used to construct the per capita variables.)

"Capital stock." Found by summing gross domestic investment over the period 1948–75 and depreciating appropriately. Included in this measure are the value of dwellings, the assets of government, and the stock of inventories, as well as the types of capital more usually associated with productive activity. The data on investment were obtained from national accounts statistics, cumulated using a fifteen-year asset life and double declining balance depreciation, and then converted into U.S. dollars using current exchange rates. Leamer (1984, pp. 233–34) comments: "Of all the variables included in [the] study, CAPITAL is the one that causes this author the greatest discomfort, both for conceptual and measurement reasons." However, after making the most obvious improvement in the capital variable, Leamer (1988, p. 422) concludes that there is no "dramatic improvement in our understanding of the determinants of the commodity structure of trade."

"Technical labor." The number of workers in category 0/1 of the International Standard Classification of Occupations. This category includes a wide variety of professionals from scientists to athletes, economists to religious workers.

"Educated labor." Derived as a residual after subtracting "technical labor" and "illiterate labor" from the economically active population.

"Illiterate labor." The number of economically active workers multiplied by the illiteracy rate.

"Tropical land." The total land area in the zone of a tropical rainy climate. For this and the following three variables, no attempt was made to adjust for fertility, because there was no data. This climate is typical of Brazil or Indonesia, for example.

"Dry land." The total land area in the zone of desert or steppe climate.

"Warm land." The total land area in the zone of humid mesothermal climate. Includes Mediterranean, humid subtropical, and marine west coast climates. Dominates in such countries as Italy or the United Kingdom.

"Cold land." The total land area in the zone of humid microthermal climates, those experienced in continental land masses in temperate or subarctic zones. Dominates in Sweden or Austria, for example.

"Coal." Value of production of coal, lignite, and brown coal. Physical production data for each country is multiplied by world price in order to obtain monetary values.

"Ores." The value of production of thirteen minerals, of which the most important are copper (18% of the total world value of ore production), iron ore (18%), zinc (10%), and phosphate (7%). Physical production data for each country is multiplied by the world price in order to obtain monetary values.

"Oil and gas." The value of crude oil production (62%) and natural gas production (38%). Physical production data for each country is multiplied by world price in order to obtain monetary values.

Data for all years on gross domestic product, population, and central government spending were collected by the author. Summers and Heston (1984) provided the GDP. They took national accounts figures denominated in local currencies and converted the figures into U.S. dollars using a procedure that avoids the worst pitfalls of employing current market exchange rates. Population was obtained from the *Demographic Yearbook* of the United Nations. And Data from the International Monetary Fund's *International Financial Statistics* and *Government Finance Statistics* was used to construct CGS.

C H A P T E R 3

International Trade Theory and
the Centrally Planned Economies

In that time he learned that the world is all of one piece. He learned that the world is like an enormous spider web and if you touch it, however lightly, at any point, the vibration ripples to the remotest perimeter and the drowsy spider feels the tingle and is drowsy no more but springs out to fling the gossamer coils about you who have touched the web and then inject the black, numbing poison under your hide. It does not matter whether or not you meant to brush the web of things.
—**Robert Penn Warren, *All the King's Men***

The ultimate goal of the present work is not primarily to analyze the international trade of socialism, but rather to use trade data to understand the effect of economic system on economic behavior. The central assumption underlying this methodology is that the world is a seamless web, with trade patterns inevitably reflecting the internal character of economies. Those who doubt the reasonableness of this assumption for Eastern Europe should consider whether they would predict that the Soviet Union exports as many video-cassette recorders as barrels of oil. The question is not *whether* trade depends on the character of the domestic economy, but *how*. Theoretical ideas on the nature of that dependence are the subject of the present chapter.

I first examine the relationship between internal characteristics and trade patterns in the most venerated trade model, the Heckscher-Ohlin model. Consideration is given to the assumptions that make that model a description of the centrally planned economies. If these assumptions approximate reality, then the HO model can provide the theoretical structure for the data analysis of later chapters. Discussion of the reasonableness of these assumptions for centrally planned economies is reserved for the end of this chapter, after an examination of the institutions relevant to CPE trade.

Section 3.2 analyzes a recent departure in neoclassical trade theory—a model examining the effect of product differentiation and economies of scale on trade patterns (henceforth, the PE model). Although similar in methodology, the HO and PE models produce markedly different conclusions, in particular on the structure of the equations used to analyze trade patterns.

Moreover, below the surface of the two models' assumptions lies a crucial difference in emphasis. For the HO model to describe reality, it is not necessary that nations have any fundamental ability to innovate. In contrast, the PE model assumes that each nation is able to generate a unique set of products. This difference between the two models leads to a crucial element in the interpretation of the empirical results to be presented in later chapters.

The literature on the centrally planned economies has tended to emphasize institutional description and to downplay neoclassical trade models. Sections 3.4–3.9 discuss the predictions on the pattern of trade that can be extracted from that literature. To examine whether those predictions are based on sound logic, the discussion is given a simple structure that focuses on the underlying assumptions and on the variables considered to be the crucial exogenous factors in the analysis. Section 3.4 explains this structure, which distinguishes four main areas in which existing trade theories make assumptions: endowments, preferences, technology, and the decision-making environment.

Economic system can influence elements in all four areas, as shown in Section 3.5, which provides an overview of the institutions of the CPEs. For example, specifying the nature of incentives can help one characterize the environment facing decision-makers, or acknowledging the effect of bureaucratic organization on the size of enterprises can aid in describing the nature of technology. In each of the four areas, I use information about the differences between CPEs and market economies (MEs) to formulate hypotheses on the nature of CPE trade. These hypotheses serve as a focus for the empirical results of later chapters. They center especially on the comparisons of capitalism and socialism that are particularly constructive if one wants to distinguish between the neoclassical and Schumpeterian views outlined in Sections 1.3–1.4.

Section 3.10 argues that theoretical considerations alone are not sufficient to conclude that neoclassical models of trade are irrelevant to centrally planned economies. The argument draws on two elements. First, I point out that all economic models are idealizations of reality. One cannot deny the applicability of neoclassical models to CPEs merely by noting some deficiency in planning, for example. Second, I show that the typical arguments for not applying the standard trade models to CPEs are equally applicable, mutatis mutandis, to the MEs. One can only resolve whether neoclassical trade theory is more applicable to the CPEs than to MEs by recourse to empirical information. This is the information presented in Chapter 7.

3.1. The Heckscher-Ohlin Model

The present section examines the standard multicountry Heckscher-Ohlin model, focusing on implications for patterns of trade across countries. The purpose of examining the HO model, and related neoclassical models in Section 3.2, is twofold.[1] First, that model provides an ideal, a view of how an efficient economy trades. That ideal can then be used as a yardstick against which to compare the behavior of real-world economies. Second, the HO model provides a complete general equilibrium characterization of the nature of trade between countries. It admits a set of equations that can be applied to the examination of cross-country trade patterns.

The complete set of assumptions for the model is detailed in Appendix B of this book. Readers who are unfamiliar with the basic model are referred to Bhagwati and Srinivasan (1983) and then to Leamer (1984), which the Appendix B closely follows. Here I mention in passing only two aspects of the model—the extent to which economies are assumed to be similar and the characterization of producer behavior.

Heckscher-Ohlin theory assumes that technology and preferences are identical across economies. It therefore examines only one basic cause of trade: differences in the structure of resource endowments between countries. One could debate endlessly whether these assumptions on technology and preferences are justified, but the purpose here is to highlight the assumptions for readers. The issue is discussed in Sections 3.3 and 3.4.

In the usual exposition of the HO model, producers are assumed to be competitive profit maximizers, facing prices undistorted by any government interventions. As Batra (1976) shows, one could just as easily interpret the model to be one in which central planners make efficient production decisions.[2] Thus, the HO model is one of ideal capitalism (perfect competition) or of ideal socialism (perfect computation). There is therefore nothing in the internal logic of the model that makes it more applicable to MEs than to CPEs. Because relative applicability is something that cannot be addressed by examining the model alone, discussion of that issue is postponed until after information on the trade processes of CPEs is introduced.

Given the assumptions listed in Appendix B, one can derive the following equation system:

$$W_{ij} = \sum_{k=1}^{s} b_{ik}V_{kj} \qquad i = 1, \ldots, N \qquad j = 1, \ldots, T, \qquad (3.1)$$

where

W_{ij} is the net exports of good i by country j,
V_{kj} is the endowment of resource k in country j,
b_{ik} is a parameter, constant across countries,

[1] The new theory of international trade, based on models of product differentiation and economies of scale, is a radical break with Heckscher-Ohlin in terms of some of its economic implications, but the methodology of the two approaches is very similar.

[2] Similarly, Ishii 1986 shows that long-run equilibrium in self-managed societies produces the same relationships.

N is the number of goods produced,
S is the number of resource endowments, and
T is the number of countries.

The system of equations given by (3.1) is the element of the Heckscher-Ohlin model to be used in the present work. One can predict a country's net exports of each of the N goods traded in the world economy solely from a knowledge of its resource endowments and of parameters that are constant across countries. The constancy of the parameters means that they can be estimated in a cross-country regression framework.[3]

3.2. Models of Product Differentiation and Economies of Scale

It was precisely the prediction mentioned in the previous paragraph—that either exports or imports are zero—which spurred the development of new trade theories. Contrary to this prediction, there is a great deal of intraindustry trade, in which a country both exports and imports different varieties of the same good. The presence of such trade has long caused economists to doubt that Heckscher-Ohlin told the complete story of trade between advanced industrial nations.[4] However, it was only recently that advances in the analysis of monopolistic competition and product differentiation led to complete general equilibrium models of trade admitting the possibility of intraindustry flows. To date, the culmination of these attempts is the work of Helpman and Krugman (1985), on whom the following discussion draws heavily.

There are many similarities between the HO model and the new theories combining product differentiation and economies of scale (PE model). First, both theories assume that production decisions are made as if they were being made by profit-maximizing firms, powerless to earn profits in the long run because of the forces of entry and exit.[5] (Whether those decisions come about because of the conscious actions of planners or because of the pressures of competition is not addressed at present.) Second, both theories assume that technology is the same across all countries. Third, in both cases, aggregate demand functions are taken to be the same in every economy.

Given the above similarities, the two models are species of the same genus. The methodologies are very similar. The essence of the similarity is that the assumptions lead to the prediction of factor-price equalization.[6] Then, the choice of technique for the production of every good will be identical world-

---

[3] These parameters do change when world endowments or technology change, but they are constant across countries at any point in time.

[4] See, e.g., the references cited in Krugman 1979.

[5] This is not usually stated explicitly in the HO model, where the focus instead is on the zero-profit implication of constant-returns-to-scale. However, one interpretation of that model is that constant returns result from the entry of small identical firms.

[6] In the context of the PE model, factor-price equalization is taken to include also the equali-

wide. Given the assumptions on preferences, consumption decisions are also similar across countries. Then, the only difference between the countries that is relevant for the pattern of interindustry specialization is the structure of factor endowments. Predictions on interindustry trade are therefore the same in each model. It is the implications for intraindustry trade and specialization that separate the two models.

The difference between Heckscher-Ohlin and the product differentiation theories results from assumptions about the nature of products and on consequent changes in the specification of technology and preferences. The PE model assumes that products come in many varieties. Because of either an individual love of variety or heterogeneity of preferences across individuals, there is a demand for diversity within any economy. Any producer has an incentive to sell a variety different from all competitors, so there would be an infinite number of varieties if production at an infinitesimal scale were economic. The demand for variety must be combined with an assumption of economies of scale in order to generate realistic predictions.

In the PE model, every country produces a different set of varieties, and every country consumes all varieties. Therefore, if product differentiation occurs in all sectors, every country both exports and imports varieties produced in every sector: intraindustry trade results, in contrast to the HO model. Given the assumptions made on demand, and given the prediction of factor-price equalization, exports are a linear function of factor endowments weighted by the rest-of-the-world's share of GDP:

$$X_{ij} = \left[\sum_{k=1}^{S} b_{ik}^* V_{kj} \right] \cdot \left[1 - \frac{G_j}{G_w} \right]$$

$$i = 1, \ldots, N \qquad j = 1, \ldots, T, \quad (3.2)$$

where G_j is the national income of country j, a "w" subscript denotes the world, and the asterisk on the coefficients of the equation is intended to remind the reader of the difference between the source of equation (3.1) and that of (3.2).

An equation for imports analogous to (3.2) is derived in Appendix B. Then an equation for net exports, W_{ij}, in any sector is found as the difference. The resultant equation is exactly the same as that developed within the HO framework, equation (3.1) above.

The fundamental difference between the predictions of the two theories is in the existence of intraindustry trade. There is no such trade within the Heckscher-Ohlin framework; the alternative model predicts that a country both exports and imports goods that are subject to product differentiation. With product differentiation in all sectors, exports are given by (3.2). This

---

zation of the size of firms within one industry across economies. See especially Helpman 1981, pp. 321–22.

equation cannot be derived from HO theory. Under both theories, the equation for net exports, (3.1), is correct.

Behind the assumptions of the two theories lurk some major implications, which lead to a difference in the domain of applicability of the two models. This difference will be the subject of much discussion throughout the remainder of the book. Here I begin with a few remarks.

For both models, it is assumed that producers act as if they maximize profits and that the presence or absence of profits determines the entry and exit of new firms. In the HO model, the assumptions on producer behavior can be rationalized in two alternative ways. In a market economy, either capitalist or self-managed, one could postulate perfect competition with costless entry and exit. For a centrally planned economy, one could assume that planners have the requisite amount of information to produce welfare-maximizing decisions. If the assumptions of the HO model hold, the set of equations generated by that model are equally applicable to the ideal forms of the two types of economic system.

The same argument cannot be made for the PE model. When there is product differentiation and economies of scale, the profit-maximizing equilibrium does not necessarily coincide with the welfare maximization. From the viewpoint of efficiency, there is a trade-off between large-scale production, which reduces costs, and increases in the number of products, which enhance utility through variety. As Dixit and Stiglitz (1977) show, this trade-off is not necessarily resolved at the welfare-maximizing point in a market economy. There can be either too many or too few varieties. Therefore, if the assumptions of the PE framework hold, trade decisions in a perfectly planned socialist economy cannot be described by the same set of equations generated by competitive capitalism.

I believe that an even more important difference between the HO and PE models is buried within the assumptions. In the HO model, all countries produce identical goods. Therefore that model does not require that each country be a fundamental innovator. The assumptions of the HO model could be rationalized by positing that countries can obtain the most advanced technologies in the form of licenses and turnkey plants or by imitation. The ability to imitate, but not necessarily to innovate, is implicit in the Heckscher-Ohlin model.

The PE model is fundamentally different from the HO model in one important respect that relates to the acquisition of technology. The PE model assumes that a country produces a unique set of varieties of any good. Therefore each country must have, to some degree, developed its own technology.[7] Imitation or the use of a foreign patent cannot lead to the types of behavior

---

[7] Here I ignore the role of multinational corporations in using domestic R & D facilities to develop products to be made on foreign territory. The statement in the text therefore applies most directly to countries that do not allow MNCs to operate on their territory.

assumed in the model. Because the PE model implicitly assumes that a country does some innovation of its own, some divergence between the CPEs and the MEs in their ability to innovate is sufficient to predict that the PE model might not be equally applicable to both systems.

3.3. Further Elements of Trade Theory

All too often the trade literature is strong on insight but weak on ways in which the insights can be embodied in empirical models of trade.[8] The fact that some theories cannot be easily represented in a rigorous empirical model does not mean that they must be disregarded. It is important to know the criticisms of the HO and PE models in order to judge the meaning and robustness of the results. Moreover, if some theory pinpoints an important deficiency in the HO or PE models, one might be justified in making appropriate ad hoc adjustments to those models in empirical applications. In this section, therefore, I briefly review some elements of neoclassical trade theory that seem particularly relevant when considering empirical applications of the HO and PE models.

Technology   Newcomers to trade theory will usually spontaneously reject the assumption that technology is constant across countries. But as Leamer (1984, p. 36) points out, this reaction is probably due to confusion over the difference between technique and technology. One sees different techniques (e.g., capital-labor ratios) used in different countries because impediments to trade have inhibited factor-price equalization, not necessarily because the set of techniques available to the two countries is different.

By making the distinction between a "meta-technology" and a production function, one can perhaps remove some of the difficulty in accepting the assumption that all countries have access to the same technology. The meta-technology includes all the production functions consistent with known science. A firm chooses one of those functions from the set, the choice depending crucially on the availability of R & D personnel. In such a way, all countries have access to the same technology, but choice of technique depends crucially on the availability of one particular resource endowment: trained scientists.[9]

The advantage of the foregoing approach is that one can consider technology (or rather the ability to use it) just another resource endowment within the context of a general equilibrium HO or PE model. This solves the problem of embodying theory in a rigorous empirical model. [10]

Despite the above, the assumption that technology is a special input that

[8] The difficulty of finding the appropriate empirical representation of particular trade theories is a theme running throughout Deardorff's (1985) review of the empirical trade literature.

[9] For the case of the United States, Sveikauskas 1983 examines a number of different measures of endowments that affect the ability to adopt the latest techniques.

[10] The real problem, which has been glossed over in the discussion, is whether factor-price

must be treated differently from others has been an inescapable element of the trade literature for many years. The implicit assumption many authors make is that some causes of difference in technology cannot be accommodated within the HO framework.[11] For example, the product-cycle theory (Vernon, 1966) postulates that the development of new products will most likely take place near the most advanced markets. Krugman (1979) has embodied such notions in a systematic trade model. He assumes that innovating countries develop new varieties of goods, which can be made in noninnovating countries only after a lag. Then the innovator exports new products and imports older products. In a very real sense, the more sophisticated country exports the services of a factor that one might call the ability to innovate.

In turning to empirical analysis, one is forced to look for new explanatory variables that measure a country's ability to develop new technologies. As Hufbauer's (1970) analyses make clear, the upshot is essentially that "sophistication" of some sort is an ingredient of trade performance. Because it is difficult to measure such a phenomenon precisely, GDP per capita is the most obvious proxy. Therefore, the content of technology theories of trade is so rudimentary when applied empirically in a cross-country context that there is no gain from dwelling any further on theoretical details here.

Information and Multinational Corporations. The typical international transaction envisaged in the standard trade models is a transaction at arm's length between two national corporations. In contrast, the descriptive literature on trade has emphasized the role of multinationals, reflecting the large amount of trade that occurs within firms. Only in the 1980s, have trade theorists begun to embody multinationals in their general equilibrium models in a meaningful way.

Any analysis of the multinationals should begin with the reasons for their existence. One must ask what is unique about multinationals' trade, compared with other forms of transactions. The answer is almost immediate from the question: the fact that trade is internalized (Helpman 1984b; Ethier 1985). At least in terms of general principles, there is much agreement on the reasons for conducting activities within firms. Following Williamson's (1975) now classic analysis, one would emphasize the problems arising from asymmetrical information, especially under conditions of bargaining and bounded rationality.

At present, when economists have only just begun to analyze the phe-

---

equalization is at all likely, given the view of technology presented. The relative endowment of scientific personnel probably varies much more than other relative endowments. Hence, it is exactly the variation in numbers of scientists that makes it likely that Appendix B's assumptions HO-5 and PE-5 are violated.

[11] Authors advancing the cause of technological differences have not always explicitly stated whether they view their theories as inconsistent with Heckscher-Ohlin, but that viewpoint seems to be implicit in much of the literature.

nomenon of internalization in trade models, there would not be much gain from summarizing detailed analytical results. Indeed, given the lack of consensus on the most appropriate modeling strategy, the results often differ in important ways.[12] One important area of consensus has arisen, however—the possibility of cross-national organization leads to trade flows that otherwise would not occur (Helpman-Krugman 1985, p. 237). This conclusion is of central interest in the present context, because socialist countries are much less receptive to multinationals than capitalist nations are.

Once the role of multinationals is highlighted, one must ask in which activities they are likely to be important. Internalization is most likely to be beneficial when information is valuable and distributed asymmetrically. For example, in Ethier's (1985) model, the less information held by users of a good, the more common multinationals are. Informational asymmetry is most likely to be a problem when technologies are being transferred and when product quality is not easily ascertainable.

In previous work (Murrell 1982), I emphasized the role that informational constraints play in East-West trade and showed that, under special circumstances, there are institutions that can provide the same services as multinational corporations. Buy-back agreements, in which purchases of Western technology are financed by agreeing to supply goods manufactured with that technology, might solve the problem of informational asymmetry. The pattern of such agreements was found to be consistent with the hypothesis that buy-back is a substitute for the internalization of trade flows. Hence, the absence of multinational enterprise affects CPE trade patterns if these alternative institutional arrangements cannot play a role completely equivalent to that of the multinationals. This important topic is discussed at much greater length after the characteristics of the CPEs are examined.

Economies of Scale and Country Size   Economies of scale have already appeared in the analysis. In the PE model, such economies cause nations to specialize in different products, but in that model there is no interaction between country size and trade patterns because the advantage of scale works only in a limited region: the desire for product diversity by consumers places a natural economic limit on the scale of any single plant. But as Helpman (1984a) emphasizes, economies of scale can take a variety of forms, and in some cases country size might become a determinant of trade structure.

Panagariya (1981) constructs a model of a two-sector economy in which one sector has increasing returns and the other has decreasing returns. He shows that free trade can result in large countries exporting the product made in the increasing-returns sector. The essential reason for the trade patterns is that the smaller country is in some sense "too small" for one of the industries.

[12] Compare Helpman 1984b and Ethier 1985 on the relation between multinational activity and differences in relative factor endowments.

With different reasoning, Krugman (1980) suggests similar results for a world with differentiated products and significant transport costs. By concentrating production of the decreasing-cost products in the large country, scale economies are realized while transportation costs are minimized through proximity to the larger market. This result does not depend on one industry being "too large" for a small country, but rather on the asymmetry between domestic and foreign consumers.

Nonhomothetic Preferences The standard form of trade theory assumes that preferences are homothetic, so that the structure of consumption is independent of per capita income and, in particular, factor endowments. The many objectors to this assumption base their arguments on such venerable works as Engel's law. Indeed, Markusen (1986) has claimed that one can understand the relative size of trade between the world's different regions only by invoking nonhomotheticity.

For Heckscher-Ohlin, the introduction of nonhomotheticity does not cause profound changes in the model to be analyzed, as Leamer (1984, pp. 39–41) has shown. In Appendix B, I derive a modified version of equation (3.1). The change arises from assuming that the consumption of a good is a linear function of per capita income, rather than simply a constant proportion of income. With this assumption, one obtains the following equation:

$$W_{ij}/r_j = b_{i0} + \sum_{k=1}^{S} b_{ik}v_{kj} \qquad i = 1, \ldots, N \qquad j = 1, \ldots, T, \qquad (3.1')$$

where v_{kj} is the per capita endowment of resource k in country j, and r_j is the population of country j.[13] Thus, the equation relating resource endowments to trade flows maintains its simple form even after relaxing the assumption of homothetic preferences. With the change, one can see that it is natural to use per capita endowments in the equation.

3.4. Thinking about the Trade of CPEs: An Introduction

This book is concerned with the structure of trade and what that structure implies about the character of centrally planned economies. The HO and PE models are idealizations, and, an important use of these models is in comparing predictions to results. When the results deviate from predictions, one needs an alternative theoretical blueprint to be able to interpret the meaning of the deviation. For the countries of interest in this study, that interpretation can come only from a model relating the organizational features of CPEs to trade outcomes. However, as Hewett (1980, p. 49) remarks, existing analyses of

---

[13] Of course, the b_{ik} are different from those in the original version of equation (3.1).

CPE trade have usually paid little attention to commodity structure. Indeed, there is a tendency in the Western literature to view CPE trade as an irrational, unpredictable process.[14]

Once one looks below the surface of the literature, however, there are many theories of CPE trade. These theories are not usually viewed as such because they are typically cast in the form of ad hoc remarks or anecdotes. They lack a systematic underpinning within a framework that allows one to proceed easily from basic cause to precise effect. The underlying causal mechanism in these remarks is therefore often obscure, with the consequence that they provide little help in interpreting empirical results.

This section and those that follow summarize hypotheses on CPE trade within a consistent framework. By imposing a theoretical structure, albeit very weak, one can better understand the basic causal forces assumed to be present in the economy, thereby facilitating interpretation of empirical analyses. To demonstrate that such a framework is helpful, I present an example of a case where I believe the existing literature comes to unjustified conclusions because the basic causal forces embedded in an argument were not identified. The example was easy to choose because I am among the guilty (see Murrell, 1981).

Consider the ability of the CPEs to meet world quality standards. The traditional argument is simple. In CPEs, goods are of poor quality because producer incentives do not reward quality sufficiently and because buyers do not have the motivation to refuse delivery of shoddy items in a shortage economy. From this it is usually concluded that CPEs fare poorly in international markets where quality is important, even after one controls for level of development and technological sophistication.

Let us examine the argument more closely. First, if one is to conclude anything from observing the general low quality of goods sold in CPEs, it must be assumed that producer incentives are the same for those goods as for exports. However, we do know that there are large special incentives for export producers (Treml 1981). Second, the usual arguments do not take into account the fact that the weak quality requirements of domestic buyers are not relevant for export producers. In fact, an implication of the usual argument is that effective demand for high-quality goods in a shortage economy is *lower* than it is in other economies. Therefore, demand side considerations, taken alone, lead to conclusions that are the opposite of those usually made: other things being equal, a shortage economy exports high-quality goods.[15]

I certainly do not want to place myself in the position of claiming that the

[14] That is how I interpret the remarks of Wilczynski 1965, p. 65, and Holzman 1968, p. 820, for example.

[15] This "others things being equal" is particularly strong, of course. In particular, it effectively implies that different quality levels can be produced for export and for the domestic market.

conclusion in the previous sentence must be correct.[16] The sole claim is that the conclusion contained in the conventional wisdom evaporates when one uses the notions of demand and supply to dissect the conventional argument on quality. That conclusion might be true, but it does not inevitably follow from the set of facts usually cited and the standard partial equilibrium analysis that is used. The argument above reveals the existence of opposing forces that affect trade in high-quality goods. Empirical analysis is then needed to decide which force is the stronger. In this connection, one should note that Brada and Wipf (1976, pp. 37–38) claim to show that quality problems are not evident in the trade patterns of Romania.

In arguing that the discussion be conducted within a theoretical framework, I am simply proposing that some elementary principles of economic discourse be applied. In the present context, these principles are three in number. First, one must be clear about which variables are endogenous and which are exogenous.[17] Second, one should analyze economic outcomes in terms of how the behaviors of individual agents interact, and be explicit about their motivations and the environment they face.[18] The third principle, derivative of the others, is that separating the analysis of supply and demand is a very useful mode of discourse. Indeed, it is the absence of this separation in the usual arguments on quality that leads to inappropriate conclusions.

To set up a framework for the discussion, it is helpful to reflect on the nature of the assumptions of the neoclassical trade models. The assumptions describe the following components of an economy:

1. The decision-making environment faced by producers, their objectives, and their constraints
2. The types of goods for which supply is exogenous (i.e., resource endowments) and the types that are producible
3. A description of technology and the relationship between the technologies available in different countries
4. The preferences of those making consumption decisions and the relationship between the preferences of individuals in different countries

When describing a theory of trade, one must make assumptions in all four areas. Thus, the discussion in Sections 3.6–3.9, which examines hypotheses

[16] For example, it might be the case that a single factory cannot produce two different levels of quality simultaneously because quality control requires factory-wide procedures. In that case, conventional wisdom on the quality of goods in trade probably holds.

[17] Of course, as one's perspective changes, say from the individual to the economy, the classification of any variable might change. However, acknowledging such a change, as in elementary demand and supply, leads to a deeper understanding of economic forces.

[18] The reader should note that I use the term "agents" rather than "individuals." There is no methodological problem in talking about the behavior of a collection of individuals, such as Gosplan.

on the nature of CPE trade, is organized around these four categories, making the underlying causal mechanisms readily transparent. Then, empirical results have much clearer implications for the analysis of the nature of CPEs. Before turning to this discussion, however, it is instructive to review the structure of institutions in CPEs, in order to bring to the fore the features of organization relevant to foreign trade.

3.5. A Brief Overview of the Institutions of CPEs

One cannot analyze foreign trade decisions by merely examining the structure of the institutions designated to conduct trade. As neoclassical models make clear, trade reflects all decisions. However, one can only highlight significant features. Thus, this summary is an idealization of reality, and, as in any model, the primary objective is to isolate the phenomena that are particularly pivotal. These features are identified (in italic) in the following, and their implications for foreign trade are analyzed in subsequent sections.

The most important distinguishing feature of the centrally planned economies is the virtual *absence of capitalist firms*. As a consequence, multinational corporations are not free to conduct their operations. Although there have been attempts to encourage joint ventures in which multinationals participate, these have not been notably successful. At a first approximation, one can treat CPEs as having *no multinational corporations* trading on their soil.

Centrally planned economies have a *hierarchical organization* that is based on a philosophy that decisions emanate from the central authorities. Consequently, there is a large degree of *centralization of decisions*. (The degree of centralization has declined in the reformed economies of Hungary and Yugoslavia, but it still remains much higher than in typical market economies.) From this fact flow many consequences. For example, the decision-making overload at the center, with the consequent need to reduce the amount of information processing, probably accounts for some lack of variety in consumer goods. Moreover, once one combines centralization with the absence of capitalism, *profit-oriented price competition* will have little role in the economy.

The absence of private firms and the presence of centralization seem to imply, although this is not inevitable, that *entry of firms (or enterprises) is slow*, compared with market economies. Moreover, the *exit of firms is also ruled out* by the fact that workers seem to have been bestowed with property rights in their existing jobs in the CPEs (Granick 1987). This has important consequences for the rate and direction of innovation. It also implies that existing producers are not usually challenged by new ideas, especially those generated in foreign markets.

A characteristic of CPEs that has endured through increases in the level of development and reform of the economic mechanism is the presence of *macro-*

economic shortage. While there is much disagreement about whether such shortages exist on consumer markets (see Portes and Winter 1980 and Kornai 1980), there seems to be a consensus that there is shortage within the industrial system: enterprises face an excess demand for their products. The causes of macro-economic excess demand are also the subject of debate. The most complete argument focuses on the absence of financial discipline in socialist enterprises (Kornai 1980).

Having described a few general features, we turn to the apparatus of economic decision-making.[19] A simple description of the hierarchy would distinguish four levels: the political and bureaucratic leaders set basic economic goals; the planners work out the consequences of those goals and ensure that the orders given subordinates are consistent with economic balance; the ministries translate the aggregate targets of the plan into operational tasks and supervise the operations of the lowest level of the hierarchy, the enterprises, whose task is to convert inputs into outputs.[20] For our purposes, one of the most important ministries is the Ministry of Foreign Trade, whose subordinate "enterprises" produce imports from foreign exchange or produce foreign exchange from domestically produced goods.

Because of the existence of hierarchy, any analysis of the economic decisions of CPEs must begin with the political leaders. The *leaders' preferences* are certainly not identical with those derived from some mechanical aggregation of consumer preferences—for example, the savings rate is higher in CPEs than in most equivalent market economies. Moreover, Communist Party leaders sometimes seem to have a specific conception of the type of trade structure they would like (Montias 1977, p. 877), a conception that is not always justified by objective economic facts. One must be wary, however, of overemphasizing the extent to which the leaders' preferences influence the pattern of effective demand, especially between consumer goods. Many procedures in the CPEs are designed to elicit information on consumer's preferences and to incorporate that information into the plan. In economies where price signals are absent, the effectiveness and accuracy of these procedures are probably more significant influences on the structure of the demand for consumer goods than any deviation between leaders' preferences and those of consumers.

The task of the planners is to take the goals of the leaders, interpret them in terms of some basic economic targets, obtain information on production possibilities from the lower levels of the hierarchy, and endeavor to ensure balance in the plan. Although Western observers have commented in detail

[19] Here, I focus solely on the traditional organization of CPEs as in the Soviet Union, instead of making remarks about reforms.

[20] I can only apologize to those scholars who believe that this description is overly simplified and omits some crucial entity or fact. Given the amount of space devoted to the topic, much of importance had to be ignored.

on the nature of the planners' procedures (Levine 1959; Granick 1975), one can draw surprisingly few general lessons about the structure of foreign trade from knowledge of the details. One important feature of the planning process is certainly the degree of information overload and the consequent need to use short-cut techniques. As Birman (1978) shows, this results in planning *"from the achieved level,"* in which this year's plan is obtained by adding increments to last year's results. In a remarkable article, Manove (1971) proves that such procedures can lead to the balancing of plans, albeit slowly. Thus, although the Western literature usually emphasizes the dysfunctional aspects of central planning, the existence of planning from the achieved level should focus our attention more on the *slowness of adaptation*, than on fundamental incoherency.

Annual planning is in essence a process for achieving balance. But the yearly figures take as given the existing size and structure of the industrial plant. Previous investment decisions therefore have a significant effect on present plans. Investment decisions must perforce use information on *prices, interest rates, and wages*. Quantities measured in different physical units can be made comparable only by employing some common denominator, which is usually a price. Goods produced in different years are made comparable by using interest rates, either explicit or implicit. Therefore the use of prices is inevitable in any system that aims to choose sensibly between investment projects with varying payoff periods, producing different goods, and employing alternative input combinations.

Beneath the planners, in function if not in status, are the ministries, with their own many levels of internal hierarchy. The ministries are responsible for supervising enterprises and for channeling information and plans between the planners and the enterprises. The latter process confers much power on the ministries through control of information and the ability to make decisions, as data are disaggregated in the flow of information down the hierarchy. Nove (1980) designates the outcome as "centralized pluralism," with the ministries competing among each other for scarce resources. Indeed, Granick (1980) has argued that the ministry should be viewed as the fundamental decision-making unit in planned economies.

Given ministerial power, one must reflect on the nature of ministerial decisions. Ministries are usually assumed to be quantity maximizers, with bureaucratic aggrandizement their basic goal.[21] From this assumption two significant consequences follow. First, there is a bias toward a *high rate of investment* as ministries strive to enlarge their economic role. Second, because quantity of output, rather than consumer satisfaction, is emphasized, there will be a *lack of focus on quality, product variety*, and other less easily quantifiable facets of economic activity.

Enterprises form the base of the hierarchy. The enterprises are units with

---

[21] For example, this assumption drives Kornai's (1980) analysis of shortage under socialism.

an independent accounting identity, responsible for making operational the goals set by superiors. In the most decentralized economies, this means the maximization of profits, while in the more traditional CPEs a myriad of plan figures demands attention. But it is traditional in economics, and in the CPEs, to assume that the "soul of man under socialism" has not yet arrived, that managers are interested in their own welfare. Hence, one should focus attention on the *incentive system*, which affects the degree to which managers follow their superiors' orders and determines outcomes in the interstices of the plans, where the orders are unclear. To the extent that those incentives contain targets denominated in value terms, one should also consider the influence of the *price system* on enterprise managers.

In exploring the nature of enterprise decisions, one should remember that managers in CPEs are more isolated from customers and suppliers than firms in market economies are. Enterprises most often interact with superiors, who are essentially in the same trade. This remoteness from agents on the same level of the hierarchy must lead to poor information flows, especially with regard to the special needs of customers and the availability of technological opportunities. The *remoteness from the customer or supplier* has been especially important in international activities.

Up to now there has been little reference to the institutions created specifically to conduct foreign trade. The reason for this omission is that one can view such institutions within the framework outlined above. The Ministry of Foreign Trade is akin to any other ministry. It aids in the planning process, channels information about the activities of its operational units to the planners, implements the relevant part of the plan by disaggregating the plan figures, and supervises a group of "producers." The foreign trade bureaucracy is usually treated as a very special unit because its "enterprises," the foreign trade organizations (FTOs), either use or produce a very special resource—foreign exchange. The unique nature of this resource should not blind one to the fact that foreign trade fits into a general structure that applies to all economic activities (Gruzinov 1979, p. 73).

The Ministry of Foreign Trade receives export and import plans that are coordinated with the activities of other ministries. The decision process that leads to these plans is intensely bureaucratic and therefore resistant to any simple characterization. It is subject to the same influences adumbrated above for planning in general. The use of simple benefit-cost ratios to evaluate decisions is perhaps more common in the foreign trade sphere than elsewhere, although even in this area the extent of their influence is by no means paramount (Gardner 1983, pp. 117–19). Because these ratios, or *foreign-trade efficiency indicators*, use data denominated in monetary units, their existence points again to the price system as one determinant of trade patterns.

One can draw few general lessons relevant to the structure of trade from knowledge of the internal organization of the Ministry of Foreign Trade. Indeed, the comments of an inside observer (see Gruzinov 1979) give the impression that nobody can understand the workings of the central administration of that ministry. However, certain features of the operational units, the FTOs, are worthy of comment.

The most important target in the export plans of the foreign trade organizations is the total value of exports within a specific commodity category (Gardner 1983, p. 71). The FTOs have discretion in choosing the product mix that best accomplishes their goals, given that the plan target is met. Therefore, the *incentive system of the FTOs* is an important determinant of trade patterns. These incentives are such that FTOs are encouraged to export goods with a high foreign-to-domestic price ratio and to import goods with the opposite property (Gardner 1983, p. 72). One's attention is drawn again to the price system.

Gruzinov's (1979) description of the workings of the Ministry of Foreign Trade is somewhat reminiscent of Zaleski's (1971) characterization of the planning process, which emphasizes the bureaucratic focus on management, rather than any conception of efficiency or optimization. Bureaucratic superiors have the objective of maintaining control in the implementation process, instead of encouraging the FTOs to consider alternative techniques for increasing the gains from trade. Thus, given the incentives implicit in the traditional career structure, there is little encouragement to develop expertise in marketing, quality control, and advertising: the system lacks what one might call *nonprice product-promotion* tools.

3.6. The Decision-Making Environment for Producers

This and the following three sections examine the implications of CPE organization for foreign trade patterns, focusing on features that generate fairly transparent hypotheses about trade structure. These hypotheses are derived on the assumption that the centrally planned economies interact with market economies that conform to the assumptions of the neoclassical models of trade. Therefore, the focus is on how organizational features of CPEs bring about deviations from patterns of trade predicted for MEs.

The listing of hypotheses serves mainly as a background to the empirical work in ensuing chapters, for these are the hypotheses examined using trade data in Chapters 4, 6, and 7. The identification of a hypothesis should not be taken as an endorsement. Indeed, at different junctures in the following I examine arguments that have diametrically opposite implications for trade structure. Empirical analyses are then needed to evaluate which underlying causal force is stronger. The listing of a hypothesis is also no indication that the hypothesis has withstood empirical tests conducted by previous authors. Comments on previous empirical results are reserved for later chapters, when they can be directly compared with the new results generated here.[22]

---

[22] Because appropriate data are absent, not all hypotheses will be tested.

At a very simple level, three classes of production decisions are made in centrally planned economies. The ministry-planner nexus determines the basic structure of input-output relations. The enterprises help to determine the finer details, especially product quality, product mix within narrow ranges, and short-run input combinations. The planners and the Ministry of Foreign Trade choose the mix of goods to be traded internationally. The ways in which organizational structure affects these decisions is described below. In that description, I have ignored the way these decisions are influenced by preferences, the size of endowments, and the level of technology, factors that are analyzed separately in later sections.

Hierarchy and Centralization   Given the complexity of modern economies, shortcut techniques must be used to make planning decisions. The best-known of these techniques is planning from the achieved level. As Manove (1971) shows, the result of such planning can be coordination, but coordination achieved with a lag. Production decisions take some time to adjust to changing conditions. For example, Lacko (1984) finds that investment allocation in Hungary follows a pattern in which the share going to each sector remains remarkably stable in the long run. Such facts can be reflected in trade patterns, as observers of the centrally planned economies have long emphasized (Brown 1968, pp. 66–69) and as shown in Wolf's (1982) empirical analysis of Soviet data:

> *Hypothesis 1.* Planning from the achieved level causes the CPEs to respond slowly to changes in world market conditions.

The Absence of Profit-Motivated Price-Competition   In centrally planned economies, enterprises usually do not have the authority to set their own prices, so there is no incentive for monopoly enterprises to restrict output because such actions do not raise managerial bonuses. Powerful enterprises in CPEs just do not use their economic leverage in such ways; they are much more likely to bargain to obtain increased input allocations. In contrast, capitalist firms in sectors with higher concentration ratios can obtain monopoly profits by restricting production. As Helpman and Krugman (1985) theorize and Marvel (1980) shows empirically, sectors in market economies with higher concentration ratios have lower net exports. Thus, as trade reflects relative differences, we have:

> *Hypothesis 2.* The absence of profit-oriented price competition in CPEs gives those economies a comparative advantage in sectors that have high levels of concentration in MEs.

Efficiency Indicators   When investment decisions require a comparison of processes with differing capital intensities, or when foreign trade decisions depend on evaluating the merits of trading different goods, any reasonable decision criterion must compare the costs and benefits of the alternatives.

Because the alternatives involve physical variables expressed in noncomparable units, costs and benefits must be measured in value terms. These facts have long been acknowledged by planners. That recognition has resulted in the development of foreign-trade efficiency indicators and investment efficiency indicators in all CPEs (Boltho 1971, pp. 71–90). Of course, the extent of use of such indicators is still an open question.[23]

The present work is not the place to review the literature on the indicators. The crucial point is that they are a means of introducing rigorous cost-benefit (i.e., profit maximization) criteria into decision-making. If the indicators were perfectly designed and universally employed, the resultant decisions would then allocate resources efficiently. Many authors have criticized specific aspects of the design. However, as Abouchar (1985, p. 346) comments, "It is all too easy to impose unrealistic expectations on Soviet criteria, insisting that Soviet investment decision-making pass a test that Western rules have not completely met." Indeed, Abouchar concludes that most of the Soviet rules for application of the indicators in investment decisions are consistent with welfare maximization (p. 361). Thus, in looking for ways in which CPE trade differs from the structure implied by the neoclassical models, one should not focus on the use of efficiency indicators. Instead, attention should be directed at the data entering into the indicators: prices.

The Price System   On the basis of empirical evidence, Gardner (1983, p. 152) concludes that relative prices play a more important role in Soviet trade decisions than is commonly assumed by Western analysts who focus on the inefficiencies and complexities of bureaucratic organization. If this is the case, systematic biases away from efficiency prices are likely to be reflected in trade decisions. Rosefielde (1973, p. 126) has based an explanation of the commodity structure of Soviet trade on such considerations.

Throughout their history, the socialist countries have wrestled with the dilemma of using interest rates because such practice could be construed as inconsistent with Marx's Law of Value. An uneasy compromise has led to an undervaluation of capital. If comparative costs affect trade patterns, then one can follow Rosefielde and, surprisingly, a Romanian analysis (Popa 1986, p. 59) in postulating:

Hypothesis 3. The undervaluation of capital in CPEs leads to greater net exports of capital intensive goods than would be the case with efficiency-maximizing decisions.

But this argument is incomplete.[24] If capital is undervalued, the quantity demanded of both capital and capital-intensive goods increases, to the extent

---

[23] See, e.g., Dyker 1983, p. 100, on Soviet investment decisions, and Gardner 1983, p. 117, on Soviet foreign trade.

[24] I thank Arvind Panagariya for making this point clear to me.

that prices affect domestic factor proportions and product demand. Unless the quantity of capital and capital-intensive goods supplied responds perversely to the undervaluation, a rationing mechanism is needed for capital. This mechanism determines which sectors obtain capital and therefore whether capital-intensive exports are encouraged.

The incompleteness in the argument leading to Hypothesis 3 will be inherent in any discussion focusing solely on prices. The artificial lowering of a price affects both the quantity demanded and the quantity supplied. Without counter-vailing forces or perverse responses, disequilibrium results. The choice of rationing method, used to resolve the disequilibrium, then helps to determine the outcome. If the nature of the rationing method is not addressed, then the argument is incomplete. The ensuing hypothesis also derives from such in-complete analyses.[25]

A standard criticism of the price-setting process in CPEs focuses on the use of average rather than marginal costs. Using the *ceteris paribus* assumption (to be questioned later) that the optimal number of enterprises in each industry has been chosen, such pricing policy most affects the sectors where the ex-istence of a scarce resource means that marginal costs greatly vary across enterprises—the natural resource sector. Hence, in the CPEs land and natural resources have not been priced at their true opportunity cost (Dyker 1983, p. 102). Using arguments similar to those justifying the previous hypothesis, one obtains:

> *Hypothesis 4.* Average-cost pricing encourages the export of goods embodying land and natural resources.

Incentive Systems   Enterprise managers are employees of ministries, and managerial careers are very much dependent on ministerial decisions. Because the bonus formula governing managerial pay is designed outside the ministries but administered by the ministerial hierarchy, there is an ambiguity in the incentives facing managers. Present incomes are supposed to be determined by a mechanical formula, but long-run welfare depends on the attitude of superiors. The same ambiguity must be present in any analysis of managerial decision-making.

It is clear from standard analyses (Berliner 1957, 1976) that ministries are interested in growth of physical output and regular fulfillment of the most important plan targets. Because the most important plan indicator is a quantity index, these two motives do not conflict. In the traditional bonus scheme, the central element is also a quantity target, so ministerial pressures and the bonus scheme both persuade the manager to focus on quantity and ignore quality (Kornai 1959, pp. 57, 67–68). According to Pryor (1963, p. 174), Western customers were aware of this fact from the earliest days of central planning.

---

[25] It would take us too far afield to specify how the gap could be filled.

Hence, noticing that demand considerations are postponed for later discussion, one postulates:

> *Hypothesis 5.* Other things being equal, particularly the pattern of domestic demand, the traditional incentives in CPEs lead to less production of, and fewer exports of, high quality goods.

Two forces countervail the hypothesized effect. First, demand considerations remain to be analyzed in Section 3.9. Second, the traditional pattern of incentives is eroding. This is the case most clearly in the decentralized systems of Yugoslavia and Hungary, but also in the traditional CPEs, where quality has long been recognized as a problem. Special bonuses for quality have been used for more than twenty years and have reportedly had a significant effect (Akhmedev 1980; Wilczynski 1975). Hill and McKay (1988, p. 113), for example, claim that quality is the same in the Soviet Union and the United Kingdom, for the goods they tested. These bonuses are especially important for goods destined for export (Treml 1981, p. 214). Hence, Hypothesis 5 might well be a reflection of CPE past rather than CPE present.

One aspect of CPE organization that must be emphasized is the relative remoteness of the producer from customer and supplier. This is especially the case in international trade, and it leads to an absence of normal features of Western business conduct, such as responsiveness to customers' special needs, awareness of changing styles, and manufacturer-provided after-sales service (Pryor 1963, pp. 174–76; Tardos 1976, p. 296). These features of commercial behavior can be viewed as aspects of quality, and therefore Hypothesis 5 is reinforced. However, distinctive aspects of quality are referred to here. In empirical tests, one should bear in mind differences between the properties imparted to the product in manufacture and the properties of the process of selling the product. It is quite possible that one aspect of quality could be below par while the other is at international standards.

We now come to the incentives of those implementing international trade, the foreign trade organizations. Like all enterprises, the FTOs are given a plan to follow, but within the confines of this plan there are decisions for the FTOs to make. Because the FTOs incentives are tied to the size of their net income, they choose to export goods with a high ratio (or import with a low ratio) of foreign price to domestic price.[26] At a first level of approximation, then, the FTOs attempt to maximize profits subject to the many constraints imposed on them by their organizational superiors.

In anticipation of objections to the conclusion in the previous sentence, by

---

[26] See Gardner 1983, pp. 72–73. My summary of the basic incentives driving the FTOs is consistent with the information in Gruzinov 1979, pp. 196–98, which discusses indicators of export effectiveness (efficiency indicators) used by the FTOs. I have ignored some of the intricacies of the calculation of the income of FTOs, discussion of which would lead to no particular hypotheses on the structure of foreign trade.

scholars knowledgeable about the intricacies of foreign trade management, I would like to clarify the sense in which the conclusion is offered. I do not intend to imply that FTOs focus single-mindedly on the goal of profit maximization, many other factors affect their behavior. However, in trying to understand the empirical implications of the workings of a complex bureaucracy, one must simplify and concentrate on the aspects from which clear implications can be drawn. Once one removes the chaff of detail, the maximization of net income—profits—stands out. Hence, to understand the ways in which CPE trade deviates from efficient trade patterns, it is not of prime importance to examine the incentives of the FTOs.[27]

3.7. The Nature of Production Technology

The present focus is on how economic system dictates the nature of the assumptions to be made in trade models. Technology is a stock, the result of history, much of which has been made by agents acting within the confines of the economic system. The nature of that stock impinges on trade behavior by setting constraints on present decisions. This section examines the link between trade and system that occurs because of the peculiarities of the process of accumulation of technology in centrally planned economies.

The Level of Technology The analysis of technology must begin in a general manner, not by focusing on a single systemic characteristic, as is the case elsewhere. The reason for this difference in approach is that system affects technology in many ways. Nevertheless, two distinct analyses are possible, and it was the difference between these two that was the center of discussion in Sections 1.3 and 1.4, where they were named "neoclassical" and "Schumpeterian."

The traditional view focuses on the structure of bureaucracy and the lack of incentives. Amann and Cooper (1982, pp. 11–19) provide a review of the types of factors that are usually emphasized:

- The importance of the gross output target in the incentives of enterprises distracts attention from cost-cutting innovations.
- The limited direct contact between supplier and customer stifles the diffusion of technological information.
- The unresponsiveness of a centralized price-setting process means that enterprises are often not sufficiently rewarded for the development of new products.
- Centralization hampers the introduction of new technology, because implementation requires the assistance of a large number of the most important

---

[27] This does not exclude the possibility of examining the data that they use—prices, for example.

economic institutions, who are themselves preoccupied with the immediacy of routine decisions.

The resulting conclusion is that CPEs are technologically backward.[28]

The Schumpeterian view does not focus on the properties of existing institutions, but rather on the ability of the society to generate and to choose between new alternatives (see Chapter 1). From this perspective, one would emphasize the lack of entry of new enterprises in CPEs, the inability of enterprises to cross sectoral lines, and the impossibility of transnational internal organization. Nevertheless, the Schumpeterian view reaches the same conclusion on technological level as the traditional view: the CPEs lag.

Direct empirical evidence on the relationship between aggregate technological level and economic system is not conclusive. Bergson (1978) placed the Soviet Union at approximately the same level of total factor productivity as Italy in 1960. Brubaker (1972) reached essentially the same conclusion when comparing labor productivity. (One can interpret measures of productivity as indicating the aggregate level of technology.[29]) In that case, the Soviet Union in 1960 had approximately the level of technology one would expect, given the time at which the process of modern economic development began. This conclusion is consistent with Davies's (1977, p. 15) summary of the econometric evidence: while the level of technology in the Soviet Union is behind that in the Western countries, the rate of accumulation has been on a par with that in the West.

Bergson's (1987) views differ. He assumes that the size of the capital stock measures stage of development. In that case, total factor productivity measures the level of technology (or in Bergson's preferred terms, the level of efficiency) controlling for any differences in historical experience. Bergson (1987) shows that total factor productivity in four socialist economies in 1975 lies approximately 30% below that of a sample of developed market economies. Bergson attributes this 30% to the inefficiency of socialism, including lags in adopting modern technologies. Given that the sampled MEs are among the most developed countries in the world, one's acceptance of Bergson's results depends largely on the degree to which one embraces the notion that capital accumulation proxies development.

Because existing evidence on the technological level of the Soviet Union does not give a clear picture, and because little evidence on the other socialist countries is available, it is worthwhile to examine what trade data reveal on the level of technology in centrally planned economies. Such an examination is based on the fact that the application of modern technology has a differential

[28] See Amann and Cooper 1982, p. 18, for this conclusion on the Soviet Union. The information on the other CPEs is less complete.

[29] Bergson 1978 and 1987, however, interpret differences in total factor productivity as representing differences in efficiency.

effect across sectors. As technological level rises, relative costs change because some processes are more conducive to the application of knowledge than others.[30] The changing pattern of costs is then reflected in changes in the pattern of trade. Hence, if one subscribes to either the traditional view or the Schumpeterian perspective, one would conjecture:

> *Hypothesis 6.* The pattern of trade exhibited by CPEs evidences a lower level of technology than in comparable market economies.

The Lack of Free Entry   Like Sherlock Holmes's dog that didn't bark, the importance of entry to the CPEs might have been somewhat overlooked because of entry's most significant feature—its absence. Lack of entry of new firms could result from the fact that hierarchy likes a stable structure. Entry is also likely to be diminished by the protection of failing enterprises emphasized by Kornai (1980) and the protection of job rights emphasized by Granick (1987). However, the absence of individually owned enterprises is probably even more important. In CPEs, new alliances of individuals cannot form to promote new ventures; existing institutions must be relied upon to create the new. Moreover, entry from foreign countries, in the form of multinationals, is effectively barred.[31] Whatever the reasons, it seems that new firms arise rarely in Eastern Europe. Nowhere can one find the Apples and the Hondas that come to be major forces in the world economy within only a decade of their entry into an industry. Even in Yugoslavia, with its market-oriented economy and special provisions to encourage semicapitalist new firms, entry has been trivial (Lydall 1986, p. 273).

The importance of new entrants to the process of technological change is fundamental to the Schumpeterian perspective. Mansfield et al. (1977, p. 16) summarize the relevant information: "There is a great deal of evidence that new firms and firms entering new markets play a very important role in the promotion of technological change. Existing firms can be surprisingly blind to the possibilities of new ideas. They can become bureaucratized and tradition-bound. An important way that their mistakes and inertia are overcome in our economy is through the entry of new firms."

The importance of free entry is not uniform across sectors because of the differing properties of the technological process at various stages of an industry's development. As Nelson (1981, pp. 1051–52) notes: "Particularly in new industries, or in industries where the technology is relatively new, small firms and often new entrants are important sources of new technology. . . . In such a context, small scale R & D is often productive. The ability of a new firm to enter the industry and grow then may be vital to rapid innovation. As a technology matures, experience begins to count more and the effort

---

[30] Compare making steel to making sculptures, or harvesting wheat to harvesting raspberries.

[31] Foreign firms are not allowed to hold a majority stake in any Eastern European country.

needed to make further improvements often becomes more expensive.
. . . Entry becomes more difficult. Large size becomes a requirement for the
support of efficient R & D.'' In countries that do not have significant entry,
a distinctive pattern of technological change must result. This could be the
reason for one significant feature of technological change in the Soviet Union,
summarized by Davies (1977, p. 62): "At all stages of the research-production
cycle Soviet industry displays a particular aptitude for improving and scaling-
up existing processes, rather than bringing basically new processes and products into full-scale operation.'' Hence, in those industries in which free entry
is vital to the process of innovation, capitalist countries have lower relative
costs than socialist countries. One postulates:

> *Hypothesis 7.* CPEs have a comparative disadvantage in sectors in
> which entry of firms is most significant in capitalist economies.

Absence of Multinational Corporations   One particular form of entry is completely foreclosed in Eastern Europe: entry by firms majority-owned by for-
eigners—multinational corporations (MNCs). These firms play a very
important role in the transfer of technology, advancing such transfer between
developed countries by an average of seven years, according to the estimates
of Mansfield et al. (1982, pp. 14, 36). Brada (1980) has therefore emphasized
the constraints on East-West technology transfer imposed by the absence of
the operations of the MNCs.

Multinational corporations promote the spread of technology by using internal organization. Where rewards and costs are highly indeterminate, transactions can be best effected by eschewing negotiation over the division of
profits between two separate entities (Williamson 1975). The importance of
such situations varies across sectors, and that variation is evidenced in the
cross-sectoral importance of MNC activity. For example, Blomstrom et al.
(1988) find that nearly 50% of the exports of electrical machinery of less-
developed countries is attributable to the operations of MNCs.[32] The corresponding figure for metal products is only 8%. Hence the absence of MNCs
in centrally planned economies will lead to a distinctive pattern of trade.

At this stage it is tempting to conclude that CPEs must have a comparative
disadvantage in sectors in which MNC activities are most important. But this
conclusion might be inappropriate. Multinational corporations encourage
trade, both imports and exports. The use of a technology might require the
importation of a particular good that is so new and difficult to price that market
exchange is impossible. For example, Brada (1980, pp. 44–45) found that,
although MNCs help to spread the technology of pharmaceutical production,
the use of this technology often required the importation of bulk chemicals
by MNC subsidiaries. Thus, the central effect of MNCs might not lie in be-

---

[32] Their data summarize the operations of U.S., Japanese, and Swedish MNCs only.

stowing a comparative advantage, but rather in increasing the total amount of trade. To explore the effect of the absence of MNCs in CPEs, one would examine:

> *Hypothesis 8.* Centrally planned economies evidence a lower level of trade in sectors in which MNCs are most important in MEs.

However, one can leave open the possibility that MNCs actually confer a comparative advantage by examining:

> *Hypothesis 9.* The CPEs have a comparative disadvantage in sectors in which MNCs are most important in MEs.

New Products versus New Processes   The above hypotheses separating traditional and Schumpeterian views on technological advance focus on causal factors—entry and MNCs—not on results. However, these two views also have differing implications for the structure of technological change, which can be examined with trade data. These implications focus on differences between the capacity to develop new products and the ability to create new manufacturing processes.

Proponents of the traditional view do not focus on whether product or process changes are most discouraged by the organization of CPEs. Berliner (1976, pp. 418, 440) notes that the classical Soviet incentive structure favored process over product innovation, but that changes in incentives in the 1960s did increase the incentives for product innovation. Moreover, such benefits have been particularly emphasized for export activities (Wilczynski 1975). After reviewing the systemic factors influencing technological change in the Soviet Union, Amann (1982, p. 18) concludes that there is no firm evidence that product innovation is less successful than process innovation.

For a variety of reasons, the Schumpeterian perspective leads directly to the conclusion that CPEs will be deficient in product innovation relative to process innovation. First, the absence of entry is critical. New products are often generated outside a particular sector, whereas new processes tend more often to arise in existing firms (Utterback 1979, pp. 48, 50). Second, decisions on new processes can be cast much more easily into the rational cost-benefit framework favored by CPEs than can decisions on new products. For example, Beardsley and Mansfield (1978, p. 130) found that the profits from process innovation are easier to predict than profits from product innovation, where the extra uncertainty of consumer reactions to the new good must be taken into account. Survival of the fittest might be the only possible decision-making mechanism for choosing between new products.

Third, new process technologies are easier to disseminate without internal organization than new product technologies (Brada 1981, p. 211). Thus, new product technologies must be spread by the relatively rapid rise of innovators, rather than by communication between sovereign enterprises. The presence of a rigid structure of growth in CPEs might inhibit the ability of the economy to adapt quickly to the rise of new products. Finally, the need for internal organization means that importers of technology must rely critically on MNCs for new product technologies. For one sample of R & D projects, Mansfield et al. (1982, p. 61) found that 72% of new product ideas were transferred overseas through affiliates, whereas only 17% of new processes were transferred in the same way.

Thus, in examining differences between technological change in CPEs and MEs, the Schumpeterian perspective applies most directly to new products. For the generation and spread of new processes, the Schumpeterian view has much weaker implications. Hence, to detect differences between the traditional and Schumpeterian perspectives, one would examine:

> *Hypothesis 10.* The CPEs have a comparative disadvantage in sectors in which technological change in new products is most important.

> *Hypothesis 11.* The CPEs have a comparative disadvantage in sectors in which technological change in new processes is most important.

If the Schumpeterian perspective is correct, one would expect to see Hypothesis 10 succeed and Hypothesis 11 have little success. The traditional view could not explain such a result.

Hierarchy and Centralization   The type of economic system affects not only technological advance but also the choice of technique from the set available with a given technology. When decisions are made at the apex and implemented through a hierarchy, some attention must be paid to the costs of organizational complexity. The simplest way to reduce those costs is to limit the number of operational units. Pryor (1973, pp. 143, 162) suggests that this is one reason production units are larger in CPEs than in MEs. Recent evidence from Ehrlich (1985, p. 293) suggests that the difference in size is by as much as a factor of four. When there is a bias toward large scale, relative costs increase in industries in which firms are subject to diseconomies of scale.[33] If such costs affect trade patterns, one obtains:

> *Hypothesis 12.* The desire to reduce the costs of hierarchy leads to a comparative disadvantage in decreasing-returns-to-scale sectors and a comparative advantage in sectors with increasing returns-to-scale.

Essentially the same analysis pertains to product variety, to the extent that such variety increases the number of production units or the complexity of input-output relations. In the presence of hierarchy, efficient economic de-

---

[33] It is the comparative element in comparative advantage which produces this conclusion. Relative costs can change in some sectors solely because absolute costs change in others.

cisions call for a reduction in the number of varieties. Moreover, the sectors in which extensive product variety exists in market economies will be those in which new product ideas are common. We have already seen that, because of the absence of free entry and multinational corporations, the CPEs will be deficient in such sectors. Hence:

> *Hypothesis 13.* The desire to reduce the costs of hierarchy and the absence of free entry, including that of MNCs, lead the CPEs to have a comparative disadvantage in sectors characterized by a large amount of product variety and a comparative advantage in industries producing a homogeneous product.

One direct consequence of this hypothesis is the following:

> *Hypothesis 14.* Because CPEs produce a narrow range of varieties, intraindustry trade will be less significant for CPEs than for MEs.

3.8. The Stock of Endowments

The levels of some endowments, such as mineral deposits, are set by nature.[34] Others, such as capital stock, are the result of past decisions and therefore reflect the nature of the economic system. This section focuses on endowment differences between MEs and CPEs that can be traced to the effects of economic organization, not on those attributable to nature.

Capital Stock　The emphasis on growth and development runs to the very core of the socialist ideology, so, it is not surprising that CPEs have maintained very high levels of capital accumulation. For example, Moorsteen and Powell (1966, p. 182) show that the rate of growth of capital in the Soviet Union far exceeded the rate in the United States at an equivalent stage of the industrialization process. For the early postwar years, Bergson's (1971, p. 443) figures clearly show that the Eastern European countries had higher rates of investment than market economies at the same level of development.

If a country is a latecomer to industrialization, higher investment rates take many years to be translated into higher capital stocks. It was only in the 1970s that the quantity of investment in the Soviet Union reached that in the United States (Edwards, et al. 1979, p. 386). Thus, it takes many years for the quantity of capital to catch up, and one should therefore not exaggerate the size of the capital stock in CPEs. A simple average of the per capita stocks of the Soviet Union, Poland, Hungary, and Yugoslavia in 1975 was only a fraction higher than that of Spain and only two-thirds that of Italy (Bergson 1987, p. 346). In examining whether the emphasis on capital accumulation

---

[34] This is not to say that the rate at which these endowments are exploited is not independent of system.

affects trade patterns and whether the CPEs have a bias toward capital-intensive exports, as suggested by Hypothesis 3, one should remember to compare MEs and CPEs that are appropriately matched.

Scientific Labor   The use of modern industrial processes requires skilled personnel, who cannot be trained overnight. The implemented level of technology is therefore a function of the stock of such personnel. One means of judging the efficiency of innovation processes in CPEs is to examine whether trade patterns are consistent with endowments of scientists and research workers.

The socialist countries have placed great emphasis on the creation of large stocks of scientists and engineers. Nolting and Feshbach's (1979, pp. 746–47) careful calculations show that the Soviet Union had 40% more R & D workers per capita in 1975 than the United States did. A Polish source gives Eastern Europe 80% more scientists and engineers per capita than Western Europe in 1965.[35] Bulgaria, Czechoslovakia, and the GDR all spend a greater proportion of GNP on R & D than the United States spent.[36] Only Yugoslavia spends an amount consistent with that of its capitalist peers. However, Dezsenyi-Gueullete (1983, p. 204) claims that R & D workers in centrally planned economies are less efficient than such workers in MEs because of the nature of their incentive system. Similarly, Rapacki (1982, p. 64) argues that CPEs use R & D workers inefficiently because they are allocated to too high a level in the economic hierarchy. Hence, one should examine:

> *Hypothesis 15.* If R & D workers are used as efficiently in CPEs as in MEs, the factor content of CPE trade should embody at least as much R & D labor as the trade of the most developed market economies.

Quality Reputation   In the past decade, a major focus of economic theory has been on the way market behavior changes when there is asymmetric information between buyer and seller (Stiglitz 1987). A standard example of this asymmetry occurs when the seller knows product quality but the buyer ascertains quality only after use. In such circumstances, the seller has an incentive to build up a reputation for producing high-quality products (Shapiro 1983). In international trade, reputation is equivalent to a specialized capital stock, allowing a country to increase national productivity by charging a price commensurate with quality.

In the immediate postwar years, the CPEs were viewed as producing low-quality goods (Pryor 1963, p. 174). In the headlong rush to develop, the

[35] These figures show Europe to be far behind the United States, which is marginally lower than the Soviet Union. The data are cited in Wilczynski 1974, p. 78.

[36] Because the data source (UNESCO 1986) relies on national numbers, one must doubt strict comparability. Notwithstanding this point, the difference between CPEs and MEs is striking.

deterioration of quality went far beyond the expectations of planners (Wilczynski 1975, p. 135). Now, there are many procedures encouraging the production of high-quality goods, especially those for export (Wilczynski 1975; Treml 1981), but any attempt to build a better reputation must take decades. Thus, the reputation for low quality has certainly persisted long after the quality-oriented schemes were first introduced (Murrell 1982). Moreover, the CPEs have not availed themselves of the services of multinational corporations, which could provide the service of signaling higher quality.

The main implication of acknowledging the importance of quality reputation is in interpreting the results of tests examining trade in high-quality goods. The existence of reputation means that such tests can just as easily reflect the past as the present. Because reputation lags behind reality, it is important to examine whether the test results show change over time. Given that the quality reputation of CPEs was uniquely bad in, say, 1965, any significant improvement in quality-control procedures in the 1970s would evidence itself in a gradual, rather than dramatic, increase in ability to export high-quality goods.

Marketing Skills The volume of resources devoted to marketing in the CPEs has been small, compared to that in the MEs. This is demonstrated most generally in Ofer's (1973, pp. 128–32) regression analysis, which shows that the share of the labor force devoted to trade and finance in CPEs is half that to be expected, given level of development. In specific activities, the data are even more dramatic. Advertising expenditures as a percentage of consumption in the United Kingdom are nearly fifty times those in the Soviet Union, ten times those in Poland and Czechoslovakia, and three times those in Hungary and Yugoslavia (Hanson 1974, p. 51). Similarly, retail workers in Eastern Europe are 50% fewer, as a percentage of the population, than in market economies (Skurski 1983, pp. 149–50).

It is reasonable to assume that skills relevant to marketing, such as advertising and package design, take time to acquire. If in the past few resources have been devoted to these skills, one cannot immediately reverse the situation. For example, Brada (1973, p. 333) argues that when sellers are familiar only with markets characterized by shortages, they can hardly be expected to adapt to the conditions in Western markets. Given the past lack of commitment to marketing activities, there must be an effect on present performance.[37] In the international arena, this effect is combined with the consequences of the absence of multinationals and their well-developed marketing networks.

Because certain goods require larger services of ''salesmanship'' than others, the lack of marketing skills in the CPEs must affect trade patterns. Hence, Holzman (1979, pp. 300–301) has argued that the CPEs have a comparative disadvantage in salesmanship. One caveat must be stated, however. The ar-

[37] Lakos 1982, p. 169, shows the effect of poor marketing, supply reliability, and after-sales service on Hungarian export performance.

gument holds only to the extent that supply-side factors account for the observed lack of marketing activity in the CPEs. If that is the case, one can postulate:

> *Hypothesis 16.* The small endowment of marketing skills in CPEs leads to a comparative disadvantage in goods requiring large amounts of salesmanship.

Implicit Resource Endowments   Marrese and Vanous (1983) have argued that the Soviet Union engages in unconventional exchange with the remainder of Eastern Europe. They assume that the Soviet Union pays for the defense services implicit in the use of its neighbors' soil. The payment comes in the form of subsidies on Soviet exports of raw materials, especially fuels. Although the Marrese-Vanous thesis has attracted a number of criticisms,[38] it is not the intention to discuss them here; the thesis itself can be examined using trade data.

If the smaller Eastern European countries do obtain resource endowments at concessionary rates from the Soviet Union, one would expect to see an effect on East-West trade patterns. The concessionary rates amount to an extra endowment of the resource in question. The results of Chapter 6 contain estimates of the size of endowments implicit in East-West trade patterns, and one can check these results against expectations based both on data on actual resource endowments and on the implications of the Marrese-Vanous thesis. That thesis implies:

> *Hypothesis 17.* The pattern of East-West trade for the smaller Eastern Europe countries is more intensive in natural resources than could be justified by levels of domestic production. The reverse is the case for the Soviet Union.

"Sophistication"   Implicit in much of the CPE trade literature is the notion that the level of development characterizes patterns of trade. This notion is most often invoked in criticisms of CPE trade performance. One often encounters claims that CPE patterns of trade match those of the developing countries rather than those of their neighbors to the West. For example, both Balassa (1978, p. 252) and Kadar (1977, p. 158) have made comments to this effect on Hungary, and Oblath and Pete (1985, p. 165) come to the same conclusion after examining Soviet trade with Finland.

The theory behind such empirical statements is usually vague, at best. The level of development is assumed to proxy certain resource endowments that are acquired in the process of development and that, unlike standard inputs such as capital, remain unmeasured. Hufbauer (1970, p. 146) summarizes the implications of several theories by saying that industrial sophistication

---

[38] See esp. Brada 1985, p. 87.

affects trade patterns and that the level of sophistication can be proxied by GNP per capita. Hence, the empirical observations referred to in the previous paragraph can be further examined by testing:

Hypothesis 18. The pattern of trade of the CPEs more closely approximates that of the developing countries than that of the developed market economies.

3.9. Preferences

In centrally planned economies, political leaders carry far more weight in determining the final mix of goods than political leaders in market economies. It is fair to assume that the preferences of a political leader concerning the development of the economy are different from a mere aggregation of individual preferences. Hence, one is justified in postulating differences between CPEs and MEs based on observations on the nature of leaders' preferences. Such differences constitute a basis for trade.

One general point must be aired before turning to specifics. Suppose one observes an important property of a domestic economy, say, the seeming abundance of widgets. The implications for trade that follow from that observation depend crucially on whether the abundance results from supply or from demand. If the country has a large endowment of widget-making resources, then the abundance reflects a comparative advantage, which results in net exports of widgets. However, if the abundance represents a local taste for widgets, then the country has a comparative disadvantage, resulting in imports. Stated at this level, the point seems very obvious, as indeed it is. But this point has often been overlooked in discussion of CPE trade patterns, as the example of quality in Section 3.4 makes clear. The importance of correctly interpreting the relation between domestic abundance and trade patterns becomes paramount here, where preferences are examined.

Investment versus Consumption　Political leaders in the CPEs have vigorously pursued growth throughout history, which leads them to seek a high rate of investment. It has often been claimed that this preference is reflected in foreign trade decisions. For example, Wiles (1968, p. 187) states that foreign exchange is essentially an investment resource in CPEs. Koves (1985, p. 91) remarks that for many years imports of consumer goods were regarded as detrimental to society.

The tendency to favor investment does not seem to change if the locus of decision-making is decentralized. Ministries and enterprises also have strong preferences for investment. They are able to give vent to these preferences by taking advantage of the lax financial discipline that arises from the paternalism inherent in socialism (Kornai 1980).

The higher rate of investment must affect trade patterns. For example, Hewett (1980, p. 67) attributes the large amount of machinery imports to this factor. As the high investment rate results from demand pressures, it leads to a comparative disadvantage in investment goods:

> *Hypothesis 19.* Because of the leaders' taste for growth, the CPEs have a comparative advantage in consumer goods and a comparative disadvantage in investment goods.

The Environment   If comparative cost helps to determine trade flows, trade will reflect differing policies on how costs are calculated. One such policy is the degree to which enterprises are forced to internalize the costs of environmental damage. In a world becoming more sensitive about environmental despoliation, countries that ignore such damage have a comparative advantage in goods whose production entails a large degree of pollution.

There is no clear consensus on whether the effective demand for environmental protection is greater or less in CPEs than in MEs. Goldman (1970) claims that the different systems are similar in this regard, while later he suggests that CPEs might have features tending to encourage despoliation (Goldman 1972, pp. 70–75). To the extent that leaders pursue strong growth policies, environmental quality might decrease, just like the supply of consumer goods. McIntyre and Thornton (1978), however, argue that CPE institutions hold a greater potential for creating efficient environmental policies than MEs institutions.

Gorizontov and Prokudin (1978) reveal an awareness of environmental problems throughout Eastern Europe and detail many schemes undertaken to reduce pollution. Both Mote (1976), for air pollution, and ZumBrunnen (1976), on water pollution, conclude that levels of pollution in the Soviet Union are what one would expect, given the stage of development. In perhaps the most rigorous comparative study, Slama (1986) shows that sulfur dioxide pollution per unit of GDP in Eastern European countries is three times as much as in Western Europe.

Given the lack of consensus on the relative strengths of environmental policies in CPEs and MEs, but given the emphasis of CPE leaders on growth, it is reasonable to examine the following:

> *Hypothesis 20.* The preferences of leaders are such that CPEs have a comparative advantage in goods whose production generates large amounts of pollution.

The Structure of Consumption   The presence in MEs of taxes on alcohol and tobacco and their absence on food and medicine attest to the effect of paternalism on the structure of consumption.[39] Hence, it is not surprising that the

---

[39] Those who would argue that such a structure of taxes is not paternalistic, but rather enhances efficiency, would be hard-pressed to justify their arguments using the values of elasticities of supply and demand.

leaders of CPEs have influenced consumption patterns. At the grossest level, there is a marked tendency to favor food consumption over that of industrial consumer goods. For example, Schroeder (1983, p. 322) shows that the proportion of food in consumption in the Soviet Union is far greater than in countries at an equivalent level of per capita income. Similarly, Koves (1985, p. 91) remarks that industrial consumer goods are always hit hardest when trade restrictions are imposed. Hence, one postulates:

> *Hypothesis 21.* Demand-side factors imply that the CPEs have a comparative advantage in industrial consumer goods.

Two countervailing forces are relevant to the pattern of trade in food products. The leaders' preference for investment diminishes total consumption, but food's share of that total is greater. However, it is probable that the latter effect dominates. For example, Weidemann (1984) and Cook (1987) present evidence showing that protein and meat consumption is higher in Eastern Europe than in a group of comparable MEs.[40] To see which effect is the stronger influence on trade patterns, one must examine the following:

> *Hypothesis 22.* Demand-side factors imply that the CPEs have a comparative disadvantage in food.

The same paternalism that emphasizes food also probably inhibits the consumption of luxury consumer items. (In my youth, British governments, both true blue and deep red, subsidized orange juice and taxed gramophones.) Moreover, any policies to reduce income inequality have the same effect. Hewett (1980, pp. 66–67) hypothesizes that trade patterns will be affected. Hence, one would predict:

> *Hypothesis 23.* Demand-side considerations argue that the CPEs have a comparative advantage in luxury goods.

Shortages We now consider the effect of shortages from the perspective of the demand side. When faced with shortages, buyers become less sensitive to the characteristics of goods. Consider the example of quality. A small depreciation in quality does not result in fewer purchases when there is a shortage, because consumers are not on their demand curves. Hence, the existence of shortage gives the producer some degree of monopoly power with respect to product characteristics.

Consider now producer reactions to the demand-side effects of shortages. Suppose that producers can vary sales on foreign markets by varying quality. Assume also that a limited amount of resources is available to produce goods of high quality. Because of shortages, quality on the domestic market can be reduced without reducing sales. Thus, the producer has the incentive to trans-

---

[40] The figures for groups were calculated from Cook's raw data. The group of MEs is the one referred to as "lower-income OECD" in later chapters, but in this case excludes Turkey.

fer the quality-producing resources to the manufacture of goods bound for export and, as a consequence, to reduce the quality of items sold domestically.

Shortages, through the effect on buyers, can cause quality on the domestic market to be inversely correlated with the quality of exports. Thus, arguments relying on a simple extrapolation from domestic conditions to a prediction of the properties of exports are incomplete. If the observed domestic conditions are produced by demand-side factors, the arguments are incorrect.

The foregoing discussion means that there is a force countervailing the postulated effect in Hypothesis 5. Any predictions on whether CPEs have a comparative disadvantage in high-quality goods depends on the relative strengths of the effects analyzed here and those examined in Section 3.6. One cannot decide which force is the stronger without recourse to empirical studies.

The present discussion has focused on quality, but its arguments are easily adapted to any other nonprice characteristic of output that can be changed by the decisions of enterprises—for example, technological level, product assortment, or use of marketing. Thus, the present argument has identified forces that countervail the effects analyzed in Hypotheses 6, 14, and 17.

3.10. The Relative Applicability of Neoclassical Trade Models in CPEs and MEs

The Heckscher-Ohlin model summarizes the patterns of trade that lead to efficiency in the static allocation of resources when products are undifferentiated. Economists readily assume that this model, or variants thereof, is applicable to market economies. But the analogous assumption for centrally planned economics has few adherents. The large majority of Western economists seem ready to conclude that the CPEs are so riddled with the inefficiencies of bureaucratic decision-making that one could not possibly apply the Heckscher-Ohlin model.[41]

The way economists would justify the conclusion embodied in the previous sentence is best described by presenting a caricature of the typical methodology.[42] It begins with a stroll through the institutions that comprise the economic system. In passing, one observes many features of those institutions that are incompatible with decisions that would be made in efficient markets. For example, one might remark on the problems arising from average-cost pricing or from inadequate incentives for producing high-quality goods. The number of facts to be accumulated on such "irrationalities" can be overwhelming. Overcome by the sheer weight of evidence, one must conclude that such economies are grossly inefficient. And because the features causing the inefficiencies have been implicitly compared with those of market systems,

---

[41] For an exception, see the works of Rosefielde (1973, 1981), which are discussed later.

[42] Montias 1976, p. 7, calls the approach caricatured here the "invidious comparison with an all-purpose ideal."

it is natural to conclude that the economies are inefficient relative to Western economies. In the international trade arena, this conclusion implies that a model of trade summarizing the decisions of market economies could not be applicable to the socialist economies.

That the previous paragraph is a caricature cannot be denied, but it does not do too much violence to the prevailing methodology that many scholars seem to use. For example, one of the most perceptive observers of the Eastern European economies arrives at the following conclusion:

> Another "literary" opinion . . . is that the detailed and the broad allocations are much more sub-optimal [in a Soviet-type economy] than in a market. This follows immediately from [an examination and evaluation of the institutions of Soviet-type economies]. It can also be observed at once by any tourist. . . . It can also be confirmed as to the broader allocations by perusing even superficially the technical press, which is always full of Communist self-criticism as to choice of location, choice of technology, etc. . . . The impression that the system is sub-optimal rests upon a mountain of evidence. (Wiles 1977, pp. 302–3)

One cannot argue with the conclusion that the evidence proves the suboptimality of the socialist economies, but once one reflects on its true nature, that conclusion is less important than it seems.

The typical reasons for concluding that the socialist economies are suboptimal, and hence for not applying the standard trade models to CPEs, are equally applicable, mutatis mutandis, to the MEs. The waste produced by the bureaucratic inertia of a foreign-trade ministry in the East might be matched against the costs of special-interest tariffs in the West. The effects of oligopolistic pricing in market economies could be compared to the distortions induced by average-cost pricing in Soviet-type economies. The undersupply of public goods in the market might be compared with the excess demand for investment goods in the East. One could proceed further, but the point is obvious. One cannot conclude anything about the relative applicability of models of efficient decision-making merely by identifying myriad distortions in socialist economies. This point was made most forcefully by one who was hardly noted for his sympathies toward the socialist system, Harry G. Johnson (1969, p. 13):

> Western scholars . . . have been too easily inclined to point to the irrationality of the price structure in socialist economies, without recognizing the manifold irrationalities in pricing in their own economies produced by such typical phenomena as agricultural price support policies, fixing of wages by collective bargaining and minimum-wage laws, tariffs and other restraints on international trade, and complex subsidies to particular industries provided by defence contracts, foreign-aid tying, and governmental support of scientific research in particular fields.

There is one simple problem with the conventional argument that the Heckscher-Ohlin model of efficient decision-making is not applicable to the socialist economies. This argument proceeds on the implicit assumption that a model is a straightforward description of reality. But models do not describe—they simplify. They are idealizations, used to facilitate comprehension. Hence, nobody would seriously contend that the assumptions of the HO model are exactly satisfied by any capitalist society. Thus, in arguing that those assumptions are not satisfied in socialist economies, one really establishes little about the relative applicability of the model.

The above argument leads immediately to the conclusion that judgments about the relative applicability of models in different settings can only come from an approach that takes seriously a rigorously comparative methodology. Hence, Chapter 7 examines the following hypothesis, which reflects the traditional view of the CPEs:

> *Hypothesis 24.* The trade pattern of the MEs conforms more closely
> to the Heckscher-Ohlin model than does the trade of CPEs.

In the existing literature, one author has been consistently willing to challenge the conventional analysis implicit in the above hypothesis. Rosefielde (1973, 1981) argues that one can use the lens of Heckscher-Ohlin to understand CPE trade. His notion of "fundamental comparative advantage" entails the idea that cost considerations, of the type witnessed in market economies, also play a role in planned economies. If this is the case, then relationships summarizing the trade decisions of the market economies would also be relevant for CPEs.

The above discussion would apply equally well if one were to examine the relative applicability of the product differentiation and economies of scale model. Hence, parallel to the previous hypothesis, one can postulate:

> *Hypothesis 25.* The trade pattern of the MEs conforms more closely
> to the PE model than does the trade of CPEs.

Hypotheses 24 and 25 are examined empirically in Chapter 7. They are particularly important in this work because the HO model is the standard neoclassical model, while the product differentiation and economies of scale model (PE model) reflects certain aspects of the Schumpeterian theory. (However, the PE model is still far from being one based purely on Schumpeterian reasoning.)

The theory behind the HO model concentrates on the static allocation of physical endowments. That theory does not reflect upon the nature of product development, the role of marketing, the importance of quality control, and so forth. In contrast, the PE model focuses on the types of behavior that occur in industries subject to product differentiation. In such industries, the rapid creation of new products is important, as well as the ability to sell these new products on world markets. An economy's prowess in manufacturing new products is dependent on the extent of free entry in the economy and on the degree to which multinationals are willing and able to function within the domestic economy. The ability to sell those new products is dependent on marketing skills, a reputation for quality, and on access to the resources of multinational corporations. Thus, while the derivation of the PE model does not use Schumpeterian analysis, one can easily see that Schumpeterian factors are important in the types of sectors to which the PE model is most applicable.

CHAPTER 4

Qualitative Information on Nonstandard Trade Determinants: Summary Statistics from Trade Data

Ivan Yakovlevich . . . had remembered where he had seen the nose before and it was on none other than the Collegiate Assessor Kovalev, whom he shaved regularly each Wednesday and Sunday. . . .

Like every self-respecting Russian tradesman, Ivan Yakovlevich was a terrible drunkard. And although he shaved other people's chins every day, his own looked permanently unshaven.
—**Nikolai Gogol,** *The Nose*

In empirical applications of the standard theory of international trade, economists have tended to emphasize a narrow range of trade determinants. The great triumvirate—land, labor, and capital—usually span the spectrum of factors analyzed.[1] However, differences in the economic performance of nations are plausibly the product of a much wider set of influences. For example, Gogol's Yakovlevich reminds us that lack of sensitivity to quality of service might be a more enduring determinant of Russian economic performance than the more usual factor endowments.

Nothing in the standard theory restricts its application to the usual narrow range of variables. One can speak just as easily of an endowment of entrepreneurship or of quality orientation as of an endowment of capital.[2] If these alternative endowments were given a place in the national production function, the usual results would apply to these factors also.

The reason the nonstandard factors have been ignored in empirical work is obvious. Such factors are difficult, often impossible, to measure. But one should be clear about the properties of empirical work ignoring these factors.

---

[1] See, e.g., Leamer 1984.

[2] In speaking of such factors as national differences in entrepreneurship, there is no implication that these are inherited. Religions, educational systems, family structure, and historical experience, which vary enormously from country to country, could all influence the acquisition of such talents as entrepreneurship.

Such work is second-best, with no claims to optimality. Thus, it might be appropriate to use alternative second-best procedures—ones that include the nonstandard variables but that do not use statistical techniques requiring extensive quantitative information on factor endowments. When the absence of data means that the most sophisticated procedures must omit variables, simple summary statistics can be just as valuable as maximum likelihood estimates.

The sections that follow present measures of trade performance obtained by subjecting trade data to simple transformations that are based on rudimentary information about the characteristics of the sectors in which goods are produced. These transformations are simply ones producing the revealed comparative advantages (RCAs) discussed in Chapter 2. Section 4.1 examines the information content of the RCAs in the light of international trade theory. Section 4.2 describes the information employed in forming commodity aggregates that are particularly informative about the phenomena of interest.

Sections 4.3–4.6 contain the empirical results. Table 4.1 offers a road map to the presentation of those and all other results in the book. That table summarizes all the hypotheses developed in the previous chapter. It notes the sources of the hypotheses, their relevance in differentiating between Schumpeterian and neoclassical paradigms, and the section of the book in which each hypothesis is examined empirically. Section 4.3 examines which theories of trade can best explain the types of goods in which CPEs specialize. For organizational purposes, I divide the remainder of the results into three sections, each focusing on a different aspect of economic activity. Section 4.4 explores the way economic system interacts with technological characteristics to affect trade patterns. Section 4.5 asks whether the trade of CPEs reflects the properties of the markets in which goods are sold. And Section 4.6 focuses on the link between CPE trade and the properties of goods, including the effect of systemic differences in preferences for specific commodities.

4.1. Measures of Economic Performance Based on Trade Statistics Alone

As throughout this book, the basis of the analysis here is the relation between the trade performance of a country and the characteristics of its domestic economy. Sometimes those characteristics describe fundamental features of a country's economic system. For example, Holzman (1979) has suggested that CPEs tend to breed managerial personnel who have little ability for salesmanship and that this fact is reflected in trade patterns.[3] An empirical examination of Holzman's theory would therefore be valuable in furthering one's understanding of the nature of CPEs. However, formal econometric testing

---

[3] Salesmanship is one variety of human capital that can be acquired through the investment of effort. The low level of salesmanship therefore follows from the lack of incentive to undertake such effort in a shortage economy.

Table 4.1

Summary of the Hypotheses, Indicating Their Relevance in Comparing the Schumpeterian and Neoclassical Paradigms

Hypothesis Number	Where Introduced	Where Empirically Examined	Summary statement of hypothesis	Relevance in evaluating predictive power of Schumpeterian and neoclassical models
1	Sec. 3.6	Sec. 6.4	Planning "from the achieved level" causes CPES to react slowly to changes in world conditions.	Both models are consistent with this hypotheses.
2	Sec. 3.6	Sec. 4.4; Table 4.14	CPES have a comparative advantage in sectors having high concentration in MES.	Neoclassical model predicts that static resource allocation decisions of CPES are not rational enough for the CPES to take advantage of inefficiencies in MES.
3	Sec. 3.6	Sec. 6.3 and 6.4; Tables 6.3 and 6.6	Pricing policy leads CPES to export capital-intensive goods.	Neoclassical model predicts bias in trade patterns resulting from pricing policies.
4	Sec. 3.6	Sec. 6.3 and 6.4; Tables 6.4, 6.5, and 6.10–13	Pricing policy leads CPES to export goods embodying land and natural resources.	Neoclassical model predicts bias in trade patterns resulting from pricing policies.
5	Sec. 3.6	Sec. 4.5; Tables 4.18 and 4.19	CPES have an inability to export high-quality goods.	Both models make a similar prediction, although the Schumpeterian model focuses more on the difficulties of marketing such goods at arm's length.
6	Sec. 3.7	Secs. 4.4, 6.3, and 6.4; Tables 4.9, 4.10, 4.11, 4.12, and 6.7	CPES implement new technologies slowly and have a comparative disadvantage in sectors in which technological change is fastest.	Both models make a similar prediction on comparative advantage; the Schumpeterian model predicts much lower levels of both exports and imports of high technology goods for CPES than for MES.

Table 4.1 (*continued*)

Hypothesis Number	Where Introduced	Where Empirically Examined	Summary statement of hypothesis	Relevance in evaluating predictive power of Schumpeterian and neoclassical models
7	Sec. 3.7	Sec. 4.5; Table 4.17	CPES have a comparative disadvantage in sectors in which free entry is important in MES.	The Schumpeterian model emphasizes the importance of the lack of new firms in CPES.
8	Sec. 3.7	Sec. 4.5; Table 4.16	CPE trade is lower than ME trade in the sectors in which MNCS are most important.	The Schumpeterian model predicts that the MNCS facilitate trade, both imports and exports.
9	Sec. 3.7	Sec. 4.5; Table 4.16	CPES have a comparative disadvantage in sectors in which MNCS are most important.	Examines whether the presence of MNCS leads to a comparative advantage rather than solely the facilitation of trade.
10	Sec. 3.7	Sec. 4.4; Table 4.11	CPES have a comparative disadvantage in sectors in which new products are important.	The Schumpeterian model predicts that free entry and MNCS are crucial in the process of introducing new goods; the neoclassical model makes the same prediction, emphasizing different causes.
11	Sec. 3.7	Sec. 4.4; Table 4.12	CPES have a comparative advantage in sectors in which new processes are important.	The Schumpeterian model predicts that CPES might not have poor relative technological performance in such sectors, and especially emphasizes the contrast with sectors in which new products are important; the neoclassical model has no such emphasis.

Table 4.1 (*continued*)

Hypothesis Number	Where Introduced	Where Empirically Examined	Summary statement of hypothesis	Relevance in evaluating predictive power of Schumpeterian and neoclassical models
12	Sec. 3.7	Sec. 4.4; Tables 4.7 and 4.8	The costs of hierarchy cause CPES to have a comparative disadvantage in industries subject to diseconomies of scale.	The neoclassical model predicts that CPES will be poor performers in decreasing returns-to-scale sectors.
13	Sec. 3.7	Sec. 4.5; Table 4.15	The costs of hierarchy and the lack of free entry cause CPES to have a comparative disadvantage where there is much product differentiation.	Both models predict that the CPES suffer from lack of product variety; the Schumpeterian model predicts that lack of variety is particularly important in sectors relying on free entry and MNCS.
14	Sec. 3.7	Sec. 4.4; Table 4.6	CPES have less intraindustry trade than MES.	The Schumpeterian model predicts only that intraindustry trade is low for CPES in sectors in which free entry and MNCS are necessary; the neoclassical model predicts that CPE intraindustry trade is low everywhere. Hence, contrast results of Hypotheses 7, 8, and 14.
15	Sec. 3.8	Secs. 6.3 and 6.4; Tables 6.3 and 6.7	CPES have as large a stock of R & D workers as the MES.	Both models predict that effective stock is lower in CPES than in MES.
16	Sec. 3.8	Sec. 4.5; Tables 4.20 and 4.21	CPES have a small endowment of marketing skills.	Both models are consistent with this hypothesis.

Table 4.1 (*continued*)

Hypothesis Number	Where Introduced	Where Empirically Examined	Summary statement of hypothesis	Relevance in evaluating predictive power of Schumpeterian and neoclassical models
17	Sec. 3.8	Secs. 6.3 and 6.4; Tables 6.5 and 6.10–13	Because CMEA fuel prices are relatively low, the exports of fuels of the EE6 to the West are higher than justified by domestic endowments.	Both models are consistent with this hypothesis.
18	Sec. 3.8	Chaps 4, 6, and 7 generally	The character of CPE trade resembles that of the developing countries more closely than that of the developed countries.	Both models are consistent with this hypothesis.
19	Sec. 3.9	Sec. 4.6; Table 4.23	The emphasis on growth causes CPES to have a comparative disadvantage in goods used by industry.	Both models are consistent with this hypothesis.
20	Sec. 3.9	Sec. 4.4; Table 4.13	The emphasis on growth causes CPES to have a comparative advantage in sectors producing much pollution.	Both models are consistent with this hypothesis.
21	Sec. 3.9	Sec. 4.6; Table 4.22	The leader's preferences cause CPES to have a comparative advantage in industrial consumer goods.	Both models are consistent with this hypothesis.
22	Sec. 3.9	Secs. 4.6 and 6.3; Tables 4.24 and 6.4	The leader's preferences cause CPES to have a comparative disadvantage in food.	Both models are consistent with this hypothesis.
23	Sec. 3.9	Sec. 4.6; Tables 4.25 and 4.26	Egalitarian policies cause the CPES to have a comparative	Both models are consistent with this hypothesis.

Table 4.1 (*continued*)

Hypothesis Number	Where Introduced	Where Empirically Examined	Summary statement of hypothesis	Relevance in evaluating predictive power of Schumpeterian and neoclassical models
			advantage in products consumed by those in the upper tail of the income distribution.	
24	Secs. 3.1, 3.2, and 3.10	Chap. 7; Tables 7.1 and 7.3	The trade data of the MES conform to the Heckscher-Ohlin model more closely than the data of the CPES.	Strong prediction of the neoclassical analysis. The Schumpeterian model is agnostic.
25	Sec. 3.1, 3.2, and 3.10	Chap 7; Tables 7.2 and 7.4	The trade data of the MES conform to the PE model more closely than the data of the CPES.	Inconsistent with both models. The Schumpeterian model predicts a strong contrast with the results for the previous hypothesis, the neoclassical model does not.

Note: CPE = centrally planned economy; ME = market economy; PE = product-differentiation and economies-of-scale.

of the effect of salesmanship on trade would be difficult even for Western countries. We do not have measures of any country's endowment of salesmanship, nor is there an obvious proxy.

Qualitative information can provide a basis for empirical work when the "resource endowment" of interest cannot be quantified. Often one knows which goods use a particular endowment intensively in production. If one creates measures of the trade performance of a country for these goods, then one might be able to deduce some facts about the endowment of interest. The present section examines the construction of such measures and explores their properties.

In measuring trade performance with respect to a particular good, one must be able to make statements about whether one country was more successful than another. Insofar as possible, these statements should not be affected by differences between the countries that are extraneous to the question being examined. In particular, measures of trade performance should be normalized so that the relative size of the countries has no effect on the conclusions.[4] For example, the fact that the Soviet Union's exports of high-technology goods are larger than Finland's cannot be taken as evidence that the Soviet Union is the more advanced technologically. Fortunately, as was made clear in Section 2.2, the RCAs normalize for country size.

There is one minor adaptation from earlier definitions in the construction of the RCAs. A particular RCA now summarizes the trade performance of a composite good comprising several three-digit SITC products. For example, the composite good might include products whose manufacture requires intensive use of the factor ''salesmanship.'' Then, the relevant RCAs measure the effect of salesmanship on trade performance. The definition of the RCAs is now:

$$x_{ij} = \frac{\left[\sum_{n \in Ni} X_{nj} \Big/ \sum_{n=1}^{N} X_{nj} \right]}{\left[\sum_{n \in Ni} \sum_{t=1}^{T} X_{nt} \Big/ \sum_{n=1}^{N} \sum_{t=1}^{T} X_{nt} \right]},$$

$$m_{ij} = \frac{\left[\sum_{n \in Ni} M_{nj} \Big/ \sum_{n=1}^{N} M_{nj} \right]}{\left[\sum_{n \in Ni} \sum_{t=1}^{T} M_{nt} \Big/ \sum_{n=1}^{N} \sum_{t=1}^{T} M_{nt} \right]}$$

$$w_{ij} = x_{ij}/m_{ij},$$

where X_{ij} is the gross exports of good i by country j, M_{ij} is the equivalent figure for gross imports, T is the number of countries included in the analysis (i.e., the 77 in Table 2.2), N is the total number of goods, and N_i is the set of indices of goods having a particular property.

Section 2.2 examined whether the knowledge that x_{ij} is larger than x_{it} is sufficient to conclude that country j has the larger endowment of some composite of the factors used intensively in the production of good i. The focus here, however, is on specific endowments rather than composites. The RCAs are used in this chapter in a context in which one knows only that a certain resource endowment is used particularly intensively in producing good i. Knowledge of the intensivity of use of other resource endowments is absent. Can one then conclude from the evidence of the RCAs that j has relatively more of the endowment than t? The answer to this question in a two-good,

[4] Ideally one would want to control for many other factors, but the relevant information is not available. This issue will be addressed at the end of the section.

two-factor world is in the affirmative under fairly weak assumptions, but in a multicommodity, multifactor world the answer must be appropriately qualified.

When one ignores all but one resource endowment, the central problem in making strong inferences from revealed comparative advantages is that the clean conclusions of the $2 \times 2 \times 2$ Heckscher-Ohlin theorem are somewhat muddier in a multicommodity, multifactor world. The difficulty is easy to see using a simple example. Let us assume that costume jewelry, while being intensive in the use of salesmanship, also employs intensively the services of skilled artisans. Then a high value on the RCA for costume jewelry could be due to a very large endowment of skilled artisans in the presence of average levels of salesmanship. The RCA does not give definitive evidence on the endowment of salesmanship. The problem is simply that in a multifactor world success in exporting a particular item can result from the abundance of one of many endowments.

Of course, international trade theorists have identified conditions under which one can make the desired types of conclusions, but these conditions are stringent. In the context of the example, they would require that a *ceteris paribus* relative rise in the endowment of salesmanship must lead to a rise in the share of costume jewelry in GNP, whatever the structure of an economy's resource endowments.[5] As Ethier (1984, p. 161) comments, one is essentially in the position of assuming a 2×2 economy if such conditions are adopted.

There is, however, recourse to a different set of results, based on "restrictions no more severe than those conventionally adopted in the two dimensional environment" (Ethier 1984, p. 161). These results show that "a country tends on average to import those goods which make relatively intensive use of its relatively scarce factors in a quantity sense, where a factor is scarce or abundant according to whether the home country accounts for a smaller or greater supply of that factor than factors in general" (Ethier 1984, pp. 177–78). The important words here are "tends on average," instead of "must" in the two-dimensional environment. A functional relationship has been replaced by a probabilistic one. (Here the probabilistic element results not from some inherent uncertainty, but from subjective uncertainty on the part of the observer.)

Consider the following scenario. One knows that factor k is used intensively in the production of good i. Calculations reveal that $x_{ij} > x_{it}$. There is absolutely no information on factor endowments in either country j or country t.[6] One is then asked to choose between two hypotheses: either "j has relatively more of k than t" or "t has at least as much k as j." What should a good

---

[5] A paraphrase, this statement is a little imprecise, but it captures the basic flavor of the conditions pertaining to the relevant proposition in Ethier 1984, p. 154.

[6] In the situations examined in this chapter, ignorance on the more-usual factor endowments is not the case. Rather, there is the problem of integrating information on these endowments with the analysis of nonquantifiables, such as salesmanship.

Bayesian do? Pick the former hypothesis, of course. It would be thoroughly inappropriate, from the point of view of statistical theory, to conclude that there is no basis for judging whether j or t has more of k. Revealed comparative advantages do give information about the factor endowments of countries.

Given that the RCAs give probabilistic, not deterministic, information, one can proceed to organize that information in the manner least likely to give erroneous conclusions. Errors might arise, for example, if the structure of the "irrelevant"[7] factor endowments causes a country's RCA of interest to be far different from that expected when assuming that the country's irrelevant endowments are at world-average levels. In order to forestall such problems, one should as far as possible use trade statistics of groups of countries rather than of individual nations. (Groups of countries are more likely than individual countries to have relative resource endowments close to world averages.) Hence, the safest conclusions are to be derived by comparing the Eastern European countries as a whole to groups of market economies. Given that the irrelevant resource endowments vary between countries, a further check is to examine whether there is consistency of results across individual countries.

To make correct conclusions more likely, one should ensure that goods have been appropriately aggregated when constructing RCAs. Because the correlation across goods of the intensity of factor use is not unity, judicious aggregation can lead to composites that use irrelevant factor endowments at average levels. Hence, judgments made using RCAs for aggregate goods are more reliable than those made using information on individual goods. Moreover, one should ensure that the aggregate is constructed using goods produced by a wide variety of industries. Then, it is less likely that the intensity of use of an irrelevant factor endowment is far from average.

As a final observation, it is necessary to point out that the conclusions of the immediately preceding paragraphs and those of the theorems of Section 2.2 are somewhat at odds. The theorems show that the RCAs are most reliable as indicators of comparative advantage when goods are least aggregated. However, in making inferences from comparative advantage to factor endowments, greater reliability derives from greater aggregation. Thus, the level of aggregation must be chosen as a compromise between these two forces. Fortunately, there is much middle ground, where both sets of requirements can be satisfied.

In the above paragraphs and in Chapter 2, the properties of RCAs were examined within the context of the standard Heckscher-Ohlin model of trade. However, HO theory describes only one type of flow—interindustry trade due to differences in relative resource endowments. As Chapter 3 showed, one must also be cognizant of the existence of intraindustry trade. For the RCAs,

---

[7] The word "irrelevant" here implies only that the focus of interest is not on these factor endowments.

such trade does not add any fundamentally new problems of interpretation, but rather implies that one should be careful when attaching meaning to particular numerical values. Hence, in Appendix C the consequences of intraindustry trade for the interpretation of RCAs are examined. The analysis shows that the presence of intraindustry trade does not change the basic information that one can extract from RCAs, provided one interprets them with care.

4.2. The Groupings of Goods Used in the Analysis of RCAs

In order to derive conclusions about any specific feature of an economy from trade data alone, it is necessary to find a composite good for which trade performance reliably reflects the level of a particular resource endowment (or a specific preference). This is not an easy task, for two reasons—one theoretical, the other empirical.

As explained in Section 4.1, one cannot assume that abundance of a certain resource endowment translates deterministically into a comparative advantage for any good using the endowment intensively. The levels of many other resource endowments affect the structure of comparative advantage. If only trade data are available, nothing can be done to solve this problem. One can merely hope that the effect of the "irrelevant" endowments is neutral. Under the best scenario, the collective results for sets of countries considered individually (or for aggregates of countries) reflect the endowment of interest, because other endowments vary randomly across countries. This assumption has been used frequently in the past, often implicitly, for example, in Gruber, et al. (1967), Balassa (1977), and Drabek (1983). Even in the framework of a multiendowment regression model, it was necessary for Leamer (1984, p. 117) to make an analogous assumption concerning the characteristics of unmeasured endowments.

After the theoretical difficulties have been removed, one faces the empirical problem of matching goods to factor endowments. Ideally, such matching uses a technology matrix (or a set of demand functions). For the types of trade determinants considered here, such information is not available. Thus, a more ad hoc approach must be taken. Outside the trade literature, there is scattered information about the character of production and consumption of many goods. This allows one to classify goods according to whether they have a certain property. For example, previous studies have identified research-intensive industries. Therefore, one can construct an RCA indicating technological level by aggregating the trade figures for goods produced in the research-intensive sectors.

Table 4.2 lists the information used to construct the aggregate goods analyzed in Sections 4.3 to 4.6. The technology example, detailed on line 9, can

Table 4.2

The Groupings of SITC Categories Used for Construction of Revealed Comparative Advantages

(The line numbers correspond to the numbers of Chapter 4's tables in which the relevant trade data appear.)

Name of Group; (Book Section Giving Results)	Phenomenon Common to Goods in Group	Property of Goods Used for Purposes of Classification (Source of Information)	Types of Goods Included in Group	SITC Codes of Goods in Group
3. Ricardo goods Sec. 4.3	Goods for which natural resources are important in production.	Judgment of Hufbauer and Chilas (1974, pp. 16–17, 35–38).	Food, wood, fibers, minerals, paper, nonferrous metals, oils, ores, raw fuels.	011–13, 022–25, 041–48, 051–55, 061, 071–72, 074–75, 121, 242–43, 251, 261–63, 271, 274, 281, 283, 285, 321, 331, 341, 411, 421–22, 431, 667, 681–87, 689
4. Heckscher-Ohlin goods Sec. 4.3	Goods produced with a standard technology and manufactured with constant returns-to-scale	Judgment of Hufbauer and Chilas (1974, pp. 16–17, 35–38).	Beverages, tobacco, cement, petroleum, floor coverings, glass, pottery, ferrous metals, metal products, domestic appliances, cars, locomotives, ships, furniture, clothing, books, jewelry, stationery.	111–12, 122, 273, 533, 551, 553–54, 611–13, 621, 629, 651–57, 661–62, 664–66, 671–79, 691–98, 724–75, 731–33, 812, 821, 831, 841–42, 851, 892–95, 897

Table 4.2 (*continued*)

Name of Group; (Book Section Giving Results)	Phenomenon Common to Goods in Group	Property of Goods Used for Purposes of Classification (Source of Information)	Types of Goods Included in Group	SITC Codes of Goods in Group
5. Product cycle goods Sec. 4.3	High technology commodities with large know-how rents.	Judgment of Hufbauer and Chilas (1974, pp. 16–17, 35–38).	Chemicals, medicines, plastics, dyes, fertilizers, explosives, machinery, aircraft, instruments, clocks, munitions.	512–15, 521, 541, 581, 532, 561, 571, 711–12, 714–15, 717–18, 722–23, 726, 729, 734, 861, 862, 864, 951
6. Intra-industry trade Sec. 4.3	Goods that are both exported and imported by the same countries.	Goods for which Grubel and Lloyd's (1975, p. 36) index of intraindustry trade is above 60% (Grubel and Lloyd 1975, pp. 30–35).	Confectionery, chemicals, plastics, cement, semiprecious stones, steel plates, leather, machinery, telecommunications equipment, aircraft, photographic equipment, books, toys, works of art.	062, 581, 661, 667, 674, 684, 611, 512–14, 711, 714–15, 724, 726, 734, 812, 862, 892–94, 896
7. Economies of scale Sec. 4.4	Producing sector is subject to large economies.	U.S. elasticity of scale is larger than 1.09 (Hufbauer 1970, pp. 212–22).	Perfumery, soaps, paper, glassware, electrical machinery, electrical appliances, road vehicles, aircraft.	551–53, 641, 665, 711, 722, 725, 733, 734
8. Diseconomies of scale Sec. 4.4	Producing sector is subject to diseconomies of scale.	U.S. elasticity of scale is below unity (Hufbauer 1970, pp. 212–22).	Explosives, leather, textiles, nonferrous metals, clothing, clocks.	571, 611, 652–54, 656, 681–89, 841–42, 864
9. High R & D Sec. 4.4	Research and development expenditures in producing sector are large.	U.S. R & D expenditures as a percentage of sales are above 5% of sales (Freeman 1982, pp. 20–21).	Pharmaceuticals, office machines, aircraft telecommunications equipment.	541, 714, 724, 734, 861

Table 4.2 (*continued*)

Name of Group; (Book Section Giving Results)	Phenomenon Common to Goods in Group	Property of Goods Used for Purposes of Classification (Source of Information)	Types of Goods Included in Group	SITC Codes of Goods in Group
10. High patent/sales Sec. 4.4	Number of patents in U.S. is large relative to industry size.	Industries with more than 0.7 patents per $1 million of shipments. For data sources, see Mueller 1986, pp. 43, 356.	Chemicals, machinery, telecommunications, railway vehicles, instruments.	512–15, 711–12, 714, 718–19, 722, 724, 726, 731, 733, 861
11. High product patent-to-sales ratio Sec. 4.4	Number of product patents in U.S. is large relative to industry size.	Industries with more than 0.5 product patents per $1 million of shipments. Measure created by combining data in line 10 and information from Scherer 1984, pp. 451–59.	Machines, telecommunications, railway vehicles, nonmotor road vehicles, instruments.	711–12, 714–15, 718–19, 722, 724, 731, 733, 861
12. High process patent-to-sales ratio Sec. 4.4	Number of process patents in U.S. is large relative to industry size.	Industries with more than 0.2 process patents per $1 million of shipments, Measure created by combining data in line 10 and information from Scherer 1984, pp. 451–59.	Chemicals, rubber, fertilizers, plastics.	512–15, 561, 581, 621, 629
13. Pollution Sec. 4.4	Production leads to large amount of pollution.	Abatement costs are over 1.2% of total costs in the U.S. in 1977 (Robison 1983).	Petroleum refining, chemicals, metals, fertilizers, paper, glass.	332, 512–14, 561, 641–42, 671–79, 681–89
14. Business concentration Sec. 4.5	Producing sector is highly concentrated in market economies.	Industries in which eight largest companies employ 50% of industry's employees in at least three of five European countries (Phlips 1971, pp. 184–194).	Tobacco, petroleum products, edible oils, tubes, office machines, telecommunications and domestic electrical equipment, road vehicles, railway vehicles, aircraft.	122, 332, 431, 678, 714, 723–25, 731, 732, 734

Table 4.2 (*continued*)

Name of Group; (Book Section Giving Results)	Phenomenon Common to Goods in Group	Property of Goods Used for Purposes of Classification (Source of Information)	Types of Goods Included in Group	SITC Codes of Goods in Group
15. Product differentiation Sec. 4.5	Goods made for the same purpose differ considerably in nature.	Coefficient of variation of unit prices between U.S. trading partners is above 1.4 (Hufbauer 1970, pp. 212–22).	Radioactive goods, drugs, nails, electric power equipment, other electrical goods, photo supplies.	515, 541, 694, 722, 729, 862
16. MNC activity Sec. 4.5	Sectors in which intra-MNC exchanges are large as a percentage of trade.	Intracompany exports of U.S. MNCS and affiliates are greater than 10% of OECD exports in 1970. (U.S. Tariff Commission 1973, pp. 357, 367).	Drugs, perfumery, soaps, plastics, rubber, paper, office machines, telecommunications, transport equipment, instruments.	541, 553–54, 581, 621, 629, 641, 642, 712, 714, 724, 725, 731–35, 861.
17. Entry into industry Sec. 4.5	Sectors in which entry of new firms is most significant.	More than 200 new firms entered in the U.S. from 1972 to 1982 (U.S., Dept. of Commerce, 1982).	Misc. organic chemicals, rubber products, wood products, paper products, glassware, pottery, machines, books, telecommunications, road vehicles, aircraft, ships, furniture, instruments.	514, 629, 632, 642, 665–66, 691, 712, 714–15, 718–19, 724, 729, 732, 734–35, 812, 821, 861, 892–93, 897
18. Convenience goods Sec. 4.5	Consumers can judge quality easily.	Goods sold in retail outlets with no sales assistance and with high locational density (Porter 1974, pp. 422–28).	Meat, dairy products, groceries, alcoholic drinks, tobacco, books, drugs, soaps.	011–13, 022–24, 032, 048, 053, 061–62, 111–12, 121–22, 421, 541, 553–54, 892
19. Experience-Durable Goods Sec. 4.5	Goods whose quality cannot be ascertained before purchase.	Classification created by Nelson based primarily on durability and high cost of after-sales service (Nelson 1974, p. 739).	Paints, tires, appliances, road vehicles, scientific instruments, clocks, communications equipment.	533, 629, 724–25, 732–33, 861, 864

Table 4.2 (*continued*)

Name of Group; (Book Section Giving Results)	Phenomenon Common to Goods in Group	Property of Goods Used for Purposes of Classification (Source of Information)	Types of Goods Included in Group	SITC Codes of Goods in Group
20. High advertising Sec. 4.5	Consumer goods that are heavily advertised in Western countries.	U.S. advertising to sales ratio above 5% (Comanor and Wilson 1974, pp. 134–35).	Wines, beers, beverages, cereals, drugs, soaps, perfumes, watches.	111–12, 048, 541, 554, 553, 864
21. Low advertising Sec. 4.5	Consumer goods that are little advertised in Western countries.	U.S. advertising to sales ratio below 1.5% (Comanor and Wilson 1974, pp. 134–35).	Meat, sugar, furniture, clothing, furs, paints, tire, footwear, vehicles.	011, 061, 523, 629, 732–33, 821, 841–42, 851
22. Industrial consumer goods Sec. 4.6	Goods used predominantly by consumers.	For Japan, percentage of total use of a good that is accounted for by consumers is above 80% (Hufbauer 1970, pp. 212–22).	Drugs, perfumes, soaps, leather, fur, clothing, travel goods, footwear.	541, 551–53, 611–13, 831, 841–42, 851
23. Goods used by industry Sec. 4.6	Goods used primarily for intermediate consumption and investment.	For Japan, percentage of total use of a good that is accounted for by consumers is below 5% (Hufbauer 1970, pp. 212–22).	Chemicals, dyes, building materials, metals, machinery, electrical equipment.	513–15, 531–32, 661–63, 671–79, 681–89, 711–18, 722–24, 726, 729
24. Food Sec. 4.6	Food products.	Category developed by the author.	Meat, dairy products, fish, cereals, fruit, vegetables, sugar, coffee, tea, spices.	011–13, 022–25, 031–32, 041–48, 051–55, 061–62, 071–75, 091, 099

Table 4.2 (*continued*)

Name of Group; (Book Section Giving Results)	Phenomenon Common to Goods in Group	Property of Goods Used for Purposes of Classification (Source of Information)	Types of Goods Included in Group	SITC Codes of Goods in Group
25. High income Sec. 4.6	Goods consumed disproportionately by high-income countries.	Goods with an income elasticity of demand above 1.5 in a cross-national study (Kravis, et al. 1982, pp. 360–63).	Frozen meat, fresh fruit, coffee, chocolate, clothing, furniture, floor coverings, domestic appliances, cars, books, recreational equipment.	012, 051, 071, 657, 725, 732, 821, 841, 892, 894
26. Luxuries Sec. 4.6	Consumption goods that can be regarded as nonessential.	Category developed by the author.	Confectionery, spices, alcoholic beverages, silk, cosmetics, lace, semi-precious stones, furs, sporting goods, jewelry.	112, 212, 062, 075, 261, 553, 611, 654, 667, 681, 894, 897

be used to illustrate the table's construction. (The line numbers of Table 4.2 correspond to the numbers of the tables in which the results are presented.) The first column of Table 4.2 provides a name for the composite good, while the second column summarizes the property common to the individual products included in the composite. It is assumed that if industries devote a large amount of resources to R & D, they use a production process relying heavily on the application of science. Next, the table lists the exact nature of the criterion used to classify industries and the source of information to which this criterion is applied. I have assumed that an industry's goods can be said to be intensive in high technology if an industry spends more than 5% of its revenues on R & D. The fourth column names some of the products included in the composite good, giving some indication of the nature of the composite.[8] The next column states that information more precisely: a group is exactly characterized by the list of the SITC codes of all goods whose trade data is used to calculate the RCAs.[9]

The empirical results are given in Tables 4.3 to 4.26, below. When inter-

---

[8] For the sake of brevity, unimportant goods are left out of the verbal description.

[9] In most cases, the classification scheme used in the source of the information (cited in

preting the results, readers should refer back to the groupings of countries listed in Section 2.4. It is important to remember that the groupings "Eastern European 6" and "Lower-income OECD" are well matched in terms of level of development. When examining the tables, readers should also bear in mind the deficiencies in the data that were discussed in Chapter 2. The possible biases in RCAs that result from these deficiencies will be discussed in Section 6.5, which develops an analytical framework within which the biases can be best examined. The argument in that section justifies the claim that data omissions cannot explain the results that follow.

The results bear upon the theories of centrally planned trade discussed in Chapter 3. Where they aid in the interpretation of the results, elements of that discussion are repeated. For the complete background to the results, readers should refer to that earlier chapter. In the following pages, continuing reference to Table 4.1 will be helpful in relating the results to the theories of Chapter 3 and the comparison between Schumpeterian and neoclassical paradigms. That table should also help the reader quickly locate the theory relevant to any particular empirical result, and vice versa.

The discussion is divided into four subtopics. The first addresses the overall nature of the trade processes of centrally planned economies.

4.3. A Ladder of Trade: The Position of the Centrally Planned Economies

Mirroring the chronological development of trade theories, the most important determinants of trade change as a country passes through the process of development. For the poorest countries, the natural resources emphasized by Ricardo exert an overwhelming influence. Then, as the ability to implement modern industrial technology rises, trade patterns begin to reflect the factor proportions used in the production of industrial goods—Heckscher-Ohlin trade. Finally, when a country becomes one of the most advanced, it develops products and processes that push forward the boundaries of industrial technology: trade patterns reflect the implementation of advanced technologies.

Hufbauer and Chilas (1974, p. 16) have divided the three-digit SITC into three categories corresponding to the three trade theories. For example, a good is called a "product-cycle good" if the product-cycle theory is the most likely of the three to predict that the good will be exported. (For the characterization of the three composite goods, see lines 3–5 of Table 4.2. The lines of that table are numbered so that any line number is the same as the number of the table in which the corresponding RCAs appear.) Of course, this classification must be imprecise because of lack of information; Hufbauer and Chilas admit

column 3 of Table 4.2) was not the SITC. Therefore, an ad hoc cross-classification had to be constructed in each case.

that it is undertaken "boldly." Nevertheless, most readers would probably agree on the broad outlines of their classification, if not the details.

For the production of "Ricardo goods," a country requires an important specific factor, usually a natural resource. For the scarce factor, country endowments are independent of the level of development. Thus, the potential to export Ricardo goods exists in all countries. "Heckscher-Ohlin goods" are produced with a standard technology based on modern industrial methods. For these goods, technology is well enough understood and sufficiently disseminated that production can occur at many levels of scale and varying factor proportions. The basis for trade in these goods is the difference between world and domestic relative factor endowments of capital and the various types of labor. "Product-cycle goods"[10] are produced using technologies that have not spread far from their country, or even company, of origin. For these goods, production is so intimately tied to the development of technology and to the specifics of demand that exports are by countries at the highest stage of development.

Although the proportions of the three types of goods in trade have been linked to the level of development, other variables affect this link. For example, Canada exports Ricardo goods to an extent greater than predicted by level of development, because of the sheer size of its natural resource endowment. More important for present purposes, the economic system influences the relative balance of trade in the three types of goods, as the hypotheses of Chapter 3 have already made clear.

Many of the hypotheses reflect on the ability to export product-cycle goods. In particular, Hypothesis 6 refers to the general backwardness of the CPEs in implementing advanced technologies, while Hypothesis 10 focuses on the absence of new product development. However, one must note the countervailing effects in Hypothesis 15, which is based on the large endowments of R & D labor in CPEs. Moreover, because the spread of new products is often undertaken by multinational corporations, the absence of these corporations will mean that CPEs lag behind other middle-income nations in beginning to manufacture product-cycle goods (Hypothesis 8).

The weight of the hypotheses tends to suggest that the CPEs have a comparative advantage in Heckscher-Ohlin goods. When decisions are made efficiently, the size of total Heckscher-Ohlin trade is positively related to the difference between a country's relative resource endowments and those of the world as a whole. Thus, a distortion in a country's decision processes increases Heckscher-Ohlin trade if and only if the country's relative resource endowments seem to be further from world averages than is actually the case. Hypothesis 3 predicts that, in the CPEs, the undervaluation of capital enhances

[10] Here I use the name chosen by Hufbauer and Chilas 1974, which was coined by Vernon 1966. The use of that name does not imply reliance on the particular theory developed by Vernon. Rather, "product-cycle" goods are the goods that would be exported by advanced countries, if any one of many "neotechnology" theories held (Hufbauer 1970, p. 195).

the share of Heckscher-Ohlin trade, if these economies are already capital-rich. Given the high saving rates of these countries throughout the postwar period, and given the enormous implicit subsidy for heavy industry in the "priority" system of decision-making, effective capital-labor ratios might well be higher than the world averages. If this is the case, centrally planned systems will generate a higher share of Heckscher-Ohlin trade than market economies at comparable levels of development.

Heckscher-Ohlin goods are produced in the older industrial sectors, where products tend to be homogeneous. Hypothesis 13 predicts that CPEs have a comparative advantage in sectors in which product variety is not important. Hypothesis 7 implicitly predicts a comparative advantage in traditional sectors, where the entry of new firms is likely to play only a small role. Thus, both these hypotheses predict that the exports of CPEs will be concentrated disproportionately in Heckscher-Ohlin goods.

There is one hypothesis that reflects directly on Ricardo goods. Hypothesis 4 predicts that the pricing system of CPEs leads to the export of goods with a high natural resource content.

The results relevant to the above discussion are contained in Tables 4.3–4.5. The RCAs are given for the nine Eastern European countries individually, plus six of the regions defined in Section 2.4. (The country grouping "All" is omitted, because by construction this group's RCAs are always equal to 1.0.) Data are listed for nine years (1975–83), enabling one to draw conclusions both about the robustness of the results and about temporal changes in trade patterns. For each cell in the table, three RCAs are presented: x indicating the export measure, m and w the import and export-import measures.

The most significant feature of Tables 4.3–4.5 is the poor performance of the Eastern European countries on the RCAs for product-cycle goods. For all twenty-seven relevant cases, the values of the RCAs are consistent with better performance in product-cycle goods for the lower-income OECD (hereafter LIO) countries than for the "Eastern European 6" (EE6). For Ricardo and Heckscher-Ohlin goods, the results are not quite as dramatic, but they are clear. A majority of the export-import indices for those types of goods are higher in the EE6 than in the LIO countries. It is obvious that the EE6 has greater comparative advantage in these groups than does the LIO group. The CPEs are further down the ladder of trade than market economies at the same level of development.

The results for individual countries are of some interest. First, East Germany's RCAs for product-cycle goods exceed those of the OECD. East Germany's trade performance on the most sophisticated goods is not only untypical of Eastern Europe, but also at the level of the most advanced countries.[11] Second, Czechoslovakia's trade pattern portrays a country that is at

---

[11] It is possible that data problems could explain this particular result, in particular the omission of trade between the two Germanys. For discussion of this point the reader must await the development of further analytics. Extended discussion is given in Section 6.5.

Table 4.3

The Revealed Comparative Advantages for Ricardo Goods, 1975–1983

	Trade Measure	1975	1976	1977	1978	1979	1980	1981	1982	1983
Market	x	0.81	0.81	0.82	0.84	0.84	0.84	0.88	0.87	0.88
	m	1.04	1.04	1.04	1.03	1.01	1.00	1.00	1.00	1.00
	w	0.78	0.78	0.79	0.81	0.83	0.84	0.88	0.87	0.89
OECD	x	0.70	0.71	0.69	0.71	0.71	0.71	0.74	0.73	0.75
	m	1.06	1.06	1.06	1.05	1.04	1.03	1.04	1.03	1.03
	w	0.66	0.67	0.65	0.68	0.69	0.69	0.71	0.70	0.72
Market minus OECD	x	1.90	1.80	1.86	1.84	1.86	1.84	1.83	1.80	1.77
	m	0.87	0.84	0.86	0.87	0.83	0.81	0.80	0.83	0.79
	w	2.19	2.15	2.16	2.11	2.25	2.27	2.28	2.18	2.25
Low-income OECD	x	0.53	0.54	0.52	0.51	0.47	0.45	0.49	0.47	0.50
	m	1.02	0.95	0.95	0.97	0.92	0.87	0.93	0.93	1.06
	w	0.52	0.57	0.54	0.53	0.52	0.52	0.52	0.51	0.47
Bulgaria	x	1.12	1.17	1.10	1.15	0.83	0.62	0.66	0.79	0.76
	m	0.54	0.70	0.61	0.77	0.82	0.78	0.82	0.57	0.78
	w	2.09	1.67	1.80	1.49	1.01	0.79	0.80	1.39	0.97
Czechoslovakia	x	0.72	0.69	0.69	0.78	0.72	0.68	0.70	0.73	0.72
	m	0.87	0.95	0.84	0.92	1.08	1.01	0.99	0.96	1.13
	w	0.83	0.73	0.83	0.85	0.67	0.67	0.71	0.76	0.64
East Germany (GDR)	x	0.49	0.40	0.38	0.39	0.38	0.22	0.29	0.30	0.34
	m	1.16	1.41	1.45	1.45	1.32	1.55	1.48	1.50	1.62
	w	0.43	0.29	0.26	0.27	0.28	0.14	0.20	0.20	0.21
Hungary	x	1.00	0.94	0.97	1.01	0.86	0.82	0.93	0.98	0.98
	m	0.72	0.73	0.71	0.65	0.70	0.69	0.71	0.62	1.05
	w	1.39	1.29	1.36	1.57	1.23	1.18	1.31	1.59	0.93
Poland	x	1.69	1.60	1.52	1.56	1.54	1.46	1.38	1.61	1.71
	m	0.90	0.99	0.99	1.19	1.35	1.43	1.96	1.53	1.30
	w	1.88	1.61	1.54	1.31	1.14	1.02	0.70	1.05	1.32
Romania	x	0.87	0.71	0.63	0.56	0.44	0.40	0.29	0.31	0.28
	m	0.96	1.21	0.97	0.86	1.05	1.31	1.87	1.43	1.75
	w	0.91	0.59	0.65	0.65	0.42	0.31	0.16	0.22	0.16
USSR	x	1.73	1.89	1.87	1.89	1.73	1.84	1.93	1.88	1.88
	m	1.11	1.10	0.95	1.03	1.22	1.36	1.37	1.42	1.36
	w	1.56	1.72	1.96	1.84	1.41	1.36	1.41	1.32	1.38
Yugoslavia	x	0.82	0.93	0.86	0.87	0.82	0.75	0.72	0.72	0.81
	m	0.46	0.61	0.55	0.45	0.56	0.58	0.60	0.59	0.74
	w	1.78	1.54	1.56	1.92	1.47	1.30	1.20	1.22	1.09
Albania	x	1.65	1.31	1.62	1.76	1.81	1.20	0.83	0.74	1.16
	m	1.20	0.75	1.37	1.37	1.28	0.95	0.95	0.99	0.90
	w	1.37	1.74	1.19	1.29	1.41	1.27	0.87	0.75	1.29
Eastern Europe 9	x	1.35	1.40	1.37	1.38	1.29	1.33	1.36	1.41	1.42
	m	0.92	1.00	0.89	0.93	1.07	1.18	1.27	1.23	1.25
	w	1.46	1.40	1.54	1.49	1.20	1.12	1.07	1.14	1.13
Eastern Europe 6	x	1.09	1.02	0.97	0.99	0.89	0.80	0.72	0.81	0.83
	m	0.88	1.01	0.94	1.00	1.12	1.20	1.38	1.11	1.26
	w	1.25	1.01	1.03	0.99	0.79	0.67	0.52	0.73	0.66

Note: x = export measure; m = import measure; w = export-import measure.

Table 4.4
Revealed Comparative Advantages of Heckscher-Ohlin Goods, 1975–1983

	Trade Measure	1975	1976	1977	1978	1979	1980	1981	1982	1983
Market	x	1.07	1.07	1.07	1.05	1.05	1.04	1.02	1.02	1.01
	m	1.00	1.00	1.01	1.01	1.01	1.01	1.00	1.00	1.01
	w	1.07	1.07	1.06	1.04	1.04	1.04	1.02	1.02	1.01
OECD	x	1.11	1.10	1.11	1.09	1.08	1.08	1.05	1.05	1.05
	m	1.02	1.03	1.03	1.03	1.04	1.03	1.02	1.02	1.02
	w	1.09	1.07	1.07	1.05	1.05	1.06	1.04	1.03	1.02
Market minus OECD	x	0.65	0.71	0.68	0.72	0.71	0.69	0.76	0.78	0.76
	m	0.88	0.87	0.87	0.87	0.84	0.93	0.96	0.92	0.90
	w	0.74	0.82	0.78	0.84	0.84	0.75	0.79	0.85	0.85
Low-income OECD	x	1.53	1.48	1.51	1.53	1.60	1.59	1.52	1.54	1.51
	m	0.84	0.88	0.92	0.92	0.96	1.01	0.96	0.98	0.90
	w	1.83	1.68	1.64	1.67	1.67	1.57	1.58	1.57	1.68
Bulgaria	x	0.81	0.92	0.98	1.04	1.44	1.63	1.63	1.39	1.40
	m	0.96	0.79	0.82	0.94	0.97	0.93	0.89	0.87	0.77
	w	0.85	1.16	1.19	1.11	1.49	1.76	1.84	1.59	1.82
Czechoslovakia	x	1.40	1.40	1.34	1.35	1.38	1.48	1.42	1.40	1.41
	m	0.60	0.65	0.59	0.58	0.57	0.52	0.59	0.64	0.62
	w	2.33	2.16	2.28	2.31	2.44	2.85	2.43	2.20	2.27
East Germany (GDR)	x	1.14	1.17	1.21	1.22	1.20	1.40	1.39	1.42	1.46
	m	0.77	0.75	0.67	0.70	0.71	0.57	0.67	0.61	0.60
	w	1.48	1.55	1.81	1.74	1.69	2.44	2.08	2.31	2.45
Hungary	x	1.20	1.20	1.19	1.18	1.27	1.29	1.19	1.13	1.18
	m	0.84	0.75	0.73	0.77	0.79	0.83	0.81	0.85	0.74
	w	1.43	1.61	1.65	1.53	1.60	1.55	1.46	1.33	1.60
Poland	x	0.71	0.86	0.92	0.95	0.99	1.03	1.03	0.90	0.84
	m	0.89	0.77	0.73	0.63	0.66	0.67	0.50	0.58	0.68
	w	0.80	1.11	1.26	1.51	1.49	1.53	2.05	1.56	1.23
Romania	x	1.40	1.60	1.64	1.71	1.91	2.01	2.05	1.96	2.02
	m	0.88	0.80	0.73	0.74	0.75	0.72	0.55	0.75	0.68
	w	1.59	2.01	2.24	2.32	2.54	2.78	3.71	2.62	2.98
USSR	x	0.85	0.74	0.73	0.76	0.90	0.81	0.87	0.95	0.95
	m	0.97	0.96	0.87	0.88	0.89	0.86	0.98	0.95	0.94
	w	0.88	0.78	0.84	0.86	1.01	0.94	0.90	1.00	1.01
Yugoslavia	x	1.49	1.37	1.40	1.44	1.47	1.54	1.53	1.59	1.58
	m	0.94	0.92	0.91	0.86	0.83	0.86	0.90	0.96	0.95
	w	1.59	1.48	1.53	1.67	1.77	1.78	1.70	1.66	1.67
Albania	x	0.98	1.21	1.07	0.99	0.93	1.06	1.28	1.15	1.13
	m	1.13	1.15	1.00	1.09	1.05	1.26	1.05	1.09	0.93
	w	0.86	1.06	1.08	0.90	0.89	0.85	1.22	1.05	1.21
Eastern Europe 9	x	1.02	1.00	1.00	1.05	1.14	1.12	1.15	1.14	1.15
	m	0.90	0.87	0.81	0.80	0.81	0.79	0.84	0.88	0.85
	w	1.13	1.16	1.24	1.31	1.42	1.42	1.36	1.30	1.35
Eastern Europe 6	x	1.09	1.19	1.20	1.24	1.34	1.43	1.46	1.36	1.37
	m	0.83	0.75	0.71	0.70	0.71	0.69	0.64	0.70	0.68
	w	1.31	1.58	1.70	1.79	1.89	2.07	2.26	1.93	2.02

Note: x = export measure; m = import measure; w = export-import measure.

Table 4.5
The Revealed Comparative Advantages of Product-Cycle Goods, 1975–1983

	Trade Measure	1975	1976	1977	1978	1979	1980	1981	1982	1983
Market	x	1.12	1.12	1.11	1.10	1.10	1.11	1.09	1.10	1.10
	m	0.96	0.96	0.95	0.96	0.97	0.98	0.99	0.99	0.99
	w	1.16	1.17	1.18	1.15	1.13	1.14	1.11	1.11	1.11
OECD	x	1.21	1.22	1.23	1.20	1.22	1.23	1.22	1.22	1.21
	m	0.91	0.90	0.89	0.90	0.91	0.93	0.93	0.94	0.94
	w	1.33	1.36	1.37	1.33	1.34	1.33	1.30	1.31	1.29
Market minus OECD	x	0.30	0.30	0.30	0.33	0.32	0.33	0.36	0.38	0.44
	m	1.28	1.34	1.31	1.30	1.37	1.28	1.24	1.26	1.31
	w	0.24	0.23	0.23	0.25	0.23	0.26	0.29	0.31	0.34
Low-income OECD	x	0.88	0.90	0.90	0.86	0.85	0.94	0.93	0.92	0.90
	m	1.15	1.15	1.12	1.11	1.10	1.07	1.08	1.06	1.06
	w	0.77	0.78	0.80	0.77	0.77	0.88	0.86	0.87	0.85
Bulgaria	x	1.09	0.91	0.99	0.81	0.64	0.70	0.63	0.76	0.71
	m	1.45	1.54	1.52	1.24	1.19	1.24	1.30	1.48	1.44
	w	0.76	0.59	0.65	0.65	0.54	0.56	0.49	0.52	0.50
Czechoslovakia	x	0.86	0.88	0.94	0.82	0.86	0.86	0.88	0.87	0.87
	m	1.56	1.49	1.58	1.56	1.46	1.55	1.47	1.41	1.37
	w	0.55	0.59	0.59	0.53	0.59	0.55	0.60	0.62	0.63
East Germany (GDR)	x	1.48	1.55	1.50	1.42	1.48	1.49	1.36	1.31	1.20
	m	1.06	0.92	0.93	0.91	1.04	0.96	0.97	1.04	1.04
	w	1.40	1.68	1.61	1.55	1.43	1.55	1.41	1.26	1.16
Hungary	x	0.73	0.78	0.76	0.75	0.82	0.84	0.86	0.88	0.80
	m	1.46	1.54	1.58	1.60	1.55	1.48	1.46	1.48	1.29
	w	0.50	0.50	0.48	0.47	0.53	0.57	0.59	0.59	0.62
Poland	x	0.63	0.54	0.55	0.55	0.51	0.54	0.62	0.49	0.47
	m	1.22	1.30	1.36	1.32	1.10	1.05	0.85	1.05	1.07
	w	0.52	0.41	0.40	0.42	0.46	0.51	0.73	0.47	0.44
Romania	x	0.74	0.63	0.69	0.64	0.54	0.54	0.57	0.64	0.57
	m	1.25	1.07	1.40	1.49	1.32	1.11	0.86	1.01	0.93
	w	0.59	0.59	0.49	0.43	0.41	0.49	0.67	0.63	0.62
USSR	x	0.37	0.33	0.39	0.41	0.40	0.34	0.26	0.23	0.23
	m	1.07	1.08	1.30	1.22	1.06	0.95	0.83	0.84	0.91
	w	0.35	0.30	0.30	0.34	0.38	0.36	0.31	0.27	0.25
Yugoslavia	x	0.57	0.55	0.62	0.60	0.61	0.64	0.67	0.59	0.51
	m	1.58	1.51	1.58	1.69	1.65	1.59	1.50	1.44	1.36
	w	0.36	0.37	0.39	0.35	0.37	0.40	0.44	0.41	0.38
Albania	x	0.05	0.07	0.06	0.06	0.05	0.12	0.09	0.13	0.16
	m	0.71	0.94	0.73	0.74	0.82	0.78	1.00	0.94	1.14
	w	0.06	0.08	0.08	0.08	0.06	0.15	0.09	0.13	0.14
Eastern Europe 9	x	0.61	0.55	0.60	0.59	0.57	0.54	0.50	0.47	0.44
	m	1.24	1.23	1.39	1.36	1.24	1.14	1.02	1.04	1.06
	w	0.49	0.45	0.43	0.43	0.46	0.47	0.49	0.45	0.42
Eastern Europe 6	x	0.83	0.78	0.81	0.76	0.74	0.77	0.81	0.82	0.76
	m	1.31	1.30	1.40	1.39	1.26	1.20	1.12	1.25	1.19
	w	0.64	0.60	0.58	0.55	0.59	0.64	0.72	0.66	0.64

Note: x = export measure; m = import measure; w = export-import measure.

the average level of development for Eastern Europe and below the level of the LIO countries. This is rather surprising, because Czechoslovakia and East Germany are usually paired in terms of level of development. Finally, the results for the two reformed economies—Hungary and Yugoslavia—seem to be typical of those of the CPEs. If reform has an effect, then, it is not to be seen in the most gross trade aggregates.

Scanning the temporal pattern of results, one can see that there is sufficient degree of robustness to be confident in drawing conclusions. The variation across countries and through time is far from random. Where temporal variation occurs, it appears to be systematic. The most significant trend is the gradual decline of Ricardo trade and increase in Heckscher-Ohlin trade in the EE6. One possible explanation for this is based on Hypothesis 17. In 1975 the Soviet Union was beginning to react to the rise of the Organization of Petroleum Exporting Countries (OPEC). From that year on, Soviet terms on oil deliveries to the council for Mutual Economic Assistance were becoming less beneficial, with regard to both price and quantity. The implicit oil endowment the Soviet Union gave the EE6 declined from 1975 on—hence, the decline in Ricardo trade. The EE6 was forced to change trade policy. It is interesting that the change led to increased emphasis on Heckscher-Ohlin goods, not on product-cycle goods. Even though most Eastern European countries had borrowed heavily to buy Western technology in the early 1970s, there is no evidence that they were able to use this technology to change trade structure.

The information given in Table 4.3 for the Soviet Union makes it clear that natural resources dominate in Soviet trade. While this is hardly surprising, it does mean that the results in the remainder of this chapter must be interpreted very gingerly for that country. The *ceteris paribus* assumption on resource endowments that is needed for the interpretation of results cannot hold for the Soviet Union. Because of the dominance of natural resources in Soviet trade, methods that take into account the multicausal determinants of trade are absolutely necessary to analyze that country. These methods are employed in Chapters 6 and 7. For the remainder of the present chapter, the focus is on the results for the Eastern European 6.

Intraindustry Trade   In closing the analysis of this section, I examine a form of trade that is not competitive with the other three, as they are with each other, but that occurs simultaneously. Intraindustry trade increases the number of varieties available to consumers when the number produced efficiently is limited by economies of scale. For this type of trade, it is somewhat misleading to talk in terms of revealed comparative advantages. Trade to accomplish an increase in the number of varieties is balanced. If the trade for any good is not balanced, that must be a reflection of factors unrelated to the causes of intraindustry trade. Thus, in examining the empirical significance of intraindustry trade, one should not focus any attention on the export-import (w)

indices. Rather, intraindustry trade is revealed to be important in a country's affairs if *both* the export (*x*) and the import (*m*) indices are large. Hence, in Table 4.6 the third line of information for each country or group of countries performs a different role from that in other tables. Rather than presenting export-import indices, Table 4.6 gives the *sum* of the export and import indices. This sum, denoted "*x* + *m*," rises with the importance of intra-industry trade; it " equals 2 when a country has a level of intraindustry trade that is at world-average levels.

It is now well accepted, both empirically and theoretically, that the share of intraindustry trade in total trade rises with the level of development. But there can be other influences on this share—economic system, for example. Hypothesis 14 predicts that CPEs undertake less intraindustry trade than MEs at equivalent levels of development. That hypothesis is based on a number of systemic factors, including the need for simplicity in hierarchy and the lack of development of new products in CPEs.

The results for intraindustry trade are presented in Table 4.6. These results give no clear message. The "*x* + *m*" indices for the EE6 are slightly below those of the lower-income OECD (LIO) group. However, especially in the 1970s, the difference between the LIO group and EE6 is small, compared with that between the LIO group and the "market minus OECD" and the OECD groups. Moreover, three Eastern European countries—Czechoslovakia, the GDR, and Hungary—have indices consistently above those for the LIO coun-tries. Indeed, it seems that only Poland in the EE6 has levels of intraindustry trade markedly below those expected on the basis of level of development.

One cannot conclude from Table 4.6 that there are large differences between the levels of intraindustry trade in the EE6 and the LIO countries. Thus, when comparing the RCAs of the EE6 and the LIO group in future analyses, one can assume that differences in RCAs are not simply a result of different systemic propensities to conduct intraindustry trade that apply to all goods. The warnings on the effects of intraindustry trade on RCAs that are given in Appendix C certainly do not apply in general to comparisons between the EE6 and the LIO countries.[12] This conclusion does not, however, apply to analyses of differences between the OECD countries and the EE6. For com-parisons of these two groups, it is necessary to use the examples developed in Appendix C in Tables C.1 and C.2 in order to draw correct implications on comparative advantage from RCAs.

4.4. The Interaction of Production Characteristics and Economic System

Economies of Scale   If a central-planning hierarchy must economize on the number of subordinate units, then increasing returns-to-scale sectors will be

---

[12] This is not to say that these warnings do not apply to analyses of particular goods for which

Table 4.6

The Shares of Intraindustry Trade in Total Trade, 1975–1983

	Trade Measure	1975	1976	1977	1978	1979	1980	1981	1982	1983
Market	x	1.12	1.11	1.11	1.09	1.10	1.11	1.09	1.10	1.09
	m	1.02	1.00	1.00	1.01	1.01	1.02	1.03	1.02	1.01
	$x + m$	2.14	2.11	2.11	2.10	2.11	2.13	2.12	2.12	2.10
OECD	x	1.18	1.19	1.19	1.16	1.17	1.19	1.18	1.18	1.16
	m	0.99	0.97	0.98	0.98	0.98	0.99	1.01	1.00	0.99
	$x + m$	2.17	2.16	2.17	2.14	2.15	2.18	2.19	2.18	2.15
Market Minus OECD	x	0.50	0.49	0.50	0.57	0.52	0.50	0.52	0.55	0.62
	m	1.14	1.20	1.19	1.16	1.20	1.16	1.07	1.09	1.12
	$x + m$	1.64	1.69	1.69	1.73	1.72	1.66	1.59	1.64	1.74
Low-income OECD	x	0.95	0.94	0.91	0.86	0.85	0.89	0.93	0.94	0.91
	m	0.99	1.00	1.00	0.98	1.01	1.00	1.03	1.03	1.01
	$x + m$	1.94	1.94	1.91	1.84	1.86	1.89	1.96	1.97	1.92
Bulgaria	x	0.92	0.98	0.94	0.83	0.79	0.78	0.87	0.96	0.93
	m	0.93	0.88	0.95	0.88	0.98	0.91	0.86	0.98	0.93
	$x + m$	1.85	1.86	1.89	1.71	1.77	1.69	1.73	1.94	1.86
Czechoslovakia	x	1.01	0.93	1.05	0.96	0.98	0.99	1.01	1.03	1.05
	m	1.22	1.06	1.07	1.06	1.03	1.05	1.01	1.00	0.93
	$x + m$	2.23	1.99	2.12	2.02	2.01	2.04	2.02	2.03	1.98
East Germany (GDR)	x	1.32	1.19	1.11	1.04	1.17	1.15	1.09	1.05	1.07
	m	1.06	0.88	0.94	0.88	0.81	0.87	0.86	0.75	0.82
	$x + m$	2.38	2.07	2.05	1.92	1.98	2.02	1.95	1.80	1.89
Hungary	x	0.91	0.94	0.89	0.82	0.94	0.92	0.93	0.92	0.85
	m	1.08	1.05	1.12	1.02	1.07	1.09	1.01	1.04	0.89
	$x + m$	1.99	1.99	2.01	1.84	2.01	2.01	1.94	1.96	1.74
Poland	x	0.52	0.52	0.49	0.57	0.53	0.53	0.66	0.50	0.44
	m	0.86	0.91	0.97	0.97	0.85	0.77	0.66	0.78	0.68
	$x + m$	1.38	1.43	1.46	1.54	1.38	1.30	1.32	1.28	1.12
Romania	x	0.81	0.58	0.78	0.75	0.58	0.60	0.66	0.75	0.60
	m	1.06	1.02	1.19	1.24	1.10	0.97	0.77	1.00	0.98
	$x + m$	1.87	1.60	1.97	1.99	1.68	1.57	1.43	1.75	1.58
USSR	x	0.36	0.50	0.52	0.58	0.52	0.54	0.29	0.28	0.28
	m	0.83	0.77	0.90	0.84	0.85	0.80	0.74	0.68	0.71
	$x + m$	1.19	1.27	1.42	1.42	1.37	1.34	1.03	0.96	0.99
Yugoslavia	x	0.57	0.56	0.54	0.53	0.58	0.54	0.59	0.59	0.63
	m	1.19	1.17	1.10	1.09	1.09	1.14	1.25	1.28	1.18
	$x + m$	1.76	1.73	1.64	1.62	1.67	1.68	1.84	1.87	1.81
Albania	x	0.11	0.12	0.07	0.10	0.07	0.11	0.09	0.14	0.14
	m	0.79	1.15	0.92	0.58	0.61	0.88	0.78	0.81	0.67
	$x + m$	0.90	1.27	0.99	0.68	0.68	0.99	0.87	0.95	0.81
Eastern Europe 9	x	0.61	0.62	0.65	0.66	0.63	0.63	0.53	0.51	0.49
	m	0.95	0.90	0.99	0.96	0.93	0.90	0.84	0.83	0.81
	$x + m$	1.56	1.52	1.64	1.62	1.56	1.53	1.37	1.34	1.30
Eastern Europe 6	x	0.83	0.76	0.80	0.78	0.77	0.78	0.85	0.85	0.80
	m	1.00	0.96	1.04	1.02	0.96	0.92	0.84	0.92	0.85
	$x + m$	1.83	1.72	1.84	1.80	1.73	1.70	1.69	1.77	1.65

Note: In this table, "$x + m$" means the sum of the export (x) and import (m) indices. x = export measure; m = import measure.

relatively favored. Hence, Hypothesis 12 predicts that CPEs have a comparative disadvantage in sectors with decreasing returns-to-scale and a comparative advantage in sectors with increasing returns-to-scale. Tables 4.7 and 4.8 present the relevant evidence. A glance at the first four rows of these tables reveals that the RCAs are related to income levels. Hence, it is important to compare the Eastern European countries with the matched group of MEs—the low-income OECD group. If that comparison is made, one can discern little effect of economic system. For the eighteen export-import indexes in the two tables, eleven are consistent with Hypothesis 12 and seven are inconsistent with that hypothesis. The oft-claimed disadvantages of large-size units in CPEs are not reflected in trade patterns in any obvious way.

The Level of Technology   Hypothesis 6 predicts that CPEs lag in the application of new technologies. This hypothesis follows from either a neoclassical or a Schumpeterian perspective. Hypothesis 15 identifies a countervailing effect due to the large endowment of R & D workers in CPEs. Tables 4.9 and 4.10 present the results relevant to these two hypotheses.

One can create commodity aggregates by using information on either the inputs or the outputs of the R & D process. Table 4.9 examines trade performance in those commodities that are produced in sectors spending large amounts on R & D inputs. Table 4.10 focuses on sectors that have gained a large number of patents relative to industry size. These two measures—R & D to sales and patents to sales—are in common use in the economics literature on technological change (Freeman 1982; Scherer 1984).

The results in Tables 4.9 and 4.10 are consistent and show an unmistakable pattern. For all comparisons of export-import RCAs in the two tables, the EE6 group always has a lower value than the LIO group. The results for the EE6 reflect a level of technological development closer to the "market minus OECD" grouping than to the LIO countries—a level of technological sophistication far below that to be expected from the usual statistics on per capita incomes.[13] The only substantive difference between the two tables lies in the levels of trade. This difference can be easily explained by the fact that all the goods in the aggregate commodity examined in Table 4.9 are goods for which the activities of MNCs are particularly important. (This is not true for all the goods that have high patent-to-sales ratios.) In the previous chapter it was argued that MNCs facilitate trade, and in Section 4.5 the results show that the absence of MNCs reduces the total level of trade.

---

there is a reason for intraindustry trade to be much lower in CPEs than in MEs. Section 4.6 contains examples of such goods.

[13] Drabek 1983 has done a smilar analysis for 1970–77. His results differ in some important respects because of differences in methodology: he compares high-technology goods with a limited subset of other goods. This leads to results that indicate a higher level of technology in Eastern Europe than my results do (see, e.g., Drabek's table 1, p. 638).

Table 4.7
Revealed Comparative Advantages for Industries with Large-Scale Economies, 1975–1983

	Trade Measure	1975	1976	1977	1978	1979	1980	1981	1982	1983
Market	x	1.12	1.12	1.12	1.10	1.11	1.12	1.10	1.11	1.10
	m	1.01	0.99	0.98	0.98	1.00	1.01	1.01	1.01	1.01
	w	1.11	1.14	1.14	1.12	1.10	1.11	1.09	1.09	1.09
OECD	x	1.22	1.23	1.24	1.21	1.23	1.25	1.24	1.25	1.23
	m	0.98	0.94	0.93	0.95	0.95	0.95	0.97	0.97	0.98
	w	1.25	1.31	1.33	1.28	1.29	1.32	1.27	1.29	1.26
Market minus OECD	x	0.23	0.23	0.24	0.26	0.25	0.25	0.26	0.30	0.36
	m	1.18	1.30	1.29	1.25	1.33	1.32	1.19	1.24	1.23
	w	0.20	0.18	0.18	0.21	0.19	0.19	0.22	0.24	0.29
Low-income OECD	x	0.92	0.95	0.91	0.87	0.86	0.94	0.91	0.92	0.95
	m	0.92	0.91	0.85	0.89	0.88	0.91	0.92	0.90	0.93
	w	1.00	1.05	1.07	0.98	0.98	1.04	0.98	1.02	1.01
Bulgaria	x	0.42	0.39	0.42	0.49	0.36	0.29	0.29	0.23	0.30
	m	0.87	0.76	0.71	0.60	0.72	0.68	0.64	0.62	0.55
	w	0.48	0.51	0.59	0.83	0.50	0.42	0.45	0.37	0.54
Czechoslovakia	x	0.94	1.09	1.18	1.02	0.93	0.95	0.95	0.90	0.90
	m	0.54	0.54	0.60	0.53	0.57	0.56	0.58	0.64	0.60
	w	1.73	1.99	1.97	1.92	1.62	1.70	1.63	1.41	1.50
East Germany (GDR)	x	0.94	0.99	0.93	0.82	0.85	0.86	0.75	0.71	0.69
	m	0.68	0.48	0.53	0.47	0.55	0.50	0.44	0.52	0.55
	w	1.38	2.03	1.75	1.74	1.54	1.73	1.72	1.36	1.25
Hungary	x	0.58	0.58	0.61	0.55	0.65	0.70	0.63	0.56	0.52
	m	0.79	0.82	0.77	0.78	0.81	0.79	0.77	0.79	0.69
	w	0.74	0.71	0.78	0.71	0.80	0.88	0.83	0.70	0.75
Poland	x	0.55	0.63	0.59	0.61	0.63	0.63	0.81	0.57	0.58
	m	0.55	0.62	0.68	0.57	0.53	0.51	0.36	0.51	0.52
	w	1.01	1.01	0.86	1.06	1.18	1.23	2.23	1.12	1.12
Romania	x	0.33	0.40	0.53	0.45	0.51	0.57	0.48	0.51	0.41
	m	0.62	0.65	0.88	0.67	0.59	0.53	0.44	0.59	0.68
	w	0.54	0.62	0.61	0.66	0.87	1.08	1.09	0.87	0.60
USSR	x	0.23	0.24	0.22	0.26	0.18	0.20	0.11	0.09	0.09
	m	0.58	0.49	0.73	0.69	0.58	0.66	0.56	0.55	0.61
	w	0.39	0.48	0.30	0.38	0.32	0.31	0.20	0.17	0.14
Yugoslavia	x	1.21	1.31	1.28	1.14	1.36	1.37	1.31	1.15	1.08
	m	1.03	1.04	1.02	0.95	0.92	0.91	0.95	0.78	0.67
	w	1.17	1.26	1.26	1.20	1.47	1.51	1.39	1.48	1.61
Albania	x	0.05	0.17	0.14	0.25	0.12	0.13	0.08	0.07	0.16
	m	0.48	0.51	0.36	0.45	0.48	0.55	0.70	0.55	0.91
	w	0.11	0.34	0.38	0.55	0.26	0.24	0.11	0.13	0.18
Eastern Europe 9	x	0.50	0.54	0.54	0.53	0.50	0.50	0.43	0.36	0.36
	m	0.66	0.62	0.76	0.70	0.64	0.66	0.60	0.60	0.61
	w	0.76	0.88	0.71	0.77	0.77	0.75	0.72	0.61	0.58
Eastern Europe 6	x	0.63	0.69	0.72	0.66	0.67	0.70	0.69	0.63	0.61
	m	0.63	0.63	0.70	0.61	0.60	0.58	0.52	0.62	0.59
	w	1.00	1.09	1.02	1.09	1.11	1.21	1.33	1.02	1.02

Note: x = export measure; m = import measure; w = export-import measure.

Table 4.8

Revealed Comparative Advantages for Industries with Diseconomies of Scale, 1975–1983

	Trade Measure	1975	1976	1977	1978	1979	1980	1981	1982	1983
Market	x	1.03	1.03	1.03	1.02	1.01	1.02	0.99	0.99	0.98
	m	1.06	1.06	1.05	1.06	1.05	1.05	1.04	1.04	1.03
	w	0.97	0.97	0.98	0.96	0.96	0.97	0.95	0.95	0.95
OECD	x	0.91	0.87	0.89	0.87	0.87	0.90	0.85	0.84	0.83
	m	1.12	1.10	1.09	1.10	1.09	1.11	1.09	1.09	1.08
	w	0.81	0.79	0.82	0.79	0.80	0.81	0.77	0.77	0.77
Market minus OECD	x	1.83	1.92	1.78	1.87	1.72	1.54	1.64	1.65	1.66
	m	0.67	0.71	0.76	0.77	0.75	0.71	0.75	0.73	0.73
	w	2.72	2.70	2.34	2.41	2.28	2.18	2.19	2.25	2.27
Low-income OECD	x	1.61	1.57	1.59	1.64	1.65	1.60	1.70	1.82	1.79
	m	0.85	0.88	0.95	0.93	0.99	0.92	0.90	0.98	0.96
	w	1.89	1.78	1.67	1.76	1.66	1.74	1.90	1.85	1.86
Bulgaria	x	1.73	1.56	1.56	1.44	1.19	1.03	0.92	1.09	1.31
	m	0.76	0.88	0.92	0.87	1.06	0.88	0.85	0.88	0.77
	w	2.28	1.77	1.70	1.65	1.13	1.16	1.09	1.23	1.71
Czechoslovakia	x	1.39	1.32	1.42	1.38	1.26	1.12	1.26	1.38	1.36
	m	1.38	1.13	1.05	1.15	1.14	1.22	1.32	1.41	1.41
	w	1.01	1.17	1.36	1.20	1.10	0.92	0.95	0.98	0.96
East Germany (GDR)	x	0.77	0.88	1.09	0.98	1.24	0.78	0.86	0.98	0.96
	m	1.31	1.32	1.43	1.38	1.11	1.23	1.03	1.41	1.52
	w	0.59	0.67	0.77	0.71	1.12	0.63	0.83	0.70	0.63
Hungary	x	2.66	2.55	2.43	2.29	2.27	2.08	2.12	2.25	2.06
	m	1.33	1.14	1.15	1.13	1.17	1.17	1.23	1.48	1.36
	w	2.00	2.23	2.12	2.02	1.94	1.78	1.73	1.52	1.52
Poland	x	1.26	1.32	1.56	1.61	1.81	2.00	2.10	1.98	1.75
	m	0.55	0.51	0.65	0.53	0.60	0.57	0.49	0.83	0.94
	w	2.29	2.60	2.39	3.02	3.02	3.50	4.29	2.39	1.86
Romania	x	1.53	1.64	1.79	1.88	1.61	1.44	1.29	1.92	1.86
	m	0.79	0.78	0.64	0.66	0.65	0.68	0.69	1.05	1.10
	w	1.93	2.11	2.77	2.84	2.45	2.13	1.86	1.82	1.69
USSR	x	0.80	0.60	0.58	0.59	0.55	0.47	0.38	0.37	0.43
	m	0.81	0.68	0.74	0.65	0.70	0.68	0.90	0.75	0.61
	w	0.98	0.87	0.79	0.91	0.78	0.69	0.43	0.49	0.70
Yugoslavia	x	4.05	3.61	3.15	2.73	2.75	2.60	2.80	2.95	3.06
	m	1.03	0.98	0.92	0.94	0.90	0.86	0.86	1.06	1.30
	w	3.94	3.69	3.41	2.91	3.07	3.03	3.24	2.79	2.36
Albania	x	1.32	2.02	1.63	2.60	1.31	1.30	0.61	0.56	0.81
	m	0.59	1.35	0.92	1.15	0.83	0.92	1.02	1.14	0.92
	w	2.23	1.50	1.76	2.27	1.58	1.41	0.60	0.49	0.88
Eastern Europe 9	x	1.39	1.29	1.30	1.28	1.22	1.07	1.00	1.02	1.06
	m	0.88	0.79	0.83	0.78	0.80	0.79	0.90	0.92	0.89
	w	1.58	1.64	1.57	1.64	1.51	1.36	1.11	1.11	1.20
Eastern Europe 6	x	1.47	1.50	1.64	1.63	1.63	1.52	1.50	1.65	1.58
	m	0.90	0.84	0.89	0.86	0.87	0.89	0.90	1.19	1.21
	w	1.64	1.79	1.85	1.89	1.88	1.71	1.66	1.39	1.30

Note: x = export measure; m = import measure; w = export-import measure.

Table 4.9

Revealed Comparative Advantages for Goods Produced in Sectors That Use
R & D Inputs Intensively, 1975–1983

	Trade Measure	1975	1976	1977	1978	1979	1980	1981	1982	1983
Market	x	1.14	1.14	1.13	1.11	1.12	1.13	1.11	1.12	1.12
	m	1.05	1.02	1.03	1.03	1.03	1.04	1.05	1.04	1.04
	w	1.09	1.12	1.10	1.08	1.09	1.09	1.06	1.07	1.07
OECD	x	1.20	1.21	1.21	1.19	1.20	1.23	1.21	1.23	1.20
	m	1.03	0.99	1.01	1.02	1.00	1.01	1.04	1.04	1.03
	w	1.16	1.23	1.21	1.17	1.20	1.22	1.16	1.18	1.16
Market minus OECD	x	0.52	0.50	0.49	0.52	0.52	0.49	0.50	0.50	0.63
	m	1.14	1.22	1.19	1.09	1.21	1.20	1.04	1.07	1.08
	w	0.45	0.41	0.42	0.48	0.43	0.41	0.48	0.46	0.58
Low-income OECD	x	0.81	0.82	0.77	0.74	0.71	0.75	0.76	0.77	0.71
	m	1.08	1.06	1.01	1.05	1.04	1.05	1.07	1.05	1.00
	w	0.75	0.77	0.77	0.71	0.68	0.71	0.72	0.73	0.71
Bulgaria	x	0.24	0.38	0.33	0.23	0.20	0.24	0.12	0.29	0.16
	m	0.50	0.43	0.67	0.52	0.50	0.52	0.41	0.52	0.46
	w	0.48	0.89	0.49	0.44	0.39	0.46	0.29	0.57	0.35
Czechoslovakia	x	0.23	0.25	0.29	0.22	0.19	0.15	0.14	0.12	0.11
	m	0.65	0.57	0.62	0.64	0.54	0.51	0.49	0.50	0.48
	w	0.36	0.45	0.48	0.34	0.34	0.30	0.29	0.24	0.22
East Germany (GDR)	x	0.75	0.77	0.77	0.73	0.78	0.62	0.51	0.43	0.37
	m	0.31	0.24	0.25	0.27	0.33	0.39	0.36	0.29	0.28
	w	2.46	3.25	3.11	2.67	2.39	1.58	1.42	1.49	1.32
Hungary	x	0.52	0.57	0.49	0.50	0.43	0.37	0.31	0.33	0.29
	m	0.54	0.55	0.53	0.57	0.58	0.60	0.52	0.56	0.41
	w	0.96	1.04	0.93	0.89	0.74	0.62	0.59	0.59	0.70
Poland	x	0.18	0.19	0.21	0.22	0.20	0.19	0.21	0.15	0.09
	m	0.37	0.41	0.38	0.36	0.34	0.31	0.32	0.55	0.52
	w	0.48	0.47	0.55	0.61	0.60	0.60	0.67	0.28	0.18
Romania	x	0.08	0.10	0.16	0.19	0.10	0.12	0.12	0.12	0.07
	m	0.61	0.51	0.69	0.55	0.51	0.54	0.38	0.48	0.51
	w	0.13	0.20	0.23	0.35	0.20	0.22	0.32	0.24	0.13
USSR	x	0.09	0.07	0.10	0.10	0.08	0.07	0.03	0.03	0.02
	m	0.25	0.24	0.26	0.28	0.32	0.26	0.29	0.26	0.25
	w	0.36	0.28	0.38	0.35	0.24	0.26	0.10	0.10	0.10
Yugoslavia	x	0.34	0.36	0.36	0.37	0.37	0.37	0.35	0.31	0.25
	m	0.92	0.88	0.90	0.96	0.91	0.87	0.84	0.79	0.67
	w	0.37	0.41	0.40	0.38	0.40	0.42	0.41	0.39	0.37
Albania	x	0.03	0.01	0.05	0.00	0.01	0.02	0.02	0.02	0.04
	m	0.60	0.75	0.61	0.47	0.72	0.43	0.43	0.48	0.60
	w	0.05	0.01	0.09	0.01	0.01	0.04	0.05	0.04	0.06
Eastern Europe 9	x	0.21	0.20	0.23	0.23	0.19	0.17	0.13	0.12	0.10
	m	0.44	0.41	0.46	0.47	0.47	0.43	0.41	0.39	0.36
	w	0.47	0.50	0.49	0.48	0.40	0.39	0.32	0.30	0.27
Eastern Europe 6	x	0.29	0.31	0.33	0.32	0.28	0.25	0.23	0.23	0.17
	m	0.47	0.45	0.50	0.47	0.45	0.45	0.41	0.49	0.44
	w	0.60	0.68	0.67	0.67	0.62	0.56	0.57	0.46	0.40

Note: x = export measure; m = import measure; w = export-import measure.

Table 4.10

Revealed Comparative Advantages for Goods Produced in Sectors Having High Patent-to-Sales Ratios, 1975–1983

	Trade Measure	1975	1976	1977	1978	1979	1980	1981	1982	1983
Market	x	1.12	1.12	1.12	1.10	1.11	1.12	1.10	1.11	1.10
	m	0.97	0.97	0.95	0.96	0.98	0.99	0.99	0.99	1.00
	w	1.16	1.16	1.17	1.15	1.13	1.13	1.11	1.12	1.10
OECD	x	1.20	1.21	1.22	1.19	1.20	1.22	1.20	1.21	1.18
	m	0.93	0.91	0.91	0.91	0.92	0.93	0.93	0.93	0.94
	w	1.30	1.33	1.34	1.31	1.31	1.31	1.29	1.30	1.26
Market minus OECD	x	0.38	0.38	0.38	0.42	0.41	0.42	0.45	0.49	0.60
	m	1.22	1.33	1.29	1.28	1.33	1.30	1.28	1.31	1.34
	w	0.31	0.28	0.30	0.33	0.31	0.32	0.36	0.37	0.45
Low-income OECD	x	0.88	0.88	0.89	0.84	0.85	0.96	0.93	0.92	0.90
	m	1.07	1.05	1.06	1.05	1.04	1.03	1.02	1.02	1.00
	w	0.82	0.83	0.84	0.80	0.81	0.94	0.91	0.91	0.91
Bulgaria	x	0.74	0.72	0.76	0.72	0.60	0.61	0.57	0.63	0.61
	m	1.40	1.34	1.28	1.11	1.03	1.10	1.14	1.28	1.19
	w	0.53	0.54	0.60	0.65	0.58	0.55	0.50	0.49	0.51
Czechoslovakia	x	0.76	0.78	0.80	0.71	0.71	0.66	0.77	0.76	0.78
	m	1.39	1.28	1.42	1.43	1.35	1.46	1.38	1.34	1.25
	w	0.55	0.61	0.56	0.50	0.53	0.46	0.56	0.57	0.62
East Germany (GDR)	x	1.20	1.18	1.16	1.06	1.14	1.07	0.95	0.94	0.89
	m	1.23	1.18	0.91	0.89	1.31	1.05	1.19	1.12	1.04
	w	0.98	1.00	1.27	1.19	0.87	1.03	0.80	0.84	0.85
Hungary	x	0.77	0.77	0.75	0.76	0.79	0.78	0.79	0.89	0.73
	m	1.22	1.28	1.34	1.39	1.36	1.30	1.29	1.35	1.12
	w	0.63	0.61	0.56	0.55	0.58	0.60	0.61	0.66	0.66
Poland	x	0.51	0.49	0.52	0.53	0.52	0.52	0.65	0.50	0.49
	m	1.11	1.16	1.19	1.13	0.97	0.96	0.74	0.80	0.87
	w	0.46	0.42	0.44	0.46	0.54	0.54	0.87	0.62	0.57
Romania	x	0.59	0.60	0.62	0.49	0.46	0.42	0.51	0.57	0.40
	m	1.10	0.86	1.10	1.14	1.11	0.97	0.74	0.86	0.72
	w	0.54	0.70	0.56	0.43	0.41	0.43	0.69	0.66	0.56
USSR	x	0.31	0.32	0.38	0.41	0.43	0.31	0.25	0.20	0.20
	m	0.96	1.00	1.25	1.21	1.05	0.86	0.78	0.84	0.89
	w	0.32	0.32	0.30	0.34	0.41	0.36	0.33	0.24	0.23
Yugoslavia	x	0.64	0.69	0.69	0.63	0.63	0.65	0.67	0.59	0.50
	m	1.50	1.45	1.57	1.64	1.64	1.56	1.37	1.38	1.26
	w	0.43	0.48	0.44	0.38	0.38	0.42	0.49	0.42	0.39
Albania	x	0.03	0.08	0.05	0.05	0.04	0.05	0.08	0.12	0.13
	m	0.67	0.58	0.63	0.56	0.73	0.74	1.04	0.87	1.16
	w	0.04	0.13	0.08	0.08	0.05	0.07	0.08	0.13	0.11
Eastern Europe 9	x	0.53	0.52	0.56	0.54	0.54	0.47	0.46	0.41	0.38
	m	1.14	1.13	1.28	1.27	1.20	1.06	0.96	0.99	0.99
	w	0.46	0.46	0.43	0.43	0.45	0.44	0.48	0.42	0.39
Eastern Europe 6	x	0.70	0.69	0.71	0.66	0.66	0.64	0.70	0.71	0.65
	m	1.20	1.17	1.21	1.20	1.16	1.11	1.05	1.12	1.04
	w	0.59	0.59	0.59	0.55	0.56	0.58	0.67	0.63	0.62

Note: x = export measure; m = import measure; w = export-import measure.

The Nature of Technological Change A key difference in the predictions of the Schumpeterian and neoclassical perspectives centers on the sectoral distribution of technological change. The Schumpeterian analysis predicts that the hindrances to technological change in CPEs will be particularly severe in sectors that rely on the development of new products. In contrast, process changes could occur as fast in CPEs as in MEs. Thus, from a Schumpeterian perspective, one would predict that CPEs have a comparative disadvantage in sectors producing new products. Any comparative disadvantage in sectors producing new processes would be much less, and given that trade is based on relative costs, the CPEs could have a comparative advantage in such sectors. As the discussion leading to Hypotheses 10 and 11 makes clear, a neoclassical analysis does not lead to this combination of predictions.

Tables 4.11 and 4.12 present a clear picture. Once one distinguishes between process and product patents, the sectoral structure of technological change in CPEs is transparent. When comparing the LIO group to the EE6, twenty-six of the twenty-seven RCAs show worse performance for Eastern Europe on new goods, while two-thirds of the RCA comparisons show better performance of Eastern Europe on new processes. The CPEs have a comparative disadvantage in sectors with large amounts of product innovations, and a comparative advantage in sectors with high rates of process innovation. It is significant that the CPEs are the only group of countries for which there is a contrast between the results of Table 4.11 and those of 4.12. For example, the group of less-developed market economies, also technological laggards, perform equally well in both tables. The message from the tables is unequivocal—the problem with CPE technology lies in the production of new goods. It is interesting that this message is not apparent in case studies of innovation processes in CPEs (Amann 1982, p. 18).

On examining the results for individual countries, the most conspicuous fact is the difference between the two most-developed CPEs: the GDR and Czechoslovakia. The GDR's results evidence a country functioning at a high technological level, although here also the difference between process and product innovation is marked; Czechoslovakia performs poorly compared with its bloc partners in both tables. Finally, nothing in the statistics for the two reformed economies, Yugoslavia and Hungary, shows any effect of reforms.

Pollution Hypothesis 20 predicts that economic system affects the link between the social costs of production and trade performance. That hypothesis is based on the widely held assumption that environmental policies are viewed as less important in CPEs than in MEs. If that assumption is correct, CPEs will tend to have a comparative advantage in goods that produce large external social costs in the form of pollution.

In order to examine whether environmental policy affects Eastern European trade patterns, I constructed RCAs for a group of goods whose cost of pro-

Table 4.11

Revealed Comparative Advantages for Goods Produced in Sectors Having High Product Patent-to-Sales Ratios, 1975–1983

	Trade Measure	1975	1976	1977	1978	1979	1980	1981	1982	1983
Market	x	1.13	1.13	1.12	1.11	1.11	1.13	1.10	1.11	1.11
	m	0.95	0.93	0.92	0.94	0.96	0.97	0.97	0.97	0.98
	w	1.19	1.20	1.21	1.18	1.16	1.16	1.13	1.14	1.13
OECD	x	1.22	1.23	1.24	1.22	1.23	1.25	1.23	1.24	1.21
	m	0.90	0.88	0.88	0.89	0.90	0.92	0.91	0.91	0.93
	w	1.35	1.40	1.41	1.37	1.36	1.36	1.35	1.36	1.30
Market minus OECD	x	0.29	0.29	0.29	0.32	0.32	0.31	0.34	0.37	0.50
	m	1.22	1.33	1.28	1.28	1.32	1.30	1.29	1.31	1.29
	w	0.24	0.22	0.23	0.25	0.24	0.24	0.27	0.28	0.38
Low-income OECD	x	0.95	0.94	0.96	0.91	0.94	1.05	1.02	1.01	1.00
	m	1.07	1.03	1.03	1.02	1.01	1.01	1.02	1.00	0.98
	w	0.89	0.91	0.93	0.89	0.93	1.03	1.00	1.02	1.02
Bulgaria	x	0.50	0.53	0.47	0.51	0.38	0.41	0.38	0.35	0.34
	m	1.54	1.53	1.42	1.13	0.98	1.08	1.17	1.48	1.45
	w	0.33	0.35	0.33	0.45	0.39	0.38	0.32	0.23	0.23
Czechoslovakia	x	0.89	0.94	0.98	0.88	0.87	0.79	0.83	0.72	0.74
	m	1.30	1.28	1.43	1.52	1.32	1.38	1.22	1.25	1.20
	w	0.69	0.74	0.68	0.58	0.66	0.57	0.68	0.58	0.62
East Germany (GDR)	x	1.23	1.26	1.28	1.18	1.30	1.16	1.00	0.97	0.88
	m	1.07	1.11	0.77	0.78	1.34	0.97	1.18	1.20	1.24
	w	1.16	1.13	1.66	1.52	0.97	1.20	0.85	0.80	0.71
Hungary	x	0.53	0.46	0.43	0.45	0.49	0.48	0.49	0.58	0.43
	m	1.02	1.16	1.26	1.31	1.32	1.16	1.16	1.21	0.98
	w	0.52	0.39	0.34	0.35	0.37	0.42	0.42	0.47	0.43
Poland	x	0.54	0.52	0.56	0.56	0.60	0.55	0.67	0.51	0.47
	m	1.26	1.38	1.38	1.37	1.04	0.95	0.79	0.79	0.84
	w	0.43	0.38	0.40	0.41	0.57	0.58	0.85	0.65	0.56
Romania	x	0.42	0.60	0.59	0.44	0.45	0.41	0.49	0.46	0.32
	m	1.19	0.94	1.38	1.59	1.31	0.94	0.65	0.60	0.46
	w	0.35	0.64	0.43	0.28	0.35	0.44	0.76	0.77	0.70
USSR	x	0.30	0.28	0.21	0.21	0.18	0.14	0.11	0.10	0.08
	m	1.14	1.26	1.49	1.44	1.18	0.92	0.80	0.93	1.06
	w	0.26	0.22	0.14	0.15	0.15	0.16	0.14	0.10	0.08
Yugoslavia	x	0.60	0.76	0.72	0.62	0.65	0.67	0.69	0.60	0.45
	m	1.61	1.56	1.73	1.81	1.85	1.64	1.42	1.43	1.23
	w	0.37	0.49	0.42	0.34	0.35	0.41	0.48	0.42	0.37
Albania	x	0.02	0.03	0.03	0.02	0.02	0.01	0.04	0.03	0.04
	m	0.68	0.49	0.46	0.39	0.69	0.72	1.09	0.90	1.29
	w	0.03	0.06	0.08	0.04	0.03	0.02	0.04	0.04	0.03
Eastern Europe 9	x	0.50	0.51	0.48	0.45	0.43	0.38	0.37	0.32	0.28
	m	1.25	1.29	1.45	1.45	1.30	1.08	0.95	1.03	1.08
	w	0.40	0.40	0.33	0.31	0.33	0.35	0.39	0.31	0.26
Eastern Europe 6	x	0.67	0.69	0.71	0.65	0.67	0.63	0.66	0.63	0.56
	m	1.23	1.25	1.31	1.34	1.21	1.06	1.00	1.08	1.04
	w	0.54	0.55	0.54	0.49	0.55	0.59	0.67	0.58	0.53

Note: x = export measure; m = import measure; w = export-import measure.

Table 4.12

Revealed Comparative Advantages for Goods Produced in Sectors Having High Process Patent-to-Sales Ratios, 1975–1983

	Trade Measure	1975	1976	1977	1978	1979	1980	1981	1982	1983
Market	x	1.09	1.10	1.09	1.07	1.08	1.08	1.06	1.06	1.06
	m	1.00	1.02	1.01	1.00	1.00	0.98	0.99	1.00	0.99
	w	1.09	1.09	1.08	1.07	1.08	1.10	1.07	1.07	1.06
OECD	x	1.18	1.22	1.21	1.18	1.20	1.21	1.19	1.20	1.19
	m	0.96	1.00	0.99	0.98	0.97	0.97	0.99	1.00	0.98
	w	1.23	1.22	1.22	1.20	1.23	1.25	1.20	1.20	1.22
Market minus OECD	x	0.28	0.23	0.24	0.27	0.24	0.27	0.29	0.29	0.28
	m	1.24	1.11	1.12	1.10	1.15	1.07	0.99	0.96	1.08
	w	0.22	0.20	0.22	0.24	0.21	0.25	0.29	0.30	0.26
Low-income OECD	x	0.95	0.96	0.95	0.89	0.85	1.00	0.98	0.97	0.95
	m	1.09	1.18	1.21	1.24	1.24	1.18	1.19	1.19	1.16
	w	0.86	0.81	0.79	0.72	0.69	0.84	0.83	0.81	0.81
Bulgaria	x	3.00	1.86	2.25	1.77	1.32	1.50	1.56	2.01	1.86
	m	1.10	1.19	1.33	1.35	1.49	1.52	1.48	1.37	1.26
	w	2.72	1.56	1.69	1.31	0.89	0.98	1.05	1.47	1.47
Czechoslovakia	x	0.89	0.87	1.07	0.96	1.07	1.34	1.52	1.72	1.77
	m	1.94	1.62	1.66	1.57	1.65	1.82	1.86	1.69	1.61
	w	0.46	0.54	0.64	0.61	0.65	0.74	0.82	1.01	1.10
East Germany (GDR)	x	2.44	2.27	2.24	2.31	2.44	2.92	2.87	2.89	2.59
	m	1.84	1.48	1.52	1.56	1.30	1.38	1.37	1.01	0.99
	w	1.32	1.53	1.47	1.48	1.87	2.12	2.09	2.86	2.63
Hungary	x	1.12	1.41	1.49	1.43	1.57	1.78	1.91	1.96	1.83
	m	2.45	2.29	2.20	2.19	2.10	2.28	2.23	2.30	2.01
	w	0.46	0.61	0.68	0.65	0.75	0.78	0.86	0.85	0.91
Poland	x	1.04	0.68	0.65	0.71	0.52	0.71	0.77	0.65	0.65
	m	0.97	1.14	1.22	1.30	1.35	1.42	1.12	1.50	1.42
	w	1.07	0.59	0.53	0.54	0.39	0.50	0.69	0.43	0.46
Romania	x	1.98	1.25	1.49	1.48	1.12	1.24	1.33	1.55	1.52
	m	1.04	1.00	0.95	0.97	1.05	1.13	1.13	1.66	1.54
	w	1.90	1.25	1.58	1.53	1.07	1.09	1.18	0.93	0.99
USSR	x	0.69	0.58	0.93	1.06	1.04	0.86	0.77	0.68	0.67
	m	0.79	0.68	0.92	0.86	0.90	1.09	1.03	0.84	0.82
	w	0.88	0.86	1.02	1.23	1.16	0.78	0.75	0.80	0.81
Yugoslavia	x	0.73	0.50	0.59	0.68	0.73	0.89	1.10	0.80	0.94
	m	1.26	1.33	1.21	1.28	1.23	1.37	1.59	1.75	1.72
	w	0.58	0.38	0.49	0.53	0.60	0.65	0.70	0.46	0.55
Albania	x	0.05	0.19	0.07	0.12	0.09	0.32	0.13	0.29	0.29
	m	1.06	1.72	1.50	1.32	0.77	0.87	0.87	0.97	0.66
	w	0.04	0.11	0.05	0.09	0.12	0.37	0.15	0.30	0.45
Eastern Europe 9	x	1.07	0.83	1.05	1.11	1.06	1.09	1.11	1.05	1.03
	m	1.12	1.06	1.18	1.18	1.18	1.32	1.28	1.19	1.15
	w	0.95	0.79	0.89	0.94	0.90	0.82	0.87	0.88	0.90
Eastern Europe 6	x	1.46	1.16	1.27	1.25	1.16	1.42	1.58	1.71	1.64
	m	1.41	1.38	1.43	1.47	1.45	1.56	1.51	1.64	1.50
	w	1.04	0.84	0.89	0.85	0.80	0.91	1.04	1.05	1.09

Note: x = export measure; m = import measure; w = export-import measure.

duction in the United States includes significant payments for pollution abatement. The assumption behind the use of such a commodity group is that countries that have not dictated abatement do not include pollution costs in their price-determination process. Those countries are predicted to have a comparative advantage in goods with high abatement costs. The results appear in Table 4.13.[14]

The results are strongly supportive of the hypothesis that environmental policy is less important in the CPEs than in any of the groupings of developed market economies. The trade of the low-income OECD countries is roughly balanced in goods having a high pollution content. In contrast, the EE6 has comparatively large export-import RCAs for these goods, and also has a large share of exports concentrated in this category. These results hold for all countries, although quite weakly for Poland and Hungary. Perhaps most interesting is the case of Yugoslavia. Among Eastern European countries, Yugoslavia's political institutions have the reputation of being most responsive to public pressure. Yet the results for this country are close to those of the EE6 and very different from those of the two groupings of less-developed market economies.

4.5. The Character of Markets and the Behavior of Economic Systems

Business Concentration   Hypothesis 2 predicts a property of CPE trade that exists because of the absence in CPEs of processes occurring in market economies. In MEs, the markup of price over marginal cost varies systematically with the degree of concentration. There is no reason to believe that this systematic relationship occurs in CPEs. Thus, the CPEs are predicted to have a comparative advantage in goods sold in markets having high concentration levels in Western economies. But one should emphasize that this prediction will be verified only if there is some degree of rationality to domestic resource allocation decisions. In particular, there must be some mechanism that allows differences between world-market prices and domestic costs to be reflected in domestic production and trade decisions.

Table 4.14 lists the RCAs for industries that have high levels of concen-

---

[14] Petroleum refining is included in the high-pollution group. Some might object to the results on the basis that the Eastern European countries obtain inexpensive crude oil from the Soviet Union, but this objection can be quickly dismissed for two reasons. First, the RCAs of Table 4.14 were also obtained with petroleum refining omitted from the group. The qualitative nature of the results remained the same. Second, the countries do have flexibility in using their ''gift'' of crude oil: it can be reexported, used for fuel to produce other goods, or consumed after refining. The argument of the text is that the export of refined goods is the most advantageous option, given the environmental policies of market economies.

Table 4.13
Revealed Comparative Advantages for Goods Produced in Industries That Have High Pollution Costs, 1975–1983

	Trade Measure	1975	1976	1977	1978	1979	1980	1981	1982	1983
Market	x	1.03	1.02	1.02	1.01	1.00	0.99	0.97	0.96	0.94
	m	0.97	0.99	1.00	0.98	0.98	1.00	1.00	0.99	0.98
	w	1.06	1.03	1.02	1.03	1.02	0.99	0.96	0.97	0.96
OECD	x	1.07	1.07	1.07	1.06	1.05	1.03	1.01	1.00	1.00
	m	0.96	0.99	1.00	0.97	0.98	1.00	1.00	0.99	0.98
	w	1.12	1.07	1.07	1.08	1.07	1.04	1.01	1.01	1.02
Market minus OECD	x	0.55	0.58	0.58	0.60	0.59	0.63	0.66	0.69	0.61
	m	1.05	0.94	0.98	1.00	1.00	0.99	1.00	1.00	1.01
	w	0.53	0.62	0.59	0.61	0.59	0.63	0.66	0.69	0.61
Low-income OECD	x	0.96	0.96	0.99	1.03	0.99	0.93	1.00	1.02	0.97
	m	0.90	0.95	1.00	0.96	0.98	1.02	0.99	1.01	0.96
	w	1.07	1.01	0.99	1.07	1.01	0.91	1.01	1.01	1.00
Bulgaria	x	2.24	2.10	2.50	2.40	2.74	2.90	2.93	2.75	2.55
	m	1.23	1.06	1.31	1.39	1.57	1.46	1.26	1.29	1.19
	w	1.82	1.98	1.90	1.72	1.74	1.99	2.33	2.14	2.15
Czechoslovakia	x	1.57	1.71	1.64	1.75	1.69	1.78	1.81	1.89	1.89
	m	1.13	1.27	1.07	1.12	1.16	1.04	1.13	1.06	1.14
	w	1.39	1.35	1.53	1.56	1.46	1.72	1.60	1.78	1.66
East Germany (GDR)	x	1.63	1.77	1.74	1.78	2.03	2.33	2.44	2.74	2.82
	m	1.37	1.24	1.24	1.16	0.95	1.08	0.92	0.93	1.01
	w	1.19	1.43	1.41	1.53	2.14	2.15	2.65	2.94	2.79
Hungary	x	1.20	1.43	1.41	1.25	1.43	1.40	1.38	1.40	1.57
	m	1.36	1.19	1.19	1.19	1.19	1.15	1.21	1.30	1.20
	w	0.88	1.21	1.18	1.05	1.21	1.22	1.14	1.08	1.31
Poland	x	1.01	1.09	1.11	1.28	1.24	1.36	1.35	1.23	1.10
	m	1.29	1.26	1.20	1.09	1.08	0.91	0.66	0.91	0.83
	w	0.78	0.87	0.93	1.18	1.16	1.48	2.04	1.35	1.32
Romania	x	2.32	2.39	2.51	2.79	2.92	2.97	3.19	2.87	3.18
	m	1.54	1.63	1.43	1.40	1.44	1.31	1.08	1.48	1.23
	w	1.51	1.47	1.75	1.99	2.03	2.26	2.96	1.94	2.59
USSR	x	1.95	1.70	1.69	1.83	1.90	1.74	1.89	2.06	2.21
	m	1.32	1.33	1.23	1.36	1.37	1.23	1.25	1.31	1.24
	w	1.47	1.28	1.37	1.35	1.39	1.42	1.51	1.57	1.79
Yugoslavia	x	1.04	1.07	0.97	1.04	1.20	1.13	1.10	1.14	1.32
	m	0.87	0.82	0.81	0.81	0.81	0.87	1.06	1.09	1.03
	w	1.19	1.31	1.19	1.29	1.48	1.29	1.03	1.05	1.28
Albania	x	1.38	1.60	1.61	1.36	1.22	1.58	2.18	2.01	1.85
	m	1.58	1.97	2.05	1.65	1.75	2.18	1.87	1.83	1.42
	w	0.87	0.81	0.79	0.82	0.69	0.72	1.17	1.10	1.30
Eastern Europe 9	x	1.66	1.61	1.60	1.72	1.83	1.79	1.92	1.99	2.10
	m	1.26	1.25	1.17	1.20	1.20	1.13	1.14	1.23	1.16
	w	1.32	1.29	1.37	1.43	1.52	1.58	1.69	1.61	1.81
Eastern Europe 6	x	1.52	1.63	1.65	1.77	1.88	1.98	2.13	2.05	2.11
	m	1.32	1.29	1.23	1.19	1.19	1.10	1.00	1.13	1.08
	w	1.16	1.27	1.34	1.48	1.58	1.79	2.12	1.82	1.96

Note: x = export measure; m = import measure; w = export-import measure.

Table 4.14

Revealed Comparative Advantages for Sectors That Have a High Level of Concentration in Western Europe, 1975–1983

	Trade Measure	1975	1976	1977	1978	1979	1980	1981	1982	1983
Market	x	1.08	1.07	1.07	1.06	1.05	1.04	1.03	1.03	1.02
	m	1.00	1.00	1.01	1.02	1.02	1.03	1.02	1.02	1.03
	w	1.08	1.07	1.05	1.04	1.03	1.02	1.00	1.01	1.00
OECD	x	1.15	1.16	1.16	1.15	1.13	1.12	1.11	1.11	1.11
	m	1.00	1.01	1.02	1.03	1.03	1.03	1.03	1.02	1.04
	w	1.15	1.15	1.13	1.12	1.10	1.10	1.08	1.08	1.07
Market minus OECD	x	0.39	0.38	0.38	0.39	0.41	0.46	0.52	0.54	0.50
	m	1.03	1.03	1.00	0.98	0.96	1.05	1.04	1.01	0.96
	w	0.38	0.37	0.38	0.40	0.43	0.44	0.50	0.53	0.52
Low-income OECD	x	0.93	0.87	0.88	0.84	0.88	0.85	0.81	0.81	0.77
	m	0.84	0.90	0.91	0.92	0.94	1.03	1.00	0.96	0.89
	w	1.11	0.98	0.97	0.91	0.94	0.83	0.81	0.85	0.86
Bulgaria	x	0.18	0.34	0.29	0.44	1.09	1.51	1.55	0.99	0.86
	m	0.69	0.50	0.52	0.73	0.53	0.50	0.58	0.50	0.46
	w	0.26	0.68	0.56	0.60	2.05	2.99	2.66	1.99	1.87
Czechoslovakia	x	0.53	0.50	0.48	0.46	0.55	0.68	0.59	0.54	0.58
	m	0.48	0.59	0.47	0.51	0.50	0.35	0.42	0.36	0.40
	w	1.09	0.85	1.02	0.90	1.11	1.94	1.41	1.49	1.44
East Germany (GDR)	x	0.96	0.88	1.00	1.05	0.88	1.22	1.32	1.38	1.33
	m	0.60	0.60	0.42	0.39	0.57	0.37	0.53	0.34	0.27
	w	1.61	1.47	2.39	2.65	1.53	3.26	2.49	4.05	4.96
Hungary	x	0.40	0.40	0.42	0.50	0.58	0.61	0.58	0.49	0.60
	m	0.41	0.37	0.37	0.42	0.42	0.39	0.36	0.38	0.29
	w	0.98	1.07	1.15	1.17	1.37	1.57	1.62	1.28	2.04
Poland	x	0.41	0.64	0.67	0.62	0.64	0.70	0.53	0.50	0.46
	m	0.69	0.54	0.51	0.42	0.42	0.48	0.38	0.33	0.34
	w	0.59	1.18	1.33	1.47	1.51	1.46	1.41	1.53	1.34
Romania	x	1.12	1.45	1.29	1.30	1.74	1.95	1.92	1.52	1.76
	m	0.65	0.44	0.55	0.49	0.45	0.41	0.26	0.33	0.30
	w	1.71	3.27	2.35	2.67	3.88	4.78	7.44	4.58	5.86
USSR	x	1.30	1.17	1.11	1.20	1.46	1.29	1.32	1.39	1.36
	m	0.85	0.85	0.71	0.77	0.75	0.56	0.61	0.71	0.72
	w	1.54	1.38	1.57	1.55	1.95	2.28	2.16	1.97	1.88
Yugoslavia	x	0.53	0.57	0.69	0.90	0.87	0.82	0.72	0.82	0.75
	m	0.74	0.79	0.83	0.77	0.76	0.69	0.74	0.73	0.65
	w	0.72	0.72	0.83	1.16	1.15	1.19	0.97	1.13	1.16
Albania	x	1.12	1.14	1.16	0.57	0.91	1.09	1.30	1.16	0.98
	m	0.90	0.65	0.59	0.76	0.86	0.66	0.73	0.76	0.54
	w	1.25	1.77	1.96	0.75	1.06	1.64	1.78	1.54	1.81
Eastern Europe 9	x	0.91	0.93	0.90	0.96	1.16	1.15	1.17	1.16	1.15
	m	0.73	0.70	0.63	0.64	0.63	0.53	0.55	0.60	0.59
	w	1.24	1.33	1.43	1.50	1.83	2.19	2.12	1.93	1.96
Eastern Europe 6	x	0.62	0.76	0.73	0.75	0.90	1.05	1.05	0.88	0.92
	m	0.61	0.52	0.48	0.46	0.47	0.42	0.40	0.37	0.34
	w	1.02	1.47	1.53	1.61	1.92	2.48	2.60	2.41	2.73

Note: x = export measure; m = import measure; w = export-import measure.

tration in Western Europe.[15] In eight of the nine years, the export-import RCAs for the EE6 are higher than those for the LIO group. Moreover, with some variation in strength, the same results apply to each individual Eastern European country. The results are supportive of the hypothesis that CPEs can capitalize on the behavior of the noncompetitive sectors of market economies. Moreover, the strength of the results increases once one examines the nature of the concentrated industries (see line 14 of Table 4.2). These industries, in the main, produce differentiated products at a fairly high level of sophistication. They are, therefore, sectors in which one would expect the CPEs to have a comparative disadvantage were it not for the effects of business concentration.

The results for individual countries also attest to the link between business concentration and comparative advantage. As an economic system moves from central planning to the market, that link changes. Under market socialism, one would expect to see some of the effects of concentration that are typical of market economies (Estrin 1983). Therefore, the results for Hungary and Yugoslavia should be less strong than those for the rest of Eastern Europe. As Table 4.14 shows, this is the case, especially for Yugoslavia.

Variety   Based on the need to reduce administrative costs and the absence of free entry and MNCs, Hypothesis 13 predicts that CPEs produce fewer varieties than MEs. The relevant evidence is contained in Table 4.15, which presents RCAs for markets in which product differentiation is particularly high.

The results are in accord with expectations. The EE6 show less ability to export differentiated products than the "market minus OECD" grouping, and their export-import RCAs are significantly below those of the less-developed OECD countries. Czechoslovakia and Poland evidence behavior that is virtually indistinguishable from that of the least developed countries. The result for Czechoslovakia is especially significant in view of the inconsistency of its rankings on the product differentiation RCAs and on per capita income. The results for Hungary and Yugoslavia are surprising for the opposite reason. The ability of these two market-socialist countries to outperform their Eastern European neighbors suggests that some features of economic reform do encourage increased trade in the sectors in which product differentiation is common.

Perhaps the relevant factor in explaining the results for Hungary and Yugoslavia is the fact that these two countries engage in more industrial cooperation agreements and countertrade than their socialist neighbors. If this is the case, then product differentiation per se might not be the real problem for CPEs. Rather, the problem could lie in the fact that the CPEs lose the

---

[15] Petroleum refining is included in the high-concentration group. Some might object to the results for the reason discussed in the previous footnote, but also for the reasons given in that footnote this objection can be quickly dismissed.

Table 4.15
Revealed Comparative Advantages in Markets in Which Product Differentiation is High, 1975–1983

	Trade Measure	1975	1976	1977	1978	1979	1980	1981	1982	1983
Market	x	1.13	1.12	1.11	1.10	1.10	1.12	1.10	1.11	1.10
	m	1.01	1.00	0.99	0.98	1.00	1.01	1.01	1.02	1.01
	w	1.11	1.12	1.13	1.12	1.10	1.11	1.09	1.09	1.09
OECD	x	1.18	1.18	1.17	1.15	1.15	1.18	1.16	1.16	1.13
	m	0.97	0.94	0.93	0.92	0.92	0.94	0.94	0.94	0.92
	w	1.21	1.26	1.26	1.25	1.25	1.25	1.24	1.23	1.23
Market minus OECD	x	0.57	0.63	0.62	0.64	0.65	0.65	0.69	0.76	0.86
	m	1.25	1.46	1.40	1.37	1.45	1.37	1.36	1.42	1.55
	w	0.46	0.43	0.44	0.47	0.45	0.47	0.51	0.53	0.56
Low-income OECD	x	0.82	0.83	0.80	0.78	0.75	0.90	0.85	0.78	0.76
	m	1.19	1.13	1.09	1.09	1.06	1.04	1.04	1.05	1.01
	w	0.69	0.74	0.73	0.72	0.71	0.87	0.81	0.74	0.75
Bulgaria	x	0.68	0.69	0.82	0.73	0.61	0.54	0.37	0.54	0.47
	m	0.94	0.85	1.01	0.95	1.00	0.92	0.99	1.02	1.02
	w	0.72	0.81	0.82	0.77	0.61	0.58	0.37	0.53	0.46
Czechoslovakia	x	0.54	0.59	0.63	0.54	0.51	0.46	0.38	0.35	0.30
	m	1.07	1.07	0.98	0.94	1.04	1.10	1.25	1.15	1.15
	w	0.50	0.55	0.64	0.57	0.49	0.42	0.30	0.31	0.26
East Germany (GDR)	x	1.09	1.11	1.03	0.92	0.91	0.82	0.73	0.59	0.60
	m	0.63	0.54	0.58	0.53	0.69	0.76	0.77	0.87	0.93
	w	1.71	2.03	1.79	1.74	1.32	1.08	0.94	0.68	0.64
Hungary	x	1.09	1.15	1.07	1.05	0.92	0.85	0.80	0.84	0.67
	m	1.12	1.09	1.11	1.14	1.12	1.09	1.13	1.07	0.88
	w	0.97	1.06	0.96	0.92	0.82	0.78	0.71	0.79	0.76
Poland	x	0.39	0.37	0.38	0.42	0.43	0.45	0.64	0.37	0.38
	m	0.89	0.98	1.02	0.84	0.80	0.75	0.65	1.03	0.96
	w	0.44	0.38	0.37	0.50	0.54	0.60	0.98	0.36	0.39
Romania	x	0.20	0.21	0.29	0.25	0.28	0.20	0.19	0.20	0.19
	m	1.01	0.79	0.90	1.00	1.03	0.89	0.57	0.59	0.57
	w	0.20	0.27	0.32	0.25	0.27	0.23	0.33	0.34	0.34
USSR	x	0.28	0.37	0.73	0.78	0.90	0.45	0.30	0.24	0.19
	m	0.69	0.67	1.08	0.97	0.91	0.79	0.70	0.59	0.60
	w	0.41	0.56	0.67	0.80	0.99	0.56	0.43	0.41	0.32
Yugoslavia	x	0.88	0.83	0.87	0.77	0.83	0.84	0.79	0.78	0.67
	m	1.26	1.21	1.19	1.15	1.08	1.19	1.06	0.96	1.00
	w	0.70	0.69	0.73	0.67	0.77	0.71	0.75	0.82	0.67
Albania	x	0.01	0.00	0.01	0.01	0.02	0.04	0.08	0.04	0.10
	m	0.42	0.44	0.42	0.54	0.66	0.66	1.00	0.91	1.28
	w	0.03	0.00	0.01	0.01	0.04	0.07	0.08	0.04	0.08
Eastern Europe 9	x	0.47	0.51	0.69	0.68	0.74	0.50	0.41	0.36	0.31
	m	0.88	0.84	1.05	0.97	0.94	0.89	0.81	0.76	0.76
	w	0.53	0.60	0.66	0.70	0.78	0.57	0.51	0.47	0.41
Eastern Europe 6	x	0.57	0.58	0.61	0.58	0.55	0.51	0.50	0.46	0.42
	m	0.95	0.93	0.96	0.91	0.92	0.89	0.87	0.98	0.94
	w	0.60	0.63	0.63	0.63	0.59	0.57	0.58	0.46	0.44

Note: x = export measure; m = import measure; w = export-import measure.

benefit of a wide variety of international trading mechanisms, most particularly the MNCs, which happen to be important in many of the sectors in which product differentiation is also important. The results in the remainder of this chapter are consistent with this conclusion.

Multinationals The raison d'être of multinationals is the facilitation of exchange when arm's-length transactions are subject to great uncertainty. Such uncertainties occur, for example, when technology, either embodied or disembodied, is the object of exchange or when the quality of a good cannot be easily verified by a buyer. Because quality is hardest to estimate when the product is new, it is obvious that technology transfer is at the heart of the operations of multinationals.

The presence of multinationals in a country does not necessarily lead to a comparative advantage in sectors in which intramultinational exchange is dominant. To see this, consider MNC affiliates that receive technology embodied in the products of, say, Sector A. Product A is then used to produce goods falling within other sectors. The country hosting the affiliates might well have a comparative disadvantage in Sector A, in which internal-MNC exchange is most prevalent. Moreover, the operations of the affiliates might be responsible for that observed comparative disadvantage. Nevertheless, the host country gains from the operations of the MNC because the affiliates provide imported technology for the production of goods in sectors other than Sector A. Hence, the effect of MNCs lies in facilitating trade, not necessarily in producing a comparative advantage.

To establish where MNC operations are most important, one must identify the sectors in which intra-MNC exchanges, the sine qua non of MNC operations, are most important. Line 16 of Table 4.2 identifies those sectors in which intracompany exchanges constitute the largest proportion of OECD trade.[16] Table 4.16 gives the relevant trade statistics.

Table 4.16 reveals that the absence of MNCs in CPEs has no clear implication for comparative advantage. The export-import RCAs of the LIO group and the EE6 are quite close to each other. However, in those sectors in which MNCs are important, the total amount of trade is considerably lower in CPEs than in MEs, a result that applies to all CPEs in all years without exception. In fact, if one calculated "$x + m$" it would be lower for the EE6 than for the least developed market economies. An instructive comparison is gained by comparing the results in Table 4.16 with those in Table 4.6, which examines levels of intraindustry trade. The levels of trade for CPEs are much lower in Table 4.16 than in Table 4.6. Hence, given that there is overlap between the sectors in which intraindustry trade is large and in which MNCs are important, it might be that the slight differences in intraindustry trade

[16] Unfortunately, because data on MNC operations are so scarce, only U.S. companies are included in the analysis.

Table 4.16
Revealed Comparative Advantages for Goods Produced in Sectors in Which Intra-MNC Exchanges Are Significant, 1975–1983

	Trade Measure	1975	1976	1977	1978	1979	1980	1981	1982	1983
Market	x	1.13	1.13	1.13	1.11	1.12	1.13	1.11	1.11	1.11
	m	1.01	1.01	1.02	1.03	1.02	1.02	1.02	1.02	1.03
	w	1.12	1.12	1.11	1.08	1.09	1.11	1.09	1.09	1.08
OECD	x	1.23	1.25	1.25	1.23	1.24	1.26	1.25	1.26	1.25
	m	1.02	1.02	1.03	1.04	1.03	1.02	1.02	1.04	1.04
	w	1.21	1.23	1.22	1.18	1.20	1.24	1.22	1.21	1.19
Market minus OECD	x	0.23	0.22	0.22	0.24	0.24	0.25	0.27	0.27	0.33
	m	1.01	1.03	1.00	0.96	0.96	1.02	1.00	0.94	0.93
	w	0.23	0.21	0.22	0.25	0.25	0.24	0.27	0.29	0.35
Low-income OECD	x	0.96	0.94	0.93	0.88	0.90	0.98	0.91	0.91	0.86
	m	0.93	0.99	1.00	1.00	1.02	1.06	1.04	1.03	0.97
	w	1.04	0.95	0.93	0.88	0.88	0.92	0.87	0.88	0.89
Bulgaria	x	0.13	0.21	0.15	0.14	0.17	0.21	0.28	0.24	0.24
	m	0.78	0.63	0.63	0.78	0.69	0.69	0.77	0.65	0.61
	w	0.17	0.34	0.23	0.18	0.25	0.31	0.36	0.37	0.40
Czechoslovakia	x	0.57	0.60	0.67	0.58	0.62	0.59	0.62	0.63	0.56
	m	0.63	0.52	0.54	0.52	0.48	0.50	0.56	0.52	0.48
	w	0.91	1.16	1.23	1.13	1.29	1.20	1.12	1.21	1.16
East Germany (GDR)	x	0.78	0.73	0.88	0.90	0.68	0.66	0.73	0.62	0.56
	m	0.63	0.58	0.43	0.38	0.55	0.41	0.58	0.35	0.30
	w	1.23	1.24	2.06	2.37	1.24	1.60	1.26	1.75	1.88
Hungary	x	0.38	0.40	0.42	0.51	0.51	0.55	0.49	0.49	0.43
	m	0.70	0.72	0.71	0.77	0.75	0.79	0.75	0.74	0.58
	w	0.54	0.56	0.60	0.66	0.68	0.70	0.66	0.66	0.73
Poland	x	0.36	0.45	0.54	0.51	0.50	0.55	0.47	0.45	0.45
	m	0.62	0.56	0.53	0.48	0.55	0.61	0.49	0.55	0.56
	w	0.58	0.81	1.02	1.06	0.91	0.90	0.96	0.82	0.81
Romania	x	0.31	0.45	0.48	0.43	0.34	0.39	0.37	0.35	0.28
	m	0.48	0.37	0.42	0.38	0.36	0.35	0.28	0.33	0.32
	w	0.65	1.20	1.16	1.12	0.96	1.11	1.31	1.05	0.88
USSR	x	0.19	0.17	0.17	0.18	0.22	0.15	0.13	0.11	0.09
	m	0.61	0.54	0.46	0.51	0.49	0.54	0.55	0.50	0.51
	w	0.31	0.32	0.36	0.36	0.44	0.27	0.24	0.21	0.18
Yugoslavia	x	0.55	0.63	0.70	0.85	0.70	0.76	0.85	0.80	0.69
	m	0.89	0.92	0.95	0.90	0.88	0.84	0.86	0.87	0.78
	w	0.62	0.69	0.74	0.94	0.80	0.90	0.98	0.92	0.89
Albania	x	0.02	0.01	0.02	0.01	0.01	0.01	0.01	0.01	0.04
	m	0.70	0.69	0.47	0.70	0.50	0.45	0.50	0.56	0.51
	w	0.03	0.02	0.05	0.01	0.01	0.03	0.02	0.02	0.09
Eastern Europe 9	x	0.34	0.36	0.39	0.41	0.38	0.35	0.33	0.30	0.27
	m	0.66	0.59	0.57	0.58	0.57	0.59	0.59	0.55	0.53
	w	0.51	0.61	0.69	0.71	0.66	0.59	0.56	0.53	0.51
Eastern Europe 6	x	0.43	0.49	0.56	0.54	0.49	0.52	0.51	0.49	0.45
	m	0.63	0.55	0.54	0.53	0.54	0.55	0.56	0.54	0.48
	w	0.69	0.89	1.04	1.02	0.91	0.94	0.91	0.91	0.92

Note: x = export measure; m = import measure; w = export-import measure.

between the LIO countries and the EE6 can be completely explained by the absence of MNCs in the CPEs.

It is possible that the most important effect on CPEs of the absence of MNCs is not captured in Table 4.16 but is a consequence of the trade flows depicted in that table. By effectively banning intraorganizational trade, the CPEs forgo many of the benefits from importing the technology embodied in goods made in the most advanced nations. Thus, the reduced trade levels in Table 4.16 could lead directly to the comparative advantages shown in Tables 4.9–12, which focus on technological advance.

Entry The Schumpeterian analysis particularly emphasizes the importance of entry of new firms (or firms new to an industry) in the process of producing and using technological advances. However, free entry is more important in some sectors than in others. Thus, if free entry is barred there will be an effect on the structure of relative costs. Hence, Hypothesis 7 predicts that CPEs have a comparative disadvantage in sectors in which entry is most significant in capitalist economies. Table 4.17 examines the RCAs for sectors in which large numbers of new firms entered U.S. markets during the 1970s.

The data in Table 4.17 are completely in accordance with Hypothesis 7. Relative to the LIO grouping, the EE6 perform poorly in sectors in which entry is a significant element of capitalist economic processes—for all countries except the GDR and for all years the export-import RCAs are much lower in the EE6 than in the LIO group. Moreover, the low level of total CPE trade evidenced in the table is consistent with the analysis that leads to Hypothesis 7. Given that entry is significant for technological change, and given that arm's-length trade of new embodied technologies is costly, one would expect that ME sectors with many new firms would find difficulties in trading with CPEs. Thus, the low levels of trade result from two effects: the absence of free entry reduces efficiency and therefore exports; the difficulty of arm's-length transactions in new products reduces the level of imports.

The results for individual countries are consistent with those in previous tables. In particular, one should emphasize that Table 4.17 shows no evidence of any payoff from economic reform in either Hungary or Yugoslavia.

Quality and Quality Reputation Hypothesis 5, based on the traditional analysis of producer incentives, predicts a comparative disadvantage in high-quality products for the CPEs. However, the discussion in Section 3.9 pointed out that the demand-side effects of shortages could produce results that are the opposite of those predicted by Hypothesis 5.

Even if the CPEs had a comparative advantage in producing high-quality goods, this would not be sufficient to establish export markets for these goods. There must also be a means of conveying quality to the buyer. Hence, the analyses leading to Hypotheses 9 and 16 are relevant. Because multinational

Table 4.17

Revealed Comparative Advantages for Goods Produced in Sectors in Which the Entry of New Firms Is Significant, 1975–1983

	Trade Measure	1975	1976	1977	1978	1979	1980	1981	1982	1983
Market	x	1.13	1.13	1.12	1.11	1.11	1.12	1.10	1.11	1.11
	m	0.98	0.97	0.97	0.98	0.99	1.00	1.00	1.00	1.01
	w	1.15	1.16	1.15	1.12	1.12	1.12	1.10	1.11	1.10
OECD	x	1.22	1.23	1.23	1.21	1.22	1.24	1.23	1.24	1.22
	m	0.97	0.96	0.96	0.97	0.98	0.98	0.97	0.98	0.99
	w	1.26	1.29	1.28	1.25	1.25	1.27	1.26	1.26	1.23
Market minus OECD	x	0.29	0.31	0.31	0.33	0.33	0.34	0.36	0.39	0.45
	m	1.07	1.13	1.08	1.07	1.10	1.13	1.15	1.11	1.11
	w	0.27	0.27	0.29	0.31	0.30	0.30	0.32	0.35	0.40
Low-income OECD	x	1.01	1.00	1.02	0.99	1.04	1.10	1.03	1.03	0.98
	m	0.95	0.97	0.98	0.96	0.97	1.01	0.99	0.96	0.92
	w	1.06	1.03	1.04	1.03	1.07	1.09	1.04	1.06	1.07
Bulgaria	x	0.34	0.38	0.37	0.40	0.40	0.49	0.45	0.39	0.31
	m	1.06	1.01	0.95	0.93	0.72	0.82	0.94	1.01	1.01
	w	0.33	0.38	0.39	0.43	0.56	0.60	0.48	0.39	0.31
Czechoslovakia	x	0.84	0.81	0.81	0.78	0.79	0.74	0.74	0.71	0.63
	m	0.96	0.90	0.98	1.00	0.88	0.95	0.88	0.88	0.81
	w	0.88	0.90	0.83	0.78	0.90	0.78	0.83	0.81	0.77
East Germany (GDR)	x	1.09	1.11	1.22	1.23	1.10	1.03	0.93	0.82	0.77
	m	0.54	0.49	0.58	0.57	0.69	0.64	0.70	0.77	0.73
	w	2.03	2.28	2.09	2.17	1.60	1.62	1.33	1.07	1.06
Hungary	x	0.53	0.51	0.48	0.59	0.57	0.60	0.57	0.54	0.51
	m	0.76	0.82	0.89	0.92	0.93	0.86	0.83	0.88	0.69
	w	0.70	0.62	0.54	0.64	0.61	0.71	0.69	0.61	0.75
Poland	x	0.48	0.54	0.63	0.61	0.61	0.65	0.62	0.54	0.53
	m	1.00	0.96	0.95	0.92	0.77	0.77	0.58	0.59	0.62
	w	0.48	0.57	0.67	0.66	0.79	0.85	1.07	0.92	0.86
Romania	x	0.58	0.56	0.59	0.54	0.47	0.51	0.49	0.57	0.53
	m	0.84	0.61	0.88	0.97	0.85	0.67	0.45	0.45	0.41
	w	0.69	0.92	0.67	0.56	0.55	0.75	1.09	1.26	1.31
USSR	x	0.25	0.23	0.20	0.21	0.21	0.14	0.13	0.10	0.09
	m	0.93	0.97	1.03	1.01	0.87	0.73	0.69	0.76	0.82
	w	0.27	0.23	0.20	0.21	0.24	0.20	0.18	0.14	0.11
Yugoslavia	x	0.56	0.57	0.67	0.77	0.67	0.75	0.83	0.84	0.74
	m	1.20	1.13	1.25	1.31	1.28	1.19	1.09	1.06	0.91
	w	0.47	0.50	0.54	0.59	0.52	0.63	0.77	0.80	0.81
Albania	x	0.04	0.07	0.07	0.09	0.07	0.08	0.08	0.11	0.12
	m	0.60	0.48	0.42	0.54	0.53	0.49	0.66	0.64	0.86
	w	0.06	0.14	0.18	0.17	0.12	0.15	0.12	0.18	0.14
Eastern Europe 9	x	0.47	0.45	0.47	0.48	0.44	0.41	0.38	0.34	0.32
	m	0.95	0.93	1.01	1.01	0.91	0.81	0.75	0.79	0.80
	w	0.49	0.48	0.46	0.48	0.48	0.50	0.51	0.43	0.40
Eastern Europe 6	x	0.64	0.65	0.69	0.69	0.65	0.67	0.64	0.62	0.58
	m	0.90	0.83	0.89	0.91	0.81	0.78	0.70	0.76	0.71
	w	0.72	0.78	0.78	0.76	0.80	0.86	0.91	0.82	0.81

Note: x = export measure; m = import measure; w = export-import measure.

corporations are absent CPEs cannot take advantage of the intracompany exchanges that are sometimes necessitated when quality is difficult to ascertain. Moreover, the CPEs themselves have insufficient indigenous talent in marketing to bypass the services that MNCs can provide.

To develop evidence relevant to quality and reputation, it is necessary to obtain two types of information. First, one must ascertain which goods embody large amounts of quality-producing inputs. Second, one needs to know for which goods seller reputation is important. Unfortunately, as far as this author is aware, there is little of the first type of information available. Data on inputs into quality control are simply unavailable.[17]

There is information available on the importance of quality reputation in the selling of goods. "Convenience" goods are goods purchased frequently that have a small unit price and are nondurables (Porter 1974, p. 422). Hence, for these goods, quality judgments are easily made by consumers through frequent purchases. For "experience-durable" goods, prepurchase quality judgments cannot be made in a direct manner. These goods are bought extremely infrequently, and after-sales service is important (Nelson 1974). Therefore, the cost of searching for quality is prohibitively high, and consumers must rely on indirect information, such as seller reputation.[18]

The results for convenience goods and experience-durable goods are given in Tables 4.18 and 4.19. In drawing conclusions for the CPEs from these tables, it is first necessary to examine the results for market economies. For convenience goods, quality reputation is, by definition, not important. But the market-economy RCAs are related to level of development, indicating that efficiency in quality control might be a factor in determining comparative advantage.[19] For experience-durable goods, inputs of quality control are important, but so too is quality reputation.

The RCAs for convenience goods, given in Table 4.18, show the EE6 with a distinct pattern, outside the range spanned by the market economies. A significant majority of the export-import RCAs for the Eastern European countries are larger than those found in any of the groupings of market economies. These results indicate that the CPEs have a comparative advantage when

[17] Of course, the proportion of value added in cost might be an indicator of the importance of such inputs. But, as we have seen, this indicator is also correlated with many other factors that could affect trade patterns. Thus, at this juncture, little would be gained by studying the results from the use of such an indicator.

[18] In early versions of this study, I also examined "search" goods, which are durables that are not bought repetitively. For these goods, quality is judged before purchase because the costs of searching among alternatives are relatively small compared with price (Nelson 1970, 1974). However, for search goods, RCAs were inversely related to level of development, indicating that ability to control quality was not an important factor in production. Therefore, little relevant to the present analysis could be concluded from the results for search goods.

[19] This statement presumes that endowments of quality-controlling inputs are correlated with level of development.

Table 4.18.
The Revealed Comparative Advantages for Convenience Goods, 1975–1983

	Trade Measure	1975	1976	1977	1978	1979	1980	1981	1982	1983
Market	x	1.04	1.06	1.07	1.06	1.06	1.07	1.06	1.07	1.07
	m	1.04	1.03	1.01	1.03	1.01	0.97	0.96	0.97	0.98
	w	1.00	1.03	1.05	1.03	1.06	1.11	1.10	1.10	1.08
OECD	x	1.01	1.06	1.08	1.08	1.10	1.11	1.10	1.13	1.14
	m	1.09	1.06	1.03	1.06	1.04	0.99	0.99	1.01	1.02
	w	0.93	1.01	1.05	1.02	1.05	1.12	1.11	1.11	1.12
Market minus OECD	x	1.14	0.90	0.86	0.79	0.76	0.72	0.75	0.67	0.62
	m	0.77	0.86	0.97	0.87	0.86	0.90	0.87	0.82	0.83
	w	1.49	1.04	0.89	0.90	0.88	0.80	0.86	0.82	0.75
Low-income OECD	x	1.26	1.33	1.31	1.31	1.33	1.34	1.35	1.29	1.32
	m	1.31	1.28	1.26	1.32	1.29	1.20	1.25	1.34	1.41
	w	0.96	1.04	1.04	0.99	1.03	1.12	1.08	0.96	0.94
Bulgaria	x	2.89	3.31	3.01	2.69	2.34	1.89	1.91	2.16	2.26
	m	0.52	0.71	0.61	0.53	0.66	0.65	0.61	0.70	1.01
	w	5.58	4.68	4.96	5.07	3.52	2.92	3.11	3.07	2.24
Czechoslovakia	x	0.92	0.85	0.81	0.89	0.79	0.70	0.73	0.78	0.83
	m	0.57	0.56	0.62	0.57	0.61	0.59	0.65	0.90	0.65
	w	1.60	1.50	1.30	1.56	1.30	1.18	1.13	0.86	1.27
East Germany (GDR)	x	1.41	1.10	0.60	0.74	0.51	0.43	0.41	0.29	0.25
	m	0.62	0.67	0.81	0.76	0.64	0.76	0.75	1.03	0.98
	w	2.28	1.66	0.74	0.96	0.80	0.57	0.54	0.28	0.26
Hungary	x	2.58	2.46	2.64	2.61	2.42	2.64	2.67	2.71	2.65
	m	0.63	0.78	0.64	0.47	0.52	0.56	0.70	0.71	0.70
	w	4.11	3.15	4.15	5.51	4.65	4.68	3.82	3.79	3.80
Poland	x	1.44	1.70	1.75	1.74	1.67	1.59	1.44	1.25	1.61
	m	0.29	0.39	0.59	0.42	0.53	0.76	1.58	1.66	1.26
	w	5.02	4.36	3.00	4.18	3.16	2.11	0.91	0.75	1.27
Romania	x	1.99	1.40	1.20	1.05	0.97	0.74	0.66	0.63	0.54
	m	0.22	0.49	0.65	0.28	0.48	0.65	1.23	0.44	0.36
	w	8.92	2.84	1.85	3.76	1.99	1.14	0.54	1.43	1.47
USSR	x	0.36	0.22	0.21	0.19	0.15	0.11	0.11	0.10	0.13
	m	0.67	0.64	0.82	0.38	0.80	1.54	1.59	1.23	1.06
	w	0.54	0.35	0.26	0.51	0.18	0.07	0.07	0.08	0.12
Yugoslavia	x	1.53	1.74	1.76	1.69	1.57	1.57	1.39	1.49	1.36
	m	0.76	0.72	0.44	0.39	0.45	0.64	0.80	0.49	0.68
	w	2.01	2.40	4.02	4.30	3.50	2.45	1.73	3.06	2.01
Albania	x	0.69	0.33	0.62	0.69	0.55	0.51	0.48	0.54	0.71
	m	0.84	1.01	1.58	0.56	0.81	0.59	0.61	0.76	0.57
	w	0.82	0.33	0.39	1.24	0.67	0.87	0.78	0.71	1.23
Eastern Europe 9	x	1.09	0.99	0.95	0.94	0.81	0.71	0.62	0.58	0.62
	m	0.57	0.61	0.68	0.42	0.64	1.06	1.26	1.06	0.95
	w	1.89	1.63	1.39	2.25	1.27	0.67	0.49	0.54	0.65
Eastern Europe 6	x	1.65	1.59	1.53	1.50	1.39	1.28	1.18	1.14	1.21
	m	0.41	0.53	0.63	0.47	0.55	0.68	1.00	0.98	0.86
	w	3.99	2.98	2.42	3.20	2.50	1.90	1.18	1.17	1.40

Note: x = export measure; m = import measure; w = export-import measure.

Table 4.19.

The Revealed Comparative Advantages of Experience-Durable Goods, 1975–1983

	Trade Measure	1975	1976	1977	1978	1979	1980	1981	1982	1983
Market	x	1.14	1.14	1.13	1.11	1.12	1.13	1.11	1.12	1.11
	m	1.02	1.02	1.03	1.04	1.03	1.03	1.02	1.03	1.03
	w	1.11	1.11	1.10	1.08	1.08	1.10	1.09	1.09	1.07
OECD	x	1.23	1.25	1.25	1.23	1.23	1.25	1.24	1.25	1.24
	m	1.06	1.06	1.07	1.07	1.07	1.05	1.04	1.07	1.08
	w	1.17	1.18	1.17	1.14	1.16	1.19	1.19	1.17	1.15
Market minus OECD	x	0.25	0.26	0.26	0.30	0.32	0.34	0.35	0.34	0.37
	m	0.85	0.88	0.90	0.86	0.85	0.95	0.95	0.81	0.76
	w	0.30	0.30	0.29	0.34	0.38	0.35	0.37	0.42	0.49
Low-income OECD	x	1.01	0.92	0.92	0.86	0.90	0.97	0.85	0.86	0.83
	m	0.87	0.91	0.96	0.96	1.01	1.08	1.02	1.05	0.94
	w	1.16	1.01	0.96	0.89	0.89	0.89	0.84	0.82	0.89
Bulgaria	x	0.06	0.06	0.06	0.07	0.07	0.04	0.02	0.06	0.06
	m	0.81	0.52	0.51	0.40	0.54	0.60	0.58	0.55	0.45
	w	0.08	0.12	0.12	0.17	0.14	0.06	0.04	0.11	0.14
Czechoslovakia	x	0.54	0.49	0.51	0.45	0.45	0.40	0.43	0.44	0.36
	m	0.45	0.38	0.42	0.44	0.40	0.41	0.39	0.40	0.41
	w	1.22	1.29	1.21	1.03	1.14	0.98	1.09	1.11	0.87
East Germany (GDR)	x	0.56	0.54	0.56	0.56	0.58	0.52	0.46	0.48	0.47
	m	0.19	0.17	0.22	0.19	0.22	0.26	0.34	0.24	0.19
	w	2.91	3.15	2.57	2.99	2.66	1.97	1.33	1.97	2.49
Hungary	x	0.32	0.37	0.33	0.45	0.42	0.51	0.48	0.39	0.41
	m	0.39	0.44	0.42	0.45	0.49	0.49	0.46	0.48	0.36
	w	0.82	0.84	0.79	0.99	0.86	1.04	1.05	0.81	1.15
Poland	x	0.24	0.23	0.27	0.32	0.39	0.52	0.52	0.38	0.29
	m	0.41	0.40	0.44	0.38	0.40	0.47	0.33	0.38	0.44
	w	0.60	0.56	0.61	0.85	0.97	1.12	1.59	1.02	0.66
Romania	x	0.18	0.16	0.17	0.19	0.15	0.16	0.14	0.17	0.12
	m	0.40	0.30	0.34	0.32	0.30	0.29	0.22	0.23	0.18
	w	0.46	0.54	0.51	0.60	0.49	0.55	0.63	0.72	0.69
USSR	x	0.18	0.16	0.15	0.16	0.19	0.13	0.12	0.11	0.11
	m	0.31	0.27	0.19	0.19	0.22	0.25	0.29	0.31	0.24
	w	0.60	0.60	0.81	0.87	0.89	0.50	0.40	0.37	0.44
Yugoslavia	x	0.64	0.60	0.56	0.77	0.69	0.83	1.01	0.94	0.84
	m	0.79	0.79	0.84	0.84	0.87	0.79	0.76	0.91	0.83
	w	0.81	0.76	0.67	0.91	0.79	1.04	1.32	1.04	1.00
Albania	x	0.03	0.02	0.01	0.00	0.00	0.01	0.01	0.02	0.03
	m	0.68	0.58	0.46	0.39	0.46	0.39	0.44	0.50	0.47
	w	0.04	0.03	0.02	0.01	0.00	0.02	0.02	0.03	0.07
Eastern Europe 9	x	0.29	0.27	0.27	0.31	0.31	0.29	0.28	0.26	0.24
	m	0.43	0.38	0.38	0.37	0.39	0.40	0.38	0.40	0.35
	w	0.69	0.71	0.71	0.85	0.78	0.74	0.73	0.65	0.70
Eastern Europe 6	x	0.33	0.31	0.33	0.35	0.36	0.40	0.37	0.35	0.31
	m	0.42	0.37	0.40	0.37	0.38	0.41	0.37	0.38	0.35
	w	0.78	0.82	0.83	0.95	0.94	0.96	1.00	0.93	0.90

Note: x = export measure; m = import measure; w = export-import measure.

quality reputation is not important. The results are particularly striking because some of the convenience goods are goods that require salesmanship, in which the CPEs are thought to have a comparative disadvantage. In contrast, for the goods examined in Table 4.19, where quality reputation is of the essence, the export performance of the CPEs is as poor as that of the less-developed market economies. Collectively, the results of Tables 4.18 and 4.19 are consistent with those of Hill and McKay (1988, p. 127), who conclude in an engineering study that Western criticisms of Soviet product quality are overstated and that quality in the Soviet Union matches that in the United Kingdom.

In Table 4.19 the levels of trade for Eastern European countries are much lower than for any grouping of market economies, indicating that the socialist countries not only have difficulty exporting goods for which quality reputation is important, but also that there is difficulty simply conducting transactions. These facts might indicate that the relevant factor explaining the data is the absence of MNC activities. In markets for experience-durable goods, MNCs are likely to be important, because quality is difficult to ascertain for such goods and arm's-length exchanges are inhibited.

Salesmanship   Hypothesis 16 predicts that CPEs have a comparative disadvantage in goods requiring large amounts of salesmanship. This prediction is based on the fact that the level of human capital in salesmanship is very low in CPEs, because marketing has been little emphasized in the past. Moreover, the CPEs have been unwilling to use the services of institutions that could provide them with such human capital—the multinational corporations.

It is not an easy task to find data on the intensivity of salesmanship in production. Therefore, a simple proxy had to be used—expenditures on advertising. Advertising is just one way of selling among many methods, but it is reasonable to assume that if one method is effective, others will be also. Therefore, the use of different selling methods will be correlated across goods. Two groups were created: products advertised intensively and products advertised little. (See lines 20 and 21 of Table 4.2. Many products fall inbetween the two groups.) By symmetry, the usual analysis of CPEs predicts a comparative advantage for goods that are little advertised, as well as a comparative disadvantage for heavily advertised goods. The relevant RCAs appear in Tables 4.20–4.21.

The results are as predicted in the usual analysis of CPEs. The trade behavior of the CPEs evidences a striking comparative advantage in goods that are little advertised in the West and, in most instances, a comparative disadvantage in goods that are heavily advertised. The export-import RCAs of the EE6 in Tables 4.20–4.21 are unlike those of any of the market groupings, indicating that the lack of salesmanship is something very peculiar to the centrally planned economies. In contrast to many of the other analyses in this chapter, the GDR seems to be typical of the CPEs in the present instance. Bulgaria's

Table 4.20.
Revealed Comparative Advantages for Goods That Are Heavily Advertised in Western Markets, 1975–1983

	Trade Measure	1975	1976	1977	1978	1979	1980	1981	1982	1983
Market	x	1.12	1.12	1.12	1.10	1.11	1.12	1.09	1.10	1.09
	m	1.04	1.03	1.03	1.03	1.02	1.01	1.00	1.02	1.02
	w	1.08	1.08	1.09	1.07	1.08	1.11	1.09	1.08	1.07
OECD	x	1.19	1.20	1.20	1.18	1.19	1.20	1.19	1.21	1.21
	m	1.04	1.01	1.00	1.02	1.01	1.00	1.00	1.02	1.02
	w	1.15	1.18	1.20	1.16	1.18	1.21	1.19	1.18	1.19
Market minus OECD	x	0.41	0.48	0.45	0.48	0.51	0.52	0.50	0.45	0.43
	m	1.12	1.22	1.29	1.18	1.15	1.13	1.07	1.01	1.05
	w	0.36	0.39	0.34	0.41	0.44	0.46	0.47	0.45	0.41
Low-income OECD	x	1.58	1.47	1.41	1.42	1.43	1.45	1.50	1.46	1.42
	m	1.17	1.19	1.11	1.18	1.14	1.09	1.13	1.16	1.19
	w	1.35	1.24	1.26	1.20	1.26	1.33	1.33	1.26	1.19
Bulgaria	x	0.96	0.93	0.96	0.73	0.79	0.94	0.70	1.16	1.08
	m	0.76	0.91	1.07	0.89	1.05	0.99	0.94	1.11	1.11
	w	1.27	1.02	0.90	0.82	0.75	0.95	0.74	1.04	0.97
Czechoslovakia	x	1.05	1.05	1.09	0.86	0.75	0.63	0.68	0.56	0.54
	m	0.68	0.69	0.66	0.59	0.62	0.66	0.83	1.04	0.87
	w	1.55	1.54	1.65	1.46	1.21	0.95	0.82	0.53	0.62
East Germany (GDR)	x	0.63	0.64	0.56	0.45	0.40	0.41	0.45	0.35	0.35
	m	0.77	0.72	0.88	0.91	0.85	0.96	0.99	0.92	0.78
	w	0.82	0.88	0.63	0.49	0.47	0.43	0.46	0.38	0.45
Hungary	x	1.23	1.21	1.19	1.04	1.00	0.96	0.94	0.95	0.85
	m	0.73	0.91	0.86	0.86	0.88	0.96	1.02	1.11	0.97
	w	1.68	1.34	1.39	1.21	1.13	1.00	0.92	0.85	0.87
Poland	x	0.32	0.31	0.30	0.24	0.23	0.21	0.22	0.16	0.13
	m	0.43	0.57	0.69	0.60	0.71	0.73	0.91	1.85	1.73
	w	0.75	0.53	0.43	0.40	0.32	0.29	0.24	0.08	0.07
Romania	x	0.16	0.16	0.21	0.22	0.27	0.30	0.41	0.27	0.21
	m	0.34	0.52	0.35	0.30	0.34	0.32	0.42	0.39	0.48
	w	0.46	0.30	0.59	0.73	0.80	0.95	0.99	0.70	0.44
USSR	x	0.19	0.15	0.16	0.14	0.15	0.12	0.10	0.09	0.16
	m	0.47	0.40	0.37	0.35	0.52	0.73	0.96	0.59	0.45
	w	0.40	0.38	0.43	0.41	0.28	0.16	0.10	0.15	0.36
Yugoslavia	x	0.91	0.69	0.78	0.72	0.80	0.89	0.92	0.82	0.74
	m	0.80	0.68	0.64	0.60	0.58	0.61	0.66	0.61	0.77
	w	1.14	1.00	1.22	1.21	1.37	1.46	1.38	1.35	0.96
Albania	x	0.29	0.40	0.16	0.05	0.14	0.11	0.07	0.01	0.11
	m	0.53	0.64	0.55	0.65	0.47	0.46	0.36	0.53	0.60
	w	0.54	0.63	0.29	0.07	0.29	0.23	0.20	0.03	0.19
Eastern Europe 9	x	0.45	0.40	0.42	0.37	0.36	0.33	0.33	0.28	0.31
	m	0.55	0.55	0.55	0.51	0.60	0.71	0.88	0.76	0.68
	w	0.82	0.73	0.77	0.72	0.59	0.47	0.37	0.37	0.45
Eastern Europe 6	x	0.61	0.60	0.62	0.51	0.50	0.49	0.52	0.48	0.43
	m	0.55	0.67	0.70	0.64	0.69	0.73	0.85	1.15	1.05
	w	1.11	0.89	0.89	0.80	0.72	0.67	0.61	0.41	0.41

Note: x = export measure; m = import measure; w = export-import measure.

Table 4.21.
Revealed Comparative Advantage for Goods That Are Little Advertised in Western Markets, 1975–1983

	Trade Measure	1975	1976	1977	1978	1979	1980	1981	1982	1983
Market	x	1.09	1.10	1.10	1.08	1.08	1.09	1.07	1.07	1.07
	m	1.03	1.04	1.04	1.05	1.05	1.02	1.00	1.02	1.03
	w	1.06	1.06	1.05	1.03	1.03	1.06	1.06	1.05	1.03
OECD	x	1.09	1.12	1.14	1.12	1.13	1.14	1.11	1.13	1.13
	m	1.11	1.11	1.12	1.13	1.13	1.09	1.08	1.11	1.12
	w	0.98	1.01	1.02	0.99	1.00	1.04	1.03	1.02	1.00
Market minus OECD	x	0.94	0.82	0.71	0.73	0.68	0.68	0.74	0.70	0.69
	m	0.60	0.60	0.62	0.60	0.56	0.66	0.70	0.56	0.49
	w	1.58	1.37	1.15	1.22	1.21	1.03	1.05	1.24	1.40
Low-income OECD	x	1.46	1.45	1.46	1.45	1.56	1.65	1.49	1.50	1.47
	m	0.84	0.87	0.93	0.93	0.97	1.04	1.01	1.05	0.96
	w	1.75	1.67	1.57	1.57	1.61	1.59	1.48	1.43	1.52
Bulgaria	x	0.76	0.74	0.78	0.75	0.75	0.64	0.56	0.62	0.65
	m	0.70	0.46	0.36	0.28	0.40	0.44	0.47	0.42	0.47
	w	1.08	1.62	2.17	2.68	1.86	1.47	1.17	1.48	1.40
Czechoslovakia	x	1.09	0.96	0.97	0.96	0.93	0.92	0.92	0.94	0.84
	m	0.40	0.33	0.39	0.36	0.35	0.39	0.38	0.47	0.42
	w	2.74	2.91	2.45	2.71	2.69	2.38	2.44	1.99	1.98
East Germany (GDR)	x	0.93	0.85	0.68	0.76	0.67	0.63	0.52	0.49	0.49
	m	0.25	0.25	0.28	0.31	0.24	0.29	0.40	0.41	0.39
	w	3.66	3.38	2.44	2.48	2.80	2.20	1.31	1.20	1.28
Hungary	x	1.88	1.66	1.67	1.81	1.78	1.95	1.77	1.67	1.57
	m	0.43	0.50	0.42	0.43	0.45	0.47	0.46	0.50	0.41
	w	4.34	3.33	4.00	4.26	3.95	4.19	3.82	3.33	3.86
Poland	x	0.72	0.76	0.87	0.91	1.02	1.15	1.18	0.94	0.87
	m	0.34	0.35	0.45	0.31	0.36	0.53	0.56	0.42	0.47
	w	2.14	2.15	1.91	2.91	2.83	2.19	2.09	2.26	1.85
Romania	x	1.57	1.52	1.41	1.43	1.37	1.39	1.17	1.54	1.39
	m	0.30	0.34	0.41	0.27	0.30	0.40	0.42	0.31	0.22
	w	5.22	4.49	3.44	5.30	4.51	3.46	2.80	4.91	6.24
USSR	x	0.14	0.13	0.14	0.15	0.17	0.11	0.11	0.10	0.09
	m	0.61	0.50	0.48	0.29	0.38	0.78	0.94	0.81	0.62
	w	0.23	0.26	0.29	0.50	0.43	0.14	0.11	0.13	0.15
Yugoslavia	x	2.41	2.13	2.12	2.13	1.97	2.29	2.33	2.33	2.21
	m	0.67	0.64	0.65	0.66	0.68	0.64	0.74	0.76	0.73
	w	3.58	3.31	3.24	3.23	2.88	3.57	3.14	3.08	3.01
Albania	x	0.48	0.89	0.63	0.86	0.55	0.51	0.24	0.21	0.34
	m	0.62	0.40	0.33	0.24	0.15	0.15	0.20	0.30	0.27
	w	0.79	2.23	1.89	3.62	3.53	3.36	1.17	0.71	1.25
Eastern Europe 9	x	0.81	0.75	0.74	0.79	0.75	0.72	0.65	0.61	0.60
	m	0.52	0.46	0.48	0.36	0.42	0.62	0.73	0.69	0.57
	w	1.56	1.63	1.56	2.17	1.79	1.16	0.88	0.90	1.05
Eastern Europe 6	x	1.12	1.07	1.07	1.12	1.13	1.18	1.08	1.06	1.00
	m	0.37	0.36	0.41	0.33	0.35	0.44	0.46	0.43	0.41
	w	2.99	2.96	2.63	3.42	3.26	2.70	2.35	2.45	2.45

Note: x = export measure; m = import measure; w = export-import measure.

results are surprising in that it appears to be one of the more sophisticated Eastern European countries on the score of salesmanship.

The market reforms in Hungary and Yugoslavia do not appear to have changed the fact that socialist countries specialize in goods that require little selling. This is of special interest when contrasted to the previous results indicating that product variety seems to have increased since the reforms. Perhaps these contrasting results are a sign of differences between the nature of cooperation agreements and of the operations of the MNCs. The MNCs, almost by definition, help to market the goods they produce, because so much of the cross-border movement of goods is within the company. Moreover, for arm's-length sales these corporations provide their reputation. In contrast, cooperation agreements for production do not provide such marketing services. Hence, the fact that Hungary and Yugoslavia have signed many cooperation agreements but do not entertain MNCs could explain the contrasts between Table 4.15 and Tables 4.20–4.21—some success in the production of variety, but little success where that production requires sophisticated marketing.

4.6. The Economic System and the Characteristics of Goods

Industry versus Consumers   Western analysts usually conclude that the consumer sector is treated as a residual in plan decisions, especially in the allocation of foreign exchange. Given also the emphasis placed on growth, one would predict that CPEs have a comparative advantage in consumer goods. But there is one element of consumption that leaders in CPEs have always been willing to protect: food consumption. Hypotheses 19, 21, and 22 reflect this analysis. Collectively, these predict a comparative disadvantage in food and investment goods and a comparative advantage in industrial consumer goods.

The relevant results are presented in Tables 4.22, 4.23, and 4.24. The first of these tables shows the RCAs for a set of nonfood consumer goods. The EE6 both export and import relatively less than the LIO countries, leaving the export-import ratios at similar values for both groups of countries. The results for goods used by industries, in Table 4.23, are somewhat more in line with the predictions of the hypotheses. The main difference between the EE6 and the lower-income OECD is that the EE6 tend to have larger RCAs for goods used by industry, leading to slightly lower export-import ratios. The results hold for all Eastern European countries individually, except the GDR. Collectively, these results weakly validate Hypothesis 19 on the priority given to investment, but do not support Hypothesis 21 on the low priority given to industrial consumer goods. The results certainly do not validate the conventional claim that foreign exchange is purely an investment resource in CPEs.

Table 4.22.
Revealed Comparative Advantages for Industrial Consumer Goods, 1975–1983

	Trade Measure	1975	1976	1977	1978	1979	1980	1981	1982	1983
Market	x	1.05	1.05	1.05	1.03	1.03	1.03	1.00	1.00	0.99
	m	1.08	1.07	1.07	1.07	1.06	1.04	1.03	1.03	1.04
	w	0.98	0.98	0.98	0.97	0.98	0.99	0.97	0.97	0.95
OECD	x	0.88	0.83	0.85	0.83	0.85	0.85	0.79	0.79	0.77
	m	1.18	1.16	1.15	1.16	1.15	1.15	1.14	1.13	1.13
	w	0.74	0.72	0.74	0.71	0.74	0.75	0.69	0.70	0.68
Market minus OECD	x	2.26	2.39	2.15	2.25	2.01	1.86	2.00	1.97	2.03
	m	0.45	0.48	0.50	0.48	0.45	0.47	0.48	0.50	0.47
	w	5.01	5.03	4.29	4.67	4.45	3.93	4.15	3.92	4.30
Low-income OECD	x	2.74	2.66	2.66	2.63	2.78	2.80	2.67	2.74	2.70
	m	0.80	0.82	0.84	0.89	0.94	0.93	0.92	0.99	0.93
	w	3.43	3.26	3.16	2.96	2.98	3.02	2.89	2.77	2.90
Bulgaria	x	1.73	1.69	1.62	1.56	1.52	1.49	1.32	1.57	1.66
	m	0.41	0.43	0.51	0.50	0.59	0.58	0.56	0.72	0.62
	w	4.27	3.93	3.19	3.11	2.56	2.57	2.35	2.18	2.67
Czechoslovakia	x	1.59	1.50	1.60	1.49	1.38	1.43	1.37	1.28	1.25
	m	0.86	0.73	0.80	0.75	0.78	0.85	0.80	1.10	1.04
	w	1.84	2.07	2.01	1.98	1.76	1.69	1.71	1.17	1.20
East Germany (GDR)	x	0.59	0.64	0.68	0.66	0.67	0.64	0.53	0.45	0.45
	m	0.81	0.73	0.80	1.09	0.86	0.78	0.72	0.89	0.78
	w	0.73	0.88	0.85	0.61	0.78	0.82	0.73	0.51	0.58
Hungary	x	4.06	3.74	3.56	3.45	3.51	3.44	3.09	3.00	2.78
	m	0.75	0.80	0.82	0.79	0.80	1.00	0.99	1.20	1.04
	w	5.43	4.69	4.33	4.37	4.37	3.43	3.13	2.49	2.68
Poland	x	1.28	1.31	1.46	1.44	1.57	1.49	1.70	1.43	1.36
	m	0.33	0.40	0.46	0.42	0.52	0.63	0.57	1.11	1.17
	w	3.89	3.30	3.14	3.45	3.02	2.37	2.97	1.29	1.16
Romania	x	2.49	2.79	2.85	2.98	2.88	2.73	2.39	3.29	2.86
	m	0.34	0.45	0.42	0.41	0.38	0.45	0.44	0.64	0.76
	w	7.25	6.25	6.85	7.20	7.53	6.09	5.47	5.18	3.75
USSR	x	0.05	0.04	0.04	0.03	0.03	0.02	0.02	0.02	0.03
	m	1.02	0.89	0.92	0.77	0.74	1.07	1.55	1.26	0.94
	w	0.05	0.04	0.04	0.05	0.04	0.02	0.02	0.01	0.03
Yugoslavia	x	6.51	4.99	4.83	4.22	4.25	4.43	4.36	4.29	4.24
	m	0.77	0.71	0.66	0.65	0.64	0.68	0.70	0.80	0.96
	w	8.43	7.06	7.30	6.48	6.59	6.52	6.25	5.35	4.42
Albania	x	1.86	3.45	2.35	3.18	1.98	1.72	0.75	0.63	1.05
	m	0.34	0.78	0.41	0.32	0.31	0.18	0.20	0.24	0.30
	w	5.42	4.43	5.79	9.81	6.39	9.72	3.79	2.69	3.54
Eastern Europe 9	x	1.47	1.35	1.35	1.33	1.26	1.15	1.04	0.98	0.99
	m	0.77	0.72	0.75	0.68	0.67	0.87	1.11	1.12	0.94
	w	1.91	1.88	1.81	1.96	1.87	1.33	0.93	0.87	1.05
Eastern Europe 6	x	1.84	1.89	1.95	1.94	1.99	1.90	1.80	1.81	1.71
	m	0.52	0.54	0.60	0.61	0.62	0.70	0.68	1.00	0.94
	w	3.57	3.47	3.24	3.21	3.18	2.70	2.64	1.82	1.81

Note: x = export measure; m = import measure; w = export-import measure.

Table 4.23.
Revealed Comparative Advantages for Goods Used by Industry, 1975–1983

	Trade Measure	1975	1976	1977	1978	1979	1980	1981	1982	1983
Market	x	1.11	1.11	1.11	1.09	1.09	1.11	1.09	1.10	1.09
	m	0.94	0.94	0.94	0.94	0.96	0.98	0.98	0.96	0.97
	w	1.18	1.18	1.18	1.16	1.14	1.13	1.11	1.14	1.13
OECD	x	1.17	1.18	1.18	1.16	1.16	1.18	1.16	1.17	1.14
	m	0.89	0.90	0.89	0.89	0.90	0.92	0.91	0.90	0.91
	w	1.31	1.32	1.32	1.30	1.30	1.28	1.28	1.30	1.25
Market minus OECD	x	0.48	0.51	0.51	0.56	0.56	0.57	0.58	0.62	0.76
	m	1.25	1.28	1.27	1.29	1.33	1.30	1.29	1.30	1.33
	w	0.39	0.40	0.40	0.43	0.42	0.44	0.45	0.48	0.57
Low-income OECD	x	0.94	0.92	0.92	0.91	0.91	1.00	1.01	1.00	0.95
	m	1.03	1.03	1.04	0.99	1.00	0.99	0.96	0.97	0.94
	w	0.91	0.89	0.88	0.92	0.91	1.00	1.05	1.03	1.01
Bulgaria	x	1.20	1.37	1.59	1.40	1.30	1.15	0.98	1.18	1.14
	m	1.44	1.32	1.41	1.20	1.35	1.33	1.25	1.33	1.28
	w	0.83	1.03	1.13	1.17	0.97	0.86	0.78	0.88	0.89
Czechoslovakia	x	1.36	1.34	1.35	1.36	1.35	1.19	1.20	1.09	1.12
	m	1.27	1.43	1.29	1.33	1.31	1.26	1.21	1.20	1.21
	w	1.06	0.94	1.04	1.02	1.03	0.94	1.00	0.91	0.93
East Germany (GDR)	x	1.44	1.49	1.49	1.36	1.50	1.23	1.19	1.15	1.17
	m	1.01	0.91	0.95	0.89	0.94	0.99	0.87	1.01	1.04
	w	1.43	1.63	1.57	1.53	1.60	1.24	1.36	1.14	1.13
Hungary	x	0.80	0.78	0.72	0.68	0.76	0.70	0.65	0.72	0.62
	m	1.11	1.07	1.18	1.17	1.17	1.07	1.05	1.07	0.93
	w	0.72	0.73	0.61	0.58	0.65	0.65	0.62	0.67	0.67
Poland	x	0.67	0.71	0.76	0.84	0.86	0.86	0.90	0.72	0.66
	m	1.39	1.33	1.36	1.23	1.11	0.93	0.70	0.79	0.77
	w	0.48	0.53	0.56	0.69	0.78	0.93	1.29	0.91	0.85
Romania	x	0.70	0.64	0.80	0.83	0.79	0.65	0.83	0.75	0.42
	m	1.54	1.48	1.66	1.72	1.60	1.29	0.98	1.09	0.98
	w	0.46	0.43	0.48	0.48	0.49	0.51	0.85	0.69	0.43
USSR	x	0.53	0.47	0.54	0.57	0.59	0.47	0.37	0.32	0.34
	m	1.32	1.38	1.52	1.48	1.49	1.22	1.19	1.29	1.34
	w	0.40	0.34	0.35	0.39	0.40	0.38	0.31	0.24	0.26
Yugoslavia	x	0.77	0.79	0.74	0.68	0.74	0.75	0.75	0.73	0.65
	m	1.34	1.30	1.37	1.36	1.33	1.32	1.26	1.26	1.14
	w	0.58	0.61	0.54	0.50	0.55	0.57	0.59	0.58	0.57
Albania	x	0.12	0.11	0.06	0.19	0.06	0.17	0.57	0.49	0.52
	m	1.10	0.96	1.11	0.92	1.42	1.60	1.48	1.59	1.58
	w	0.11	0.11	0.05	0.21	0.04	0.11	0.39	0.31	0.33
Eastern Europe 9	x	0.75	0.71	0.76	0.78	0.79	0.67	0.63	0.56	0.53
	m	1.33	1.33	1.42	1.38	1.36	1.19	1.12	1.21	1.21
	w	0.57	0.53	0.54	0.56	0.58	0.57	0.56	0.46	0.44
Eastern Europe 6	x	0.94	0.94	1.00	1.00	1.02	0.92	0.96	0.91	0.81
	m	1.32	1.29	1.33	1.28	1.23	1.10	0.97	1.05	1.01
	w	0.71	0.73	0.75	0.78	0.83	0.84	0.99	0.86	0.81

Note: x = export measure; m = import measure; w = export-import measure.

Table 4.24.
Revealed Comparative Advantages for Food, 1975–1983

	Trade Measure	1975	1976	1977	1978	1979	1980	1981	1982	1983
Market	x	1.02	1.01	0.99	0.99	1.00	1.02	1.01	1.02	1.01
	m	0.99	0.99	1.00	0.99	0.96	0.92	0.90	0.90	0.94
	w	1.02	1.02	0.99	1.00	1.05	1.12	1.13	1.13	1.07
OECD	x	0.84	0.81	0.73	0.77	0.78	0.83	0.85	0.85	0.83
	m	0.99	0.99	1.02	1.02	0.97	0.91	0.89	0.92	0.95
	w	0.85	0.81	0.71	0.75	0.80	0.91	0.96	0.93	0.87
Market minus OECD	x	2.29	2.29	2.53	2.37	2.26	1.98	1.74	1.80	1.89
	m	1.01	0.94	0.83	0.85	0.87	0.97	0.98	0.89	0.95
	w	2.28	2.42	3.04	2.78	2.61	2.04	1.77	2.02	2.00
Low-income OECD	x	1.06	1.05	1.02	1.02	1.02	1.07	1.07	1.06	1.11
	m	1.09	1.06	1.12	1.12	1.07	1.03	1.07	1.13	1.27
	w	0.97	1.00	0.91	0.90	0.95	1.04	1.00	0.94	0.88
Bulgaria	x	1.68	1.59	1.65	1.96	1.53	1.37	1.38	1.64	1.14
	m	0.44	0.75	0.53	0.85	0.78	0.89	1.02	0.52	0.75
	w	3.79	2.13	3.09	2.31	1.96	1.54	1.35	3.17	1.51
Czechoslovakia	x	0.64	0.53	0.45	0.58	0.57	0.52	0.55	0.57	0.62
	m	0.56	0.98	0.77	1.06	1.34	1.12	0.98	0.96	0.69
	w	1.14	0.54	0.58	0.55	0.42	0.46	0.56	0.59	0.89
East Germany (GDR)	x	0.91	0.59	0.26	0.38	0.24	0.17	0.21	0.13	0.09
	m	1.18	2.01	2.10	2.37	2.32	2.86	2.78	2.64	2.51
	w	0.77	0.29	0.13	0.16	0.10	0.06	0.08	0.05	0.04
Hungary	x	2.02	1.73	1.72	1.90	1.76	1.86	1.93	2.08	2.12
	m	0.44	0.85	0.66	0.55	0.49	0.56	0.52	0.40	0.71
	w	4.53	2.02	2.61	3.45	3.61	3.34	3.75	5.25	3.01
Poland	x	1.03	1.16	1.08	1.15	1.20	1.24	1.21	1.19	1.51
	m	1.00	1.45	1.28	1.79	2.20	2.59	3.88	2.82	1.77
	w	1.03	0.80	0.84	0.64	0.55	0.48	0.31	0.42	0.86
Romania	x	1.24	1.38	0.91	0.80	0.72	0.64	0.47	0.45	0.45
	m	0.80	1.12	0.86	0.57	0.84	1.46	2.37	1.28	0.77
	w	1.55	1.24	1.05	1.41	0.86	0.44	0.20	0.35	0.59
USSR	x	0.14	0.11	0.12	0.13	0.11	0.09	0.10	0.09	0.10
	m	1.79	1.84	1.46	1.56	2.03	2.69	2.69	2.62	2.08
	w	0.08	0.06	0.08	0.08	0.06	0.04	0.04	0.04	0.05
Yugoslavia	x	0.92	1.05	0.97	1.00	0.96	0.97	0.94	0.96	1.09
	m	0.27	0.59	0.56	0.31	0.58	0.56	0.55	0.50	0.45
	w	3.40	1.79	1.74	3.17	1.64	1.74	1.71	1.93	2.45
Albania	x	0.80	1.15	1.43	1.67	0.68	1.03	0.60	0.68	0.96
	m	1.70	0.14	0.62	0.45	0.33	0.06	0.13	0.33	0.26
	w	0.47	8.05	2.31	3.70	2.06	17.09	4.45	2.09	3.66
Eastern Europe 9	x	0.69	0.66	0.58	0.63	0.57	0.52	0.47	0.45	0.49
	m	1.15	1.44	1.16	1.23	1.56	2.00	2.19	2.02	1.61
	w	0.60	0.46	0.50	0.51	0.36	0.26	0.21	0.22	0.31
Eastern Europe 6	x	1.13	1.12	0.96	1.03	0.98	0.95	0.88	0.90	0.96
	m	0.81	1.26	1.08	1.25	1.49	1.76	2.12	1.50	1.26
	w	1.41	0.89	0.89	0.83	0.66	0.54	0.41	0.60	0.76

Note: x = export measure; m = import measure; w = export-import measure.

The evidence on food, presented in Table 4.24, shows that the six Eastern European countries, on the aggregate, do evidence trade patterns consistent with a bias toward food consumption. (Of course, this evidence is also consistent with relatively poor productivity in the agricultural sector. At the present level of empirical analysis, there is no way to distinguish poor production from large consumption. Results presented in Chapter 6 will partially remedy this deficiency.)

Tables 4.22, 4.23, and 4.24 are more interesting for what they reveal about differences over time and between socialist countries than for comparisons between markets and central planning. Over the period 1975–83, the export-import ratios in the three groups of goods changed considerably. The orientation toward food increases dramatically over time, and the share of consumer goods imports rises considerably. At the same time, there is a fall in the share of industrial goods imports. These trends indicate that consumers in Eastern Europe were protected more than industry from the retrenchment caused by debt problems. The leaders' priorities in times of crisis seem to have been to protect food consumption first and then, somewhat later, other consumption needs, with industry being treated as a residual. The changes in trade patterns are clearly at odds with the conventional view of the behavior of centrally planned economies. It was not consumers who seem to have suffered the burden of adjustment, as is usually assumed to be the case.

In Tables 4.22–4.24, there is more variation among Eastern European economies than between CPEs and MEs. Romania, Hungary, and Yugoslavia evidence most strongly the behavior that conventional wisdom would predict for the CPEs, especially in exporting a large share of consumer goods. Evidently one cannot conclude that reform leads to more emphasis on the needs of consumers and less on those of industry.

The Level of Income   Hypothesis 18 refers to the oft-repeated assertion that the trade patterns of CPEs are somehow more typical of less-developed countries than of middle-income countries. Hypothesis 23 focuses on the effect of income distribution in predicting a comparative advantage for the CPEs in luxury goods. Although the sources of the hypotheses are very different, the same data are relevant to each—trade patterns of goods consumed by wealthier countries and individuals. The results are contained in Tables 4.25 and 4.26.[20]

The RCAs in Table 4.25 are for goods consumed disproportionately in countries with high per capita incomes. As expected, the OECD group has export-import RCAs in these goods that are less than unity, in contrast to the

[20] RCAs were constructed for low income goods using the same source and information analogous to that in line 25 of Table 4.2. However, this grouping contained goods (rice, tea, fish) consumed disproportionately in low-income countries for reasons related as much to geography and culture as to income elasticities. Therefore, the RCAs for this group appeared to be uncorrelated with income, so they have not been employed in this study.

Table 4.25.
Revealed Comparative Advantages for Goods Consumed Disproportionately by
High-Income Countries, 1975–1983

	Trade Measure	1975	1976	1977	1978	1979	1980	1981	1982	1983
Market	x	1.09	1.09	1.08	1.07	1.07	1.08	1.06	1.07	1.06
	m	1.05	1.05	1.06	1.06	1.06	1.05	1.03	1.04	1.05
	w	1.04	1.04	1.02	1.01	1.02	1.03	1.03	1.03	1.01
OECD	x	1.08	1.07	1.05	1.05	1.06	1.08	1.07	1.08	1.08
	m	1.13	1.13	1.13	1.14	1.14	1.13	1.12	1.14	1.15
	w	0.95	0.95	0.93	0.92	0.94	0.96	0.96	0.95	0.93
Market minus OECD	x	1.10	1.11	1.11	1.09	1.01	0.97	0.93	0.95	0.93
	m	0.59	0.57	0.60	0.57	0.55	0.63	0.66	0.54	0.46
	w	1.87	1.93	1.85	1.91	1.83	1.53	1.41	1.74	2.02
Low-income OECD	x	1.53	1.42	1.39	1.36	1.43	1.54	1.42	1.40	1.38
	m	0.75	0.80	0.86	0.86	0.90	0.99	0.94	0.96	0.91
	w	2.04	1.78	1.61	1.59	1.60	1.56	1.51	1.46	1.51
Bulgaria	x	0.54	0.48	0.48	0.54	0.51	0.48	0.47	0.50	0.58
	m	0.44	0.36	0.34	0.19	0.27	0.28	0.35	0.34	0.30
	w	1.23	1.35	1.41	2.81	1.91	1.75	1.33	1.45	1.93
Czechoslovakia	x	0.79	0.70	0.70	0.71	0.69	0.67	0.68	0.67	0.58
	m	0.54	0.48	0.52	0.52	0.48	0.48	0.46	0.47	0.48
	w	1.46	1.46	1.35	1.35	1.44	1.40	1.48	1.42	1.21
East Germany (GDR)	x	0.71	0.72	0.72	0.72	0.77	0.78	0.63	0.60	0.58
	m	0.54	0.58	0.71	0.59	0.44	0.48	0.49	0.59	0.38
	w	1.31	1.24	1.02	1.22	1.74	1.61	1.28	1.02	1.51
Hungary	x	1.32	1.20	1.12	1.22	1.24	1.33	1.31	1.10	1.05
	m	0.32	0.51	0.42	0.42	0.43	0.46	0.43	0.44	0.40
	w	4.08	2.36	2.65	2.89	2.90	2.88	3.03	2.48	2.64
Poland	x	0.60	0.58	0.62	0.66	0.76	0.87	0.93	0.73	0.64
	m	0.35	0.40	0.40	0.41	0.45	0.51	0.35	0.34	0.34
	w	1.71	1.43	1.54	1.60	1.68	1.71	2.62	2.13	1.90
Romania	x	1.06	1.10	1.15	1.14	1.08	1.11	0.97	1.34	1.20
	m	0.30	0.23	0.28	0.23	0.23	0.26	0.18	0.32	0.30
	w	3.49	4.87	4.17	5.05	4.71	4.36	5.32	4.16	4.00
USSR	x	0.15	0.14	0.13	0.15	0.17	0.12	0.11	0.11	0.09
	m	0.42	0.41	0.31	0.24	0.23	0.31	0.45	0.41	0.27
	w	0.34	0.33	0.41	0.61	0.73	0.37	0.25	0.27	0.35
Yugoslavia	x	2.12	1.69	1.59	1.66	1.58	1.75	2.02	1.93	1.80
	m	0.64	0.69	0.71	0.66	0.70	0.63	0.61	0.69	0.68
	w	3.32	2.46	2.24	2.51	2.25	2.79	3.30	2.80	2.65
Albania	x	0.66	1.04	0.81	1.10	0.65	0.67	0.35	0.33	0.51
	m	0.41	0.41	0.24	0.14	0.16	0.08	0.14	0.17	0.15
	w	1.63	2.53	3.32	7.82	3.95	8.54	2.43	1.95	3.36
Eastern Europe 9	x	0.64	0.58	0.57	0.62	0.60	0.57	0.55	0.51	0.49
	m	0.44	0.45	0.42	0.37	0.38	0.40	0.44	0.44	0.35
	w	1.45	1.30	1.35	1.66	1.59	1.42	1.25	1.15	1.39
Eastern Europe 6	x	0.82	0.79	0.81	0.84	0.87	0.91	0.88	0.85	0.79
	m	0.39	0.42	0.43	0.40	0.40	0.43	0.38	0.42	0.38
	w	2.09	1.90	1.87	2.10	2.19	2.12	2.32	2.01	2.09

Note: x = export measure; m = import measure; w export-import measure.

Table 4.26.
Revealed Comparative Advantages for Luxury Goods, 1975–1983

	Trade Measure	1975	1976	1977	1978	1979	1980	1981	1982	1983
Market	*x*	1.07	1.05	1.06	1.05	1.04	1.06	1.06	1.06	1.06
	m	1.12	1.10	1.10	1.11	1.09	1.10	1.10	1.09	1.08
	w	0.96	0.95	0.96	0.95	0.96	0.97	0.97	0.97	0.98
OECD	*x*	0.99	0.98	0.98	0.97	0.99	1.03	0.99	0.99	0.98
	m	1.17	1.12	1.11	1.11	1.12	1.16	1.15	1.12	1.11
	w	0.85	0.87	0.88	0.88	0.88	0.89	0.86	0.88	0.89
Market minus OECD	*x*	1.50	1.43	1.40	1.43	1.27	1.10	1.31	1.35	1.37
	m	0.82	0.94	0.99	1.00	0.84	0.70	0.80	0.87	0.91
	w	1.84	1.52	1.42	1.44	1.51	1.57	1.65	1.55	1.51
Low-income OECD	*x*	1.76	1.56	1.44	1.36	1.45	1.32	1.61	1.65	1.53
	m	0.75	0.77	0.72	0.70	0.74	0.63	0.72	0.77	0.73
	w	2.34	2.02	2.01	1.95	1.95	2.07	2.26	2.15	2.09
Bulgaria	*x*	1.47	1.10	1.16	1.07	0.84	0.67	0.81	0.65	0.78
	m	0.28	0.46	0.48	0.41	0.46	0.45	0.41	0.56	0.48
	w	5.17	2.40	2.41	2.59	1.83	1.48	1.96	1.16	1.64
Czechoslovakia	*x*	0.70	0.67	0.63	0.52	0.52	0.47	0.58	0.54	0.48
	m	0.56	0.47	0.56	0.59	0.56	0.60	0.64	0.90	0.86
	w	1.24	1.42	1.12	0.87	0.93	0.78	0.91	0.60	0.56
East Germany (GDR)	*x*	1.31	1.28	1.57	1.26	1.52	0.85	1.23	1.42	1.27
	m	0.93	1.11	1.30	1.13	0.98	1.00	0.69	0.71	0.72
	w	1.41	1.16	1.21	1.11	1.54	0.85	1.79	2.01	1.76
Hungary	*x*	1.28	1.10	1.06	0.89	0.96	0.90	1.22	0.92	0.75
	m	0.63	0.61	0.62	0.47	0.49	0.42	0.60	0.76	0.80
	w	2.03	1.79	1.72	1.89	1.97	2.16	2.03	1.21	0.94
Poland	*x*	0.79	0.78	0.84	0.80	1.00	1.38	1.02	0.84	0.58
	m	0.26	0.30	0.41	0.32	0.34	0.29	0.22	0.53	0.47
	w	3.01	2.60	2.05	2.45	2.94	4.79	4.53	1.59	1.22
Romania	*x*	0.25	0.12	0.16	0.15	0.18	0.18	0.17	0.20	0.18
	m	0.30	0.35	0.31	0.31	0.26	0.30	0.27	0.39	0.42
	w	0.84	0.34	0.51	0.49	0.71	0.61	0.63	0.52	0.43
USSR	*x*	1.32	1.97	1.81	1.76	1.82	1.62	0.74	0.73	0.72
	m	0.42	0.32	0.41	0.30	0.36	0.26	0.33	0.25	0.18
	w	3.16	6.10	4.37	5.91	5.06	6.13	2.27	2.96	3.98
Yugoslavia	*x*	1.54	1.18	1.11	0.85	1.00	0.95	1.07	0.96	0.91
	m	0.46	0.41	0.41	0.33	0.37	0.32	0.39	0.50	0.69
	w	3.35	2.85	2.72	2.59	2.70	2.96	2.76	1.90	1.32
Albania	*x*	0.55	0.81	0.45	0.53	0.26	0.23	0.14	0.13	0.13
	m	0.18	0.25	0.19	0.12	0.09	0.16	0.14	0.16	0.29
	w	3.11	3.21	2.36	4.29	2.91	1.44	1.03	0.82	0.43
Eastern Europe 9	*x*	1.10	1.34	1.30	1.18	1.29	1.22	0.78	0.76	0.71
	m	0.43	0.40	0.47	0.38	0.41	0.35	0.38	0.40	0.39
	w	2.57	3.36	2.77	3.13	3.18	3.48	2.05	1.88	1.79
Eastern Europe 6	*x*	0.83	0.74	0.81	0.70	0.78	0.79	0.79	0.77	0.64
	m	0.42	0.47	0.55	0.48	0.47	0.46	0.45	0.66	0.65
	w	1.95	1.57	1.49	1.47	1.66	1.72	1.74	1.16	0.99

Note: x = export measure; m = import measure; w export-import measure.

less-developed market economies. Of all the regional groupings, the EE6 has the largest export-import RCAs for high-income goods. It is especially significant that these RCAs are larger than those of both the lesser-developed market groupings. Among the EE6, the ranking of countries is in accordance with expectations based on per capita incomes, with two exceptions: Hungary is much lower than expected, and Bulgaria is much higher.

The results discussed in the previous paragraph could signify either an egalitarian distribution of income or a low level of disposable income. In order to examine this possibility, one can look at the RCAs for the group of luxury goods presented in Table 4.26. If income distribution under socialism precluded the consumption of luxuries, the Eastern European export-import RCAs would be large compared with those of the less-developed OECD countries. That is not the case for the EE6 as a whole. These results are consistent with those of Morrisson (1984), who claims that income distribution in Eastern Europe is not more egalitarian than in market economies.

4.7. Summarizing the Summary Statistics

Previous chapters have distinguished "neoclassical" and "Schumpeterian" viewpoints on the differences between capitalism and socialism. Many of the foregoing results reflect on those viewpoints. Thus, a convenient way to summarize this chapter is to show that collectively the results strongly support one of these viewpoints.

There are three ways in which the different results bolster the Schumpeterian perspective as opposed to the neoclassical perspective. In reverse order of importance, they are:

1. Some tables reveal patterns that are inconsistent with the predictions of the neoclassical approach, while not bearing directly on predictions from the Schumpeterian perspective.
2. The data give results supporting Schumpeterian predictions, while not bearing directly on predictions based on the neoclassical view.
3. Some conclusions from the empirical analysis support the Schumpeterian predictions, while being inconsistent with the neoclassical approach.

Facts that fall in the first category of results are the following:

a. The results relevant to pollution indicate that cost calculations do strongly influence the pattern of trade in a direction that is "rational," under the presumption that leaders favor growth.
b. The results on convenience goods, on experience durable goods, and on advertising all show patterns of trade that are consistent across CPEs and different from those in MEs. Thus, these results evidence a pattern of rational reaction to economic circumstances that is inconsistent with the

emphasis in the traditional literature on the static inefficiency of resource allocation in CPEs. One might note that, to the extent that the CPEs differ from the MEs for these types of goods, the Schumpeterian model provides as good an explanation as the neoclassical model. Thus, these results are consistent with rational static resource allocation in the presence of the institutional rigidities on which the Schumpeterian model focuses.

c. The CPEs do not have a comparative disadvantage in decreasing-returns-to-scale industries, in contrast to the usual prediction arising from the assumed problems associated with organizational complexities in CPEs. If static resource allocation is somewhat rational, as the above results and those to follow in Chapter 7 indicate, then one must conclude that the problems of organizational complexity might not be as important as previously thought.

Results of the second type are as follows:

d. The striking comparative disadvantage of CPEs in those industries in which free entry is important is one of the fundamental Schumpeterian predictions.

e. Centrally planned economies have a low level of imports in sectors in which the MNCs are important, even though these are high-technology sectors in which the CPEs have a comparative disadvantage. This is consistent with the Schumpeterian perspective, which would emphasize that technology cannot be easily bought at arm's length by existing firms.

f. The results for high-entry sectors and for high-technology products show very low levels of trade for both exports and imports. These results stand in contrast to those for the sectors in which intraindustry trade is usually prominent, sectors in which the results for CPEs do not differ strongly from those for the MEs. Hence, the data show us that it is not the absence of product variety per se that causes relatively low levels of trade for the CPEs. Rather, the telling factor seems to be the absence in CPEs of institutions that promote trade between capitalist countries when such trade is subject to larger-than-normal transactional difficulties.

In the third category of results, one has the following:

g. The striking contrast between process-innovating sectors and product-innovating sectors immediately follows from the Schumpeterian analysis. Given that the traditional analysis predicts the same effects on technological change in both types of innovating sectors, it is difficult to see how this analysis could predict a comparative advantage for CPEs in the process-innovating sectors.

h. The CPEs can take advantage of the static inefficiencies in ME sectors in which concentration is high. This would surely argue that CPE ability in static allocation of resources could equal that of the MEs.

i. Scanning the results in Tables 4.3–4.26, the reader will immediately see that the results for Hungary and Yugoslavia are in most cases typical of the socialist countries in general. From the neoclassical view, this is inconsistent with the fact that these two economies are much more decentralized than the rest of Eastern Europe. From the Schumpeterian perspective, this is consistent with the fact that the essence of the market is a process akin to natural selection, not decentralization.

This list of facts could arise only if the Schumpeterian view was more powerful than the traditional perspective in analyzing the differences between socialist and capitalist economic behavior. Chapters 6 and 7 will add to this list.

CHAPTER 5

The Econometrics of Estimating Endowments Implicit in Trade Decisions and Measuring Country Conformity to Trade Models

"Testing" theories, as that process is generally conceived, is only one of the minor preoccupations of science. The very process that generates a theory (and particularly a simple generalization) goes a long way towards promising it some measure of validity. For these reasons, histories of science written in terms of the processes that discover patterns in nature would seem closer to the mark than histories that emphasize the search for data to test for hypotheses created out of whole cloth.
—Herbert Simon (1977)

This chapter develops methods of discovering the patterns embedded in international trade data. The patterns are summarized in estimates of the factor endowments that are implicit in trade decisions. Because these patterns are deeply hidden within the data, it is necessary to combine a complex statistical procedure with international trade theory to extract them. Moreover, given the distance between the observed phenomenon and the object of interest, the form that the statistical procedure must take is not immediately obvious. One needs a methodology for deriving that procedure—hence the use of maximum-likelihood methods in this chapter.

The primary reason for using maximum-likelihood methods here does not lie in their optimal statistical properties. Rather, the usefulness of the methods is in deriving the functional form of estimators, when the nature of the estimators is not transparent from knowledge of existing procedures. The emphasis, therefore, is not on maximum likelihood as a methodology for constructing optimal estimators and testing levels of significance, but rather on maximum likelihood as a means of showing one how to extract patterns that are deeply hidden in data.

A complete, formal description of the statistical methods requires the use of matrix algebra, not because of anything particularly abstruse in those methods, but simply because a matrix is worth a thousand words. Some readers will, understandably, not want to plow through the details of this algebra, yet it is important that all those who are interested in the empirical results of the book have some basic understanding of how those results are generated. This chapter, therefore, begins with a brief, nontechnical description of the procedures for deriving estimates of the factor endowments implicit in foreign-trade data. There follows also a summary of applications of these procedures, including the method of generating measures of the degree to which a country's foreign trade patterns fit standard trade models. Those who do not want to bury themselves in the complexities of the econometrics should read Section 5.1 and then move on to the chapters in which the results are presented. Those who are interested in the statistical methods may find the ensuing section useful as an introduction to the more formal analysis that follows.

Sections 5.2 and 5.3 develop the basic econometric techniques that underlie all the analyses of Chapters 6 and 7. Sections 5.4 and 5.5 show how one can calculate statistics that can be used to judge the accuracy of predictions derived from the use of these techniques. Section 5.6 explains how multi-year predictions can be made using a time series of trade data. In implementing the econometric procedures, it was necessary to aggregate the trade measures for each country across commodities.[1] Section 5.7 discusses the issues arising in the choice of aggregation procedure and the properties of the chosen procedure. The chapter closes with a description of the computational techniques used to derive the estimates.

5.1. A Brief Overview of the Statistical Methods

The statistical procedures begin with a relationship derived from the theory of international trade. Theory postulates that trade performance is determined by the levels of variables measuring the factor endowments of a country. There are N measures of trade performance, the endogenous variables, and S factor endowments, the exogenous variables.

The first step in the procedure is to find a set of countries for which data on both trade performance and factor endowments can be obtained.[2] Consistent with the context of the present study, let us call these the "Western" countries. With the Western data, containing both exogenous and endogenous variables, one can estimate the relationship between trade performance and factor endowments.

The next step in the procedure entails inverting this relationship. This step is easiest to envisage when the number of factor endowments, S, is assumed to be equal to the number of measures of trade performance, N.[3] Let us now

[1] The reason for the aggregation is easily seen once one follows the derivation of the theorem in Section 5.3. The number of commodity groups must be less than the number of Western countries for which one has a complete set of trade data.

[2] In the present study, these are the countries listed in Table 2.3.

[3] This assumption, invoked here for expositional reasons, will be relaxed later, with important consequences.

suppose that there is an Eastern country for which one has trade statistics but not internal data. Taking the relationships estimated for the Western countries, and entering the trade data for the Eastern country, one obtains a set of N ($=S$) linear simultaneous equations in which the unknowns are the Eastern factor endowments. One can then solve for the unknowns.

Having described the methods in their simplest context, a further complication must be addressed. It will normally be the case that the number of measures of trade performance will be greater than the number of factor endowments. It is important for the following analysis to understand why that can be the case.[4] Usually in economic models, the number of exogenous variables is greater than or equal to the number of endogenous variables. In theory, this relationship is not violated in the present study, but in practice only a subset of the full complement of variables determining trade patterns have been identified.

It has not been possible to include all variables in the analysis, for two reasons. First, there are undoubtedly omitted variables: all the data one would want are not available, even for the Western countries. Second, there might be a true white noise component—random elements that make trade patterns vary across countries.[5] Once one acknowledges the existence of these two factors, one can see that the number of explicitly identified independent variables will be smaller than the number of trade measures. In the econometric analysis, error terms are assumed to embody both the omitted variables and the white noise component.

Trade patterns are completely determined by a country's properties, both identified factor endowments and those unidentified elements included in the error term. However, one can ascertain only the relationship between trade patterns and the identified independent variables. The statistical procedures estimate these N relationships using ordinary least squares. Given N relationships and S (less than N) factor endowments, many possible sets of values of the factor endowments are logically consistent with any observed trade pattern. The estimating technique then asks which values of factor endowments are most likely to have generated the trade pattern. Obviously, the better-fitting relationships contain more information about this likelihood. Therefore, the final stage of the procedure uses information about the goodness-of-fit of the trade relationships to choose the best estimates of factor endowments. Those are the estimates presented in Chapter 6.

Once the estimates of factor endowments implicit in trade patterns are generated, there is a further and very valuable statistical exercise that one can conduct. One could plausibly postulate that there are idiosyncratic features that affect trade patterns in any country. These features are ones that cannot

[4] Especially when examining the construction of the error statistics derived in Chapter 7.

[5] The distinction between omitted variables and a true random component might actually be easier to make on an intuitive basis than to justify in a rigorous manner.

be said, in any sense, to be operating across countries.[6] For example, the distinctive features of a country's political arrangements might affect trade in a unique way. Then, the country's trade patterns are determined jointly by the identified factor endowments, the random errors, and those idiosyncratic features.

It is instructive to obtain information about the idiosyncratic features of a country. Given the amount of data available, one cannot estimate values for these features, but one can find out how important they are in determining a particular country's trade pattern. When entered into the equations relating factor endowments to trade measures, a country's estimates of factor endowments implicit in trade patterns yield a set of predicted trade measures. One can then compare the predicted trade pattern with the actual trade pattern and derive a statistic summarizing the extent to which the two patterns diverge. The amount of divergence is a measure of the degree to which the trade decisions of a country *cannot* be explained by the systematic part of the estimated trade model. This measure of divergence then summarizes the importance of both the error component and the idiosyncratic features. The size of the measure relative to that in other countries shows how important idiosyncrasies are in determining a country's trade pattern. The economic interpretation of the measures is discussed in Chapter 7.

Finally, one can calculate a time series of estimated endowments. The maximum-likelihood procedures give a set of linear relations between estimated factor endowments implicit in trade and observed trade patterns. Thus, for any period in which trade data are available, one can simply use these linear relationships to obtain a time series of estimated endowments. Of course, the interpretation of these estimates must be somewhat tentative, because one has ignored the temporal changes in the linear relationship that occur in reality. (The Western endowment data is available only for estimating the relationship in 1975.) Nevertheless, given careful interpretation, there is much information in the time series of estimated endowments, as will be shown in Chapter 7. Let us turn now to a formal presentation of the econometric procedures.

5.2. The Underlying Model

The econometric methods use as their starting point sets of equations with the following general form:

$$y_{ij} = \sum_{k=1}^{S} b_{ik} z_{kj} + e_{ij} \qquad i = 1, \ldots, N \quad j = 1, \ldots, T. \qquad (5.1)$$

---

[6] Note that it is possible to talk about the error component operating across countries in the sense that the same stochastic process operates.

The quantity y_{ij} is a measure of trade performance in good i by country j, and z_{kj} is the value of factor endowment k of country j. The b_{ik} and e_{ij} are coefficients and error terms, respectively. In the analysis, there are T countries, N internationally traded goods, and S factor endowments.

To simplify the presentation, it is convenient to introduce some notational conventions. Both column and row vectors are employed and are defined using the "dot" convention—a letter with a dot subscript indicates the vector formed by listing all possible elements obtained by varying the subscript that the dot has replaced. Column vectors have dots as their first subscript, and row vectors have dots as their second element: for example, $y'_{.j} = (y_{1j}, \cdots , y_{Nj})$ and $y_{i.} = (y_{i1}, \cdots , y_{iT})$. Matrices, denoted with capital letters, are formed from appropriate combinations of these vectors:

$Y = (y_{.1}, \ldots , y_{.T})$ is $N \times T$

$B = (b_{.1}, \ldots , b_{.S})$ is $N \times S$

$Z = (z_{.1}, \ldots , z_{.T})$ is $S \times T$

$E = (e_{.1}, \ldots , e_{.T})$ is $N \times T$

Using the above conventions, it is possible to represent equation system (5.1) in three different ways. Each of these representations has the same ultimate economic interpretation, but each is useful in its own way in the analyses that follow. The three alternatives are as follows:

$$y_{i.} = b_{i.} Z + e_{i.} \qquad i = 1, \ldots , N \qquad (5.2)$$

$$y_{.j} = B z_{.j} + e_{.j} \qquad j = 1, \ldots , T \qquad (5.3)$$

$$Y = BZ + E. \qquad (5.4)$$

The usefulness of each of the different representations is best seen by viewing each of the $N + T$ equations in (5.2) and (5.3) as matrix representations of the data for a single linear regression. Then, if a single element of (5.2) were estimated, one would be explaining the trade measure for a single good as a linear function of factor endowments. The units of observation would be countries. Because the unknown regression coefficients in (5.2) describe the relationship between trade and factor endowments, it is these equations that one naturally employs when using the Western data to estimate that relationship. Then equations (5.2) are statistically inverted to obtain values of the Eastern countries' factor endowments implicit in trade patterns. The theory behind such estimating procedures is presented in Section 5.3.

Under (5.3), goods are the units of observation, and the trade performance of a country is a linear function of a good's properties. All the data for a single country are contained in only one of the T vector equations of (5.3). Then, the estimates of any one of the T elements of (5.3) must contain information about the degree to which a single country's data fit the overall model. Thus, in examining the degree to which a specific country's trade pattern can be explained by processes common to all countries, one naturally uses (5.3). The relevant theory is explained in Section 5.5.

5.3. The Derivation of Estimators of Factor Endowments Implicit in Trade

There are two sets of countries: "Eastern" and "Western." Data on the y_{ij}'s and z_{ij}'s are available for the Western countries. However, while all y_{ij}'s are known for the Eastern countries, some, and possibly all, of the z_{ij}'s are unknown. The objective, then, is to estimate the missing z_{ij}'s.

The intuition underlying the derivation of the estimators can be easily stated. Essentially, the coefficient vectors $b_{i.}$ are estimated using the regressions (5.2). Then these estimated $b_{i.}$ and the y_{ij}'s of the Eastern countries are used to obtain the z_{ij}'s by finding the solution to an appropriate set of simultaneous equations. One difficulty, however, arises when applying this intuition in a straightforward manner by estimating $b_{i.}$ with single equation methods. The y_{ij}'s of Eastern countries contain information that can be used to improve the estimates of the $b_{i.}$, even when all Eastern z_{ij}'s are missing. Optimal use of this information requires deriving estimates of all unknowns simultaneously. Hence, in formulating the estimation theory, it is natural to turn to the matrix representation, equation (5.4).

Let the Western countries be the first T_1 and the Eastern nations be the remaining T_2 countries ($T_1 + T_2 = T$). S_1 of the factor endowments of Eastern countries are known, while S_2 are unknown ($S_1 + S_2 = S$). Nothing in the remaining theory precludes complete ignorance concerning the internal data of the East: $S_1 = 0$ is possible. Equation (5.4), then, can be rewritten using partitioned matrices:

$$[Y_1 \ Y_2] = [B_1 \ B_2] \cdot \begin{bmatrix} Z_{11} & Z_{12} \\ Z_{21} & Z_{22} \end{bmatrix} + E$$

where Y_1 is $N \times T_1$, Y_2 is $N \times T_2$, B_1 is $N \times S_1$, B_2 is $N \times S_2$, Z_{11} is $S_1 \times T_1$, Z_{21} is $S_2 \times T_1$, Z_{12} is $S_1 \times T_2$, and Z_{22} is $S_2 \times T_2$. The first column of the partitioned Z matrix contains the Western data, and the second column contains the Eastern data. The first row of Z contains the data known in all countries. Therefore, the unknown element of Z is Z_{22}.

In order to use maximum-likelihood methods, one must introduce assumptions on the distribution of the error terms. In making such assumptions, one must remember the implications of the discussion of omitted variables in Section 5.1. Such variables will be elements of the error terms in equations

(5.1). An error term that affects one country's trade performance on one good must also affect trade in other goods.[7] Therefore, $E(e_{mj} e_{nj})$ cannot be constrained to zero in the estimation procedures (i.e., country j's error for good m is likely to be correlated with j's error for good n). However, if one uses the neoclassical models of Sections 3.1 and 3.2 to drive the formulation of the econometric assumptions, these errors can be assumed to be uncorrelated across countries. For example, knowing that country p has a particular feature that gives it a comparative advantage in good i does not imply anything about the probability that country q will possess, or lack, the same feature. Thus, $E(e_{ip} e_{iq})$ is constrained to zero for $p \neq q$ and for all i. Obviously, this assumption does not hold once one steps outside the bounds of the neoclassical models. Chapter 4, for example, shows that the CPEs have certain features in common that can account for distinctive aspects of their trade behavior, but because the purpose of Chapters 6 and 7 is to investigate the degree to which neoclassical models can explain CPE trade, this assumption on errors is the appropriate one to make at the present stage.

To this juncture, no restrictions have been placed on the variance-covariance matrix of the $e_{.j}$. All that has been assumed is that no elements of this matrix should be constrained to zero. However, in order to obtain estimates, restrictions must be imposed. These restrictions are obtained by resorting to the general assumption that the same process generates trade outcomes in all countries. This assumption is obviously implicit in the maintained assumption that the neoclassical models are a complete description of the factors affecting trade patterns. Hence, the stochastic process generating the $e_{.j}$ is taken to be independent of j. The matrix $E(e_{.j} e'_{.j})$, therefore, is constant across countries and can be denoted by W. To derive the maximum-likelihood estimates, I make the usual assumption that $e_{.j}$ is normally distributed.

Using a ^ symbol to indicate an estimate of the relevant parameter or observation, define:

$$\hat{Z} = \begin{bmatrix} Z_{11} & Z_{12} \\ Z_{21} & \hat{Z}_{22} \end{bmatrix} .$$

Then, the following theorem holds:

THEOREM If $S_2 < N < T_1$, then

$$\hat{B} = Y\hat{Z}'(\hat{Z}\hat{Z}')^{-1},$$ (5.5)

$$\hat{W} = (Y - \hat{B}\hat{Z})(Y - \hat{B}\hat{Z})'/T,$$ (5.6)

and $\hat{Z}_{22} = (\hat{B}'_2\hat{W}^{-1}\hat{B}_2)^{-1}\hat{B}'_2\hat{W}^{-1}(Y_2 - \hat{B}_1\hat{Z}_{12})$. (5.7)

---

[7] Because there will be a trade balance (or similar) constraint, if trade in one good is affected, trade in others must also be.

PROOF

Given the assumptions made in the text, the following hold:

$$E(e_{.j}) = 0 \ ,$$
$$E(e_{.j} \, e'_{.j}) = W, \text{ a general } N \times N \text{ symmetric matrix,} \qquad (5.8)$$
$$E(e'_{i.} \, e_{i.}) \text{ is a diagonal matrix,} \qquad (5.9)$$
$$e_{.j} \text{ is distributed } N(0, \, W). \qquad (5.10)$$

Therefore, the likelihood of the sample is given by:

$$(2\pi)^{\frac{-NT}{2}} |W|^{\frac{-T}{2}} \exp\left[-\frac{1}{2} \sum_{j=1}^{T} e'_{.j} W^{-1} e_{.j} \right] . \qquad (5.11)$$

In order to derive the maximum-likelihood estimators, introduce L, an increasing function of the likelihood:

$$L = T \cdot \log|W^{-1}| - \sum_{j=1}^{N} e'_{.j} W^{-1} e_{.j} \ ,$$
$$L = T \cdot \log|W^{-1}| - \text{tr}(E'W^{-1}E) \ ,$$
$$L = T \cdot \log|W^{-1}| - \text{tr}[W^{-1}(Y - BZ)(Y - BZ)'] \ . \qquad (5.12)$$

Then the estimators for the unknowns, B, W, Z_{22}, can be found by differentiating (5.12) in order to find the first order conditions for the maximization of L:

$$\frac{\partial L}{\partial B} = 2W^{-1}YZ - 2W^{-1}BZZ' = 0 \ , \qquad (5.13)$$

$$\frac{\partial L}{\partial W^{-1}} = TW - (Y - BZ)(Y - BZ)' = 0 \ , \qquad (5.14)$$

$$\frac{\partial L}{\partial Z_{22}} = -2B'_2 W^{-1} Y_2 + 2B'_2 W^{-1} B_1 Z_{12} + 2(B'_2 W^{-1} B_2) Z_{22} = 0 \ . \qquad (5.15)$$

Equations (5.5), (5.6), and (5.7) are then found by rearranging (5.13), (5.14), and (5.15) and substituting estimators for the unknowns.

5.4. Measuring the Ability of the Models to Estimate Factor Endowments

In interpreting the estimates presented in later chapters, it is valuable to have information about the reliability of the models' predictions. For reasons discussed in Section 6.2, this information must come in two separate elements—reliability of the predictions for each resource endowment, and goodness-of-fit measures for countries. The construction of each of these two elements is described in this and the following section. Interpretation of the measures is left to Chapter 6, when the estimates are presented.

In deriving a measure of the predictive ability of a model, it is important to construct statistics that are readily interpretable. Most readers are familiar with within-sample goodness-of-fit measures, the most common of which is the simple R^2 of regression analysis. For purposes of simplicity and familiarity, these R^2 measures are used to summarize the ability of the trade models to predict factor endowments.

For the group of Western countries listed in Table 2.3, one has data both on trade patterns and on resource endowments. Let us suppose that (5.5) and (5.6) have been solved for $\hat{B}$ and $\hat{W}$ using only data for that group of countries. One could then take the trade patterns of the Western countries and treat these as Y_2 in applying equation (5.7). The resultant Z_{22} matrix would constitute a forecast of the factor endowments implicit in the trade of the Western countries based on the parameters of the trade model and the trade patterns of those countries. It is a within-sample forecast in the sense that the parameters have been estimated using information on the resource endowments of the Western countries themselves.

Each row of the Z_{22} matrix comprises estimates of one single resource endowment across the sample of Western countries. For each resource endowment, therefore, one can correlate actual endowments with estimated endowments. The resultant R^2 statistic is a measure of how well that particular resource endowment can be predicted using a trade model and data on trade patterns.

5.5. Goodness-of-Fit Measures for Individual Countries

Given that a number of equations have been estimated, it is possible to create a measure of how well an individual country's data fit the system of equations as a whole. Using such a measure, one can make empirically-based statements about the degree to which a country's trading pattern conforms to that observed for other countries. The economic interpretation of such statements is discussed in Chapter 7. In this section, the formulas used for the calculation of the measures are presented.

In calculating a goodness-of-fit measure, one assumes that forces, perhaps economic system, affect trade patterns in one country but not elsewhere. To incorporate these idiosyncratic features, for a specific country, denoted by c, equation (5.3) must now be modified. Assume that there is only one idiosyncratic factor and call it θ_c. Let $b_{.\theta}$ be the $N \times 1$ vector of coefficients that relates changes in trade variables to changes in θ_c. Then, for c, (5.3) must be rewritten as:

$$y_{.c} = Bz_{.c} + b_{.\theta}\theta_c + e_{.c} \tag{5.16}$$

Assuming that θ_c and $e_{.j}$ are independent, then:

$$E[(y_{.c} - Bz_{.c})'(y_{.c} - Bz_{.c})] = b'_\theta b_{.\theta} \theta_c^2 + E[e'_{.c} e_{.c}] \qquad (5.17)$$

The last term in (5.17) results from stochastic processes that are operating in all countries. Its expected size is therefore independent of c.[8] The first term on the right-hand side of (5.17) is due to the idiosyncratic features operating in country c.[9] To see whether idiosyncracies in c are more significant than those in another country, say d, one would simply want to compare $E[(y_{.c} - Bz_{.c})'(y_{.c} - Bz_{.c})]$ and $E[(y_{.d} - Bz_{.d})'(y_{.d} - Bz_{.d})]$.

Two problems are encountered in making the comparison suggested above. The first, resulting from the fact that one does not know the necessary expected values, is easily solved. Because B is unknown and $z_{.c}$ might contain some unknown elements, one simply replaces them by $\hat{B}$ and $\hat{z}_{.c}$ (the cth column of $\hat{Z}$), thus estimating $E[(y_{.c} - Bz_{.c})'(y_{.c} - Bz_{.c})]$. The economic interpretation of measures based on estimates of the resource endowments is provided in great detail in Section 7.2.

The second problem results from the desire to treat all countries in a comparable manner. If d is a Western country listed in Table 2.3, $\hat{z}_{.d}$ is identical to $z_{.d}$, which comprises actual data. In contrast, if c is an Eastern country, elements of $z_{.c}$ are unknown, and $\hat{z}_{.c}$ contains estimated values. Moreover, $z_{.d}$ has been used to estimate B and thus, one would expect, for this reason alone, that $E[(y_{.c} - Bz_{.c})'(y_{.c} - Bz_{.c})]$ would be greater than $E[(y_{.d} - Bz_{.d})'(y_{.d} - Bz_{.d})]$.[10]

The solution to the second problem is to treat all countries as if they were Eastern countries when calculating their errors. The procedure for calculating the errors of Western country d was as follows:

1. Western country d was dropped from the sample of T_1 Western countries listed in Table 2.3.
2. Western country d was added to the sample of T_2 "Eastern" countries—that is, the data on d's factor endowments were ignored.
3. Equations (5.5), (5.6), and (5.7) were solved using the modified samples of countries.
4. Hence, estimates of d's factor endowments, $\hat{z}_{.d}$, were found. The only information on country d that was used to obtain $\hat{z}_{.d}$ was d's trade data.

[8] The expected value is a function of the elements of W.

[9] The reader will notice that the assumptions made here are inconsistent with those made on W in section 5.3, but this is no problem, given the objective of the present exercise. If, in the original model, one were to assume that all countries had significant idiosyncratic features, one would not be able to derive maximum-likelihood estimates. Not enough information would be contained in the sample. Therefore, for the procedure presently being described, one derives estimates of the model under the null hypothesis of no idiosyncratic features and then tests how well this null hypothesis fits for each country separately.

[10] This is exactly analogous to the fact that one would expect within-sample forecasts to be better than out-of-sample forecasts.

This process was repeated for all Western countries separately. It is exactly equivalent to the procedure for calculating the factor endowments and errors of the Eastern countries.

The formulas for the goodness-of-fit (GF) measures can now be exactly defined. For any country, j, let $\epsilon_{.j} = b_{.\theta}\theta_j + e_{.j}$, which is a vector of error terms, including both the idiosyncratic errors and those operating in all countries. Let $\hat{z}_{.j}$ be the vector of estimated factor endowments obtained in the manner described above.[11] Then, the estimate of $\epsilon_{.j}$, which gives an N-dimensional measure of the goodness-of-fit for country j, is defined as follows:

$$\hat{\epsilon}_{.j} = y_{.j} - \hat{B}\hat{z}_{.j} \qquad j = 1, \ldots, T. \qquad (5.18)$$

That measure is simply the vector of errors generated by entering j's data into one element of equation system (5.3). Of course, it would be useful to calculate a summary one-dimensional statistic for each country. The most obvious choice is the following:[12]

$$GF = \sum_{i=1}^{N} \hat{\epsilon}_{ij}^2 / N \qquad j = 1, \ldots, T. \qquad (5.19)$$

[11] That vector could contain both estimated values and actual values of the factor endowments of country j. If actual values of some factor endowment are known for *all* countries, there is no reason for one to estimate that endowment when calculating the errors. In fact, one of the terms in that vector is always an actual value: the first element is unity because constant terms are included in all the regressions.

[12] At this stage, the reader may wonder *why* the appropriate statistic is not simply the ordinary least squares $(1 - R^2)$, obtained from element j of equation (5.3). It is important to understand why such a statistic is not suitable.

Implicit in the $(1 - R^2)$ is a normalization of the data—a deflation of the error terms by the variance of the dependent variable. In the standard setting, this normalization is applied because of the desire to create a scale-free statistic that can be used to compare the fit of equations generated in a variety of contexts. The absolute size of the error terms will vary across such equations due solely to variations in the scale of the dependent variable. The $(1 - R^2)$ statistic is not affected by such variations.

In the present context, the units of the dependent variable do not vary across countries. Therefore, there is no need to normalize the error data to adjust for differences in scale between countries. More important, such normalization would actually mask differences between the goodness-of-fit measures for the various countries. From equations (5.17) and (5.18), one can see that the expected size of the error terms will vary across countries only if there is variation in the significance of the idiosyncratic features. From equation (5.16), it is obvious that the variance of the dependent variable also increases as those features become more significant. Thus, in normalizing the error data using the variance of the dependent variable, one would inappropriately reduce the variation of the goodness-of-fit measures across countries. Moreover, the size of $y_{.j}$ also depends on $Bz_{.j}$. When two countries had no idiosyncratic features but dissimilar $Bz_{.j}$, one would obtain differences in their measures of goodness-of-fit if one normalized the error data using the variance of the dependent variable. This would be a misleading result: one would want the measures for the two countries to be the same. In such a case, the expected value of GF would be identical for the two countries, as is appropriate given the desired properties of a measure of goodness-of-fit.

Despite its intuitive appeal, there is one way in which GF might be deemed unsatisfactory. Given the assumptions on W made previously, the expected values of each element in the summation giving GF are different. The summation therefore comprises elements whose order of magnitude could vary. One might want to normalize the errors so that each term in (5.19) has the same expected value.

The diagonal elements of the variance-covariance matrix, W, are assumed to vary because some measures of trade performance can be better explained than others. Therefore, the expected values of the squares of each of the elements of the vector $\hat{e}_{.j}$ will vary in magnitude, even if θ_j is zero. This could imply, for example, that the errors in one particularly poorly fitting equation might dominate in the calculation of GF. Then GF would contain little information about the nature of a country's trade process as a whole. In order to forestall such an eventuality, one must normalize each of the elements of GF so that they have the same expected value. Hence, one derives the following statistic:

$$GF' = \sum_{i=1}^{N} \left[\frac{T\hat{\epsilon}_{ij}^2}{\sum_{k=1}^{T} \hat{\epsilon}_{ik}^2} \right].\qquad(5.20)$$

The average value of GF' for all countries is, of course, unity.

5.6 Estimating Factor Endowments Implicit in a Time Series of Trade Data

If the data on Y, Z_{11}, Z_{12}, and Z_{21} were available over a number of years, one could create a time series for the estimated endowments, $\hat{Z}_{22}$. However, while trade data is published in copious amounts, the necessary information on "Western" factor endowments is very difficult to obtain. Given the present lack of internationally comparable statistics, one must be indebted to Leamer (1984) for the availability of even one year's observations on the "Western" part of the Z matrix. Thus, for years other than 1975, Y is available, but there is no information on Western factor endowments.

Given a time series of observations on Y, one can create a time series of estimated factor endowments implicit in trade patterns by using the $\hat{B}$ and $\hat{W}$ from a year in which the Western part of Z is available. These estimates must be treated with some caution because they are produced by combining data from different years. Consideration of the economic interpretation of the multiyear estimates will be delayed until Section 6.4, where these estimates are presented. The aim here is solely to show how these estimates are produced.

Using (5.5), (5.6), and (5.7), values are available for $\hat{B}$ and $\hat{W}$. $\bar{Y}$ is a trade data matrix for some year other than the one for which the model has already been estimated. Consistent with the "dot" notation, define the matrix $Z_{1.}$ as follows:

$$Z_{1.} = [Z_{11} \, Z_{12}] \, .$$

$Z_{1.}$ is the matrix that includes observations on all variables for which information is available for all countries. Then, $\tilde{Z}_{1.}$ is the matrix for the year in which $\tilde{Y}$ is available. For most years, no information is available on factor endowments for either Eastern or Western countries. In the usual circumstances, then, $\tilde{Z}_{1.}$ will be solely a vector of 1's, created in order to deal appropriately with the constant term in the formulas.

The aim is to find estimates of factor endowments implicit in trade patterns for *all* countries—that is, the matrix

$$\hat{Z}_{2.} = [\hat{Z}_{21} \, \hat{Z}_{22}] \, .$$

Then, one simply invokes a modified version of equation (5.7):

$$\hat{Z}_{2.} = (\hat{B}_2' \hat{W}^{-1} \hat{B}_2)^{-1} \hat{B}_2' \hat{W}^{-1} (\tilde{Y} - \hat{B}_1 \tilde{Z}_{1.}) \, . \tag{5.21}$$

This formula underpins the estimates presented in Section 6.4.

5.7. Construction of Trade Aggregates for Use in the Econometric Analysis

Before the trade data could be used in the econometric analysis, an aggregation was needed. Although it would be possible to use the two-digit trade data, with sixty-one categories, to run sixty-one separate regressions of factor endowments on the trade performance of a single good,[13] one could not use all these regressions in estimating factor endowments. The econometric analysis requires combining information from all the regressions in order to form an estimate of the cross-equation variance-covariance matrix.[14] This matrix must then be inverted in order to estimate the factor endowments implicit in trade patterns. Inversion is possible only if the number of Western countries is greater than the number of trade measures used as dependent variables.[15] Hence, one must ensure that the number of trade aggregates is less than forty-six, the number of countries listed in Table 2.3.

The method of principal components is a standard technique for the purpose of aggregation. This technique allows the intercorrelations between the trade measures themselves to determine the aggregation. The method of principal components has often been used in regression analysis to combine independent

---

[13] These regressions would be the ones corresponding to equation (5.2), with the parameter N equal to 61.

[14] The matrix W of equation (5.8).

[15] If N is less than T_1, using the notation of Section 5.3.

variables when they are highly collinear (Dhrymes 1978, pp. 198–201). Here the application is to dependent variables.

The method of principal components, as embodied in the *SPSS* (Nie, 1975) routines, was used to form twenty trade aggregates. The number twenty was chosen somewhat arbitrarily within the constraint that it had to lie between the smallest number of Western countries and the largest number of independent variables used in any analysis.

5.8. Computational Procedures

This section describes the basic computational procedures used to solve equations (5.5), (5.6), and (5.7).[16] In any realistic application this system of equations has a large number of unknowns. For example, with only twenty traded goods, nine Eastern countries, and ten factor endowments, half of which are unknown for Eastern countries, 445 items must be estimated simultaneously. Standard, general-purpose, numerical, maximization algorithms are not applicable for a problem of such size. Thus, a special-purpose algorithm was programmed, one that took advantage of the structure of equations (5.5), (5.6), (5.7). The algorithm consists of the following steps:

Step 0

$$\text{Let } Z^0 = \begin{bmatrix} Z_{11} \\ Z_{21} \end{bmatrix},$$

a matrix comprising solely Western data.
Then

$$B^0 = Y_1 Z^{0\prime} (Z^{0\prime} Z^0)^{-1} \tag{5.22}$$

and

$$W^0 = (Y_1 - B^0 Z^0)(Y_1 - B^0 Z^0)' / T_1 . \tag{5.23}$$

Thus, the initial estimates of B and W, B^0 and W^0, are found by applying ordinary least squares to Western data alone.

Step 1

Initial estimates of Z_{22} are found in the following manner:

$$Z_{22}^0 = (B_2^{0\prime} W^{0-1} B_2^0)^{-1} B_2^{0\prime} W^{-1} (Y_2 - B_1^0 Z_{12}) . \tag{5.24}$$

---

[16] A copy of the computer instructions is available on request from the author, but this does not apply to the program used, TSP, which is copyrighted.

Step 2

$$\text{Let } Z^1 = \begin{bmatrix} Z_{11} & Z_{12} \\ Z_{21} & Z_{22}^0 \end{bmatrix} .$$

Derive new estimates of B and W using information from all countries, including the previously derived estimates of the factor endowments implicit in the trade of the Eastern countries. These new estimates, B^1 and W^1, are obtained using ordinary east squares with the matrices Y and Z^1 as data—that is, employing equations (5.22) and (5.23) with Y_1, B^0, Z^0, W^0, and T_1 replaced by Y, B^1, Z^1, W^1, and T, respectively.

Step 3

Derive a new estimate of the Eastern factor endowments, Z_{22}^1, by applying equation (5.24) with B^1 and W^1 substituted for B^0 and W^0.

Step 4 and After

Repeat steps 2 and 3 by continually using the new estimates of Z_{22} in step 2 and the new estimates of B and W in step 3.

Certain properties of this algorithm should be noted. First, convergence is not guaranteed. Second, even if convergence occurs, there could be more than one stopping point of the algorithm. One can test for such nonuniqueness by varying the starting point (Z^0). Despite these disadvantages, the algorithm has one very important property—it can be easily programmed using standard statistical packages that have ordinary least squares and matrix manipulation features.[17] *Time Series Processor* (TSP International) is one such package.

---

[17] Unfortunately, by using one of the standard programs, the routine becomes extravagantly expensive on computer time, partially because of the structure of the problem at hand. For this reason, and because stopping rules were difficult to program in a standard package, I picked an arbitrary number of iterations to run the procedure. This number was five for all the results obtained in Chapter 6, but only one for the exercises in Chapter 7, which are enormously burdensome on computer time.

CHAPTER 6

The Levels of Resource Endowments Implicit in Eastern European Trade Patterns: Estimates for Eleven Endowments

---

These figures show that an average million dollars worth of our exports embodies considerably less capital and somewhat more labor than would be required to replace from domestic production an equivalent amount of our competitive imports. . . . The widely held opinion that—as compared with the rest of the world—the United States' economy is characterized by a relative surplus of capital and a relative shortage of labor proves to be wrong. What is the explanation of this somewhat unexpected result?

The very high productivity of American—as compared with foreign—labor plays a decisive role in the determination of the composition of those United States exports and imports which do not reflect directly the presence or absence in this country of certain natural resources.
—Wassily Leontief (1953, 1956)[1]

There is a distinguished tradition to the notion that foreign-trade data can reveal information about the internal affairs of a country. Leontief 1953, 1956 apparently had no doubt about the meaning of his results, which others later interpreted as paradoxical. He viewed these results as demonstrating a feature of the economy that was not apparent from conventional statistics. The present chapter is written in the same spirit. I estimate the stocks of endowments implicit in the trade patterns of the CPEs and evaluate which hypotheses best explain these estimates.

The sections containing the main empirical results of the present chapter, 6.3 and 6.4, provide a wealth of new information on the socialist economies. Many of the statistics presented in those sections have no counterparts in the existing literature. The present chapter therefore contributes to the understanding of the comparative behavior of the CPEs, quite apart from the pre-

---

[1] Here quotes from two sources are combined to give the most succinct statement of Leontief's position.

sentation of much evidence that is pertinent in examining the implications of the Schumpeterian and neoclassical paradigms.[2] The evidence relevant to those paradigms comes in the form of examination of the hypotheses of Chapter 3, whose relevance to the major themes of this book was summarized in Table 4.1. The concluding section of this chapter examines the central message of this chapter's results for those two paradigms.

Section 6.3 presents estimates of the amounts of eleven resource endowments implicit in the trade patterns of nine Eastern European countries in 1975. This evidence allows one to reexamine widely accepted hypotheses using new information on all the Eastern European countries. For example, there are new insights into Rosefielde's (1973) hypothesis that there is a capital intensive bias to CPE trade. The results on resource endowments also allow one to examine widely held hypotheses that have been insufficiently investigated in the past. For example, the data reveal whether the use of land in the CPEs is affected by the low price attached to that resource. Moreover, the information presented in Section 6.4 can offer insights into the nature of the economic performance of specific countries. For example, Poland's economic difficulties are quite clearly reflected in extreme distortions in its pattern of trade at a very early stage.

Section 6.4 shows the evolving pattern of the resource content of CPE trade from 1966 to 1983. These results clearly reveal the reactions of the socialist economies to changes in the economic environment. One can detect, for example, the effects of the Soviet price reform of the mid-1960s, the changes caused by the decentralization of the Hungarian economy in 1968, and the reaction of the CPEs to the world energy price changes of the 1970s. All these events are clearly reflected in the results, which reveal characteristics of the countries' behavior that are not readily apparent in statistics constructed using more conventional techniques.

Because the methods by which the results are obtained are new, the presentation of the empirical work must be prefaced by a lengthy discussion of methodology. Readers who are interested purely in the results could skip that discussion and turn immediately to Sections 6.3 and 6.4. In doing so, they must remember that the intervening sections contain much information that allows one to place the results in perspective, especially deliberation on the critical assumptions invoked to produce the results.

The starting point of the methodology is the application of the econometric techniques developed in Sections 5.2 and 5.3 to the models described in Sections 3.1 and 3.2. Because the available trade data do not match the form of the trade variables used in those models, one must adapt the models for empirical implementation. Section 6.1 describes the equations that result from this adaptation. Section 6.2 supplies the reader with information about the

[2] The reader might profit from reviewing Table 4.1 regarding the hypotheses that are to be examined in this chapter and their relevance to the Schumpeterian and neoclassical paradigms.

reliability of the estimates of endowments embodied in trade and presents the values of the goodness-of-fit measures derived in Chapter 5. These measures are used to choose the trade model to be employed in Sections 6.3 and 6.4 to generate the central results on the implicit factor content of trade. Section 6.5 returns to methodology by considering the possible biases in the results obtained in both the present chapter and Chapter 4. In particular, that section examines in detail the effects on the results of the omission of intra-CMEA trade data. Therefore, Section 6.5 provides valuable information in evaluating the validity of the conclusions reached throughout this book. Section 6.6, in reflecting on the relevance of the results to the Schumpeterian and neoclassical models, returns to the major theme of this book.

6.1. Models for Estimating Endowment Levels
Implicit in Trade Decisions

The most interesting empirical studies that a comparative economist can undertake are studies focusing on differences in behavior between capitalist and socialist economies. In such studies, one usually is faced with problems because data published by different national authorities are not often comparable. A real dilemma often arises because the meaning of the data varies with economic system.

Faced with these problems, one must make a choice between two alternative modes of proceeding. The first is to find a means of adjustment that establishes some degree of inter-system compatibility for the data most directly relevant to the phenomena of interest. This, the most commonly used procedure, has resulted in studies that give profound insights into differences between systems—for example, Pryor (1973). Alternatively, one can use economic theory and statistical techniques to draw broad lessons from the limited data sources that are comparable between countries but that are related only indirectly to the phenomena under investigation. This second procedure is used in the present work, where I draw lessons about the nature of the domestic economy from foreign trade data.

The data used in this work—mirror trade statistics—have already been described in Chapter 2. The advantage of these statistics is that the data collection procedures are identical for all sample points. As discussed in Chapter 2, however, there is a cost, to the use of mirror trade statistics. Only some of the world's countries report information at a level of conformity and a degree of disaggregation that makes their data suitable for use here. In particular, mirror trade data statistics omit all information reported by the CMEA countries.

Given that data from the CMEA countries is not included in the mirror trade statistics, one must focus on partial trade flows rather than the preferred total flows. The cost of using a data source that is comparable across countries is that the data do not conform exactly to those entering into the standard international trade models. Those models, reviewed in Chapter 3, have total trade flows as their dependent variable.

Two main concerns arise from the use of partial trade flows. First, the international trade models must be adapted to be implemented empirically: the dependent variable must be changed from total to partial trade flows. Therefore, the present section, presents the models to be used in the empirical work and shows how they can be justified using the theory of Chapter 3. Second, the partial data might not be representative of the whole. This is especially a concern because intra-CMEA flows must be omitted to obtain a consistent set of mirror statistics. The possible biases that result from the omission of the reports of CMEA countries are examined in Section 6.5. In that section, I argue that the nature of these biases can be easily understood and that the basic conclusions from the present chapter's results cannot be a consequence of the presence of these biases.

The two versions of neoclassical trade theory gave us three sets of equations for use in the empirical analysis. The first is derived from the basic Heckscher-Ohlin model:

$$W_{ij} = \sum_{k=1}^{S} b_{ik}V_{kj} \qquad i = 1, \ldots, N \quad j = 1, \ldots, T, \qquad (6.1)$$

where

W_{ij} is the net exports of good i by country j,
V_{kj} is the endowment of resource k in country j,
b_{ik} is a parameter, constant across countries,
N is the number of goods produced,
S is the number of resource endowments, and
T is the number of countries.

However, if that model is modified slightly to take into account nonhomothetic preferences, one obtains:

$$W_{ij}/r_j = b_{i0} + \sum_{k=1}^{S} b_{ik}v_{kj} \qquad i = 1, \ldots, N \quad j = 1, \ldots, T, \qquad (6.2)$$

where v_{kj} is the per capita endowment of resource k in country j, and r_j is the population of country j.

The product-differentiation and economies-of-scale (PE) model admits a third equation. That equation relates the pattern of exports, not net exports, to the levels of resource endowments:

$$X_{ij} = \left[\sum_{k=1}^{S} b^*_{ik}V_{kj}\right] \cdot \left[1 - \frac{G_j}{G_w}\right]$$
$$i = 1, \ldots, N \quad j = 1, \ldots, T, \qquad (6.3)$$

where G_j is the national income of country j, a w subscript denotes the world, and the asterisks on the coefficients of the equation are intended to remind the reader of the difference between the source of equations (6.1) and (6.2) and that of (6.3). It bears repeating that equation (6.3) cannot be derived from the Heckscher-Ohlin theory. Thus, this relationship plays an important role in the empirical work by providing a means of establishing which neoclassical model best fits the trade data of the CPEs.

One cannot estimate any of the above equations with mirror trade statistics. Those statistics do not cover the whole of trade flows. Moreover, there is no way to estimate total trade flows from data on partial flows. One can, however, estimate the structure of trade. Thus, one must seek a means of replacing the dependent variables of the above equations with variables measuring trade structure, $\tilde{x}_{ij}$ and $\tilde{w}_{ij}$:

$$\tilde{x}_{ij} = \left[\frac{X_{ij}}{\sum_{n=1}^{N} X_{nj}} \right], \tag{6.4}$$

$$\tilde{w}_{ij} = \left[\frac{W_{ij}}{\sum_{n=1}^{N} (X_{nj} + M_{nj})/2} \right], \tag{6.5}$$

where X_{ij} and M_{ij} are the exports and imports of good i by country j. If trade is balanced, as is assumed in all the theoretical derivations, then the denominator in (6.5) is simply the total value of exports or imports.

Now the task is to derive from (6.1)–(6.3) relationships that have (6.4) and (6.5) as the dependent variables. This is not difficult because the denominators of (6.4) and (6.5)—the factors used to normalize individual trade flows for country size—are themselves trade flows. Moreover, this transformation is thoroughly in keeping with the tenor of trade theory, which, as Deardorff (1985) remarks, focuses most closely on which goods countries trade rather than how much is traded. The resultant equations, focusing on trade structure, reflect this spirit.

Let us begin with the representation of the Heckscher-Ohlin model given in equation (6.2), although (6.1) would give similar results. Dividing this equation by the sum over all goods of the absolute value of the right-hand side of equation (6.2), one obtains:

$$\frac{2W_{ij}}{\left[\sum_{n=1}^{N} (X_{nj} + M_{nj}) \right]} = \frac{b_{i0} + \sum_{k=1}^{S} b_{ik}v_{kj}}{\left[\sum_{n=1}^{N} \left| b_{i0} + \sum_{k=1}^{S} b_{ik}v_{kj} \right|/2 \right]} \tag{6.6}$$

$$i = 1, \ldots, N \quad j = 1, \ldots, T,$$

Thus, $\tilde{w}_{ij}$ is a nonlinear function of per capita resource endowments.

To obtain a version of the PE model that can be implemented with mirror trade statistics, begin by dividing both sides of equation (6.3) by population. One obtains a relationship between per capita trade and per capita resource endowments. Then, taking the resultant relationship and dividing by its own sum over all goods, one obtains:

$$\frac{X_{ij}}{\sum\limits_{n=1}^{N} X_{nj}} = \frac{\left[\sum\limits_{k=1}^{S} b_{ik}^{*} v_{kj}\right]}{\left[\sum\limits_{k=1}^{S} \left(\sum\limits_{n=1}^{N} b_{ik}^{*}\right) v_{kj}\right]} \qquad i = 1, \ldots, N \quad j = 1, \ldots, T. \quad (6.7)$$

One could now proceed to develop full maximum-likelihood methods for the estimation of equations (6.6) and (6.7), but I have chosen not to take that approach, instead opting to use linear approximations to equations (6.6) and (6.7). Then the econometric methods developed in Chapter 5 are applied to the resultant linear equations.

The decision about whether to use approximations entails a weighing of the benefits from implementing full maximum-likelihood methods versus the simplicity of alternative techniques. The simplicity of the methods of Chapter 5 is attested by the fact that the estimating equations have interpretations in terms of textbook econometric procedures and that the iterative routines could be implemented using standard programs. Against this simplicity, one matches one's confidence in the fact that the correct functional form has been identified exactly in equations (6.6) and (6.7). Equation (6.2), for example, was derived from what Leamer (1984, p. 155) has described as a "long list of incredible assumptions." This being the case, it can be argued that one should not hold particular devotion to the precise functional forms identified above. The increased complexity of the full maximum-likelihood methods does not seem to promise the types of payoffs that would compel their use.[3] This is especially the case because the parameters of equations (6.6) and (6.7), the b_{ik} and b_{ik}^{*}, have no direct interest for this study: there is no intrinsic interest in keeping the original functional forms. Therefore, to simplify the analysis, I follow the time-honored econometric methodology of linearizing the basic relationships in order to derive the model to be implemented.

Using a linear approximation to equation (6.6), one obtains:

$$\bar{w}_{ij} = \bar{b}_{i0} + \sum_{k=1}^{S} \bar{b}_{ik} v_{kj} \qquad i = 1, \ldots, N \quad j = 1, \ldots, T. \quad (6.8)$$

The bars on the coefficients of this equation are added to make clear that these coefficients are not the same as those in (6.6) above. This equation

---

[3] The complexity of the maximum-likelihood techniques is evidenced by the fact that more than 240 parameters would have to be estimated simultaneously.

system is referred to as "model H" in the remainder of the book. It is the one equation used that most closely summarizes the trade patterns predicted by the Heckscher-Ohlin model.

Turning now to the PE model, and using a first-order Taylor-series approximation to linearize the denominator of the right-hand side of equation (6.7), one obtains:

$$\tilde{x}_{ij} = \bar{b}_{i0}^* + \sum_{k=1}^{S} \bar{b}_{ik}^* v_{kj} \qquad i = 1, \ldots, N \quad j = 1, \ldots, T. \qquad (6.9)$$

Hereafter, this equation system is referred to as "model P," denoting the fact that it is a representation of the product-differentiation and economies-of-scale theory of trade.

Models H and P are by far the most important models in the empirical work to follow, but they can be adapted to take into account extensions of the basic trade theories. For example, the theories of trade reviewed in Section 3.3 could be taken to justify using GDP per capita as an independent variable in explaining trade patterns. This is the case, for example, if there are unmeasured endowments that are highly correlated with GDP per capita, such as "sophistication," which Hufbauer (1970) suggests lies at the heart of some modern explanations of trade patterns. Result 6.1, proved in Appendix D, shows that the presence of such an endowment might cause one to use the following trade equations, where g_j is per capita GDP:

$$\tilde{w}_{ij} = \bar{b}_{i0} + \sum_{k=1}^{S} \bar{b}_{ik} v_{kj} + \bar{b}_{ig} g_j \qquad i = 1, \ldots, N \quad j = 1, \ldots, T. \qquad (6.10)$$

$$\tilde{x}_{ij} = \bar{b}_{i0}^* + \sum_{k=1}^{S} \bar{b}_{ik}^* v_{kj} + \bar{b}_{ig}^* g_j \qquad i = 1, \ldots, N \quad j = 1, \ldots, T. \qquad (6.11)$$

Equation systems (6.10) and (6.11) are referred to as "model HG" and "model PG" respectively the first letter denoting the theory from which they are derived, the second denoting the addition of the GDP variable. These equations are used in Chapter 7.

This section concludes with a few brief remarks on the methodology used to derive the empirical models. Many if not most empirical exercises in economics must forsake strict adherence to theory when confronted with the hard realities of data availability. As the foregoing paragraphs make clear, this study is no better in that respect than is usual in economics, but it would be wrong to conclude that this study is an egregious offender. In the remainder of this section, I would like to justify this claim.

The overwhelming majority of empirical studies begin with theory based on either formal or informal comparative statics exercises. There is usually no recourse to the primitive elements of the theoretical problem when establishing the precise nature of the functional form to be estimated. The theory is implemented using a standard function chosen from a conventional menu—linear, log-linear, quadratic, logit, and so on. Hence, the basic methodology of empirical economics rests firmly on the use of standard approximations to unknown functional forms.

Consider, for example, Cobb-Douglas sectoral production functions.[4] The data employed in estimating these functions are linear aggregates of statistics summarizing the operations of individual firms. Yet if all firms had Cobb-Douglas production functions, one would need to use geometric aggregates in order to justify rigorously the use of sectoral Cobb-Douglas functions. Because statistical authorities do not develop nonlinear aggregates, there is no way to justify the use of the sectoral functions except by recourse to approximation. This fact does not stop economists from estimating such functions and deriving strong conclusions from the results.

The preceding paragraphs show that the methodology used to derive models H and P is clearly in the mainstream of modern economics. Because the choice of a final functional form does not rest primarily on assumptions about the primitive economic concepts used in the problem, one cannot debate that choice by appeal to the veracity of assumptions. One must make an intuitive judgment about the reasonableness of the procedures used and the resultant estimates, a judgment that depends on aesthetics as much as on logic. One might ask, for example, whether the movement from theory to estimating equations is straightforward. This the reader must judge, given the above information. Or one should consider the nature of the results—whether they present a coherent picture that is consistent with some reasonable theoretical view. The results are presented for the reader's evaluation in the remainder of this chapter and in the following chapter.

6.2. Choosing Which Model to Use in Estimating the Endowments Implicit in the Trade Patterns of CPEs

The present section provides information relevant to choosing between the HO and PE models. The interest here is clearly in how well the models estimate the factor endowments of the CPEs. However, for reasons central to the methodology of this book, there is no suitable information against which one can match these predictions. To use the analogy of simple regression analysis, the CPEs are out-of-sample observations, and the normal R^2 statistic cannot be applied to them. Hence, no single goodness-of-fit statistic can measure the predictive performance of the models for the CPEs. The required information is obtained by combining the results from two measures.

The analysis of goodness-of-fit proceeds in two steps. First, for the market

---

[4] These comments apply, mutatis mutandis, to most aggregate production functions.

economies, for which all data are available, measures analogous to the R^2's of simple regression are presented for each resource endowment. These measures provide simple, intuitively interpretable statistics on the information content of trade structure for each of the resource endowments. In the following, with some infelicity, these measures will be called R^2's. Second, one can construct measures of how closely the trade structure of any single country conforms to a pattern that could have been generated by the estimated model. Then one can compare the performance of the CPEs and the MEs on those measures. If, in this second step, the CPEs perform as well as the MEs, the R^2's derived in the first step can be used as indicators of the predictive ability of the model for the estimates of factor endowments implicit in trade of the CPEs. In the following, this second type of measure is called a country-error statistic.

This section does not attempt to go beyond simple intuition in describing the measures. Technical details have been given elsewhere, particularly in Sections 5.4 and 5.5. Moreover, all of Chapter 7 is devoted to the analysis and interpretation of the country-error statistics. Thus, the purpose of the following paragraphs is only to give the reader some flavor of the meaning of the measures, not their derivation.

Chapter 5 shows how one can obtain predictions of the factor content of trade by using estimated trade models. In that chapter, the primary focus is on the CPEs, but one can just as easily obtain predictions of the factor endowments implicit in trade of all countries. Then, for the sample of market economies, one can run an ordinary least squares regression between predicted and actual values for each of the factor endowments. The multiple correlation coefficients of these regressions show how well trade data predicts factor endowments for the sample of market economies. These correlation coefficients are the R^2's referred to above.

When evaluating the R^2's, two points must be borne in mind. First, these measures are within-sample statistics and do not apply directly to the CPEs. However, because statistical studies invariably publish within-sample R^2's these statistics are the ones with which readers are familiar. Second, sample size is obviously a relevant consideration in evaluating R^2's. Loosely speaking, the predictions are calculated from a number of regressions, each having eleven independent variables and forty-six observations. For purposes of evaluation, the R^2's can be viewed as arising from cross-sectional regressions with equivalent numbers of observations and variables.

The R^2's are listed in Table 6.1, using the resource endowment names given in Section 2.3. It is clear that model P predicts slightly better than model H, although the differences are not great. The R^2's for both models are as high as is usual in cross-sectional regression studies, and to this author at least they appear to be satisfactory.

Let us now turn to the country-error statistics, which show how well a country's data fit a model of trade estimated for the sample of Western economies. The method by which these statistics were constructed is detailed in Section 5.5, and Chapter 7 is wholly devoted to the meaning and interpretation of these statistics. Hence, the econometric and economic description of the statistics is not repeated here. Instead, I focus solely on the choice of model upon which one should rely when presenting the estimates of the factor endowments implicit in the trade patterns of the CPEs.

The country-error statistics are given in Table 6.2. (Here I present results based on the statistic GF, developed in the previous chapter.[5]) Lower values for these statistics indicate that a country fits the data better. There is no natural scale to these statistics as is the case for R^2's. Thus, the best way to judge how well the CPEs fit the data is to make comparisons between the various regional groupings of countries included in the table. Such comparisons are valid because the statistics are calculated in exactly the same manner for all countries.[6] At this juncture, two major messages can be extracted from the table. First, the trade of the CPEs fits model H much better than the trade of the market economies. Second, the CPEs perform much worse on model

Table 6.1.

The Predictive Ability of Two Models of Trade:
R-Squares between Actual and Predicted Values of
Resource Endowments for 46 Market Economies

	Trade Model Employed	
	H	P
Capital Stock	0.66	0.72
Technological labor	0.56	0.73
Educated labor	0.44	0.69
Illiterate labor	0.73	0.79
Tropical land	0.54	0.48
Dry land	0.37	0.44
Warm land	0.66	0.73
Cold land	0.33	0.49
Coal	0.39	0.53
Ores	0.57	0.74
Oil and gas	0.19	0.40

[5] The overall message from that table would not be altered if the alternative form of the error statistics were used. See the tables in Chapter 7.

[6] The resource endowment information for any specific ME was not used in calculating its error statistics. See Section 5.5 for details.

P than they do on model H. (There is much economic significance to these observations, which are the focus of Chapter 7.)

The results for the two goodness-of-fit measures show that one should place greater reliance on model H than on model P when examining the predictions for the CPEs. This judgment follows from two facts. First, model H performs only slightly worse than model P on the first criterion—the R^2's, but second, the CPEs perform very poorly on the country-error tests for model P but well on the same tests for model H. One can easily see that model H will give the most reliable results for the CPEs. Hence, for the remainder of this chapter, all results are from model H.

6.3. Estimates of Resource Endowments Implicit in 1975 Trade Patterns

The central goal in estimating resource endowments is to generate information that reflects upon the hypotheses developed in Chapter 3 (and summarized in Table 4.1). These hypotheses are all framed implicitly in terms

Table 6.2.

Measures of the Degree to Which Trade Data Conform to Patterns Predicted by Models of Trade

	Trade Model Employed	
	H	P
All	1.149	1.053
Market	1.338	1.096
OECD	0.946	0.887
Market minus OECD	1.731	1.306
Low-income OECD	0.778	0.712
Bulgaria	0.303	1.640
Czechoslovakia	0.022	1.274
East Germany	0.012	0.736
Hungary	0.361	0.872
Poland	1.566	1.826
Romania	0.159	1.455
USSR	0.336	0.245
Yugoslavia	1.340	1.027
Albania	0.008	1.259
Eastern Europe 9	0.456	1.148
Eastern Europe 6	0.404	1.300

of predictions about deviations from efficient trade patterns. Such deviations, of course, affect the endowment estimates. Thus, there are two major influences on the values of the estimates—the actual values of the resource endowments, and the effect of economic system on the use of these endowments.

On realizing that both economic organization and physical endowments affect trade patterns, one immediately understands an important element in the interpretation of the results. The results estimate the resource endowments that would be implied by a country's trade pattern, if that country had an efficient economy. Thus, if a figure of $5,000 per capita is presented for the estimated capital stock of country X, one should not necessarily suppose that country X has this amount of capital. Rather, X is behaving the same way an efficient market economy would if it had $5,000 per capita. That is why I use the terms "implicit factor content of trade" and "endowments implicit in trade patterns" when the estimates are presented.

In deriving implications from the estimates, one must separate the effects of economic system and of physical resource endowments. However, there is not enough information to do this precisely because internationally comparable data on many of the factor endowments of CPEs and MEs are not available. Indeed, it is exactly the lack of such data that led to the development of the econometric methods employed here.

Failing precise information on actual resource endowments, one must rely on common sense and judgment to detect the effect of system on the estimates. To aid in that process, I present ad hoc pieces of information on the levels of resource endowments gleaned from the existing literature on the CPEs. With that information and the estimates presented in Tables 6.3–6.5, readers must make their own judgments concerning the effect of system on trade. Due to the paucity of precise data, one cannot replace those judgments with mechanical testing procedures resulting in significance levels for individual hypotheses. Hence, no formal statistical tests are presented in the following pages. The absence of such tests is obviously not ideal, but given the lack of data in the areas presently under study, there is no alternative.

Capital   Estimates of capital endowments implicit in trade patterns are presented in Table 6.3. (As in the rest of this chapter, the estimates are derived from model H.) These estimates reflect most directly on Hypothesis 3 of Chapter 3—that the undervaluation of capital stock leads to capital-intensive exports. Rosefielde (1973) has been the strongest proponent of this hypothesis and has presented supporting empirical evidence. Applying the standard Leontief methodology to the Soviet Union, Rosefielde finds that the capital-labor ratio embodied in imports divided by that same ratio for exports is much smaller than one would predict from endowment data.

Background information on actual levels of capital stocks is highly incomplete and subject to much error. By far the best data currently available are

Bergson's (1987) estimates of the capital stock of seven MEs and four CPEs. (Even so, reading the description of the construction of these estimates, one is impressed with the number of ad hoc adjustments necessary to produce comparability.[7]) Scaling Bergson's figures to make them comparable to those in Table 6.3,[8] one places the Soviet Union's per capita capital stock at 6.58, while the equivalent figures are 6.38 for Hungary, 4.65 for Poland, and 3.23 for Yugoslavia.

Before comparing Bergson's data with the estimates, one should remember that the quality of the estimates for individual CPEs is reflected in the information in Table 6.2. That table shows that two of Bergson's countries—Poland and Yugoslavia—have very high country-error statistics. (One might

Table 6.3.
Capital and Labor Endowments Implicit in Trade Patterns, 1975

	Capital Stock	Technical Labor	Educated Labor	Illiterate Labor	Total Labor
All	4.26	2.80	25.91	9.06	37.77
Market	4.84	3.57	29.52	5.49	38.58
OECD	8.22	5.21	35.83	1.57	42.61
Market minus OECD	1.22	1.90	22.01	10.12	34.03
Low-income OECD	3.84	3.33	28.64	4.67	36.64
Bulgaria	2.38	0.72	45.97	0.27	46.96
Czechoslovakia	7.46	4.23	35.92	2.68	42.83
East Germany	7.20	4.60	35.30	2.70	42.60
Hungary	4.02	0.35	37.46	1.56	39.37
Poland	12.69	4.91	22.02	9.94	36.87
Romania	4.05	3.57	31.68	−0.94	34.31
USSR	6.75	5.38	19.07	12.08	36.53
Yugoslavia	−1.95	0.74	29.48	1.49	31.71
Albania	7.50	4.45	34.31	3.19	41.95
Eastern Europe 9	5.57	3.22	32.36	3.67	39.25
Eastern Europe 6	6.30	3.06	34.72	2.70	40.48

Note: Capital stock figures are in thousands of 1975 U.S. $ per capita; labor force figures are percentages of population.

[7] This description is in the unpublished appendix to Bergson's (1987) paper.

[8] To do this scaling, I multiplied Bergson's estimates for the CPEs by the ratio of two numbers. The numerator was the average of Leamer's (1984) actual per capita capital stocks for the seven MEs used by Bergson, and the denominator was the average of Bergson's per capita capital stocks for these seven economies.

also reflect on the economic performance of these two countries.[9]) It is therefore not surprising that estimates for these two countries are at variance with Bergson's information. Poland's trade embodies a capital stock that is nearly three times the size of Bergson's figure, while Yugoslavia's estimate in Table 6.3 is negative.

According to Table 6.2, one should expect reasonable estimates for the Soviet Union and for Hungary. If one is to take Bergson's figures as the standard, then neither of the estimates for these two countries supports Hypothesis 3. The Soviet Union's estimate is very close to Bergson's number, while the estimate for Hungary is 50% below Bergson's. Moreover, for the five Eastern European countries not covered in Bergson's study, there is little support for Hypothesis 3. Czechoslovakia and East Germany have estimates that are a little below the average for the OECD countries, about halfway between Leamer's figures for Spain and West Germany. Romania's estimate is at the average level of the low-income OECD (LIO) country grouping, and Bulgaria's is somewhat lower. Remembering that CPEs in general have higher rates of accumulation than equivalent MEs, there seems to be nothing particularly aberrant in these estimates. (Those questioning whether the omission of intra-CMEA trade affects the judgments made on the basis of these estimates will find their questions answered in Section 6.5. That section develops further analytics and shows that doubts based on such questions are largely unfounded.)

One can summarize the above discussion by presenting a rough judgment of where each country's estimate stands in relationship to expectations:

Plausible	*Too Low*	*Too High*
Bulgaria (?)	Bulgaria (?)	Poland
Czechoslovakia	Hungary	Albania
East Germany	Yugoslavia	
Romania		
USSR		

This summary lends no support to Hypothesis 3, but it also has another important implication. As a rough generalization, one could say that the more orthodox CPEs are the ones for which the estimates are plausible. Hence, as in much of this book, one finds evidence that conformity to the predictions of the HO model is a mark of the centralized socialist countries.

Does the foregoing discussion indicate an inconsistency with Rosefielde's

---

[9] In the mid-1970s both these countries were engaging in large amounts of foreign borrowing—a policy that was hiding fundamental problems in their economies, as the error statistics show. When this policy was no longer possible, in the 1980s, both these countries experienced extended periods of economic stagnation or decline.

(1973) results? At the moment, that seems to be the case. But Rosefielde's results were for the 1960s, and the ones here are for 1975. We must wait until the next section for an answer to the above question. In fact, it will be shown that the apparent inconsistency might simply be a product of the different time periods covered by Rosefielde's study and this one.

Professional and Technical Workers It is virtually impossible to obtain satisfactory measures of the level of technology that are comparable across countries, but, one might be able to use proxies. Following Leamer (1984, pp. 37–38), one can view all technologies as available everywhere, but resources are required for implementation. In particular, higher levels of technology can be implemented only if a country has a sufficiently large stock of appropriately qualified personnel. Thus, the presence of technically qualified labor is a proxy for the level of technology implemented in a country.

The variable used by Leamer (1984) measures the number of professional, technical, and related workers. This group of workers includes more than those involved in the implementation of technology. However, given the requirement that information be obtained for a wide variety of countries, there is little chance of replacing this measure by one that is more narrowly focused.

The estimates of the share of technical workers will reflect two factors: the effect of economic system on the ability of a country to implement new technology, and the stock of workers available to do that implementation. The first factor, the effect of system, is the cornerstone of Hypothesis 6 of Chapter 3, which predicts that the level of technology is lower in CPEs than in MEs. There is some scanty information that gives qualitative information on the second factor. Despite the lack of precise data, one can confidently conclude that the CPEs have a larger share of professional and technical workers than do MEs at similar levels of development. Information already presented in section 3.8 showed that the CPEs have more scientists and engineers per capita than the most developed MEs. According to UNESCO (1986), the average share of GNP used for R & D by four Eastern European countries (Bulgaria, Hungary, the GDR, and Czechoslovakia) is nearly five times the equivalent figure for the lower-income OECD (LIO) countries.[10] Even though one must doubt the precise cross-country comparability of such information, the differences between the two sets of countries are so marked that they will survive any possible refinement of the data.

The two major influences on the estimates of the implicit endowments of technical workers oppose each other. The conventional wisdom on the CPEs is that they are less effective at implementing new technology than equivalent MEs. This is the essence of Hypothesis 6. However, the CPEs have devoted

---

[10] No data on Turkey is included in the information on the LIO countries presented here. If Turkey's data were available, the point in the text would surely be strengthened.

a greater share of their resources to the implementation of technology than even the most developed countries. This is the basis of Hypothesis 15. Because the estimates show the effective amount of endowments embodied in trade, they must reflect both the stock of technical workers and the effectiveness of such workers within particular economic systems.

The second column of Table 6.3 gives estimates of the percentage of the population working in technical and professional activities that is implicit in trade patterns. The average estimate for the CPEs is at approximately the same level as the matched group of countries—the LIO grouping. The estimates for some countries seem implausible—in this case Hungary's, which is very low, and Albania's, which is high. Again it is the more orthodox CPEs whose estimates seem to be in the plausible range.

What conclusions can one make about technology in CPEs from these estimates? The presence of offsetting factors prevents any unqualified statements, but some general conclusions are possible. First, the evidence of trade data implies that there is no inconsistency between the level of technology in CPEs and that in corresponding MEs (i.e., the LIO countries). Second, there is clear evidence that CPEs are less efficient than MEs at implementing new technologies. This conclusion is reached by noting that nowhere in the estimates is there any evidence that the larger stocks of professional and technical workers in CPEs are translated into higher levels of effective economic activity. Third, nowhere do the estimates imply that the CPEs rely more heavily on high-technology imports from the West than is appropriate given their level of development.[11]

Labor   Leamer (1984) distinguishes between three types of labor: professional and technical workers, illiterate workers, and the large middle ground falling between these two groups. The estimates relevant to these three groups are included in Table 6.3. The last column of that table, a simple sum of the three percentages, is an estimate of total labor force participation.

In a consideration of the labor force estimates, two pieces of information are relevant. First, the CPEs report high levels of literacy, especially compared with countries at the same stage of socioeconomic development (Taylor and Jodice 1983). If trade truly reflects resource endowments, and if literacy rates are an indicator of productive efficiency of workers, then the estimates in the "illiterate labor" category should be lower for the CPEs than for equivalent countries. Second, there is information on labor force participation rates. It is clear that these rates are much higher in CPEs than in all MEs. Using a

---

[11] The present conclusions should receive one final qualification. Some factors that could effect the estimates cannot be taken into account in the present analysis. For example, Western restrictions on high-technology exports might reduce the CPEs imports of high-technology items. In such a case, the estimates would be upwardly biased. According to Martens (1986, pp. 92–93), these restrictions are not quantitatively significant.

regression model, Pryor (1985, pp. 82–85) finds that CPEs have participation rates that are 120% of those in equivalent MEs.

The penultimate column of Table 6.3 reflects the amount of illiterate labor embodied in trade flows. The average values for Eastern Europe are approximately in accordance with expectations, perhaps somewhat higher than would be expected given literacy rates: the estimated share of illiterate labor in population in the CPEs lies between that of the OECD group as a whole and that of the group of LIO countries.

The estimates for one individual country deserve special comment. The Soviet Union has a higher implicit factor content of illiterate labor than any other country or region in the table. This result is significant because, in general, the estimates for the Soviet Union seem very reliable: the error statistics in Table 6.2 are low, and the predicted values of the Soviet Union's other endowments conform to expectations. If this result is correct, then the quality of Soviet nontechnical labor is very low, compared with all developed countries, including other CPEs. As far as I am aware, no other study has pinpointed this characteristic of Soviet labor.

The "educated workers" category is a residual—that great mass of workers with some education but without technical or professional qualifications. Given the broadness of this category, the main value in estimating it is in obtaining information on effective labor force participation. The estimated total participation rates are found by summing the three categories of labor, the result appearing in the last column of Table 6.3. These rates are very slightly lower than would be expected given, for example, Pryor's (1985) result quoted above.

Land   The resource endowment data distinguish four types of land, according to climate. The first two—tropical and dry—are of little interest here, because only the Soviet Union among the CPEs has either of these types of land. The smaller CPEs lie wholly in the temperate (WARM) and continental (COLD) categories. Data from the U.N.'s Food and Agriculture Organization (1975) show that on average the EE6 countries have about 5% more arable land per capita than the LIO countries and about 15% less than the OECD countries. Of the EE6, only Hungary and Bulgaria have more land per capita than the average of the OECD countries.[12] The Soviet Union has about 85% more land per capita than the average for the OECD.

The relevant results are presented in Table 6.4. The last column of that table is the sum of the estimates of endowments of WARM and COLD land

[12] For closer examination of Table 6.4, it is useful to know that Bulgaria's arable land per capita equals 101% of the OECD average, while the corresponding figures for other countries are Czechoslovakia 71%, the German Democratic Republic 56%, Hungary 103%, Poland 88%, Romania 98%, Yugoslavia 75%, and Albania 52%.

implicit in trade patterns. That column therefore estimates the total agricultural land embodied in trade for the climatic zones present in the smaller CPEs. By making comparisons with the groupings of capitalist countries and using the information in the previous paragraph, it is obvious that all these estimates are higher than can be justified on the basis of land availabilities. Only the Soviet Union is an exception to this statement, with its land estimate roughly appropriate, at least if the OECD figures are used as a benchmark.[13]

The information in the last column of Table 6.4 shows that all CPEs, with the possible exception of the Soviet Union, have a trade balance in agricultural products that is much too high, given the available stocks of agricultural land. (The estimates in the second column serve only to reinforce this conclusion. The trade patterns of the CPEs predict stocks of land that the countries do not

Table 6.4.
Land Endowments Implicit in Trade Patterns, 1975

	Tropical Land	Dry Land	Warm Land	Cold Land	Total Warm and Cold Land
All	0.65	5.11	1.97	2.03	4.00
Market	1.21	1.41	1.47	0.93	2.40
OECD	0.12	1.31	2.08	2.26	4.34
Market minus OECD	2.23	1.15	0.71	−0.43	0.28
Low-income OECD	−0.38	−0.19	0.16	−1.00	−0.84
Bulgaria	−1.57	10.03	0.88	18.33	19.21
Czechoslovakia	0.50	7.10	1.74	2.90	4.64
East Germany	0.12	1.78	1.05	3.09	4.14
Hungary	0.31	22.85	5.11	8.33	13.44
Poland	0.14	64.60	11.50	−6.63	4.87
Romania	−1.24	2.88	−0.11	10.03	9.92
USSR	−0.50	19.15	2.22	5.71	7.93
Yugoslavia	−5.56	10.17	4.37	21.70	26.07
Albania	0.58	2.76	0.76	2.36	3.12
Eastern Europe 9	−0.80	15.70	3.06	7.31	10.37
Eastern Europe 6	−0.29	18.21	3.36	6.01	9.37

Note: Figures are in hectares of land per capita.

[13] As Section 6.5 shows, the omission of intra-CMEA trade might account for some of the differences between the Soviet Union and the EE6, but it cannot account for the fact that the average value of the land content of trade is higher than anticipated.

possess.) These results bear on two hypotheses formulated in Chapter 3. Hypothesis 4 predicts a bias toward the export of agricultural products because the pricing system does not accurately reflect the marginal cost of land. In contrast, the opposite effect is predicted by Hypothesis 22, which is based on the fact that CPEs consume large amounts of food relative to their level of development. Both hypotheses could be correct, with the empirical results reflecting the balance of the hypothesized effects. The evidence in Table 6.4 indicates that the pattern of CPE trade results from Hypothesis 4 being dominant.

The results on the land variables are in contrast to those on food in Chapter 4, which indicated that the CPEs have a comparative disadvantage in food. There is a way in which the results could be consistent, however. The present estimates show solely that the CPEs are net exporters of land, while those in Chapter 4 show that the CPEs are net importers of food. If CPE pricing and agricultural organization encourages land-intensive crops at the expense of other crops, then there is no conflict between the two sets of results. Hypotheses 4 and 22 could both be correct.

Minerals   The results for three mineral aggregates are presented in the first three columns of Table 6.5. These results are relevant to two of the hypotheses of Chapter 3. Hypothesis 1 predicts that CPE trade patterns lag behind those of the rest of the world. Because world energy prices were rising rapidly in 1973–74, domestic CPE prices were lagging behind. Hence, one would expect that the CPEs would have an apparent comparative advantage in energy in 1975. Hypothesis 4 predicts that the price system of CPEs leads to a bias toward the exportation of natural resources.

Some extra information is presented with the estimates in Table 6.5 in order to enable the reader to place the results in perspective. Columns 6 and 7 list the actual values for the production of coal plus lignite and for oil plus natural gas. Column 5 sums the information in columns 6 and 7. The amount in column 5 can be interpreted as the per capita dollar fuel endowment of the CPEs.

The most insightful comparison is between column 4, the estimate of the total energy content of trade, and column 5, the actual endowment of energy. A quick glance at this column reveals that there is a bias within Eastern Europe toward the export of either fuels or goods containing a high embodied fuel content. But, this bias is not uniform. Bulgaria, Hungary, and Yugoslavia are the most extreme cases, with exports three or more times the amount that could be justified by endowments; in Romania and Poland the equivalent ratio is two, and in the Soviet Union it is less than one and a half. In contrast, however, the predicted values for the GDR and Czechoslovakia are in the region of the actual values. The results in column 1, on minerals, seem to be consistent with those on fuels. The pattern of predictions on the embodied ore content of trade shows again that Czechoslovakia and the GDR behave very differently from their neighbors.

The results in Table 6.5 provide somewhat ambiguous evidence. On average, of course, CPEs seem to have a bias toward the export of fuels, but as the results on Czechoslovakia and the GDR attest, that bias is not inevitable. Moreover, given that these estimates are for 1975, there is no means of distinguishing between the effects identified in Hypothesis 1 and those identified in Hypothesis 4. The next section, however, will enable us to distinguish clearly between these hypotheses.

Table 6.5.

Endowments of Ores and Mineral Fuels Implicit in Trade Patterns and Actual Endowments, 1975

	(1) Est. Ores	(2) Est. Coal	(3) Est. Oil	(4) Est. Fuels	(5) Actual Fuels	(6) Actual Coal	(7) Actual Oil
All	34	32	79	111	N.A.	N.A.	N.A.
Market	24	14	32	46	50	14	36
OECD	30	21	47	68	79	26	53
Market minus OECD	14	5	20	25	24	1	23
Low-income OECD	15	−6	−28	−34	15	7	8
Bulgaria	126	77	411	487	57	56	1
Czechoslovakia	48	71	106′	177	153	153	0
East Germany	25	51	109	160	159	152	7
Hungary	109	116	175	291	71	37	34
Poland	213	330	68	397	197	188	9
Romania	38	62	225	287	155	22	133
USSR	111	119	232	351	268	82	186
Yugoslavia	82	89	375	464	39	25	14
Albania	31	46	103	149	64	7	57
Eastern Europe 9	87	107	200	307	129	80	49
Eastern Europe 6	93	117	182	300	132	101	31

Note: All figures are in 1975 U.S. $ per capita. Figures for regional groupings are averages of country figures. N.A.-not available. Columns (1) to (4) are estimates from trade data. Columns (5) to (7) for the CPEs are derived using production data taken from the U.N. *Yearbook of Energy Statistics* (1979), conversion factors for coal equivalents from the same source, and price data from Leamer (1984, p. 91). For the MES, these data are taken directly from Leamer (1984, pp. 221–27). Data for MES and CPES are comparable. Columns (3) and (7) include oil and natural gas. Columns (2) and (6) include coal and lignite. Column (4) = column (2) + column (3). Column (5) = column (6) + column (7).

6.4. Time Series of Endowment Levels Implicit
in Trade Patterns: 1966–1983

The results of the previous section are based on relationships between trade
and endowments for one year, 1975. Using time series of trade patterns, these
relationships can be employed to generate time series of estimated factor
contents. Of course, these estimates must be treated rather gingerly, because
the relationships between trade and endowments do change over time with
changes in technology, world endowments, and so forth. (It is not possible
to estimate the changes in these relationships, because endowment data exist
for only one year.) Nevertheless, given a sensitive reading of the results, the
time series of estimated factor contents reveal interesting qualitative information on temporal changes in the socialist economies.

Given that the relationships between trade and endowments are not updated
yearly, one should not attribute any precise meaning to the absolute values
of estimated factor contents in years other than 1975. Rather, one can reasonably only hope to discern changes in the relative behavior of different
countries. Thus, I normalize all countries' estimates for each year in such a
way that the estimated factor contents of the "market" economies remain
constant over time. I chose the market grouping for the normalization so that
the results would not be affected by variations in behavior that were particular
to a narrow range of capitalist countries. (The market grouping is the largest
set of market economies.) In any case, the tables contain sufficient information
to allow readers to carry out their own preferred way of normalizing the data.

The relevant results appear in Tables 6.6 to 6.13. These results show the
implicit factor contents of trade (relative to those of the market grouping)
under the assumption that the relationship between trade and endowments
remains constant over time. The results are for 1966, 1972, and 1975–83.[14]
Because the time-series results for the land variables do not give any more
information than is contained in Table 6.4, they are omitted for the sake of
brevity.[15]

Table 6.6 presents the time series for the capital stock embodied in trade.
There is surprisingly little trend in the results for most of the countries.
Poland's strong bias toward capital-intensive trade is evident in all years. The
reverse bias in Yugoslavia also remains throughout the period. There is little
to remark upon for the other countries, except for Hungary and the Soviet
Union.

Table 6.6 clearly shows that the results from the present study are consistent
with those of Rosefielde (1973), even though those of Table 6.3 seemed to

---

[14] Only two-digit data were available to me for the years 1966 and 1972. Data at this level
are sufficient for the results in the present chapter, but then could not be used in Chapter 4
because that chapter required three-digit data.

[15] Copies of the results for these variables are available from the author on request.

be in conflict. Rosefielde's results, which were for 1968 and before, show a capital-intensive bias in Soviet exports. The same bias is clearly present in Table 6.6 for 1966 and, though less marked, for 1972, but is either absent or insignificant by 1975. The most obvious theory explaining the downward trend in capital-content of trade focuses on changes in Soviet pricing policy. In the 1966 reforms, a charge for capital was introduced for the first time (Hewett 1984, p. 134). Accounting for the cost of capital has evidently helped make Soviet trade more consistent with objective economic facts.

From 1966 to 1975 the capital content of Hungarian trade decreased a great deal. As stated in the previous section, the 1975 figure is almost certainly smaller than Hungary's actual capital stock. The bias toward low capital intensivity in Hungary's trade has apparently been introduced since 1966. It is tempting to associate this change with the introduction of reforms in Hungary, and this temptation increases when one realizes that the same bias is a constant feature of Yugoslavian trade patterns, while absent in all other socialist countries. However, no theory is available to explain why market-socialist economies should have such a bias in trade patterns. For the moment,

Table 6.6.
Capital Stock Per Capita Embodied in Trade Patterns: 1966, 1972, 1975–83

	1966	1972	1975	1976	1977	1978	1979	1980	1981	1982	1983
All	4.69	4.64	4.26	4.31	4.18	4.10	4.13	4.32	4.23	4.28	4.33
Market	4.84	4.84	4.84	4.84	4.84	4.84	4.84	4.84	4.84	4.84	4.84
OECD	7.82	7.99	8.22	7.85	7.97	7.84	7.76	8.00	7.80	7.69	7.74
Market minus OECD	1.33	1.59	1.22	1.61	1.50	1.62	1.75	1.50	1.68	1.80	1.76
Low-income OECD	3.56	3.93	3.84	3.88	4.13	4.78	4.56	4.38	4.42	4.91	5.17
Bulgaria	2.46	3.95	2.38	4.61	3.83	2.66	2.82	2.34	1.90	4.52	5.32
Czechoslovakia	7.87	7.82	7.46	7.50	7.20	6.68	6.67	7.46	7.30	7.25	7.38
East Germany	7.43	7.57	7.20	7.34	6.93	6.50	6.47	7.31	7.08	6.97	7.15
Hungary	6.19	5.71	4.02	5.28	4.84	4.44	3.87	4.28	3.71	3.83	4.53
Poland	15.39	14.71	12.69	12.81	12.57	13.25	13.47	15.13	14.17	16.29	16.35
Romania	4.58	4.05	4.05	4.86	3.91	3.39	3.02	3.60	4.22	4.83	5.40
USSR	12.76	9.84	6.75	6.65	6.23	3.67	3.52	6.31	6.84	5.39	5.15
Yugoslavia	0.53	2.19	− 1.95	0.66	0.81	0.86	0.07	0.43	0.38	0.85	0.86
Albania	7.20	7.41	7.50	7.32	6.80	6.30	6.40	7.72	7.70	8.15	7.55
Eastern Europe 9	7.16	7.03	5.57	6.34	5.90	5.31	5.15	6.07	5.92	6.45	6.63
Eastern Europe 6	7.32	7.30	6.30	7.07	6.54	6.15	6.05	6.69	6.40	7.28	7.69

Note: Figures are in thousands of 1975 U.S. $ per capita, normalized so that the "market" grouping remains constant at its 1975 value.

the low capital-intensivity of Hungarian and Yugoslavian trade patterns must remain facts in search of a theory.

The results for the three types of labor appear in Tables 6.7–6.9. Surprisingly little information is revealed beyond that appearing in the previous section. Hungary's low figure for professional and technical labor, just like its capital figure, seems to be a product of the reform era. Again, the comparison with Yugoslavia raises thoughts about the effects of reforms.

The strongest time trend in the labor content figures are in those for the Soviet Union. Throughout the period from 1966 to 1979, both the downward bias in the skilled-labor estimates and the upward bias in the unskilled-labor content increase. The results for these two labor variables are dramatically different from those expected, and very different from those of any other CPEs (with the possible exception of Poland). Although the changing demography of the Soviet Union (Feshbach 1983) might help explain these results, it seems that more than a shifting regional balance of workers is required to explain the changes in the labor content of trade from 1966 to 1983.

Tables 6.10–6.13 provide the results for raw material endowments. All these tables provide essentially the same message about the nature of temporal

Table 6.7.
Professional and Technical Labor Embodied in Trade Patterns:
1966, 1972, 1975–1983

	1966	1972	1975	1976	1977	1978	1979	1980	1981	1982	1983
All	3.25	3.01	2.80	2.82	2.82	2.77	2.76	2.78	2.72	2.70	2.74
Market	3.57	3.57	3.57	3.57	3.57	3.57	3.57	3.57	3.57	3.57	3.57
OECD	5.36	4.96	5.21	5.17	5.08	4.95	4.82	4.98	4.92	4.87	4.96
Market minus OECD	1.66	2.31	1.90	1.97	2.02	2.13	2.32	2.15	2.18	2.25	2.21
Low-income OECD	2.46	2.58	3.33	3.17	3.03	3.14	2.75	2.99	3.07	3.24	3.59
Bulgaria	1.31	2.12	0.72	0.54	1.57	1.44	1.38	1.24	0.74	−0.01	−0.12
Czechoslovakia	4.71	4.54	4.23	4.24	4.17	4.18	4.18	4.39	4.36	4.48	4.78
East Germany	4.90	4.72	4.60	4.67	4.60	4.47	4.48	4.68	4.59	4.69	4.92
Hungary	3.10	2.28	0.35	0.79	1.65	1.53	1.54	0.77	1.05	1.45	1.74
Poland	6.94	4.62	4.91	4.98	4.89	4.77	4.81	5.48	4.56	4.25	4.38
Romania	3.63	3.30	3.57	3.78	3.70	3.23	3.50	3.63	3.66	4.09	4.27
USSR	6.17	5.64	5.38	6.41	5.50	3.46	3.86	5.37	5.66	5.65	5.91
Yugoslavia	1.80	0.99	0.74	1.01	0.89	0.76	0.75	2.36	1.91	1.52	1.29
Albania	4.71	4.57	4.45	4.63	4.54	4.36	4.37	4.48	4.25	4.16	4.55
Eastern Europe 9	4.14	3.64	3.22	3.45	3.50	3.13	3.21	3.60	3.42	3.37	3.52
Eastern Europe 6	4.10	3.60	3.06	3.17	3.43	3.27	3.31	3.36	3.16	3.16	3.33

Note: Figures are percentages of population normalized so that the "market" grouping remains constant at its 1975 value.

changes. Therefore, the main focus of the present discussion will be on the last of these tables, that for fuel.[16]

Table 6.5 revealed that in 1975 the CPEs had a structure of trade whose implicit content of both coal and oil was higher than could be justified on the basis of present production levels. The discussion of that table left open three possibilities for explaining that bias: Hypothesis 4 focusing on the effect of average-cost pricing policies on the use of natural resources, Hypothesis 1 predicting a slow adjustment to the 1973 fuel price increases, and the effect on the estimates of the omission of intra-CMEA trade. The last possibility is examined, and receives little support, in the next section. Here, the focus is on the choice between the two other possibilities.

One basic fact stands out above all others from Tables 6.10–6.13—1975 is a very special year. For fuels, the factor content of net exports of most socialist countries rises by more than 50% from 1966 to 1975. Then, from

Table 6.8.
Skilled Labor Embodied in Trade Patterns: 1966, 1972, 1975–1983

	1966	1972	1975	1976	1977	1978	1979	1980	1981	1982	1983
All	27.0	26.4	25.9	25.7	26.2	25.8	25.9	25.9	25.8	26.2	26.1
Market	29.5	29.5	29.5	29.5	29.5	29.5	29.5	29.5	29.5	29.5	29.5
OECD	36.1	36.8	35.8	35.3	35.2	35.4	35.8	36.7	36.1	34.7	33.9
Market minus OECD	21.6	21.1	22.0	22.5	22.6	22.3	22.2	21.2	21.6	23.0	23.9
Low-income OECD	26.7	27.2	28.6	27.6	26.2	28.2	29.4	30.8	30.9	28.7	29.9
Bulgaria	35.7	43.3	46.0	46.7	50.2	44.3	40.4	36.5	32.7	39.1	29.7
Czechoslovakia	38.0	38.4	35.9	35.1	34.8	35.4	35.1	36.3	36.4	36.1	35.9
East Germany	37.2	37.8	35.3	34.9	34.8	35.6	35.6	36.8	36.6	36.6	36.2
Hungary	42.2	41.0	37.5	37.7	38.3	37.8	37.4	39.5	37.8	39.0	38.9
Poland	24.3	34.8	22.0	20.8	26.3	25.6	25.3	24.4	22.2	29.3	28.9
Romania	31.6	35.3	31.7	32.4	32.6	33.3	32.1	33.7	34.4	35.9	37.3
USSR	29.4	25.0	19.1	10.6	16.2	12.4	9.6	9.0	12.2	9.4	9.6
Yugoslavia	28.0	34.2	29.5	34.0	30.0	32.5	28.2	24.6	29.1	32.1	38.3
Albania	36.4	36.8	34.3	33.6	33.9	35.1	34.9	36.0	35.5	34.2	35.6
Eastern Europe 9	33.7	36.3	32.4	31.8	33.0	32.4	31.0	30.8	30.8	32.4	32.3
Eastern Europe 6	34.8	38.4	34.7	34.6	36.2	35.3	34.3	34.6	33.3	36.0	34.5

Note: Figures are percentages of population normalized yearly so that the "market" grouping remains constant at its 1975 value.

[16] Much more information is available for fuel production levels than for ore production. Moreover, because several countries in Eastern Europe rely on indigenous fuel resources as much as possible and therefore use coal where oil would be used in market economies, it seems that the fuels estimates would contain a more balanced picture of temporal changes than estimates on coal and oil separately.

1977 onward the fuel factor content falls steeply. By 1980, and thereafter, the EE6 countries behave in a manner consistent with actual production levels (compare column 5 of Table 6.5 with the entries in Table 6.13). Hence, Table 6.13 presents unequivocal evidence in the choice between Hypotheses 1 and 4. The CPEs seem to act with a lag, but once reactions to the oil price rises were in place in the 1980s, there seems to have been little evidence of fuel price distortions in trade patterns.

It is appropriate to make one final remark on the time-series estimates of the factor contents of trade. In most of the tables, there is a remarkable stability in the year-to-year estimates. (The only estimates for which there are large movements are the ones for fuels. For those estimates, systematic time trends are easily discernible and are easily explained because world energy prices were highly volatile in the 1970s.) This stability increases one's faith that the estimates in this chapter really do capture essential features of the behavior of the socialist economies. It is unlikely that such stability would occur if trade decisions were made on the basis of year-to-year stopgap measures, as is sometimes implied in the literature on the socialist economies. Thus, one can feel confident in concluding that Tables 6.3–6.13 do represent an un-

Table 6.9.
Illiterate Labor Embodied in Trade Patterns: 1966, 1972, 1975–1983

	1966	1972	1975	1976	1977	1978	1979	1980	1981	1982	1983
All	7.6	8.3	9.1	9.6	9.2	9.0	9.1	8.9	9.7	10.0	9.9
Market	5.5	5.5	5.5	5.5	5.5	5.5	5.5	5.5	5.5	5.5	5.5
OECD	1.6	2.4	1.6	1.7	1.4	1.9	1.9	0.9	1.0	1.7	2.2
Market minus OECD	9.6	9.0	10.1	10.1	10.5	9.9	9.7	10.7	10.9	10.2	9.7
Low-income OECD	4.8	6.0	4.7	5.9	4.6	5.5	4.7	4.1	4.1	4.8	4.2
Bulgaria	3.6	−1.2	0.3	0.7	−0.5	1.7	3.2	5.0	8.9	2.4	9.6
Czechoslovakia	3.2	1.5	2.7	2.8	3.3	1.8	1.5	0.4	0.6	1.2	0.6
East Germany	3.5	1.8	2.7	2.5	2.9	1.5	1.1	0.2	0.5	0.6	0.2
Hungary	1.0	0.6	1.6	2.8	2.0	1.3	1.1	−0.9	0.3	1.0	−0.2
Poland	10.1	5.6	9.9	12.6	7.8	10.8	11.3	10.0	15.8	18.1	13.3
Romania	3.4	−1.1	−0.9	−0.6	0.9	−0.6	−0.8	−1.9	−1.8	−2.7	−3.5
USSR	7.6	6.9	12.1	15.0	11.9	17.1	17.4	17.7	23.6	21.3	17.7
Yugoslavia	1.1	−0.5	1.5	−1.2	0.1	0.0	1.8	3.2	−2.2	−1.8	−6.0
Albania	4.1	2.4	3.2	3.2	3.6	1.8	1.4	0.4	0.9	1.6	0.6
Eastern Europe 9	4.2	1.8	3.7	4.2	3.6	3.9	4.2	3.8	5.2	4.6	3.6
Eastern Europe 6	4.1	1.2	2.7	3.5	2.7	2.8	2.9	2.1	4.0	3.4	3.3

Note: Figures are in percentages of population normalized yearly so that the "market" grouping remains constant at its 1975 value.

derlying reality—behavioral, organizational, and physical—of the socialist economies. This conclusion is reinforced in the next section.

6.5. On Possible Criticisms of This Book's Interpretations of the Results

I have not yet considered the most plausible objection that might be made against my interpretations of the results presented in Chapters 4 and 6. I have not confronted the fact that there are imperfections in the data which critics might seize upon to reject the book's conclusions. These critics might claim that all the highlighted results can be explained by omissions in the data that produce biases in the estimates.

The presence of imperfections of data and the consequent possibility of biases are not in themselves sufficient reasons to dismiss a large number of consistent results. All nonexperimental empirical work is less than perfect and could be subject to the same criticism. Thus, any reasonable objection to this book's conclusions must rest on an argument that shows how the specific

Table 6.10.
Value of Ores Per Capita Embodied in Trade Patterns: 1966, 1972, 1975–1983

	1966	1972	1975	1976	1977	1978	1979	1980	1981	1982	1983
All	34	33	34	30	30	27	28	28	29	32	30
Market	24	24	24	24	24	24	24	24	24	24	24
OECD	17	30	30	28	28	27	28	22	22	21	22
Market minus OECD	27	11	14	16	17	18	17	22	23	23	22
Low-income OECD	12	21	15	22	17	19	24	21	19	22	15
Bulgaria	51	80	126	129	120	83	75	73	79	148	131
Czechoslovakia	62	48	48	39	37	29	29	29	31	29	19
East Germany	38	30	25	21	19	16	17	16	20	18	12
Hungary	71	77	109	99	88	79	70	89	82	87	84
Poland	183	255	213	186	192	186	180	173	165	257	224
Romania	52	51	38	29	25	20	9	3	5	13	12
USSR	142	125	111	64	101	108	75	76	73	47	37
Yugoslavia	65	107	82	91	93	88	80	74	60	90	99
Albania	38	31	31	21	16	14	17	20	28	32	20
Eastern Europe 9	78	89	87	76	77	69	61	61	60	80	71
Eastern Europe 6	76	90	93	84	80	69	63	64	64	92	80

Note: Figures are 1975 U.S. $ per capita normalized yearly so that the "market" grouping remains constant at its 1975 value.

results might arise from data problems. If such an argument exists, then there are two *theories* explaining the results: the one I have offered in this book and the "data-omission theory." An evaluation of which theory is most powerful must focus on how well each explains the evidence.

This section evaluates the objections that are most likely to be offered by critics. I examine the most significant problems with the data and consider how data omissions affect the results. In other words, I begin the process of constructing the alternative data-omission theory and consider the predictions that arise therefrom. These predictions are then examined in the light of the results already presented. I then reach an evaluation of whether the data-omission theory should cause one to reject the interpretations that have previously been placed on the results.

The introduction of some terminology is helpful at this stage. "Reporting" countries will be those whose data are used to construct the mirror trade statistics, the countries listed in Table 2.1. "Estimating" countries will be the Western countries used to estimate trade equations—the ones for which resource endowment data are available, listed in Table 2.3. As before, the

Table 6.11.
Coal Per Capita Embodied in Trade Patterns: 1966, 1972, 1975–1983

	1966	1972	1975	1976	1977	1978	1979	1980	1981	1982	1983
All	27	24	32	26	26	19	19	20	21	23	21
Market	14	14	14	14	14	14	14	14	14	14	14
OECD	11	20	21	21	20	20	22	20	21	23	24
Market minus OECD	14	3	5	4	6	6	4	6	5	3	2
Low-income OECD	−8	3	−6	4	−3	7	8	10	9	11	10
Bulgaria	54	45	77	64	67	42	33	33	33	53	44
Czechoslovakia	71	49	71	54	50	34	33	32	33	35	27
East Germany	50	35	51	40	38	25	25	24	26	29	24
Hungary	78	59	116	85	77	51	46	47	47	57	63
Poland	263	272	330	270	252	199	199	195	196	260	210
Romania	50	41	62	42	44	20	13	6	8	20	18
USSR	154	99	119	76	91	77	61	50	34	34	36
Yugoslavia	89	76	89	86	72	48	39	41	29	51	54
Albania	48	33	46	34	33	21	21	20	22	24	21
Eastern Europe 9	95	79	107	83	80	57	52	50	48	63	55
Eastern Europe 6	94	83	117	92	88	62	58	56	57	76	64

Note: Figures are in 1975 U.S. $ per capita normalized yearly so that the "market" grouping remains constant at its 1975 value.

"EE6" or the "CPEs" will refer to the countries whose predicted implicit factor content of trade is of most interest.

The possible problems from data omissions can be divided into three categories. The first arises from the fact that not all the world's countries could be used to construct the mirror trade statistics. Due to nonreporting of trade to the United Nations and the immense cost of processing and procuring data for all the world's countries, only a subset of the world is included in the reporting countries.[17] However, the proportion of the world's countries included as "reporting" does not accurately represent the coverage of the data. India, for example, has over 40% more population than the forty-six countries of Africa. Thus, the reporting countries cover a large share of world trade— from 80% to 90%.

The second possible problem stems from the fact that nonreporting countries are particularly important in the affairs of the CPEs. The CPEs themselves,

Table 6.12.
Oil Per Capita Embodied in Trade Patterns: 1966, 1972, 1975–1983

	1966	1972	1975	1976	1977	1978	1979	1980	1981	1982	1983
All	37	46	79	69	86	53	49	53	48	50	41
Market	32	32	32	32	32	32	32	32	32	32	32
OECD	32	44	47	53	55	40	38	34	38	35	33
Market minus OECD	31	12	20	12	11	24	25	28	26	26	28
Low-income OECD	17	12	−28	−1	6	11	7	18	20	5	9
Bulgaria	165	173	411	341	391	198	128	166	117	189	116
Czechoslovakia	64	75	106	103	112	70	67	61	52	44	35
East Germany	56	69	109	102	114	76	80	71	69	64	49
Hungary	87	98	175	124	158	112	104	85	77	87	85
Poland	−60	115	68	52	83	38	7	−37	−27	−51	−53
Romania	94	144	225	182	234	145	136	143	106	92	87
USSR	47	107	232	150	285	249	184	103	65	124	133
Yugoslavia	200	237	375	297	372	196	204	222	156	152	188
Albania	55	64	103	94	104	74	76	67	63	54	47
Eastern Europe 9	79	120	200	160	206	129	110	98	75	84	76
Eastern Europe 6	68	112	182	151	182	107	87	81	66	71	53

Note: Figures are in 1975 U.S. $ per capita normalized yearly so that the "market" grouping remains constant at its 1975 value.

[17] Readers might not know the size of the data bank on which a complete set of the world's mirror statistics would be based. One year's data would have upward of 5 million elements.

and the Soviet Union in particular, do not report data to the United Nations.[18] Therefore, readers might suspect that biases could arise because of differences between the nature of the data omitted from the CPEs trade and the data omitted from that of the estimating countries.

The third difficulty is that the mirror statistics of two CPEs exclude the data of particularly important trade partners. Because West German politicians still subscribe to the myth of one Germany, data on trade flows between the two Germanies are not reported to the United Nations. In 1975, trade between these two countries amounted to 33% of East Germany's trade with the capitalist world (Stahnke 1981, p. 344). Before the Sino-Albanian split, trade with the Chinese amounted to more than 40% of Albanian trade (Kaser 1977, p. 1329). Since China does not report to the United Nations, this element of Albanian trade is missing. Because the omission of intra-German and Sino-Albanian trade raises issues that are different from the issues raised by the

Table 6.13.
Value of Fuel Per Capita Embodied in Trade Patterns: 1966, 1972, 1975–1983

	1966	1972	1975	1976	1977	1978	1979	1980	1981	1982	1983
All	64	70	111	95	112	72	69	73	69	72	62
Market	46	46	46	46	46	46	46	46	46	46	46
OECD	43	64	68	74	75	60	59	54	58	58	57
Market minus OECD	44	15	25	17	17	30	29	34	31	29	30
Low-income OECD	9	15	−34	3	4	18	14	28	29	16	20
Bulgaria	219	218	487	406	458	240	161	199	150	242	159
Czechoslovakia	135	124	177	157	162	103	101	93	85	79	62
East Germany	105	104	160	142	153	101	105	95	95	93	73
Hungary	165	157	291	209	235	163	150	132	124	143	149
Poland	203	386	397	322	335	237	206	158	168	209	158
Romania	144	184	287	223	277	166	149	149	114	111	105
USSR	201	205	351	225	376	326	245	153	100	159	168
Yugoslavia	289	313	464	383	444	244	243	263	185	202	243
Albania	102	97	149	128	136	95	97	87	85	78	68
Eastern Europe 9	174	199	307	244	286	186	162	148	123	146	132
Eastern Europe 6	162	196	300	243	270	168	145	138	123	146	118

Note: Figures are in 1975 U.S. $ per capita normalized yearly so that the "market" grouping remains constant at its 1975 value.

[18] When this project began, only Czechoslovakia claimed to report the relevant data to the United Nations. Even if all the CMEA reported to the United Nations, there would be vast problems arising in converting intra-CMEA data to world values (see Murrell 1986).

omission of intra-CMEA trade, this third possible problem is discussed separately from the second.

The First Possible Problem The mirror trade statistics omit the reports of a large number of countries that account for a small share of world trade. The reporting countries are the forty most important industrialized and industrializing countries. The countries omitted are, apart from the CPEs, small developing and less-developed countries. Thus, if there is an important bias in the mirror statistics of all countries, it would lie in the fact that the net exports of the omitted reporting countries have a large share of primary materials and a low share of industrial goods.[19]

The effect of the omission of reporting countries is less significant than might seem at first glance, because one is interested in the model's predicted factor contents rather than in the coefficients of trade equations. Result 6.2 of Appendix D shows that predictions of endowments are unbiased for the sample of estimating countries as a whole. Therefore, if a nonestimating country has a structure of endowments that lies in the same region as that of the estimating countries, the predicted factor contents for the nonestimating country will be unbiased. The intuition of this point is simple. If omissions of trade data are similar in estimating countries and in nonestimating countries, the relationships between the observed trade data and resource endowments will be the same for all countries.[20] Therefore, one can use the relationships for the estimating countries to obtain an unbiased prediction of the implicit factor content for any nonestimating country. (Remember that, at the present stage, it is assumed that countries with similar endowments are missing similar trade reports from their mirror statistics. When one drops this assumption, the second possible problem arises.)

In conclusion, the systematic omission of a small amount of trade data for all countries should not lead one to have great concerns about the quality of the estimates. Rather, it is only if the nature of the omitted data varies greatly between the estimating countries and the CPEs that concerns should be raised.

The Second Possible Problem In early reactions to the present work, I have found one comment typical. Critics focus on the absence of intra-CMEA trade data and assume that there are large biases in the estimated factor contents. Although it is tempting to make such an assumption, in fact the assumption need not be correct. As previously discussed, there are data missing from the trade measures of all countries. If the character of these missing data does not vary systematically across countries, then there are no biases in the es-

[19] Notice, for example, that several important oil producers are omitted from the reporting countries.

[20] On the maintained assumption that the relationship between actual trade patterns and endowments is the same in all countries.

timates. Thus, those who point to problems arising from the omission of intra-CMEA trade are making an assumption about differences in the character of the missing trade data of the "estimating" countries and the CPEs.

The omitted reporting countries (apart from the CPEs) are primarily less-developed nations whose net exports are disproportionately concentrated in raw materials and raw-material-intensive industries. For a typical member of the EE6 or for Yugoslavia, net imports from the rest of the CMEA are disproportionately concentrated in the same areas (Vanous 1981a, p. 688).[21] Therefore, for the EE6 and for Yugoslavia, one cannot make the immediate presumption that the mirror trade statistics have systematic omissions that are substantially different from those of the "estimating" countries. For these seven countries, then, the hypothesis of bias in estimated factor contents is not one that is obviously correct or incorrect. Further evidence is needed to form a conclusion.

The first piece of evidence is a simple logical point. The estimates in Tables 6.11–6.13 are derived from net export data. Because by definition intra-CMEA trade as a whole must be balanced, a bias from the omission of intra-CMEA data cannot produce the same effect on all socialist countries simultaneously. Hence, any general conclusion on the nature of socialist trade supported by the results for all countries cannot be caused by the omission of intra-CMEA trade data. Moreover, because the Soviet Union is so dominant in CMEA trade, if a conclusion is supported by a majority of countries that includes the Soviet Union it is unlikely that a bias in mirror trade statistics is the cause.

The next piece of evidence is derived formally in Appendix D, where I investigate the effects of omission of one country's trade reports on the estimated factor contents of a trading partner. (As discussed in the previous paragraphs, the theoretical investigation in Appendix D is relevant only to the extent that the effect of omission of intra-CMEA trade on the CPEs mirror statistics is different from the effect of omitted trade data on the estimating countries' statistics. If there is no such difference, then there are no biases in the estimated factor contents.) The effects depend, of course, on the type of trade that occurs between the specific partners. Two results in Appendix D show the possibilities. If the trading partner whose reports are missing from mirror statistics is typical of a country's trading partners, Result 6.3 in Appendix D shows that there is no effect on the estimates of implicit factor contents. In contrast, if trade between two nations is typical of the nonreporting country, Result 6.4 shows that the estimated factor contents will be a weighted average of the nonreporting country's endowments and those of the country under examination. In this last case, the implicit factor contents of the trading partners become compounded in the estimates.

The discussion above shows that there is one important possibility that must

---

[21] These net imports are of course dominated by trade with the Soviet Union.

be considered. The omitted EE6-Soviet trade might be different in character from the trade omitted from the mirror statistics of the "estimating" countries.[22] If that is the case, the estimated endowments of Hungary, for example, could actually be estimates of weighted averages of Hungarian and Soviet per capita resource endowments. (As the difference between Results 6.3 and 6.4 makes clear, this is not necessary but possible. Another possibility is that the estimates for Hungary are unbiased. One cannot tell which is correct without knowing the exact nature of the omitted trade data.) Thus, in the light of these possibilities, one should reconsider the meaning of the estimates presented in earlier sections of this chapter, concentrating not on the precise estimates themselves, but rather on the basic qualitative conclusions drawn therefrom.

For some important factor endowments, the Soviet Union can be expected to be within the range spanned by the EE6. This is certainly the case for capital stock per capita and the three labor force endowments. Hence, if there is bias in the estimates of these endowments for the EE6, these should appear as a narrowing of the range of the estimates, close to those for the Soviet Union. Examining Table 6.3 and the accompanying discussion, one can see little to suggest that such a narrowing has occurred. Insofar as one can judge with available information, there are no capital stock estimates that are significantly closer to those of the Soviet Union than one would expect. Indeed, the opposite seems to be the case for Hungary and Bulgaria. In summary, there is much variety across the capital stock estimates and little evidence of biases that make the values all center closely on the estimate for the Soviet Union.

The Soviet Union has more arable land per capita than any other socialist country.[23] Because the estimates of land per capita for the Soviet Union are lower than those for half of the EE6, which are much higher than expected, the most important qualitative features of the estimates contained in Table 6.4 certainly cannot be explained by the omission of intra-CMEA trade data. However, since the estimates for Czechoslovakia, East Germany, and Poland are overestimates (compared with land endowments) but lower than the Soviet estimate, it is possible that the absence of intra-CMEA trade causes the overestimation for these three countries. But this possibility follows logically only if these countries have a negative trade balance with the Soviet Union in land-intensive products. Because Polish-Soviet food trade was roughly balanced in 1975 (Marrese and Vanous 1983, p. 176), the data-omission theory cannot explain the Polish estimate; it can at most explain the nature of the German and Czechoslovak land estimates.

The estimates for fuels are obviously the ones for which one would most

[22] The concentration on Soviet-EE6 trade is due to the dominance of the Soviet Union within the CMEA.

[23] The data on which this statement is based appear in Food and Agriculture Organization 1975.

likely suspect a bias due to omissions in trade statistics, for two reasons.[24] First, a glance at Table 6.5 tells us that the estimated implicit fuel content of Eastern European trade is much larger than could be justified by domestic production levels. Second, Soviet fuel net exports to the CMEA are large. Thus, the following paragraphs examine whether a bias is present in the fuel estimates. Throughout the following, one must remember that the issue is whether the estimates are distorted by biases in trade statistics or whether they reflect fundamental features of domestic economic arrangements. If one concludes that the latter is the case, this does not necessarily imply that the estimates represent domestic production levels. Other features of the economy could be responsible—features that cause trade patterns to be distorted toward the net exports of fuel-intensive products.

The relevant facts are contained in Tables 6.5 and 6.13. The following comments are based on comparisons between the estimated factor contents for 1975–83 and the production levels for 1975. (Because very gross judgments are being made, it is not necessary to calculate relative production levels for 1976–83. The fuel production levels of the EE6 did not change dramatically during that period.) Let us use the word "overprediction" to mean that the estimated factor content of trade is larger than production levels. Underprediction is used analogously. The question, then, is whether these overpredictions or underpredictions are due to biases in mirror statistics or to organizational features of the domestic economies.

In pursuit of autarky, several Eastern European countries have tended to use coal where oil would normally be used, so it is sensible to examine predictions for fuels as a whole. For the majority of countries during 1975–78, there are overpredictions for fuels, but the East German and Czechoslovak estimates are roughly in line with production levels. From 1979 to 1983, estimated fuel factor contents decline—with underprediction, on average, being the case during the 1980s.

These basic facts are interpretable in terms of hypothesis that says that the socialist countries reacted slowly to world price changes in the 1970s. The relevant argument has already been provided in the discussion of Tables 6.6 and 6.13. A possible counterargument focuses on the alternative hypothesis that the estimates of fuel factor contents reflect biases in trade data, rather than fundamental features of the socialist economies. However, those results contain information that is inconsistent with the alternative hypothesis. Consider the following facts:

1. Nothing in the figures on Soviet fuel trade can explain the contrasts between the 1970s and 1980s in Table 6.3. The net exports of Soviet fuel to the EE6 increased from 1975 to 1981 and remained roughly constant thereafter.[25] The decrease in estimated factor contents is inconsistent with what

---

[24] The following discussion could apply, *mutatis mutandis*, to ores. I concentrate on fuels because much more information exists on fuel trade.

[25] *PlanEcon Report* 1986, nos. 12–13 pp. 16–17.

would be expected if the results solely reflected biases due to the omission of Soviet trade.

2. In 1975 and 1977–79, the Soviet estimated fuel content of trade is higher than production levels. The "data omission" theory would predict the opposite for all years.

3. During the 1970s, Polish and Romanian fuel estimates are overpredictions. However, these two countries have balanced trade in fuels with the rest of the CMEA (Vanous 1981b, pp. 546–47). The data-omission theory would therefore predict no bias in estimates for these countries.

4. During 1975–83, the fuel estimates for East Germany and Czechoslovakia are either roughly in accord with production levels or below those levels. Both these countries obtain significant net imports of fuels from the rest of the CMEA (Hewett 1984, p. 207). The data-omission theory is inconsistent with these underpredictions.

5. Yugoslavia has the most extreme overestimate, but in contrast to the EE6, Yugoslavian net imports of fuel are equally divided between CMEA and non-CMEA countries.[26]

6. In 1975, Yugoslavian, Hungarian, Bulgarian, and Polish estimated fuel contents are higher than Soviet production levels. Because the data-omission theory says that estimates are, at worst, a weighted average of the per capita endowments for the relevant countries, that theory cannot explain the extent of the overpredictions for these four countries.

The above facts imply that the data-omission theory cannot explain the main features of the results on the estimated fuel content of trade, but one should not immediately conclude that there are no biases in the estimates at all. The appropriate conclusion seems to be that biases do not dominate the results and certainly cannot be present for all countries. If one ranks the countries according to the proportion of energy needs satisfied by net imports from the CMEA, then the order would be Bulgaria, Hungary, Czechoslovakia, Yugoslavia, East Germany, Poland, and Romania.[27] While one might argue that the size of Bulgaria's and Hungary's estimated fuel contents are upwardly biased, this argument becomes more difficult as one proceeds down this list. For Czechoslovakia and East Germany, underpredictions are dominant in Table 6.13, so it would be difficult to argue that the estimates for these two countries are upwardly biased and, a fortiori, the same conclusion applies to countries with the same or smaller percentages of fuel requirements satisfied by net imports from the CMEA.

Summarizing these above arguments, one can reach a coherent conclusion. The socialist countries were slow to react to changed conditions in world oil markets in 1973, but by the 1980s their reactions had been embodied in trade patterns. The omission of the Soviet Union from the list of reporting countries

[26] Ibid.

[27] This ordering is based on rough calculations using information from Hewett 1984, p. 207; Watson 1981, p. 479; and *PlanEcon Report* 1986, nos. 12–13, pp. 16–17.

might imply some upward bias in estimates for socialist countries that relied heavily on the Soviet Union for fuels, especially Bulgaria and perhaps Hungary, but there seems to be nothing to indicate that such biases dominate the qualitative features of the results for the whole of the Eastern Europe. In fact, the composite results for the EE6 indicate little overprediction or underprediction as a whole from 1978 onward.

The data-omission theory can do little to explain the basic features of the results for fuels presented in this chapter. Because the effects of omissions in trade data would be most likely to appear in estimated fuel factor contents, it would seem reasonable to conclude that the basic qualitative features of all results in this chapter would not be altered if one could obtain trade reports from all countries in the world.

The above information is helpful in analyzing whether incorrect conclusions could be derived from the results of Chapter 4. The methodology of that chapter, necessitated by the nature of the data, meant that the results were not adjusted for the presence or absence of large amounts of extraneous factors (in contrast to the present chapter, which used a multiendowment methodology). Hence, Chapter 4 used the *ceteris paribus* assumption that the effects of the extraneous endowments could be ignored. In order to make this assumption most plausible, conclusions were drawn on the basis of comparisons between the EE6 and the LIO countries.

One must now ask whether the *ceteris paribus* assumption is in fact acceptable. Again, as in the previous argument, the exact information necessary to answer this question is not available, for the simple reason that it is precisely the omission of information that is the problem. However, there is much circumstantial information to draw upon, from both Chapter 4 and Chapter 6. Consider the following:

1. The information presented in Tables 6.3 and 6.4 and the discussions of these tables shows that the differences in capital, land, and labor endowments between the LIO group and the EE6 are not large enough to create any doubts about the validity of the *ceteris paribus* assumption.

2. If there is a problem with that assumption, it appears that fuel endowments would be the main difficulty. However, the estimated relative fuel content of EE6 trade declined by more than 60% between 1975 and 1983, without any major change in the qualitative features of the results of Chapter 4. This robustness in the results of Chapter 4, over nine years, during which the decisions of the Eastern Europeans changed a great deal, is one of the major reasons to believe that these results cannot be due to problems with the *ceteris paribus* assumption on endowments.

3. If one scans the results of Chapter 4, it is obvious that they are all supported strongly by Poland, Yugoslavia, Bulgaria, and Czechoslovakia. Yet those four countries differ considerably from the point of view of the fuel endowment variable. Poland has high production levels, and Yugoslavia has low production levels. Czechoslovakia has a low estimate of relative fuel

factor content, while Bulgaria has a high estimate. Given the cross-country stability of the results in the face of differing performance on the fuel variable, one can reasonably assume that variable to be irrelevant to Chapter 4's conclusions.

4. If relatively smaller endowments of natural resources in the LIO countries than in the EE6 were responsible for the types of results that appear in Chapter 4, one would expect to see relatively small EE6 imports of raw materials. As Table 4.3 makes abundantly clear, this is not the case. The EE6 countries seem to import a large amount of raw materials. This is true even for the three biggest producers of energy, Poland, Romania, and the Soviet Union. Endowments cannot explain these import figures, but one can construct an explanation with a theory showing how the socialist countries must concentrate their industrial power in old, resource-based, new-process-technology-intensive industries. The Schumpeterian perspective provides exactly that theory.

5. If one subscribes to the theory that the *ceteris paribus* assumption of Chapter 4 is wrong, then one holds certain assumptions about the way in which the RCAs are biased. As it turns out, for several of the hypotheses examined in Chapter 4, these biases would tend to make the hypotheses more difficult to verify. This is certainly the case for the results that show that the CPEs have a comparative disadvantage in convenience goods, no comparative disadvantage in goods produced under economies of scale, and a comparative advantage in goods that are little advertised.

6. Certain results of Chapter 4 depend upon the fact that the CPEs have low levels of trade, both exports and imports, in some goods categories (see, in particular, the results relevant to MNC's and product differentiation). Given the extremely low level of CPE trade in these goods, relative to levels in other products, particularly products subject to much intraindustry trade (Table 4.6), it is apparent that these results could not be explained by a failure of the *ceteris paribus* assumption on resource endowments.

In summary, the most obvious criticism of the empirical results in this book is based on the omission of data—data on extraneous resource endowments in Chapter 4 and on intra-CMEA trade in both Chapter 4 and Chapter 6. A theory attempting to explain the results based on data omissions could be constructed, but the arguments above show that such a theory can do little to explain the basic features of the results. Furthermore, much in this data-omission theory is inconsistent with the results. Therefore, critics who doubt the conclusions of this study must do more than simply question the results because of problematic data. They must provide a theory showing how the results are determined by data omissions, even though the most plausible effects of omissions do not seem to be present in the data. I am skeptical that such a theory could be constructed.

The Third Possible Problem   The results for Albania are simply not important for this study because of that country's small size, low level of development, and unique politico-economic experience. Therefore, the following remarks apply only to East Germany.

This last data problem is much more difficult to evaluate than the previous one, because the variety of evidence that can be brought to bear is limited: the trade between the two Germanys is obviously a unique phenomenon. Judging by the results in this chapter—the fact that East Germany's results seem so close to those of Czechoslovakia—one would not want to worry about biases from the omission of intra-German trade. In contrast, however, the results of Chapter 4 seem to mark East Germany as different from the rest of the CPEs and from the MEs. Perhaps the omission of data has had an effect on the results for the GDR. At this point, I prefer to remain agnostic and simply not rely on any of the GDR's results for this book's central conclusions. Readers can readily verify that this has been the case in the previous pages.

6.6. Summarizing the Results

Tables 6.3–6.13 constitute a large body of new evidence on the behavior of the socialist economies. It is no exaggeration to say that nothing like this information has previously appeared in the comparative systems literature. Thus, the implications of the new evidence presented here cannot be easily and succinctly summarized. The most important contribution of this chapter to the understanding of the nature of the CPEs lies in the details of the results— details that provide much information both for country specialists and for scholars of comparative economic behavior.

Although the foregoing discussion places much of the evidence in context, particularly using the hypotheses developed in Chapter 3, many of the detailed results of Tables 6.3–6.13 still require further explanation. For example, it is important for future research to investigate why the reformed economies have such a low capital stock implicit in trade patterns (see Table 6.6), or it is important to understand exactly why the Soviet Union evidences such a low-quality labor force (see Table 6.9). Thus, some of the most important results of this chapter might be called "facts in search of theories," which, it is hoped, will spur future research on the behavior of socialist economies.

One central message does present itself in the chapter's results. This is the reasonableness of the estimates, given currently available information on the CPEs. Especially for the more orthodox CPEs, the estimated factor contents present a coherent picture, and one that is largely consistent with objective economic circumstances. Certainly, the results do not lead to the characterization of CPE trade as irrational, as is often the case, even in academic writing. To be sure, there are some consistent signs in the estimates of behavioral causes of inefficiencies. Particularly strong examples are the tendency to overexport land-intensive products and the relatively slow adjustment to changing world energy prices in the 1970s. But these abnormalities are surely much less significant than one would expect, given the general tenor of current writing on the socialist economies.

A central conclusion emanating from the chapter's results is that the basic neoclassical model of trade—the Heckscher-Ohlin model—is eminently applicable to the socialist economies.[28] For the orthodox CPEs—Czechoslovakia, East Germany, and the Soviet Union—one applies that model and obtains sensible results. The picture is certainly not a picture of irrational resource allocation. This conclusion, however, does not apply to the two reformed economies—Hungary and Yugoslavia. The results, for the latter country especially, do not present a picture that one would readily characterize as evidence of rational decision-making. Yugoslavia shows an extreme bias toward the importation of capital-intensive products and a concentration on exportation of products intensive in natural resources, fuel, and land. Thus, there is little evidence that decentralization and price rationalization, as currently practiced in socialist reforms, can improve the rationality of static resource allocation of the socialist economies. Therefore, to diagnose the economic failures that might be present in CPEs and to suggest remedies, one cannot use the lens of neoclassical theories. The measures generated in the next chapter will overwhelmingly back up this conclusion.

[28] This conclusion is consistent with that of Rosefielde 1981, which is in contrast to the tenor of the prevailing literature.

CHAPTER 7

■■■■■■■■■■

Measuring How Closely the Trade Patterns
of Socialist and Capitalist Economies
Fit Standard Trade Models

All happy families are like one another; each unhappy family is unhappy
in its own way.
—Leo Tolstoy, *Anna Karenina*

This chapter presents estimates of the degree to which the trade patterns of
capitalist and socialist countries fit standard models of trade. The econometric
groundwork for the calculation of these estimates has already been presented
in Section 5.5. Here the emphasis is on economic interpretation.

If the statistical results from neoclassical models show that the trade patterns
of MEs and CPEs are very similar, in that they both fit the same model, how
might one construe the results? Two possibilities are outlined in Section 7.1
and given detailed elaboration in Sections 7.4 and 7.5. "Coherency" reflects
the notion that the behavior of the socialist economies fits a pattern found
when applying some particular theory empirically. In this chapter, coherency
measures the degree to which socialist trade behavior conforms to trade patterns found when a neoclassical model is estimated for the market economies.
"Static efficiency" extends the notion of coherency and interprets the results
as measuring the extent to which an economy's behavior approximates that
which optimizes the allocation of resources.

The concepts of coherency and static efficiency really represent the weakest
and strongest interpretations of the results to be presented. (One could, in
fact, find a continuum of interpretations between these two.) The objective
in the present chapter is not to argue for one of these interpretations, but
rather to present the assumptions that underlie each. Even if one construes
the results in the weakest possible manner, they are surprising and very informative. The chapter's empirical results show that the trade structure of
CPEs approximates that predicted by Heckscher-Ohlin theory. However, once
one applies the product differentiation and economies of scale model, the PE
model, the CPEs trade behavior does not fit the pattern found for market

economies. The results for the HO model, describing as it does rational allocations, and the contrast between the results for the two models certainly would not be expected from the traditional analyses of centrally planned economies.

The next section begins the chapter's analysis with a brief introduction to the two possible interpretations of the measures of the degree to which trade patterns fit estimated models. That section also examines the relation of the present analysis to previous empirical work. Section 7.2 examines the justification for the construction of the measures, motivating them in a diagrammatic framework. The following section details how the measures were calculated and presents the basic results. Sections 7.4 and 7.5 delve more deeply into the two interpretations of the measures, focusing especially on how one might justify the claim that the measures indicate comparative levels of static efficiency. Section 7.6 considers the robustness of the measures with respect to changes in assumptions.

Because the measures produced in this chapter are derived from a methodology that is wholly new, a large proportion of the following pages is devoted to the description and analysis of that methodology. For those who are interested primarily in following the major theme of this book—what the data tell us about the socialist countries—the most important parts of this chapter are Sections 7.1 and 7.3. The concluding section of the chapter relates the results to the major theme of the book—the relative applicability of the Schumpeterian and neoclassical paradigms.

7.1 Possible Interpretations of Measures of How Closely Trade Patterns Fit Standard Trade Models

Although there are many claims concerning the differences between socialist and capitalist societies, surprisingly few studies have tested such claims by applying theoretical models in a rigorously comparative empirical framework. One set of studies has made a beginning in examining these claims in such a setting. The typical study in this set estimates a cross-section relationship using a sample of both capitalist and socialist countries. Then, with dummy variables or a similar methodology, there is a test of whether the regression coefficients for the socialist countries are different from those for the rest of the sample.[1] Highly informative results can be obtained from such studies. Outstanding examples are contained in Pryor (1973, 1985), Ofer (1973), and Bergson (1987).

Often the results of such studies are given strong normative interpretations. Pryor (1973) provides a good example. He examines the extent to which the structures of wages, of establishment size, and of enterprise size are similar

[1] Often the sole focus is on the constant term in the regression. See Hewett 1980 for a discussion of the properties of different econometric methodologies.

between East and West. A large degree of similarity is found. Pryor's arguments imply that the structures in the West result from rational economic decision-making.[2] Similarity therefore must be taken to indicate some degree of rationality in the economic processes of Eastern Europe. In the same way, one could construe the results of Stollar and Thompson (1987) as bearing upon economic performance, although the conclusions are the opposite of those of Pryor.

The weakest interpretation of this chapter's results is that they follow in the same vein as the aforementioned studies—searching for differences between socialist and capitalist economies. Therefore, "coherency" just measures the closeness with which a particular country's data fits a particular estimated model. Many measures of coherency are possible, depending on the particular model that has been used and the data employed to estimate it. Thus, the significance that can be attached to a particular measure depends upon the intellectual force that stands behind the particular theoretical model, the closeness with which the empirical implementation is tied to that model, and the quality of the data used.

The strongest interpretation of this chapter's results—"static efficiency"— is based on the normative implications of one of the theoretical models employed in the empirical work. The details needed to justify this interpretation must be left to later sections. However, the idea is simple. Under strong assumptions, deviations from rational trade patterns indicate deviations from static efficiency. These strong assumptions are those of the HO model, plus particular characterizations of the way static inefficiencies are introduced into an economy. Given those assumptions, the mapping from trade patterns to resource endowments is the same for all countries. The relationship summarizing that mapping has an error term, which shows the size of the factor causing the static inefficiency. Then, the residuals in estimated Heckscher-Ohlin relationships are monotonically related to inefficiencies. Hence, one can use the Heckscher-Ohlin relationships for market economies and the trade patterns of all countries to construct indicators of static efficiency, comparable across MEs and CPE's.

Given the importance attributed to static efficiency by economists, and given the tendency to emphasize the superiority of the market in achieving efficiency, it is perhaps surprising that there is a dearth of studies that give cross-country comparable measures of static efficiency. Bergson (1971, 1987) can be interpreted as claiming that his studies give such results. However, as the criticism by Domar (1971) makes clear, this interpretation can be seriously questioned, and Bergson's estimates probably reflect much more than just static efficiency.[3] Hence, as Pryor (1985, p. 193) has concluded: "Compu-

[2] This is my interpretation based on remarks by Pryor 1973, pp. 78–80, 164, and 194–95.

[3] Studies related to this topic are Collier 1986, Desai and Martin 1983, Brada 1973a, 1973b, 1974, Sturm 1977, and Pryor 1985. However, none presents measures of *static* efficiency that are comparable between socialist and capitalist countries.

tations of relative efficiency of different nations are very difficult and we have no unambiguous empirical evidence that price allocation systems are any more efficient than physical allocation systems.''

In a recent paper, however, Whitesell (1987) has followed the methodology of Thornton (1971) and Desai and Martin (1983) in measuring static efficiency by using estimated production functions to calculate sectoral misallocation of capital and labor. Whitesell's extension of this methodology was in carrying out comparable empirical work across four countries, and his results show that losses from misallocation average 2.7% of total production in the United States, 4.1% in the Soviet Union, 8.1% in West Germany, and 13.0% in Hungary.[4] Although these are controversial results and need to be verified by further work, they are interesting here because they are consistent with the general view of economic processes that was laid out in Chapter 1. In this view, the performance of economies on static efficiency is regarded as an unimportant feature of their economic prowess. Hence, even if one views the socialist countries as having an economic character very different from that of the capitalist countries, one should not be disturbed to find little difference between the countries in the matter of static efficiency.

7.2. A Diagrammatic Exposition of the Calculation of the Measures

The formulas for calculating the measures have already been presented in Section 5.5, but that section concentrated on the econometric and computational aspects of the problem, rather than on the economic aspects. The economic theory underlying the construction of the measures is most easily understood through diagrams. Moreover, the intuition behind the method of calculation can be seen at the same time. Therefore, in this section, I present a diagrammatic analysis of the construction of measures of coherency or static efficiency using trade data. As for all diagrammatic analyses, one should remember that several special assumptions that are not necessary in the more general algebraic analysis are made to facilitate exposition.

Figure 7.1 examines the behavior of different countries at one point in time, when each is faced by the same world trade equilibrium. There are assumed to be three endowments K, L, and M and three produced goods X, Y, and Z. For reasons that are most easily understood when the conclusions from the analysis are presented, use of the diagrammatic method entails examining a set of countries whose patterns of resource endowments exhibit some similarities.[5] Figure 7.1 examines countries across which variations in resource endowments exhibit only one degree of freedom—a set of countries whose

---

[4] These are approximate figures, based on some of Whitesell's interpretations.

[5] For readers who cannot wait, here is the reason: The aim of the diagram is to show that the space spanned by the vectors of efficient trading combinations cannot be higher than the dimension of the space spanned by the vectors of resource endowments. In contrast, the space spanned by

resource endowments span a space of one dimension. Two assumptions define this set of countries. First, all countries have resource endowment levels that produce the same level of GNP when used efficiently. Second, the endowments of labor and capital all lie on some arbitrary straight line in $K–L$ space.[6] (At this juncture, the reader should remember that these assumptions are needed only for the diagrammatic exposition.)

Quadrant I of Figure 7.1 depicts levels of resource endowments. The endowments of the countries under consideration all lie on the same straight

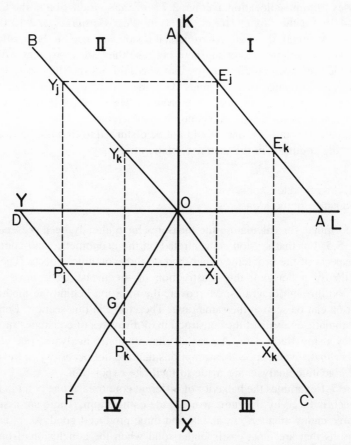

Figure 7.1. Cross-Sectional Relationships between Trade and Endowments

the vectors of inefficient trading combinations can easily be of a higher dimension than the space spanned by the vectors of resource endowments. To show this point diagrammatically, it is necessary to have a diagram that is one dimension higher than the space spanned by the vectors of resource endowments. Hence, given two-dimensional diagrams, the vectors of resource endowments must be confined to a one-dimensional space.

[6] The position of this line cannot be completely arbitrary. It must be consistent with the assumption on GNP.

line—*AA* in the diagram. Once a point on this line is chosen, the level of the third resource endowment, *M*, is implied, but not shown on the diagram. Hence, the patterns of resource endowments occupy a one-dimensional line in three-dimensional space, of which two dimensions are shown. Quadrants II and III depict production relationships. *OB* shows the relationship between the quantity of good *Y* produced and the level of resource endowment *K*, when countries are in efficient equilibria, when their resource endowment lies on *AA*, and when their endowments allow them to produce the assumed level of GNP. *OC* shows the analogous relationship between good *X* and resource endowment *L*.[7] Given the assumptions made on the resource endowments of the countries under examination, and given equation (B.3) of Appendix B, *OC* and *OB* are straight lines.

Consider country *j*, with endowment point E_j, which conducts its affairs efficiently. Y_j and X_j show the production choices of this country, with P_j being the production point of the economy. If *k* is another country, then E_k, Y_k, X_k, and P_k are the analogous points. Thus, it is easily seen from the diagram that P_k and P_j are on a straight line, *DD*, as are the production points of all efficient countries whose resource endowments are in the assumed set. Given any point on *DD*, there is associated a single level of production of the third good, *Z*. Hence, the set of production points spans only one dimension of three-dimensional space.

OF shows the locus of consumption points traced out by countries in efficient Heckscher-Ohlin equilibrium. All efficient countries with the same GNP consume at the same point on *OF*—in this case, point *G* (chosen arbitrarily in the diagram). Therefore, all countries trade in order to move from their production point to *G*. (Simultaneously, good *Z* is also traded.) Hence, view *G* as the origin of a separate diagram, Figure 7.2. On the axes, one has net imports of *X* and *Y*. The line *DD* now appears as the locus of trade patterns for efficient economies whose resource endowments lie in the assumed set. Moreover, for each point on *DD* there corresponds one and only one value of the net exports of *Z*.

We reach the first conclusion of this diagrammatic analysis. The analysis began by analyzing only efficient economies whose resource endowments could be viewed as lying in a space of one dimension. Then, the space spanned by the vectors of efficient trading patterns—the locus of efficient trading patterns in diagrammatic terms—is of the same dimension as the space spanned by the vectors of resource endowments. (One can now see why the analysis had to restrict the dimensions of the space in which the endowments lay. Without using a space of endowments of lower dimension than the diagram, this conclusion could not have been generated.)

Consider now an inefficient economy, *n*, which has endowments in the

[7] The linking of *Y* and *K* in one quadrant and *X* and *L* in the other is of no importance. One could just as easily have the *Y*–*L* and *X*–*K* linkages. The positions of *OC* and *OB* are therefore somewhat arbitrary at the present level of abstraction.

same set as the countries previously examined. E_n is the relevant endowment point in Figure 7.3. Suppose the nature of the inefficiency lies on the production side and involves a shifting of production possibilities from OB and OC to OB^n and OC^n, with an implied change in the production of Z also. Hence, the production point lies at P_n. Assuming that country n makes efficient consumption decisions given levels of production, n will trade to a point on OF consistent with n's GNP.[8] On Figure 7.3 this point is denoted G_n (which is arbitrarily placed on OF). By placing G_n at the origin of Figure 7.2 and then maintaining the relative position of P_n and G_n, one obtains P_n as a trading point on that diagram. Consider a different country, m, also inefficient but with a different cause of inefficiency. E_m is the relevant endowment point, the relevant production relationships are now OB_m and OC_m, with a production

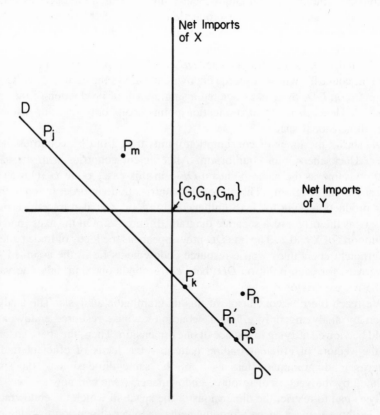

Figure 7.2. Trade Patterns of Efficient and Inefficient Economies

[8] In the analysis, there is the implicit assumption that the world trade equilibrium has been established, given n's behavior and that of any other inefficient economy. Then n faces the same terms of trade as all other economies and can trade toward OF.

point at P_m and a consumption point G_m. Hence, one obtains P_m on Figure 7.2.

The second conclusion now immediately arises. One could generate a large variety of points such as P_n and P_m, by varying the nature of the inefficiency. These points would not be confined to any single line; they would occupy a space of dimension higher than one. Because all efficient economies are like one another and each inefficient economy is inefficient in its own way, the trading patterns of inefficient economies are not confined to a space of the same dimension as that of the set of efficient trading combinations. In terms of our diagram, Figure 7.2, the efficient economies all have trade patterns that lie on DD, but the points representing the inefficient economies span the complete two-dimensional space.

A means of measuring the divergence between the trading patterns of a CPE and those common to MEs immediately suggests itself. One has trade

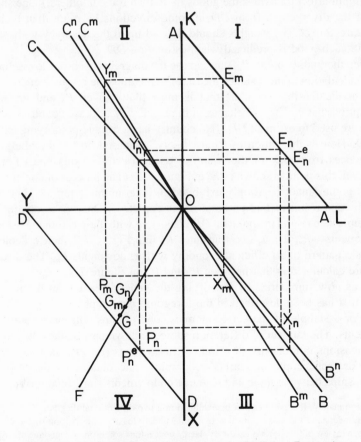

Figure 7.3. Trade Related to Endowments for Inefficient Economies

and endowment data for the MEs and only trade data for the CPE. Assume that one can use ME data to estimate the higher-dimensional analog to line *DD*—the space of efficient combinations of traded quantities. Then, in all probability, the point generated by a CPE will not be contained in this space. The distance between this point and the space of market-economy trade patterns is an indicator of the extent to which CPE and ME trade patterns diverge. Many distance measures are possible. In the following, the diagrammatic analysis is used to explain how one particular distance measure can be justified.

Consider the point P_n in Figure 7.2. The most obvious measure of distance between this point and the line *DD* is obtained by locating P'_n, the point on *DD* that is the smallest Euclidean distance from P_n. Then, one could obtain the sought after measure as the distance between P'_n and P_n. But this measure does not take into account the fact that *DD* is an estimate. Divergence from *DD* might be much more likely in one direction than in the other. (Random error might affect trade in some goods more than trade in others.) One should weight the divergences from *DD* in some directions by more than those in other directions.[9] The weights should depend upon the accuracy with which trade in each good is predicted when estimating *DD*.

Given the trading point, P_n, one can use the diagrams to show the mechanics of the calculation of the distance measure.[10] One finds the resource endowment point in the feasible set (*AA*) that is most likely given P_n and given the assumption that country n behaves in the same way as those countries whose data were used to estimate *DD*. (No country has a trading point lying exactly on *DD*. Hence, the notion of ''most likely'' is based on the distribution of divergences from *DD* for the countries used to estimate this line.) For our country n, this point is shown as E_n^e in Figure 7.3. (The process of construction of this point cannot be simply exhibited in diagrammatic terms. Therefore, only the end result of that process, E_n^e, is depicted.) Once E_n^e is obtained, it is a simple step to find the point on *DD* consistent with these estimated resource endowments—P_n^e. Then, one translates P_n^e into Figure 7.2, hence depicting the trade pattern of an efficient economy with endowments E_n^e. The distance measure calculated is that between P_n^e and P_n on Figure 7.2.

Let us now summarize by identifying the general features of the methodology that has been described in the foregoing paragraphs:

1. For a sample of market economies, one obtains data on resource endowments. The number of different resource endowments defines the number of dimensions in the space of resource endowments (i.e., the analog to *AA*).

2. For that sample of market economies, one obtains estimates of the relationships between trade and resource endowments (i.e., relationships em-

[9] Unfortunately, this point cannot be exhibited in a two-dimensional diagram.

[10] To understand the exact statistical reasoning underlying the construction of the distance measure, a review of Chapter 5 is necessary. Here I concentrate solely on an economic description of the mechanics, not on the statistical rationale.

bodying information analogous to that in *OB, OC,* and *OF*). These relation-ships implicitly define the space of market-economy trade patterns (i.e., *DD*), which is of the same dimension as the space of measured resource endowments and of lesser dimension than the space of feasible trade patterns.

3. For any CPE, calculate the factor endowments (i.e., E_n^e) that are most likely to have generated its trading pattern, given the assumption that the relationship between trade and endowments in this country is the same as that estimated for the market economies.

4. Calculate the trade pattern that would be generated by a country with the "predicted" endowments (i.e., E_e^n) if that country's behavior conformed exactly to that summarized in the estimated relationships between trade and endowments (i.e. P_n^e).

5. Measure the distance between the centrally planned economy's actual trade pattern and the one calculated at the previous step.

Given that this study can use only data on trade patterns, not data on levels of trade, the procedures for construction of the distance measures must be modified somewhat from the above. Once one uses trade structure, the simple straight lines in two-dimensional space, necessary in a diagrammatic analysis, cannot be used to describe the method of construction of the distance measures. However, the distance measure actually used is completely analogous to the one defined above. The only essential change is that higher-dimensional non-linear relationships replace the straight lines in two-dimensional space of the diagrammatic presentation. Therefore, the intuition conveyed by the diagrams is an accurate rendering of the basic properties of the measures given below.

7.3. How the Measures Were Obtained, and the Basic Results

By linking the analysis of the previous section with the economic and econometric theory presented in previous chapters, the following ten steps show exactly how the methodology motivated by the diagrams is implemented in practice:

1. The dimension of the set of feasible resource endowment vectors is defined by the number of endowments for which data are available for market economies. Section 2.3 described the available data, which comprised the values of eleven major resource endowments. The eleven-dimensional space spanned by the values of these endowments is analogous to line *AA* in Figure 7.1.

2. The theoretical link between resource endowments and trade levels is provided by the equations derived from the HO model, which is given formally in equation system (3.1) of Section 3.1. These equations effectively contain all the information embodied in *OB, OC,* and *OF* of Figure 7.1.

3. As discussed in Section 2.1, the available trade data does not conform

to that needed for the dependent variable in equation system (3.1) of Section 3.1. That equation system requires levels of trade; structure of trade is all that is available for the CPEs. Therefore, in order to implement the HO model for the CPEs, one must transform that model's relationships to conform to data availability. The resultant equations are given as (6.6) of Section 6.1.

4. The transformed equations are highly nonlinear in resource endowments. In order to obtain equations for estimation, they are linearized. The resulting equations, (6.8) of Section 6.1, have the structure of trade as a linear function of per capita resource endowments. These are the equations referred to as model H.

5. In moving from the formal HO model to the estimating equations, a number of transformations of the data have been made. Each of these transformations must alter the properties of the estimates obtained. One point in particular must be noted. The transformation of the model entails a transformation of the scale of the estimates of deviations between a CPEs trade pattern and that estimated for model H. In particular, the estimates should now be interpreted as per capita measures rather than levels.

6. Equation system (6.8) of Section 6.1 is estimated using the econometric techniques developed in Section 5.4. The estimated model implicitly contains information analogous to that embodied in curves OB, OC, and OF that appear in Figure 7.1.

7. In the estimated model, the number of goods is larger than the number of resource endowments. Hence, the set of feasible trade combinations is larger than the set of trade combinations that can be generated as predictions from the estimated model using all feasible resource endowment vectors. (The former set is analogous to the two dimensions of Figure 7.2, the latter set to DD.) This property of the model is analogous to the fact that line DD in Figure 7.2 is only one-dimensional, while all two-dimensional trade patterns exhibited in that figure are possible. Hence, actual trade patterns will in all probability not lie in the space generated by the predictions from the estimated model.

8. Employing equation (5.7) of Section 5.3, one can use the estimated model to generate predicted resource endowments for any CPE. In Figure 7.3, these estimates are represented as the point E_n^e for country n, which has trade pattern P_n. By entering the estimated resource endowments as dependent variables in the estimates of equation (6.8) of section 6.1, one obtains a "predicted" trade pattern. In the simple case depicted in the diagrams, this is P_n^e in Figure 7.2.

9. The difference between the predicted trade vector and the actual trade vector for any country is an estimate of a vector of errors in equation (6.8) of Section 6.1. (These two trade vectors are analogous to P_n^e and P_n in Figure 7.3.) There is one such vector of errors for each country. One then aggregates the elements of any one vector to find the desired measure for any country.

Two approaches to this aggregation were suggested in equations (5.19) and (5.20) of Chapter 5, giving the alternative measures called *GF* and *GF'*.

10. There is no natural scale against which readers can compare the absolute size of the measures *GF* and *GF'*. Therefore, comparisons among countries provide the most informative use of these measures.[11] Naturally, the most interesting comparisons are between CPEs and MEs. However, the MEs are used to estimate the trade equations. Therefore, a bias could be present in the comparisons if statistics for the ''in-sample'' MEs were compared with the statistics for the ''out-of-sample'' CPEs. In order to remove this bias, each ME was treated in exactly the same manner as the CPEs when its *GF* or *GF'* measure was created. As discussed in detail in Section 5.5, each ME was individually dropped out of the set of countries used to estimate the trade equations when the measures were calculated for the particular ME. Thus, all results in this chapter are generated for the CPEs and the MEs in an exactly equivalent manner.

Having now summarized the elements of the analysis that are used in creating the estimates, the results themselves can be presented. Table 7.1 gives the basic results.[12] The groupings of countries are as used throughout the book and as defined in Section 2.4. Model H is the basic Heckscher-Ohlin model as embodied in equation system (6.8) of Section 6.1. As discussed in that section, there is a simple way in which one can attempt to handle the problem of important omitted variables. Such an attempt leads to model HG, equation system (6.10) of Section 6.2, which adds GNP per capita to model H. With results for both types of error statistics, *GF* and *GF'*, and both models, H and HG, Table 7.1 has four sets of estimates for the error statistics.

There is no natural scale for the measures presented in Table 7.1. The precise numerical values depend upon the several data transformations that lead to the final results. Therefore, conclusions should be drawn only by comparing the relative positions of countries within one set of results. In making such comparisons, readers should remember that lower values of these country-error statistics indicate that a country more closely fits the relevant model—the country has a more ''rational'' structure of trade.

All four columns of Table 7.1 give consistent results. The Eastern European countries, on average, have much lower error statistics than the groupings of market economies. Seven Eastern European countries have error statistics that lie below those of comparable capitalist economies. Only two countries stand out as having poor performance: Poland and Yugoslavia. The performance of these two countries is absolutely consistent with that in Chapter 6, where predicted factor endowments for Poland and Yugoslavia were perhaps further

[11] The absolute size of these measures (but not the ranking of countries) is dependent on some arbitrary assumptions employed in the process of aggregating the trade data. See Section 5.7 for details.

[12] These are for 1975.

from expectations than those for other Eastern European countries.[13] The results for these two countries are also consistent with what one would expect on the basis of their economic performance in the years following 1975.

Yugoslavia's results force one to doubt whether decentralization, as presently envisaged in reforms, improves the allocation of resources in socialist societies. These doubts are increased by the observation that Hungary has higher error statistics than all its neighbors, except Poland and Yugoslavia. The results in Table 7.1 lead one to have grave doubts about the idea that market-socialist reforms can increase the rationality of trade structures.

The most striking results from Table 7.1 are those for the orthodox centrally planned economies, excluding Poland. Each of these economies has error statistics lower than those of any of the groupings of market economies. Nowhere in the table is there evidence supporting Chapter 3's Hypothesis 24,

Table 7.1.
Error Statistics (*GF* and *GF'*) Calculated from Equations Reflecting the HO Model

	Model H		Model HG	
	GF	*GF'*	*GF*	*GF'*
All	1.149	1.000	1.181	1.000
Market	1.338	1.150	1.355	1.148
OECD	0.946	0.840	0.944	0.839
Market minus OECD	1.731	1.459	1.766	1.457
Low-income OECD	0.778	0.692	0.712	0.649
Bulgaria	0.303	0.240	0.342	0.250
Czechoslovakia	0.022	0.019	0.026	0.023
East Germany	0.012	0.011	0.016	0.014
Hungary	0.361	0.353	0.494	0.324
Poland	1.566	1.503	1.543	0.881
Romania	0.159	0.132	0.245	0.170
USSR	0.336	0.368	0.337	0.242
Yugoslavia	1.340	1.072	1.375	0.946
Albania	0.008	0.007	0.006	0.005
Eastern Europe 9	0.456	0.412	0.487	0.317
Eastern Europe 6	0.404	0.376	0.444	0.277

[13] This consistency between the results of Chapters 6 and 7 is of some importance in choosing between the interpretations of the results. Countries with lower error statistics seem more likely to have a factor content of trade that is consistent with actual endowments. This argues that error statistics indicate behavior consistent with economic rationality—the static efficiency interpretation. I shall return to this point later.

which embodies a view that seems to be overwhelmingly supported by economists who study Eastern Europe. That hypothesis states that the HO model, the most widely used neoclassical model of trade, fits the MEs better than the CPEs. Insofar as can be ascertained, given the data available, this hypothesis must be rejected.

To this point I have focused the reader's attention on the Heckscher-Ohlin model, rather than on the product-differentiation and economies-of-scale model, the PE model. However, the description of the ten steps in creating the country-error statistics, with which this section began, is easily adapted to the PE model.[14] Because the econometrics of Chapter 5 is applicable to both models, all one need do in the description is to replace references to the HO model with references to the PE model. Hence, in step 2, the reference to equation system (3.1) of Section 3.1 must be changed to (3.2) of 3.2. In steps 3 and 4, the references to (6.6) and (6.8) of section 6.1 must be changed to (6.7) and (6.9) of the same section. Then one has a complete description of how to apply the country-error procedure to the PE model.

Table 7.2 contains the results relevant to the PE model. That model is implemented as in equation system (6.9) of Section 6.1. A further equation system, (6.10) of the same section, is created by adding GNP per capita to the equations. The two resultant equation systems are denoted P and PG in Table 7.2, whose construction is otherwise identical to that of Table 7.1.

The results in the two tables present a striking contrast. The relative performance of the CPEs has now been reversed. The groupings of Eastern European economies have higher error statistics than all the market-economy groupings. Of individual countries, only the Soviet Union can be said to have lower error statistics than those of the market economies.

The interpretation of the contrasting results in the two tables arises naturally from the intuition underlying the HO and PE models. The former model focuses on the ability of a country to allocate physical endowments rationally. That model does not reflect upon the nature of product development, the role of marketing, the importance of quality control, and so on. In contrast, the PE model focuses on the types of behavior that occur in industries subject to product differentiation. In such industries, the rapid creation of new products is important, as is the ability to sell these new products on world markets. As shown in Chapter 3, the ability to produce new products is dependent on the extent of free entry in the economy and on the degree to which multinationals are willing and able to function within the domestic economy. The ability to sell those new products is dependent on marketing skills, on a reputation for quality, and on access to the resources of multinational corporations.

The components of economic performance referred to in the previous sentence are not included in the list of endowments for which data were available,

---

[14] The diagrams in Section 7.2 would have to be changed, but as those diagrams only provide motivation for the econometrics, rather than define the procedure, there is no need to show how they would be adapted in order to show that the procedure works for the PE model.

but it is plausible to argue that across market economies these factors are correlated with the observed endowments that are used in the estimating process. (This is especially the case for equation system PG, which includes GNP per capita as a variable.) Given the lack of free entry, marketing skills, and multinational corporations in the CPEs, the correlation between observed and omitted endowments cannot be the same as that for the MEs. Hence, one can conjecture why the error statistics for CPEs are so high in Table 7.2. The error terms estimated from equations P and PG capture the fact that the values of the omitted endowments in the CPEs are really very different from those in the MEs. Given the types of economic behavior on which the PE model focuses, that means that the error statistics reflect differences between the CPEs and the MEs in performance in industries in which new product development, marketing skills, and product differentiation are all important. Hence, the differences between the results of Tables 7.1 and 7.2 clearly show that the contrasting behavior of the CPEs and the MEs can be best understood from a Schumpeterian perspective.

Two details in the results justify the foregoing interpretation. First, the difference in the results for the HO and PE models does not appear for the

Table 7.2.
Error Statistics (*GF* and *GF'*) Calculated from Equations Reflecting the PE Model

	Model P		Model PG	
	GF	*GF'*	*GF*	*GF'*
All	1.053	1.000	1.072	1.000
Market	1.096	1.036	1.076	1.026
OECD	0.887	0.853	0.887	0.814
Market minus OECD	1.306	1.219	1.264	1.238
Low-income OECD	0.830	0.818	0.883	0.778
Bulgaria	1.640	1.589	1.900	1.955
Czechoslovakia	1.274	1.356	2.069	1.766
East Germany	0.736	0.699	1.167	0.976
Hungary	0.872	0.917	1.390	1.093
Poland	1.826	1.888	2.713	2.374
Romania	1.455	1.424	1.599	1.439
Soviet Union	0.245	0.251	0.311	0.266
Yugoslavia	1.027	0.902	0.953	0.782
Albania	1.259	1.161	0.869	0.860
Eastern Europe 9	1.148	1.132	1.441	1.279
Eastern Europe 6	1.300	1.312	1.806	1.600

Soviet Union. This is natural. For an economy with stocks of raw materials similar to those in the Soviet Union, it would be quite rational to specialize in the sectors in which product differentiation is not important. Hence, any supposed lack of ability in creating new products would not necessarily be an outstanding feature of the trade data of the Soviet Union.

In order to bolster the interpretation of the results, examine the effect of introducing GDP per capita into the trade models. There is very little difference between the results for model H and model HG in Table 7.1. In contrast, the CPEs seem to fare much worse in their error statistics for model PG than in those for model P. (In moving from P to PG, the ME statistics do not change much, but the EE6 statistics rise by 40%.) Now, because omitted variables are likely to be much more important for model P than for model H and because GDP per capita is introduced in order to ameliorate the effects of such variables, the results seem to say that the elements missing from the standard set of resource endowments are very important in differentiating between the CPEs and the MEs. What is missing is of course the "endowments" that could capture a country's ability to be successful in a world in which the Schumpeterian model provides the most powerful explanation of success.

7.4. The Coherency Interpretation of the Measures

All the information necessary to understand the nature of the coherency interpretation has already been presented. The elements of the construction of a measure of coherency comprise the following steps:

1. Formulate mathematical equations representing a theoretical model.
2. Inventory the available data.
3. Derive a form of the mathematical model that contains only the data that are available.
4. Derive an econometric method that can be used to estimate the model derived at the previous step.
5. If necessary, introduce approximations to the model that are necessitated by constraints imposed by the statistical techniques and the availability of computational technology.

Hence, the evaluation of a particular measure of coherency rests upon two factors. First, there is the prominence of the theoretical model with which the exercise began. Second, one must examine how closely the estimated version of the model approximates the original theoretical model and evaluate how stringent are the assumptions needed to justify the approximation.

The evidence is before the reader on both these counts. First, there is no need to justify the importance of the HO model; one can hardly exaggerate its significance in international trade theory. Second, given presently available data and the limits of computational capacity, the implemented form of the model is as close to the HO equations as possible. Other authors might choose assumptions that would give them slightly different empirical representations of the theory, with consequently different estimates, but it is unlikely, especially in view of data availability, that any different representation would clearly dominate the one I have used above. What is more likely is that the different representations would have differing properties that are not easily comparable. In that case, a final evaluation of the collective results would depend upon assessing the weight of evidence. At the moment, however, I believe that there are no estimates that could appear as rivals to the ones in Tables 7.1 and 7.2. Given the controversial nature of these results and their significance, I look forward to seeing challenges to the above analysis based upon different assumptions and approximations.

7.5. The Static Efficiency Interpretation of the Measures

In this section I raise the possibility that one can interpret the error statistics derived from the HO model as indicating the level of static inefficiency in the economy. The analysis is merely suggestive, because a formal justification in a general setting would be impossible. As Leamer remarks, his use of the HO model—in a context more favorable to data analysis than to the study of the CPEs—requires a host of "incredible" assumptions.[15] Thus, one must view the present application of that model simply as a device to motivate the methods in a heuristic fashion. (Indeed, the heuristic nature of the argument is assured by the fact that the estimated trade model is actually a nonlinear transformation of the equations used in the present section.)

The approach in the present section is to show that the desired result occurs at least in the case of two simple examples. For these two examples, divergences from optimal economic policy result simultaneously in a decline in static efficiency and a change in the pattern of trade. The extent to which trade deviates from the efficient pattern is monotonically related to the decline in efficiency. Therefore, the magnitude of this deviation is an indicator of static inefficiency. Moreover, the appropriate way to calculate the deviation's size is to estimate the errors in equations relating trade flows to the factor endowments of a country (i.e., applying the methodology of Section 7.2).

In the following, I use the simplest $2 \times 2 \times 2$ HO model of trade to consider the consequences of divergences from optimal policies. The equations derived from that model in Chapter 3 are as follows, when simplified for the two-good, two-endowment case:

$$W_1 = b_{11}V_1 + b_{12}V_2 , \qquad (7.1)$$

$$W_2 = b_{21}V_1 + b_{22}V_2 , \qquad 7.2)$$

---

[15] Both the econometric and economic assumptions are described in the same manner (Leamer 1984, pp. 117, 155).

where W_i is net exports of good i, V_i is the endowment of resource i, and the country subscript is omitted in the present analysis. These equations arise in a world of either perfect competition or perfect computation (i.e., optimal planning). In keeping with the spirit of the present study, I examine the implications for these equations when a central planning authority produces an inefficient plan. To begin, it is useful to describe the planning procedure that leads to the efficient outcome.[16]

The country has stocks of the endowments V_1 and V_2. From these stocks, outputs of the two goods, Q_1 and Q_2, are produced. Given the levels of endowments, the feasible output combinations are described by the production possibility frontier $Q_2 = F(Q_1)$. The price of good 2 relative to good 1 on world markets is p. With homothetic preferences, decisions can be made using a single utility function, $U(C_1, C_2)$, where C_i is the aggregate consumption of good i. Thus, planners maximize $U(\cdot)$ subject to the constraints $Q_2 = F(Q_1)$, $C_i = Q_i - W_i$, and $pQ_2 = Q_1$. This maximization leads to trade decisions conforming to equations (7.1) and (7.2) above, the coefficients (b_{ik}) being constant across all countries.[17]

The planners' decisions can be represented in the standard trade diagram, which is useful to motivate the discussion at later points. On Figure 7.4, PP is the production-possibility curve, C_e and C_a are community indifference curves, and TT shows international trading possibilities. The economy produces at point D, exports DB of good 2, imports BE of good 1, and consumes at E, the efficient point.

If the planners made inefficient decisions, the economy would consume on a lower indifference curve, say C_a. Given full information, one could compare C_a and C_e to measure inefficiency. But information is incomplete, So, one must measure efficiency indirectly. As is obvious from the diagram, if the economy did not reach E, trade decisions would differ from those represented by DB and BE. Hence, a method of indirectly estimating inefficiencies immediately suggests itself—one should compare actual trade decisions with those predicted by the Heckscher-Ohlin equations. At least in the cases of the two examples that follow, this suggestion can be shown to be correct.

Example A: Planners Use the Wrong Utility Function Suppose that planners misestimate the utility function in some way. They issue a consumption plan based on this mistake and a production plan based on correct information about technology.[18] Figure 7.5 depicts the resultant situation. The efficient points are labeled as in Figure 7.4. The dashed line C_m represents a miscalculated indifference curve, which planners use to make consumption deci-

---

[16] See Batra 1976 for a fuller treatment.

[17] This last point follows directly from Batra's (1976) observation that the trade decisions of small CPEs are identical to those predicted by the HO model and from Leamer's (1984, pp. 8–9) derivation of the equations that result from that model.

[18] Nonoptimal production plans will be considered in Example B.

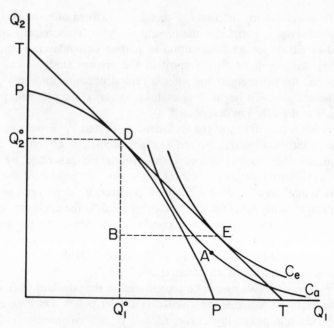

Figure 7.4. The Efficient Trading Outcome

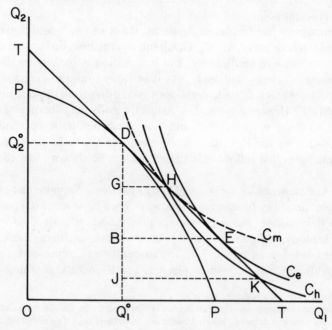

Figure 7.5. The Relation between Trade Decisions and Efficiency When an Incorrect Utility Function Is Used

sions. Trade is less than optimal: DG of good 2 is exported in exchange for GH of good 1. The efficiency loss is measured by the difference in welfare along the curves C_h and C_e. It is transparent from the diagram that the size of that loss is monotonically related to the deviation of trade patterns from the optimal. The same conclusion results if planners miscalculate in the opposite direction. The resultant consumption plan is at point K. Trade (DJ and JK) is larger than optimal by an amount related to the efficiency loss, which is the difference in welfare along C_h and C_e.

One can formalize the analysis by representing the planners' miscalculation of the utility function by a single parameter. Suppose that the planners use $U(C_1 - \alpha, C_2)$ instead of $U(C_1, C_2)$. The parameter α indicates the size of the planners' error. (For economies at the same level of static efficiency, α will vary in proportion to the size of the economies because it is on the same scale as consumption.) Then if the production plan is given by Q_i^o, trade decisions are found using the following first-order condition (where subscripts on $U(\cdot)$ indicate partial derivatives—that is, $U_i = \partial U / \partial C_i$):

$$pU_1(Q_1^o - \alpha - W_1, F(Q_1^o) + \frac{W_1}{p})$$
$$- U_2(Q_1^o - \alpha - W_1, F(Q_1^o) + \frac{W_1}{p}) = 0 .$$

Then the relation between the deviation of trade from optimal (dW_1) and changes in the degree of miscalculation is (where $\partial^2 U / \partial C_i \, \partial C_j = U_{ij}$):

$$\frac{dW_1}{d\alpha} = \frac{pU_{11} - U_{21}}{-pU_{11} + 2U_{12} - (U_{22}/p)} . \tag{7.3}$$

The change in welfare is given by:[19]

$$\frac{dU(\cdot)}{d\alpha} = \frac{pU_{11} - U_{21}}{-pU_{11} + 2U_{12} - (U_{22}/p)} \cdot \frac{(U_2 - U_1)}{p} . \tag{7.4}$$

Given usual conditions on utility functions,[20] $dW_1/d\alpha$ everywhere has the same sign. When $\alpha = 0$, $dU(\cdot)/d\alpha$ is zero; when $\alpha < 0$, $dU(\cdot)/d\alpha$ is positive; and when $\alpha > 0$, $dU(\cdot)/d\alpha$ is negative. Hence, the absolute size of the deviation of trade from optimal values is monotonically related to the degree of inefficiency. Already, one sees that error statistics can be interpreted as indicating the level of static inefficiency. This conclusion is more forcefully developed in conjunction with the lessons drawn from the second example.

Example B: Nonoptimal Production Decisions   Suppose that planners miscalculate $F(\cdot)$ in some way: they issue orders on Q_1 and Q_2 that are not feasible.

---

[19] In the following expression, the term $(U_2/p) - U_1$ is calculated with $\alpha = 0$ whatever its actual value.

[20] If the utility function is quasi-concave and both goods are everywhere normal, the numerator and denominator of (7.3) have opposite signs.

Assume that 1 is the priority sector. Then the planned amount of good 1 will be produced and Q_2 will be determined, as a residual, by the equation $Q_2 = F(Q_1)$.[21] Assume that consumption decisions are made optimally on the basis of actual production levels.

Figure 7.6 shows the resultant situation. The efficient points are labeled as in Figure 7.4. The inefficient production combination is $(\bar{Q}_1, \bar{Q}_2)$. The economy will trade to point A, exporting GH of good 2 and importing HA of good 1. It is easy to see that trade is greater than optimal by an amount that is monotonically related to the efficiency loss. Similarly, if the planners' miscalculation has the opposite sign and (Q_1^*, Q_2^*) is the chosen combination, the economy consumes at F and trade is less than optimal by an amount related to the efficiency loss.

To formalize the analysis, consider the consequences when planners fix the level of production of good 1 at $Q_1^o + \beta$, where Q_1^o is the optimal level and β is some deviation from it. The parameter β indicates the size of the planners' error. (For economies at the same level of static efficiency, β will vary in proportion to the size of the economies because it is on the same scale as production.) Maximizing $U(\cdot)$ subject to some arbitrary level of β, one obtains

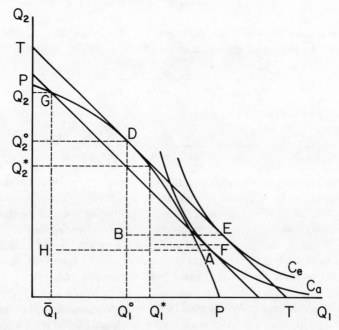

Figure 7.6. The Relationship between Efficiency and Trade Decisions When an Incorrect Estimate of the Production Function Is Used

[21] The analysis is simplified immensely by assuming production on the possibility curve.

the following condition (where subscripts on $U(\cdot)$ again indicate partial derivatives):

$$pU_1(Q_1^o + \beta - W_1, F(Q_1^o + \beta) + \frac{W_1}{p})$$

$$- U_2(Q_1^o + \beta - W_1, F(Q_1^o + \beta) + \frac{W_1}{p}) = 0 .$$

Totally differentiating this equation, one obtains:

$$\frac{dW_1}{d\beta} = \frac{pU_{11} + pF'U_{12} - U_{21} - F'U_{22}}{-pU_{11} + 2U_{12} - (U_{22}/p)} . \tag{7.5}$$

At the optimal position, since $F' = -1/p$:

$$\frac{dW_1}{d\beta}\bigg|_{\beta=0} = 1 . \tag{7.6}$$

The change in welfare is given by:

$$\frac{dU}{d\beta} = \frac{pU_{11} + pF'U_{12} - U_{21} - F'U_{22}}{pU_{11} - 2U_{12} + (U_{22}/p)}$$

$$\cdot \left[U_1 - \frac{U_2}{p}\right] + (U_1 + F'U_2) \tag{7.7}$$

$$= U_1 + F'U_2 .$$

Given the usual assumptions on $U(\cdot)$, $dW_1/d\beta$ has the same sign at all points.[22] Also $dU/d\beta \gtreqless 0$ as $0 \gtreqless \beta$.[23] Thus, the conclusion is exactly the same as in Example A: the absolute value of the deviation of trade levels from optimal values is monotonically related to the level of inefficiency.

Conclusions Drawn from the Two Examples To derive the conclusions, it is useful to define notation for the solutions of the two differential equations (7.3) and (7.5). Write these solutions as $W_1 = \theta^A(\alpha) + W_1^o$ for (7.3) and $W_1 = \theta^B(\beta) + W_1^o$ for (7.5), where W_1^o is the net trade flow when efficient decisions are made—that is, $\theta^i(0) = 0$.

As noted previously, the signs of the first differentials of both the $\theta^i(\cdot)$ are independent of the values of α and β, respectively. In contrast, from (7.4) and (7.7), one can see that efficiency declines with an increase in the absolute value of either α or β, whether these variables are positive or negative. Thus, the level of inefficiency is an increasing function of the absolute values of

[22] This follows, again, from the normality of both goods.
[23] This point follows from the fact that $U_2 = pU_1$, that $F' = -1/p$ when $\beta = 0$, and that $\partial F'/\partial\beta < 0$.

the $\theta^i(\cdot)$.[24] A first conclusion follows: if one can estimate the size of the $\theta^i(\cdot)$, one has an indicator of the level of inefficiency.

Given that α and β reflect not only the degree of planners' errors but also the size of the economy, the $\theta^i(\cdot)$ vary across economies of different size, even if they have the same degree of inefficiency. Hence, to compare inefficiencies in economies of different sizes, the estimates of the $\theta^i(\cdot)$ must be normalized for country size. For the estimates presented here, this normalization is automatic, given the use of trade equations in which trade structure and per capita endowments are the variables.

Because $\theta^A(\alpha)$ and $\theta^B(\beta)$ are unknowns, they must be estimated. Examine $\theta^A(\alpha)$, for example. Equation (7.1) predicts the optimal level of trade. Therefore, when inefficiencies of type A are present, that equation becomes:

$$W_1 = b_{11}V_1 + b_{12}V_2 + \theta^A(\alpha) . \qquad (7.8)$$

Thus, $\theta^A(\alpha)$ can be treated as part of the error term in obtaining an estimate of (7.8). However, one must first examine whether $\theta^A(\alpha)$ satisfies the most important assumptions on error terms used when deriving the estimators of the trade equations in Chapter 5.

The integral $\theta^A(\alpha)$ is the integral of the expression on the right-hand side of equation (7.3). Both the numerator and the denominator of that expression depend on the total value of factor endowments (i.e., national income) and not on the structure of those endowments. Moreover, given homotheticity of the utility function, increases in national income change second-order partial derivatives only by a scale factor. As the scale factor in numerator and denominator cancels, (7.3) is independent of national income. Thus, if α is random, then (7.3) and its integral, $\theta^A(\alpha)$, are independent of the factor endowments, V_i. Hence, the model satisfies the basic necessary condition for treating $\theta^A(\alpha)$ as an error term when obtaining the estimates of the system of trade equations—errors are uncorrelated with the independent variables. Note, however, that this condition requires that α be distributed across countries independently of factor endowments.

The conclusion for Example B is not quite as strong. As can be seen from (7.5), $dW_1/d\beta$ depends on $F'(\cdot)$, which is a function of the levels of resource endowments. One cannot claim that $\theta^B(\beta)$ is everywhere independent of the V_i, but in a neighborhood of the optimum point, $dW_1/d\beta$ is independent of $F'(\cdot)$ because the product mix in efficient economies is chosen so that the marginal rate of product transformation equals the world price level. If β is randomly distributed across countries, one can treat $\theta^B(\beta)$ as independent of resource endowments close to the optimal point. Thus, in Example B, the assumption on independence of error terms and exogenous variables applies, but only as an approximation in the region of the efficient point.

---

[24] This statement is slightly imprecise, in a way that will be made clear at the end of the present section.

To derive the conclusions in the immediately preceding paragraphs, it was necessary to assume that α and β—the sources of inefficiencies—were distributed across countries independently of resource endowments. To justify such an assumption, one would need to argue that inefficiencies arise as a result of peculiarities of the institutional character of an economy. Such an argument might be derived from Olson (1982), who theorizes that interest groups are primarily responsible for inefficiencies and that interest-group formation is heavily influenced by chance events. The pattern of inefficiency in an economy might then be largely a product of the idiosyncrasies of a particular environment: all efficient economies are like one another; each inefficient economy is inefficient in its own way.

One cannot push the argument too far. There are systematic variations in the pattern of interest-group formation across economies (Murrell 1984; Kennelly and Murrell 1988), and some of the variables producing these patterns are related to factor endowments. Hence, it is important to investigate whether the results of Section 7.3 are critically dependent on the assumption that the causes of inefficiency are randomly distributed across economies. This investigation is undertaken in the next section.

It is appropriate at this juncture to bring together the conclusions developed in the present section. First, the analysis has shown that the errors in estimated trade equations can measure the degree of static inefficiency in an economy. It is important to emphasize here that the estimates reflect not only trade distortions but also inefficiencies in the economy as a whole. Second, if one uses the normalized form of the trade equations, one estimates a per capita efficiency loss. Such an estimate is comparable across economies. Third, in order to justify the econometrics, one must assume that the source of inefficiencies is distributed across countries independently of resource endowments. The robustness of the estimates with respect to violations of this assumption are examined in the following section.

7.6. Examining the Robustness of the Results

As shown in Section 5.5, the error estimates were derived by first estimating an equation of the following form:[25]

$$y_{ij} = \sum_k b_{ik}z_{kj} + b_{i\theta}\theta_j + e_{ij} . \tag{7.9}$$

Equation (7.9) is a general representation of equations 6.8 and 6.11 of Chapter 6, with the added country-error term: $b_{i\theta}\theta_j$. Because the variables in the equations differ according to the trade model used, the variables are denoted by the generic symbols y_{ij} and z_{kj}, which were employed when discussing the econometrics of estimationg the errors. For the estimates presented in Section

---

[25] This equation is taken from (5.16) of Chapter 5. It is consistent with (7.8) of the present chapter, in which $b_{1\theta}$ was normalized at unity.

7.3, the term $b_{i\theta}\theta_j + e_{ij}$ was treated as a composite error term on the assumption that it was uncorrelated with the z_{kj}. Given that assumption, consistent estimates ($\hat{\epsilon}_{ij}$) of $b_{i\theta}\theta_j + e_{ij}$ were obtained by using the formula developed in Section 5.5:[26]

$$\hat{\epsilon}_{ij} = y_{ij} - \sum_k \hat{b}_{ik}\hat{z}_{kj} \,. \tag{7.10}$$

The validity of these estimates is in question if the independence assumption on the error terms does not hold. In that case, the estimates of the b_{ik} are inconsistent.

Given the discussion in the previous section, it is important to examine whether the results change when one considers that the inefficiency element of the error terms might be correlated with the exogenous variables. Let us suppose that $z_{\theta j}$ is a proxy for the term θ_j. Then one would estimate the following equation:

$$y_{ij} = \sum_k b_{ik}z_{kj} + b_{i\theta}z_{\theta j} + e_{ij} \,. \tag{7.11}$$

If $z_{\theta j}$ is a good enough proxy, it would purge the error terms of the elements that are correlated with the z_{kj}'s. Then, one would obtain consistent estimates of the b_{ik}, and (7.10) could be used to derive consistent estimates of the errors. Note that equation (7.10) is still used to calculate the error estimates, where the summation in that equation does not include the value $k = \theta$ (that is, $\hat{\epsilon}_{ij} = \hat{b}_{i\theta}\hat{z}_{\theta j} + \hat{e}_{ij}$). Hence, the use of $z_{\theta j}$ has been solely to improve the estimates of the b_{ik}.

To apply the above procedure, one needs a proxy for the variables that cause inefficiencies. Because the aim of the present section is to convince skeptics, I chose a proxy directly based on the likely source of skepticism. An assumption that usually lurks behind economists' discussions of efficiency under socialism is that any departure from free-market institutions causes a decline in efficiency. Government is the institution primarily responsible for such deviations, so the chosen proxy is a measure of government intervention in the economy.

The measure used as a proxy was CGS, central government expenditures as a proportion of GDP, the source of data for which was described in Chapter 2. This measure is a highly imperfect proxy because there is not a perfect correlation between the size of a distortion induced by a government action and the financial resources the action uses. However, there are no available alternatives to CGS, or similar measures.[27]

That CGS is an imperfect proxy is not fatal to the present exercise. Here, the purpose is to add a variable to the analysis that will help to reduce the

---

[26] The term "consistent" is used in the precise statistical sense.
[27] Mueller and Murrell (1986) examine the available measures on the size of government activity.

possible biases in estimating the b_{ik}'s. The robustness of the results can then be examined. By using a proxy for government intervention, one reduces the correlation between the residuals and the z_{kj}'s, lessening biases. If the results then remain just as strong, one can have more confidence in their validity.

Tables 7.3 and 7.4 list the new error estimates. These estimates are obtained by using the econometric methods of Section 5.5 on equations (7.11) and then applying (7.10) to derive the errors. It is important to emphasize here that the measured errors are deviations of trade patterns from the predicted efficient pattern, *not* deviations from the pattern predicted with CGS in the model. (Note that $z_{\theta j}$ is omitted when moving from (7.11) to (7.10).) Thus, the estimates are exactly comparable to those in the previous tables—the only difference being the way the efficient trade pattern has been estimated.

There is no need to summarize in detail the results that appear in the new tables.[28] The relative sizes of the errors in Tables 7.3 and 7.4 are approximately the same as those in Tables 7.1 and 7.2. Certainly the two major conclusions—

Table 7.3.
Error Statistics (*GF* and *GF'*) from the HO Model with a Proxy for Government Intervention

	Model H		Model HG	
	GF	GF'	GF	GF'
All	1.982	1.000	2.036	1.000
Market	2.258	1.147	2.257	1.097
OECD	1.641	0.843	1.501	0.819
Market minus OECD	2.876	1.451	3.014	1.374
Low-income OECD	1.856	0.856	1.708	0.774
Bulgaria	0.213	0.132	0.338	0.201
Czechoslovakia	0.198	0.072	0.179	0.059
East Germany	0.273	0.090	0.243	0.074
Hungary	0.391	0.237	0.539	0.286
Poland	1.714	0.895	2.202	1.056
Romania	0.319	0.191	0.332	0.178
Soviet Union	0.524	0.226	0.630	0.263
Yugoslavia	1.327	0.917	1.215	0.841
Albania	0.254	0.082	0.222	0.065
Eastern Europe 9	0.579	0.316	0.656	0.336
Eastern Europe 6	0.518	0.270	0.639	0.309

[28] In comparing the first or third columns of Tables 7.1–7.2 with those of Tables 7.3–7.4, one first notices that the absolute size of the errors has increased. This is exactly what one would

the better performance of the CPEs using the HO model, and the worse performance of the CPEs using the PE model—are completely unaltered. There is no way the results of Tables 7.3 and 7.4 would force one to qualify the conclusions of the previous section. The conclusions do not seem to depend critically on the assumption that the sources of inefficiencies are not correlated with resource endowments across countries.

7.7. Conclusions

The results of this chapter show that the trade patterns of the socialist and capitalist economies are quite similar when examined using the Heckscher-Ohlin model. However, when the product differentiation and economies of scale model is employed, the opposite is the case. The results of Chapter 4

Table 7.4.
Error Statistics (*GF* and *GF'*) from the PE Model with a Proxy
for Government Intervention

	Model P		Model PG	
	GF	*GF'*	*GF*	*GF'*
All	1.580	1.000	1.568	1.000
Market	1.586	1.025	1.341	0.970
OECD	1.338	0.892	1.279	0.907
Market minus OECD	1.835	1.157	1.403	1.034
Low-income OECD	1.204	0.911	1.436	0.928
Bulgaria	2.026	1.392	4.571	2.270
Czechoslovakia	1.620	1.416	3.956	2.111
East Germany	0.879	0.651	3.169	1.360
Hungary	1.808	0.920	2.514	0.975
Poland	2.077	1.786	5.950	2.929
Romania	2.143	1.595	5.120	2.339
Soviet Union	0.738	0.424	1.336	0.560
Yugoslavia	3.087	1.339	2.979	1.284
Albania	6.051	3.081	3.231	2.064
Eastern Europe 9	2.270	1.400	3.647	1.766
Eastern Europe 6	1.759	1.293	4.213	1.997

expect if the addition of CGS improved the estimate of the efficient trade pattern. Hence, one can have some confidence in the fact that CGS is playing the role of a proxy for government intervention.

also showed marked differences between the two sets of economies. Thus, despite the results for Heckscher-Ohlin, the conclusion of the chapter *cannot* be that the trade patterns of MEs and of CPEs are similar in general. Rather, the conclusion must be that the two systems are similar only in the aspects of economic performance captured by the HO model. In other aspects, they are quite different.

The HO model focuses on the static allocation of physical resources. But, as has been argued repeatedly in the foregoing pages, there are many other important—perhaps more important—elements in economic performance. The HO model, as conventionally formulated, omits these aspects of performance. Therefore, when that model is estimated, differences between the economies on these aspects will not be captured in the resultant comparisons of goodness-of-fit measures. Instead, the measures will capture the aspects of performance that are the focus of the HO model—rationality in the allocation of physical resources.

The theory underlying the PE model includes some consideration of the elements of economic performance that are the focus of the Schumpeterian analysis. To be sure, the PE model is not formulated from a Schumpeterian perspective, but it is closer to that perspective than the HO model. Hence, when the socialist economies fare much worse on the goodness-of-fit tests for PE than for HO, one can clearly interpret the differences in trade patterns between MEs and CPEs as reflecting differences in the aspects of economic performance emphasized by the Schumpeterian model, but not by the neoclassical model.

EPILOGUE

▬▬▬▬▬▬▬▬

The Results and Some Questions They Raise

Do not speak lightly of the three volume novel, Cecily. I wrote one myself
in those earlier days. . . . The good ended happily, and the bad unhappily.
That is what Fiction means.
Miss Prism in *The Importance of Being Earnest*

In this epilogue I summarize the principal features of the preceding pages—
the nature of the differences between Schumpeterian and neoclassical paradigms, and the empirical results that most directly reflect on those differences.
I then reflect briefly on an issue that has been ignored thus far—the significance
of the results for the future of the socialist countries. I do this by posing a
number of questions about the process of economic reform, questions that
arise naturally only on acceptance of the Schumpeterian framework.

The central message of this book has focused on the differences between
two views of the nature of economic activity. The neoclassical approach
emphasizes analysis of the equilibrium allocation of physical resources in an
environment in which there is a fixed set of institutions. That approach leads
one to stress the incentives facing economic agents who make production
decisions, the informational role of prices, and the cumbersomeness of large-
scale bureaucracy in allocating resources in a complex modern economy.

The Schumpeterian approach downplays the significance of analysis of the
equilibrium allocation of resources. Instead, as the key aspect of economic
performance, Schumpeterians emphasize the generation of technological and
organizational innovation, the adoption of those innovations, and the means
by which the economy adapts to those innovations. In the Schumpeterian
view, the process of economic innovation under capitalism is best characterized as an evolutionary mechanism in which many new ideas are generated,
often by new entrants into an industry, and in which the economic system
chooses the most successful innovations. A major component in the spread
of innovations is change in the relative size of organizations—the growth of
the successful organization and the possible demise of those that made the
wrong choices or that were less innovative. Thus, in analyzing the economic
performance of socialist economies, Schumpeterians would emphasize the
rigidity of institutional structure and the absence of mechanisms to select
efficient organizations and foster their growth.

When viewed in the composite, the evidence in this book shows that the essential differences between capitalist and socialist economies lie in the factors emphasized in the Schumpeterian perspective and not in those stressed by the neoclassical model. Some of the principal features of that evidence are the following:

- When examining how closely the trade data of different countries fit a neoclassical model of efficient static resource allocation (the Heckscher-Ohlin model of trade), the socialist economies appear to be as efficient as the capitalist economies. Moreover, the socialist countries have a comparative advantage in sectors whose behavior leads to static inefficiencies in Western economies—the sectors with high concentration levels. Hence, it is difficult to argue that inefficiency in static resource allocation is the particular problem of the socialist economies.
- When one examines a model of trade that better captures aspects of the Schumpeterian paradigm, the peculiarities of the socialist economies become apparent. Capitalist trade data fit much better than the socialist data.
- Many of the traditional hypotheses formulated from a neoclassical perspective are not evidenced in trade data. For example, trade patterns do not evidence a strong capital-intensive bias. In contrast, the hypotheses of the Schumpeterian model fare well. For example, the socialist countries perform less well on product innovation than on process innovation and have a comparative disadvantage in sectors in which there is a large amount of entry of new firms.
- When one uses the HO model, the decentralized socialist economies, Hungary and Yugoslavia, seem to be less efficient than the orthodox centrally planned economies. On most of the results reflecting the Schumpeterian perspective, these two economies look very much like their socialist neighbors. Hence, decentralization as presently undertaken in Eastern Europe— the type that is consistent with the neoclassical model—does not seem to improve the allocation of resources. This is a prediction of the Schumpeterian model, which emphasizes that natural selection, not decentralization, is the essence of the market.
- In many sectors in which the socialist countries have a low level of exports, because of intrinsic weaknesses in their economies, there is also a low level of imports. This is the case, for example, where multinationals are important, even though these are high-technology sectors. The low level of imports is consistent with the Schumpeterian perspective, which emphasizes that new technologies cannot be easily transferred at arm's length, but instead must be spread by the expansion of existing firms.

In summary, this book's results show that the real difference between capitalism and socialism is that the latter, as presently constituted, does not possess a mechanism that is able to generate new institutions, select the productive ones, and foster their growth. The results do not lead one to focus, as is traditional, on the process of allocation of resources between a fixed set of institutions.

In many ways, this summary raises more questions than it answers, because there is no systematic account of the implications of the Schumpeterian view of the world for the future of the socialist economies and for their possibilities for reform, and no such account can be given here because it would surely require another book. In closing, however, I offer some preliminary thoughts on those implications. These thoughts are in the form of questions about the reform of socialist economies that seem to follow immediately from the empirical conclusions. Although I only pose these questions and do not answer them, the very fact that they can be entertained shows the profound implications of accepting the Schumpeterian view.

Is the market-socialist model irrelevant in designing reforms? As Chapter 1 makes clear, the market-socialist model of Lange has played a significant role in guiding economists' thoughts on the reform of the socialist economies. This model lies at the center of the neoclassical tradition and thus emphasizes the very features that this book claims are of secondary importance. If the market-socialist model places emphasis in the wrong place, one might conclude that use of that model is counterproductive in understanding the issues in economic reform. Indeed, one might conjecture that reforms based on that model actually worsen performance, because the discipline of central planning is lost, without any gain in the features emphasized by the Schumpeterian view. There is some evidence for this conjecture in the results for Hungary and Yugoslavia presented in the preceding chapters.

Is price reform the sine qua non of general economic reform? One often encounters the argument that all attempts to reform must fail if reformers do not begin by reforming the price system. But this book argues that the effects of irrational prices in the economic data of the socialist countries cannot easily be detected. This is not to argue that present prices are rational, but rather that existing irrationalities perhaps do not have a profound effect on the performance of the economic system. Moreover, if price reform occurred, the most important problems identified by the Schumpeterian perspective would remain—for example, the lack of free entry.

There are very important costs in adjusting prices. As Granick (1987) emphasizes, the existence of stable relative prices is a major factor in guaranteeing the system of job rights in the Soviet Union. A radical change in prices therefore implies that workers will lose one of the most important benefits they gain from the existing economic system. Moreover, any use of scarcity prices would lead initially to enormous inequalities in a system that is not presently at equilibrium.

Price reform in the present institutional environment would therefore have large immediate costs and, if this book's argument is correct, few immediate benefits. The real benefits of price reform could come only after a long period of institutional reform. Scarcity prices created at the beginning of that period would hardly be relevant to the economic environment at the end of that period. Thus, given the timing of the benefits and costs of price adjustments, one might conjecture that these adjustments are better delayed until the process of institutional reform is well under way.

Which should be the first steps in an economic reform? If there are many changes to be made in an economic system, reformers must pay attention to the chronological sequence of change. Because each alteration in the system has a cost—the reduction in some group's income or status, for example— it is important to consider which changes reap the highest reward.

Analyzing the issue from a Schumpeterian perspective, one should focus upon the extent to which a particular change can produce new organizations that are automatically evaluated by the economic system and that can be removed if they prove unfit. It seems clear that design of organizations is not a process that can rely solely upon the application of intellectual cost-benefit analysis, given the present state of knowledge. Present-day policy-makers just do not have the theory and the information to decide on an a priori basis whether managerial socialism, self-management, leasing of state capital by private entrepreneurs, a joint venture, or a multinational corporation is most appropriate in a particular economic sector, given the existing economic environment. Hence, a variety of alternatives must be tried and evaluated *ex post*. The benefits from organizational change under socialism will, therefore, depend crucially on the extent to which the system is able to create and evaluate a variety of organizational forms.

The initial costs of an organizational change lie in the threat posed by the new organizations to existing institutions. Moreover, as some of the new forms of organization succeed, large costs will arise if the inefficient organizations cannot be swiftly removed from the economic system.

Given the sources of the costs and benefits of organizational change, one can identify areas in which reforms might be the most productive. For example, reformers should encourage the formation of new institutions in the rural sector, particularly for light industrial production. The inevitable small size of the new institutions and their geographical isolation would facilitate the process of generation of a variety of organizational forms. Moreover, small size and rural location probably imply weak political power, so that these new organizations are much more likely to be evaluated according to their productive potential rather than their political influence. It is surely no coincidence that the successful part of the Chinese reforms largely lies in the countryside, where agriculture and associated light industry have been allowed to advance, or fail, independently of the many political constraints that affect urban industry. This success is exactly consistent with the Schumpeterian emphasis on the effectiveness of a process that searches for and selects suitable organizational forms.

Given the nature of the costs and benefits of reforms identified by the Schumpeterian model, the initial reforms could also be aimed at using the ready-made lessons about economic activity that foreign organizations have learned. And as the Schumpeterian model emphasizes, the only sure way to learn these lessons is to invite the multinational corporations to participate in the domestic economy. To create as little domestic opposition as possible, the MNCs could participate in sectors in which the socialist countries have not previously specialized, particularly in the production of light industrial consumer goods. With the use of foreign organizations in nontraditional sectors, it is likely that the growth of such organizations could be largely dependent on their own success, a necessary component of the Schumpeterian process. Moreover, foreign entities would surely have less weight in bargaining for subsidies if they are unsuccessful. Thus, the gradual demise of the unsuccessful, another Schumpeterian component, is assured.

Need reforms be comprehensive? It is a common assumption that the only successful reforms are comprehensive reforms, but the analysis in the above paragraphs effectively argues the opposite. That analysis emphasizes not blanket reforms but rather the search for sectors in which the process of free entry is least likely to damage established interests and in which the process of selection of the most productive organizations is least likely to be impeded.

It is intellectual hubris to suppose that efficient organizational forms can be designed anew for all existing institutions in the economy. Experiment is the only way to discover efficient institutional structures. It is political folly to think that the status of large institutions, such as the most important heavy industrial plants, can be radically changed in the near future. A gradual process, in which political power is eventually checked by the transparent efficiency of the new organizations, is necessary. Therefore, a policy following from the Schumpeterian perspective emphasizes identifying the areas of activity where the search for efficient organizational alternatives can take place through trial and error, unimpeded by existing rigidities. Existing areas of activity that do not have these conditions would not be changed initially. The argument for such a policy, of course, relies upon the finding that it is not intersectoral resource allocation that is the basic problem of the socialist economies. By definition, the problem of efficiency in economy-wide resource allocation could be addressed only by a comprehensive reform.

Can the socialist systems produce the types of reforms that are necessary for success in a Schumpeterian world? This question can best be considered by asking some more limited questions. Could one imagine a situation in which a new organization arose because of the discovery of a very successful product, where this institution's growth was astounding, and where that growth was determined principally by the institution's own success? Examples of such phenomena can be found in all capitalist economies that have the standard of living to which the socialist countries aspire. Could this happen in a country where all the institutions were publicly owned?

It seems clear that such changes could not really occur in the socialist nations of Eastern Europe as these countries are presently constituted. If organizational growth and decline of the type witnessed in capitalist countries were to occur, some very basic mores of economic behavior would need to change in the socialist countries. A very different institutional structure would have to be built. In existing economic thought, there is no blueprint for a socialist system that is designed on Schumpeterian principles. Nobody has confronted what it means to implement the Schumpeterian model in the socialist societies in the same way that Lange and the Hungarians faced the issue of what market socialism means. Hence, the answer to one of the most important questions on the future of the socialist economies must await future developments in economic thought. The existing literature provides not even the seed of an answer.

What is the essential trade-off in the implementation of reforms? The standard neoclassical answer to this question is that reforms provide an increase in allocative efficiency while creating a decrease in equality. The Schumpeterian perspective focuses on the problem of institutional rigidity under socialism rather than on resource allocation. One concomitant of this rigidity is a significant benefit that the socialist countries provide their workers—a security of employment that is not matched by capitalist countries. It seems clear that any increase in the flexibility of the institutional structure would lead to some loss in that security. There simply is no way that the relative size of different organizations can change radically without some mechanism that forces workers to move between jobs. Thus, the trade-off the Schumpeterian model would emphasize is "dynamism versus security" rather than "efficiency versus equality."

When the essential trade-off is presented in this manner, the choices facing the socialist countries seem much more difficult. If security of employment is one of the paramount goals of workers, as is my guess, then acceptance of the Schumpeterian model would cause economists to undertake a fundamental reevaluation of the nature of the benefits and costs of economic reform under socialism. Moreover, that reevaluation must also apply to the conventional economic analysis of the relative properties of capitalism and socialism.

APPENDIX A

▃▃▃▃▃▃▃▃▃▃

Do RCAs Reveal Comparative Advantage?

Section 2.2 used a diagrammatic analysis to examine whether the numerical values of revealed comparative advantages (RCAs) reflect differences in comparative advantage across nations. This appendix strengthens the conclusions of that analysis by examining the same question within an algebraic framework that is more general than the diagrammatic one.The analysis is conducted assuming that the standard Heckscher-Ohlin model explains the pattern of trade. For that model, the term ''comparative advantage'' is usually used in a binary fashion: a country either has a comparative advantage in a good or it does not. Given this usage, the RCAs obviously indicate comparative advantage, but for the purposes of empirical work, one would like to make stronger statements than binary ones.

Ultimately, the aim of using RCAs is to translate observations on trade into statements about factor endowments. For some of the empirical analyses, such statements require a judgment concerning which country has been relatively more successful in exporting a particular good. That is, one would like to say which of two countries has a ''greater comparative advantage'' in a particular good.[1]

To examine whether the RCAs give an appropriate indication of degree of comparative advantage, one must construct a *ceteris paribus* scenario in which export performance unambiguously rises. It is not sufficient solely to postulate an increase in the value of exports in the good in question, however. If the increase is small and occurs simultaneously with large increases in the exports of other goods, it is not clear that the increase in exports represents a rise in the degree of comparative advantage.[2]

In the following discussion, it is assumed that the resource endowments of

---

[1] Such statements become absolutely necessary in a world in which intraindustry trade occurs, because in that case one cannot rely on either exports or imports being zero as in a pure Heckscher-Ohlin world. See Section 4.2.

[2] It is easy to construct a scenario in which the exports of a good i increase even if the relative endowment of the factors intensive in its production decrease. This would be the case if, for example, the endowments intensive in some importables decreased a great deal at the same time as the endowments intensive in i declined relative to the average. The exports of i might then increase because of the increase in total trade in the economy as a whole.

country j have changed in such a way that, if world prices were to remain constant, country j's production of good i would increase, j's production of all other goods would decline, and the value of j's aggregate production would remain constant. If world prices remained constant, then, j's exports of i would increase and the exports of all other goods would decline. This is exactly the scenario under which one would say that j's comparative advantage in good i increases. The following analysis examines whether, after all the resultant changes in the world economy, the increased comparative advantage is reflected in an increase in the value of the appropriate RCA.

The difficulty in the analysis, the one ignored in Hillman (1980), is that world prices react to the initial change in endowments, the effect being a decline in the price of i. All countries then react to this price change. In the final equilibrium, j still produces more i than before the change in resource endowments, and its exports of i have increased by dX_{ij}. I examine the effect of dX_{ij} on x_{ij}, the revealed comparative advantage.

In constructing the following argument, it was first necessary to decide on a mode of discourse. A diagrammatic analysis would be impossible, because at several points the argument involves changes in the trade flows of at least three goods.[3] A complete algebraic treatment would involve more mathematical, theoretical, and notational setup costs than could be justified, given the status of the argument in the present work. Moreover, the conclusions to be derived are in themselves unexceptionable. Thus, most readers would be willing to accept a discourse at a lower level of rigor than that of a full general equilibrium analysis. In the following I eschew the use of a formal model and employ a combination of verbal and mathematical arguments. Obviously, such arguments require strong simplifying assumptions.

There is only one way in which the simplifying assumptions alter the basic economic content of the problem at hand. At some stages it is assumed that aggregate non-i exportables do not differ greatly from aggregate importables in any manner other than in the differing intensities of resource use in production. That is, I assume that many properties that hold for the aggregate of all goods also hold for aggregate importables and aggregate exportables separately. The reason such assumptions are necessary is that x_{ij} accounts for only half of trade behavior. If exportables and importables differed in their properties, then the behavior of x_{ij} might reflect shifts in aggregate trade patterns even though net exports do not change. Thus, one reason x_{ij} might fail to reflect comparative advantage is that it ignores half of trade behavior—imports. One can therefore immediately conclude that the w_{ij} are more likely to be well behaved than the x_{ij} or the m_{ij}.

The argument leading to the two theorems proceeds in two separate steps.

[3] Readers should note, however, that a diagramatic analysis using only two goods is extremely helpful in providing the basic intuition behind some of the reasoning that follows.

First, some basic simplifying assumptions are made. These assumptions lead to five inequalities.[4] Then, in the proofs of the two theorems, the inequalities combine with some simple calculus to establish the conditions sufficient to conclude that dx_{ij}/dX_{ij} is positive.

Two basic assumptions facilitate the ensuing discussion. First, it is assumed that the prices of all goods other than i do not change relative to each other when j's factor endowments change. This assumption is much stronger than would be needed if one were to employ a full general equilibrium argument to prove the two theorems. For such a proof, one would only need to assume that the relative changes within the non-i prices are "relatively small" compared with the change in the price of i relative to any of the non-i prices.

Given the above assumption, one can use the price level of the non-i goods as the numeraire in the discussion that follows. Thus, after the change in j's factor endowments, the price of i falls and the prices of all other goods remain constant.

The purpose of the second assumption is to ensure that aggregate exports and aggregate imports are separately Hicksian substitutes for good i in consumption and also substitute outputs for i in production. If this were not the case, then it would be conceivable, for example, that the aggregate exports of a country could precipitously decline in response to the *ceteris paribus* decrease in the price of i. Unfortunately, because the argument requires that these substitute relations hold for all countries separately, and because each country exports a different set of goods, a strong assumption is needed, solely in order to reduce the complexities of the argument. It is assumed that i is a Hicksian substitute for all other goods in consumption and also a substitute in production.[5]

Before proceeding to the derivations of the five inequalities, it is helpful to define notation. First, remember that x_{ij} is given by:

$$x_{ij} = \frac{\left[X_{ij} \bigg/ \sum_{n=1}^{N} X_{nj} \right]}{\left[\sum_{t=1}^{T} X_{it} \bigg/ \sum_{n=1}^{N} \sum_{t=1}^{T} X_{nt} \right]}.$$

---

[4] If one were to give the argument a mathematical gloss, the deductions of the five inequalities would be called lemmas.

[5] When the reader encounters the use of this assumption, it will become apparent that it could be replaced by much weaker conditions, if a more detailed argument were used. All one really requires is that, for any country, two weak conditions hold: (1) the derivative of the aggregate consumption of exportables, excluding i, with respect to the price of i has the same sign as the similar derivative of the aggregate consumption of importables, excluding i; (2) the derivative of the aggregate production of exportables, excluding i, with respect to the price of i has the same sign as the similar derivative of the aggregate production of importables, excluding i.

Define X^i as world exports of good i excluding X_{ij}, X_j as the total exports of country j excluding X_{ij}, and X as world exports of all goods excluding X_{ij}. Then, x_{ij} can be rewritten as:

$$x_{ij} = \frac{X_{ij}/(X_{ij} + X_j)}{(X_{ij} + X^i)/(X + X_{ij})} .$$

For the arguments below, it is important to remember that the RCAs are calculated using trade flows measured in value terms. Thus, all the X variables in the formula for x_{ij} are value, not quantity, measures.

Inequality (A.1) examines the way the rest-of-the-world's exports of good i change as country j exports more i. The initial change is one in j's factor endowments, which caused j's exports of i and world supply of i to increase. Therefore, the price of i falls. Now examine the set, S, of countries (omitting j) that were net exporters of i in the original situation. Relative price changes affect the consumption of these countries in two ways—through the usual route of substitution and income effects on demand, and also because there is a decline in real income suffered by the net exporters of i. Both these effects imply that S's consumption of non-i goods must decline. Production of non-i goods must rise in S. Therefore the quantity, and hence the value, of the net exports of non-i goods by each country in S must rise. To maintain balance in trade, the value of net exports of i by each of these countries must fall.[6] Because S is the set of exporters of i omitting j, the value of world non-j exports of i (X^i) will fall:

$$\frac{dX^i}{dX_{ij}} \leqq 0 . \tag{A.1}$$

The intuition behind (A.1) is obvious. Country j has become relatively better suited to exporting good i. The rest of the world then becomes less suited to exporting i: non-j exports of i do not rise.

Total trade must remain balanced for country j. Hence, the aggregate value of the net exports of goods other than i declines when the value of exports of good i rises. Thus, j's aggregate consumption of all goods other than i decreases less than the aggregate production of these goods. Let us assume that this is separately the case for exported goods (except i) taken in the aggregate and for imported goods taken in the aggregate.[7] This assumption would hold if those goods that are exported, taken in the aggregate, do not have demand-and-supply elasticities that differ greatly from those goods that are imported, taken in the aggregate. This is not a strong assumption in the

[6] It is quite possible that the quantity of i exports by S will rise. That is why it is important to bear in mind that X_{ij} is measured in value terms.

[7] Here again one finds an assumption needed to ensure that a property that holds for all goods holds for exportables alone.

case when there are many goods, and when some of the exogenous determinants of the elasticities can vary independently of some of the determinants of whether a good is exported or imported. If this assumption holds, then the aggregate value of i's exports of goods other than j (that is, X_j) must decline as a result of the increase in X_{ij}:

$$\frac{dX_j}{dX_{ij}} \leqq 0 . \tag{A.2}$$

Inequality (A.2) has a clear intuitive interpretation. When the comparative advantage in good i has increased relative to all other goods, one would expect the aggregate exports of other goods to decline.

Inequality (A.3) considers the change in the total value of world exports other than j's of i (that is, X). First, consider the element $X - X^i - X_j$—the non-i exports of all countries other than j. There are three influences tending to change the levels of these exports:[8]

1. The increase in the production of non-i goods due to the change in the price of i (p_i).
2. The usual substitution and income effects on consumption resultant from the reduction in p_i.
3. An extra income effect on consumption because the value of a country's national income changes as p_i changes. This effect works in opposite directions on net exporters and net importers of i.

Influences 1 and 2 tend to increase exports of non-i goods, as does influence 3 in net-exporting countries. Thus, to place a lower bound on the change in $X - X^i - X_j$, one must examine the possible size of influence 3 on net importers of i.

The possibility most likely to be harmful for the properties of the RCA of good i is if the net importers used all the money saved on imports of i (from the reduction in p_i) to increase their consumption of their own exportables and therefore reduce their exports of non-i goods. Then good i might appear more important in world exports, increasing the denominator of x_{ij}.[9] We must establish conditions such that the increase in the denominator does not lead to a decrease in the ratio as a whole.

When the price of i changes, the money income saved by the net importers of i is $-dp_i$ times the quantity of world imports of i. Thus, $X - X_j - X^i$ cannot decline by more than dp_i times world imports of i. To create an

[8] Remember that the effect on non-j countries of the change in X_{ij} could only come through changes in prices.

[9] At this point, one can see that the possibility of problems with x_{ij} is solely due to the fact that it includes only half of trade behavior. Under this "worst case" scenario, imports also decline. Therefore, any measure that used both imports and exports would not be adversely affected by this worst case.

inequality that is usable in Theorem A.1, one must relate the resultant reduction in exports to dX_{ij}.

The scenario under consideration is one in which an exogenous change in
j's resource endowments causes a change in the world price of i and consequent
changes in world production, consumption, exports, and imports. Let η_i be
the absolute value of the demand elasticity which summarizes the general
equilibrium relationship between world consumption of i and p_i that is consequent on these changes.

Because non-j production of i declines, non-j consumption of i rises by
less than dX_{ij}. Using this fact and the knowledge that identical homothetic
preferences imply that consumption is proportional to GNP, the following
inequality holds:

$$dX_{ij}/p_i > \frac{(1 - \text{GNP of } j)}{\text{world GNP}} \cdot (\text{change in quantity of world consumption of } i).$$

Combining the information in the preceding paragraphs:

$$d(X - X^i - X_j) > \frac{-1}{\eta_i} \cdot dX_{ij} \cdot \frac{(\text{world imports of } i)}{\text{world consumption of } i}$$

$$\cdot \frac{(\text{world GNP})}{(\text{world GNP} - \text{GNP of } j)}.$$

Because total imports must be less than total consumption:

$$\frac{dX}{dX_{ij}} > \frac{-1}{\eta_i} \cdot \frac{(\text{world GNP})}{(\text{world GNP} - \text{GNP of } j)}. \tag{A.3}$$

The intuition behind inequality (A.3) is easily seen. The smaller is η_i the
greater is the change in the price of i resultant from a given change in j's
resource endowments. Therefore, the smaller is η_i the more able is an importer
of i to reduce exports of other goods and still maintain a trade balance.[10]
Thus, the lower bound on the change in X is closer to zero the larger η_i is.
Similarly, the smaller world GNP is, the greater will be the effect on p_i of a
given change in j's resource endowments, and hence the further the bound
from zero.

Given some extra notation, we are ready to prove Theorem A.1, which
examines the conditions under which x_{ij} has the desired properties. Define:

$1/u = j$'s exports of i as a proportion of world trade in i,
$1/v = j$'s exports of i as a proportion of j's total exports,
$1/g = j$'s GNP as a proportion of world GNP.

[10] Net exporters of i will increase their exports of non-i products.

THEOREM A.1

$$\text{If } 1 - \frac{2}{3(u + v) + 2|u - v| - 2} \cdot \frac{1}{\eta_i} \cdot \frac{g}{g - 1} - \frac{1}{v} - \frac{1}{u} > 0,$$

then

$$\frac{dx_{ij}}{dX_{ij}} > 0 .$$

Proof

If both u and v are greater than 1, there must be at least three countries in the world. Normalizing X_{ij} at 1 unit, i exports $\{v - 1\}$ of non-i, a second country exports $(u - 1)$ of i, and there must be, at least, further trade flows involving a third country of $[u - v]$ and v (if $u > v$) or $[v - u]$ and u (if $v > u$). Hence, world trade must be at least $[3(u + v)/2] + |u - v| - 1$. Differentiating x_{ij} with respect to X_{ij}:

$$\frac{dx_{ij}}{dX_{ij}} = x_{ij} \left[\frac{1}{X_{ij}} + \frac{dX/dX_{ij} + 1}{X_{ij} + X} - \frac{dX_j/dX_{ij} + 1}{X_{ij} + X_j} - \frac{dX^i/dX_{ij} + 1}{X_{ij} + X^i} \right] .$$

Now

$$\frac{dX}{dX_{ij}} = \frac{d(X - X^i - X_j)}{dX_{ij}} + \frac{dX^i}{dX_{ij}} + \frac{dX_j}{dX_{ij}} .$$

Thus, dx_{ij}/dX_{ij} is purely a function of the derivatives appearing in inequalities (A.1), (A.2), and (A.3) and of u, v, g, and η_i. One immediately obtains the theorem by substituting those inequalities into the above expression. Q.E.D.

The meaning of the inequality contained in the theorem is not very transparent, but in some simple cases its implications can be seen. Suppose $u = v = g$. Then, one can easily show that dx_{ij}/dX_{ij} must be positive if $(u - 4)$ is greater than $1/3\eta_i$. If u is 5 (i is 20% of j's trade and j accounts for 20% of world trade and production), then η_i must be greater than $1/3$ for the sufficient condition to hold. If the percentage figure drops to 10%, then η_i need only be larger than $1/18$. It easy to see that the overwhelming majority of situations will be consistent with the inequality established in the theorem.

Theorem A.2 examines the relationship between changes in x_{ij} and x_{it}, where t is a country that also exports good i. For this theorem, one must establish bounds on the change in X_t, the total exports of t minus X_{it}. The reasoning is the same as in establishing (A.3), but much simpler, because t is an exporter of i. The three effects on X_t due to the decrease in p_i—the change in production of non-i goods, the change in the consumption of non-i goods due to the substitution effect, and the change in consumption due to the income effect—all act in the same direction, to increase non-i exports. Thus, it is immediately clear that:

$$\frac{dX_t}{dX_{ij}} \geqq 0 \ . \tag{A.4}$$

Inequality (A.5) is implied by the arguments justifying (A.1), which apply to the non-i countries both individually and collectively:

$$\frac{dX_{it}}{dX_{ij}} \leqq 0 \ . \tag{A.5}$$

Theorem A.2 analyzes the conditions under which the relative change in the RCAs of the two countries is appropriate, given the assumed change in factor endowments. The restrictions in this theorem are much less stringent than those in the previous one, because t's change in behavior with respect to good i is completely reflected in x_{it}.

THEOREM A.2

If v is greater than 2, then an increase in X_{ij} causes x_{ij}/x_{it} to rise.

Proof

Because the denominators in the expressions defining x_{ij} and x_{it} are identical, their ratio simplifies to:

$$\frac{x_{ij}}{x_{it}} = \frac{(X_{ij}/X_{ij} + X_j)}{(X_{it}/X_{it} + X_t)} \ .$$

Therefore,

$$\frac{d}{dX_{ij}} \left[\frac{x_{ij}}{x_{it}} \right] = \left[\frac{x_{ij}}{x_{it}} \right] \cdot \left[\frac{1}{X_{ij}} + \frac{dX_{in}}{dX_{ij}} \left[\frac{1}{X_{it} + X_t} - \frac{1}{X_{it}} \right] \right.$$
$$\left. + \frac{dX_t}{dX_{ij}} \cdot \frac{1}{X_{it} + X_t} - \left[\frac{dX_j}{dX_{ij}} + 1 \right] \cdot \frac{1}{X_{ij} + X_j} \right]$$

Using inequalities (A.4) and (A.5) and the definition of v:

$$\frac{d}{dX_{ij}} \left[\frac{x_{ij}}{x_{it}} \right] = \left[\frac{x_{ij}}{x_{it}} \right] \cdot \frac{1}{X_{ij}} \cdot \left(1 - \frac{2}{v} \right) \ .$$

The right-hand side is positive if v is greater than 2. Q.E.D.

APPENDIX B

██████████████

Derivation of Equations Representing Trade Models

This appendix presents the assumptions and the analysis necessary to derive the relations between trade and endowments that are given in Chapter 3.

The Heckscher-Ohlin Model

This section derives equation (3.1) of Section 3.1. Because the Heckscher-Ohlin model is now the standard in trade theory, there is no need here for a complete derivation that painstakingly fills in all intermediate steps.[1] Instead, the focus here is on details that are particularly pertinent in obtaining equation (3.1). The analysis follows that of Leamer (1984, pp. 2–10, 158–160).

The basic assumptions are as follows:

HO-1. There are fixed endowments of S primary factors, which are mobile within countries but cannot cross borders. V_{kj} denotes the jth country's endowment of factor k.

HO-2. Each country produces N goods. The amount produced of each good is a function of the total endowments used in the sector, where that function exhibits constant returns-to-scale. Q_{ij} is the amount of good i produced by country j.

HO-3. $S = N$, the number of goods equals the number of factors. In a more general analysis, one could assume that $N \geq S$. For the ways in which models with $N > S$ can be converted to ones with $N = S$, one should consult either Leamer (1984, pp. 16–18) or Anderson (1987, p. 147).

HO-4. Technology is the same across all countries. A discussion of the meaning and validity of this assumption is in Section 3.3.

HO-5. The structure of factor endowments varies among countries less than the structure of factor input intensities varies across industries.[2]

---

[1] Such an analysis can be found in standard textbooks—for example, Bhagwati and Srinivasan 1983.

[2] For the meaning of this assumption the reader is referred to either Bhagwati and Srinivasan 1983, pp. 56–58, or Leamer 1984, pp. 5–7. Although the assumption is important in deriving

HO-6. Production decisions are made *as if* profits are being maximized. The conditions under which this is the case are considered in Section 3.1.

HO-7. The structure of income distribution and demand functions is such that the consumption of any particular good, at given prices, is the same proportion of national income in all countries.

HO-8. Transportation costs are zero.

HO-9. Trade is balanced for all countries.

HO-10. There are no tariffs, export subsidies, or other trade impediments.

The analysis begins with equations for the demand and supply of resources. Given identical technologies in all countries and factor price equalization, which is implied by the assumptions, input-output coefficients are identical across countries. Let a_{ki} be the amount of resource k used to produce one unit of good i. Then:

$$V_{kj} = \sum_{i=1}^{S} a_{ki} Q_{ij} . \tag{B.1}$$

Given factor-price equalization and constant returns-to-scale:

$$G_j = \sum_{i=1}^{N} p_i Q_{ij} = \sum_{k=1}^{S} \gamma_k V_{kj} , \tag{B.2}$$

where G_j is the national income of country j, p_i is the price of good i, and γ_k is the price of endowment k. It is convenient here to use the "dot" notation to form vectors: an entity with a dot subscript indicates the column vector formed by listing all the variables obtained by varying the subscript that is replaced by the dot. For example $V'_{.j} = (V_{1j}, \ldots, V_{Nj})$. The input-output coefficients can be taken to form the matrix $A = \{a_{ki}\}$. Then if A is invertible, (B.1) becomes:

$$Q_{.j} = A^{-1} V_{.j} . \tag{B.3}$$

Net exports, W_{ij}, are the difference between production and consumption: $W_{.j} = Q_{.j} - C_{.j}$, where $C_{.j}$ is the consumption vector of country j. Given assumption HO-7, and introducing the parameters c_i, which represent the proportion of national income spent on good i, the following equation describes the cross-country pattern of consumption:

$$C_{.j} = c_. G_j . \tag{B.4}$$

Denote world values with a w subscript. Because the world production of every good must equal world consumption:

$$c_. = \frac{A^{-1} V_{.w}}{G_w} ,$$

---

the conclusions, detailed discussion, which would involve a greater diversion into the mechanics of production economics than is merited in the present context, is not appropriate here.

then

$$W_{.j} = Q_{.j} - C_{.j}$$

$$= A^{-1}V_{.j} - c_.G_j \qquad (B.5)$$

$$= A^{-1}V_{.j} - A^{-1}V_{.w}(G_j/G_w) .$$

Denoting the elements of A inverse by $\bar{a}_{ij}$ and using equation (B.2):

$$W_{ij} = \sum_{k=1}^{S}\left[\bar{a}_{ik} - \frac{\gamma_k}{G_w}\left(\sum_{s=1}^{S} \bar{a}_{is}V_{sw}\right)\right]V_{kj} . \qquad (B.6)$$

Noting that the term in square brackets is independent of j and thus constant across countries, one obtains equation system (3.1) of Section 3.1.

The Product Differentiation and Economies of Scale Model

I now undertake a similar analysis in a model that allows for product differentiation in consumption and economies of scale in production, the PE model. The analysis results in equation system (3.2) of Section 3.2. Here, I follow closely Helpman and Krugman (1985), although I emphasize different elements of the trade equilibrium. The reader is therefore directed to that work for many of the details that have been omitted from the necessarily brief exposition given here.

The assumptions which follow parallel those of the Heckscher-Ohlin model. The notation "PE" signifies the two elements that constitute the main differences between the two models—*product differentiation* and *economies of scale*:

PE-1. Assumptions on factor endowments are the same as HO-1.

PE-2. There are N goods. Each of these N goods can be produced in an infinite number of varieties. The production function for each variety exhibits economies of scale, at least at low levels of output. Each variety of a single good has the same production function, but such functions vary between goods. Q_{ij} is the jth country's aggregate output of all varieties of the ith good.

PE-3. Assumptions on the relation between the numbers of goods and factors are the same as HO-3.

PE-4. As in HO-4, technology does not vary across economies.

PE-5. As in HO-5, variation in relative factor endowments is less than in relative input intensities.

PE-6. Production decisions are made as if profits are being maximized. The number of firms (and hence varieties) in each sector is such that no firm makes profits.

PE-7. The structure of income distribution and demand functions is such that, if all varieties of any single good have the same price, (1) the demand functions for all varieties of any specific good are identical and (2) the aggregate consumption of any particular good, at given prices, is the same proportion of national income in all countries. (For the large number of details on the assumptions about preferences, the reader is referred to Helpman and Krugman [1985, Chap. 6]. Here I have only summarized the essential implications of these assumptions, but the reader should be warned that the exigencies of modeling producer decisions under conditions of product differentiation call for particularly strong assumptions.)

PE-8. As in Heckscher-Ohlin, transportation costs are zero.

PE-9. As in Heckscher-Ohlin, trade is balanced.

PE-10. As in Heckscher-Ohlin, there are no trade impediments.

Assumptions PE-8 and PE-10 imply that the price of any specific variety is the same across all countries. Assumptions PE-2, PE-6, and PE-7 imply that each producer sells a unique variety, that there is a finite number of varieties produced, and that each variety of the same good is produced by employing the same technique of production. Assumptions PE-4 and PE-5 imply that all countries produce some amount of every good, that factor prices are equalized across countries, and that the size of firms within any specific sector does not vary across countries. Hence, the prices of all varieties of the same good are identical.

Given the above conclusions, input-output coefficients do not vary across countries or across varieties. Thus, equations (B.1) and (B.3) hold in this new model.[3] The quantities of output in those equations are now to be interpreted as aggregate production figures: Q_{ij} is equal to the number of varieties of good i produced in country j times the output of each variety of good i. Equation (B.2) also holds because of factor-price equalization and the fact that profits in all countries have been driven to zero either by planner's decisions or by the forces of entry and exit.

With the assumptions on preferences embodied in PE-7 and the conclusions concerning producer behavior, each country will consume a proportion of each variety equal to the country's share of world income. The exports of good i by country j, X_{ij}, are then the amounts remaining of the varieties of i produced in j after consumption:

$$X_{.j} = A^{-1}V_{.j}\left[1 - \frac{G_j}{G_w}\right]. \tag{B.7}$$

---

[3] The factors influencing the values of the a_{ki} are somewhat different in the present context from those in the HO model. But given the manner in which the model is used, that difference is inconsequential.

Noting that the elements of A do not vary across countries, one obtains equation (3.2) in Chapter 3.

Country j consumes a proportion of every variety produced in the rest of the world equal to its share of world income. Thus, the imports of good i by country j, M_{ij}, are equal to the production in the rest of the world times the income share:

$$M_{.j} = (A^{-1}V_{.w} - A^{-1}V_{.j}) \cdot (G_j/G_w) . \tag{B.8}$$

Hence, by subtracting (B.7) from (B.8), one obtains an equation explaining the cross country pattern of net exports, which is identical in structure to that obtained from the HO model, (B.5).

The Effect of Nonhomotheticity on the Heckscher-Ohlin Model

Use assumptions HO-1—HO-10, replacing HO-7 by:

HO-7'. The structure of income distribution and demand functions is such that per-capita consumption, at given prices, is the same linear function of per capita income in all countries.

Then equations (B.1)–(B.3) hold, but (B.4) now becomes:

$$C_{.j} = c_{.0}r_j + c_{.1}G_j , \tag{B.4'}$$

where the $c_{.0}$ and $c_{.1}$ are vectors of parameters and r_j is the population of country j. It is at this juncture that the analysis differs slightly from that of Leamer (1984), who assumes that population is the same as labor force. I assume that the two are independent variables. This difference accounts for the extra term in my equation (3.1') compared with those appearing in Leamer (1984, p. 39).

Because world consumption must equal world production, one obtains using (B.3) and (B.4'):

$$c_{.0}r_w + c_{.1}G_w = A^{-1}V_{.w} ,$$

$$c_{.1} = (A^{-1}V_{.w} - r_w c_{.0})/G_w .$$

Then

$$W_{.j} = Q_{.j} - C_{.j}$$

$$= A^{-1}V_{.j} - c_{.0}r_j - c_{.1}G_j$$

$$= A^{-1}\left[V_{.j} - \sum_{k=1}^{S}\left(\frac{\gamma_k V_{kj}}{G_w}\right)V_{.w}\right] + c_{.0}\sum_{k=1}^{S}\frac{\gamma_k V_{kj}}{G_w}r_w - c_{.0}r_j .$$

Denoting the elements of A inverse by $\bar{a}_{ij}$:

$$W_{.j} = \sum_{k=1}^{S} \left[\bar{a}_{ik} - \frac{\gamma_k}{G_w} \left(\sum_{s=1}^{S} \bar{a}_{is} V_{sw} \right) + r_w \gamma_k \left(c_{i0}/G_w \right) \right] v_{kj} - c_{i0} r_j \;.$$

Dividing by population and denoting per capita endowments by v_{kj}:

$$\frac{W_{ij}}{r_j} = \sum_{k=1}^{S} \left[\bar{a}_{ik} - \frac{\gamma_k}{G_w} \left(\sum_{s=1}^{S} \bar{a}_{is} V_{sw} \right) + r_w \gamma_k (c_{i0}/G_w) \right] v_{kj} - c_{i0} \;,$$

which is equation (3.1') of Section 3.3.

APPENDIX C

███████████████

Interpreting the Values of RCAs in
the Presence of Intraindustry Trade

In Chapter 2 and in Section 4.1, the properties of revealed comparative advantages were examined within the context of the standard Heckscher-Ohlin model of trade. However, HO theory describes only one type of flow: interindustry trade due to differences in relative resource endowments. This appendix examines the consequences of intraindustry trade for the interpretation of RCAs.

The product-differentiation and economies-of-scale theory (the PE theory) reviewed in Section 3.2 views trade flows as comprising two components (Helpman and Krugman 1985, pp. 141–42). Intraindustry flows increase the number of varieties available for consumption, when the number efficiently produced domestically is limited by economies of scale; interindustry trade compensates for differences in resource endowments across countries. One can view the first component as balanced for each good, while any imbalance in the second reflects relative resource endowments.[1] The second component is the focus of interest in attempts to draw conclusions about the factor endowments of a country.

The way in which a particular RCA reflects differences in resource endowments depends on the size of intraindustry trade in the countries in question, but there is no way of knowing the amount of intraindustry trade precisely. Theory, however, helps. Helpman and Krugman (1985, p. 173) predict that countries with higher per capita incomes have larger shares of intraindustry trade. Balassa and Bauwens's (1984) empirical study strongly confirms this prediction. Furthermore, one can predict the types of goods in which intraindustry trade is particularly important—goods for which style and quality are important and differ between manufacturers. Thus, for example, one would expect intraindustry trade to be important for cars and clothes, but not for crude oil or raw cotton. Finally, and perhaps most importantly, theory tells

---

[1] Of course, the flows that make up the first and second components are in the same products, so the distinction between the two types of trade in a single industry is theoretical rather than anything that can be observed empirically.

us that any trade imbalance in any specific commodity category reflects resource endowment differences, not product differentiation.

Armed with the lessons of theory, one can proceed to examine the possibilities for the RCAs. Let us begin with an example. Countries A and B trade
in a multicommodity, multicountry world. Country A conducts more intraindustry trade than country B (perhaps Country A has a higher per capita income
than B). Good i is subject to a larger-than-average amount of intraindustry
trade. Assume that interindustry trade in i reflects imbalances in the endowments of a specific resource, which both A and B have in relative abundance.
Then A will certainly export more than an average amount of i, because both
interindustry trade and intraindustry trade will be high. As assumed, country
B has an insignificant amount of intraindustry trade. Thus, one can conclude
that $x_{ia} > 1$, but no condition on x_{ib} can be established. For the import RCAs,
the reverse case holds. B imports little of i, but A has large intraindustry
imports. Then, m_{ib} is certainly less than unity, but one cannot predict the size
of m_{ia}.

The argument is simpler for the export-import measures. Intraindustry exports and imports are equal for each commodity. The export figure is in the
denominator, the import figure is in the numerator. Thus, the size of intraindustry trade does not affect the ordering of w_{ij} and unity. In the present
example, both w_{ia} and w_{ib} are greater than one. However, the presence of
intraindustry trade affects the relative ordering of the two countries' indices.
Because intraindustry trade is more important in country A, its index will be
closer to 1 than B's is. Hence, $w_{ia} < w_{ib}$, even though the two countries were
assumed to have similar relative endowments of the resource that interindustry
trade in the good reflects.

One can make similar arguments for all relevant cases by varying the
example's assumptions about the abundance of the relevant resource endowment and by examining a good for which intraindustry trade is insignificant.
Of course, this is a trivial exercise, but one that is tedious and time consuming.
Therefore, I have already done the relevant work for the reader. The results
appear in Tables C.1 and C.2. (The first line of Table C.1 repeats the information developed in the two preceding paragraphs.) The examples in the
tables cover some stark alternatives. There is no attempt to examine the gamut
of possibilities. Rather, the aim in constructing the tables has been to give
the reader some idea of the range of possibilities.

Tables C.1 and C.2 consider three critical levels of the resource endowments
intensively used in the production of the good under examination. When the
level is denoted "large" in the tables, it is assumed that the country has a
larger comparative advantage in this good than in any other.[2] (Similarly,
"average" indicates no comparative advantage, and "small" betokens a large

[2] This large comparative advantage is assumed to exist no matter which criterion is adopted
to measure comparative advantage.

Table C.1

The Structure of RCAs for a Good, i, for Which Intraindustry Trade Is Large, and for Two Countries, A (Which Conducts a Large Amount of Intraindustry Trade) and B (Which Undertakes No Intraindustry Trade)

A's Relative Endowment of the Factors Intensive in i's Production	B's Relative Endowment of the Factors Intensive in i's Production	A's RCAs	B's RCAs	A's RCAs vs. B's RCAs
Large	Large	$x_{ia} > 1$ $m_{ia} ? 1$ $w_{ia} > 1$	$x_{ib} ? 1$ $m_{ib} < 1$ $w_{ib} > 1$	$x_{ia} ? x_{ib}$ $m_{ia} > m_{ib}$ $w_{ia} < w_{ib}$
Large	Average	$x_{ia} > 1$ $m_{ia} ? 1$ $w_{ia} > 1$	$x_{ib} < 1$ $m_{ib} < 1$ $w_{ib} = 1$	$x_{ia} > x_{ib}$ $m_{ia} > m_{ib}$ $w_{ia} > w_{ib}$
Large	Small	$x_{ia} > 1$ $m_{ia} ? 1$ $w_{ia} > 1$	$x_{ib} < 1$ $m_{ib} ? 1$ $w_{ib} < 1$	$x_{ia} > x_{ib}$ $m_{ia} ? m_{ib}$ $w_{ia} > w_{ib}$
Average	Large	$x_{ia} ? 1$ $m_{ia} ? 1$ $w_{ia} = 1$	$x_{ib} ? 1$ $m_{ib} < 1$ $w_{ib} > 1$	$x_{ia} ? x_{ib}$ $m_{ia} > m_{ib}$ $w_{ia} < w_{ib}$
Average	Average	$x_{ia} ? 1$ $m_{ia} ? 1$ $w_{ia} = 1$	$x_{ib} < 1$ $m_{ib} < 1$ $w_{ib} = 1$	$x_{ia} > x_{ib}$ $m_{ia} > m_{ib}$ $w_{ia} = w_{ib}$
Average	Small	$x_{ia} ? 1$ $m_{ia} ? 1$ $w_{ia} = 1$	$x_{ib} < 1$ $m_{ib} ? 1$ $w_{ib} < 1$	$x_{ia} > x_{ib}$ $m_{ia} ? m_{ib}$ $w_{ia} > w_{ib}$
Small	Large	$x_{ia} ? 1$ $m_{ia} > 1$ $w_{ia} < 1$	$x_{ib} ? 1$ $m_{ib} < 1$ $w_{ib} > 1$	$x_{ia} ? x_{ib}$ $m_{ia} > m_{ib}$ $w_{ia} < w_{ib}$
Small	Average	$x_{ia} ? 1$ $m_{ia} > 1$ $w_{ia} < 1$	$x_{ib} < 1$ $m_{ib} < 1$ $w_{ib} = 1$	$x_{ia} ? x_{ib}$ $m_{ia} ? m_{ib}$ $w_{ia} < w_{ib}$
Small	Small	$x_{ia} ? 1$ $m_{ia} > 1$ $w_{ia} < 1$	$x_{ib} < 1$ $m_{ib} ? 1$ $w_{ib} < 1$	$x_{ia} > x_{ib}$ $m_{ia} ? m_{ib}$ $w_{ia} > w_{ib}$

Note: Question Mark (?) denotes, that given available information, either $>$ or $<$ is possible.

Table C.2.
The Structure of RCAs for a Good, k, for Which Intraindustry Trade Is Insignificant, and for Two Countries, A (Which Conducts a Large Amount of Intraindustry Trade) and B (Which Conducts No Intraindustry Trade)

A's Relative Endowment of the Factors Intensive in k's Production	B's Relative Endowment of the Factors Intensive in k's Production	A's RCAs	B's RCAs	A's RCAs vs. B's RCAs
Large	Large	$x_{ka} ? 1$ $m_{ka} < 1$ $w_{ka} > 1$	$x_{kb} > 1$ $m_{kb} < 1$ $w_{kb} > 1$	$x_{ka} < x_{kb}$ $m_{ka} ? m_{kb}$ $w_{ka} ? w_{kb}$
Large	Average	$x_{ka} ? 1$ $m_{ka} < 1$ $w_{ka} > 1$	$x_{kb} < 1$ $m_{kb} < 1$ $w_{kb} = 1$	$x_{ka} > x_{kb}$ $m_{ka} ? m_{kb}$ $w_{ka} > w_{kb}$
Large	Small	$x_{ka} ? 1$ $m_{ka} < 1$ $w_{ka} > 1$	$x_{kb} < 1$ $m_{kb} > 1$ $w_{kb} < 1$	$x_{ka} > x_{kb}$ $m_{ka} < m_{kb}$ $w_{ka} > w_{kb}$
Average	Large	$x_{ka} < 1$ $m_{ka} < 1$ $w_{ka} = 1$	$x_{kb} > 1$ $m_{kb} < 1$ $w_{kb} > 1$	$x_{ka} < x_{kb}$ $m_{ka} ? m_{kb}$ $w_{ka} < w_{kb}$
Average	Average	$x_{ka} < 1$ $m_{ka} < 1$ $w_{ka} = 1$	$x_{kb} < 1$ $m_{kb} < 1$ $w_{kb} = 1$	$x_{ka} ? x_{kb}$ $m_{ka} ? m_{kb}$ $w_{ka} = w_{kb}$
Average	Small	$x_{ka} < 1$ $m_{ka} < 1$ $w_{ka} = 1$	$x_{kb} < 1$ $m_{kb} > 1$ $w_{kb} < 1$	$x_{ka} ? x_{kb}$ $m_{ka} ? m_{kb}$ $w_{ka} > w_{kb}$
Small	Large	$x_{ka} < 1$ $m_{ka} ? 1$ $w_{ka} < 1$	$x_{kb} > 1$ $m_{kb} < 1$ $w_{kb} > 1$	$x_{ka} < x_{kb}$ $m_{ka} > m_{kb}$ $w_{ka} < w_{kb}$
Small	Average	$x_{ka} < 1$ $m_{ka} ? 1$ $w_{ka} < 1$	$x_{kb} < 1$ $m_{kb} < 1$ $w_{kb} = 1$	$x_{ka} ? x_{kb}$ $m_{ka} > m_{kb}$ $w_{ka} < w_{kb}$
Small	Small	$x_{ka} < 1$ $m_{ka} ? 1$ $w_{ka} < 1$	$x_{kb} < 1$ $m_{kb} > 1$ $w_{kb} < 1$	$x_{ka} ? x_{kb}$ $m_{ka} < m_{kb}$ $w_{ka} ? w_{kb}$

Note: Question Mark (?) denotes that, given available information, either $>$ or $<$ is possible.

comparative disadvantage). When the value in the first column is "large" (average/small), the results in columns 3 and 5 are calculated on the assumption that country A's share of world interindustry exports is highest (zero/lowest) for the good under scrutiny. When the values in columns 1 and 2 are equal, it is assumed that interindustry trade for the good in question as a share of total interindustry trade is the same for both countries.

Tables C.1 and C.2 differ in their assumptions concerning intraindustry trade in the good under examination. In Table C.1, intraindustry trade is assumed to be relatively large for good i. Good k, examined in Table C.2, is assumed to have no intraindustry trade.[3] These assumptions become crucial when considering the differences between the two countries' RCAs because country A is assumed to engage in proportionately more intraindustry trade than country B.

Together with some rough information on amounts of intraindustry trade and characteristics of goods, Tables C.1 and C.2 can be used to help interpret the numerical values of the RCAs which are given in Chapter 4. Information on amounts of intraindustry trade is to be presented later and is also implicit in the per capita incomes provided in Section 2.4, which listed the groups of countries used in the presentation of results. Information on the goods to be analyzed is presented in Section 4.2.

Tables C.1 and C.2 are relevant with regard to a further question: Which of the three types of RCAs provides the most reliable information? Balassa's (1977, p. 327) view is that the export measure is unequivocally the best, because data on imports are likely to be affected by irrelevant factors specific to an individual country. In particular, the commodity structure of policies affecting trade varies from country to country. Then, if restrictions on imports are much more common than measures affecting exports, the import and export-import RCAs will be less reliable indicators of comparative advantage than the export RCAs.[4]

By examining the analysis leading to Tables C.1 and C.2, it is easy to see that Balassa's point is implicitly framed in a world in which intraindustry trade is absent. When all trade is due to differences in resource endowments, the meaning of a large value (or any nonzero value) on a good's export measure is clear. When intraindustry trade is present, however, a large value for an export RCA could result solely from a high per capita income, even when the country has a comparative disadvantage in the good. In contrast, the export-import measure gives unambiguous information even in the presence of intraindustry trade.

[3] No assumptions are made concerning the relative size of interindustry trade in i versus intraindustry trade in i, or concerning the relative proportions of these two types of trade in total trade.

[4] Balassa's (1977) assumptions on the relative degree of distortion in export structure and import structure seem reasonable for developed market economies. It is not clear that this assumption is equally applicable to Eastern Europe.

One cannot resolve which type of RCA measure is best on a priori grounds. There are distortions in the real world which probably affect the import and export-import RCAs more than the export measure. Counterposed to the distortions is the ambiguity in the interpretation of the export measure introduced by intraindustry trade. Given that no single measure dominates, it is prudent to present empirical results for all three, to give readers the whole spectrum of evidence.

Some remarks on the significance of particular numerical values of the RCAs are appropriate. In the tables, there is some focus on unity. The reason for this focus is obvious in the case of the export-import measure, whether or not intraindustry trade is present. If there are no distortions, the export-import RCA for a good is greater than unity if and only if a country has a comparative advantage in that good. For the export and import measures, unity has no such significance, despite claims to the contrary.[5] For the export measure, Tables C.1 and C.2 show examples both of values above unity in the presence of a comparative disadvantage and of values below unity in the presence of a comparative advantage. Comparisons with unity provide only sufficient conditions for conclusions, not necessary ones. For example, a country such as B, with little intraindustry trade, can have an x_{ib} above unity only if it has a comparative advantage in good i (see column 4 in both tables). Thus, one knows that a country having less-than-average intraindustry trade *must* have a large amount of interindustry exports if it exhibits better-than-average export performance in a commodity. A value of one is not the dividing line between comparative advantage and disadvantage, but rather an indicator of an above-average *exporter*, which is not the same phenomenon.[6]

[5] For references to articles that attribute significance to RCAs of unity, see the citations in Bowen 1983.

[6] A country with a comparative advantage is an above-average *net exporter*.

APPENDIX D

Interpreting the Estimates in
the Presence of Missing Data

This appendix explains and proves four results cited in the argument in the body of Chapter 6.

Result 6.1

Because all notation is defined at the relevant points of the text, I do not repeat definitions here. Equation (6.8) of the text stated a relationship between factor endowments and the structure of trade:

$$\tilde{w}_{ij} = \bar{b}_{i0} + \sum_{k=1}^{S} \bar{b}_{ik} v_{kj} \qquad i = 1, \ldots, N \quad j = 1, \ldots, T. \quad \text{(D.1)}$$

Equation (B.2) of Appendix B (see also Chapter 3) gives a relationship between GNP and resource endowments, which when converted to per capita variables is the following:

$$g_j = \sum_{k=1}^{S} \gamma_k v_{kj}. \quad \text{(D.2)}$$

Let us suppose that endowment S is the factor "sophistication," which cannot be measured across countries. (Of course, any other interpretation of this factor could be used in the following derivation.) However, GNP can be measured. Therefore, solving out endowment S from the above equations:

$$\tilde{w}_{ij} = \bar{b}_{i0} + \sum_{k=1}^{S-1} \bar{b}_{ik} v_{kj} + \bar{b}_{iS} \left(g_j - \sum_{k=1}^{S-1} \gamma_k v_{kj} \right) / \gamma_S,$$

$$\tilde{w}_{ij} = \bar{b}_{i0} + \sum_{k=1}^{S-1} (\bar{b}_{ik} - \bar{b}_{iS} \gamma_k / \gamma_S) v_{kj} + (\bar{b}_{iS} / \gamma_S) g_j. \quad \text{(D.3)}$$

This equation has a structure identical to that of equation (6.10) in Chapter 6. Hence, model HG is derived. Because an analogous derivation is possible for model PG, there is no need to provide the details here.

Result 6.2

In discussing possible biases resulting from the omission of reporting countries from the mirror trade statistics, I stated that, for the group of Western countries used in estimating trade relationships, the average predicted endowments would be equal to the average of those countries' actual endowments (see Chapter 6). Here, I prove this statement. The proof uses the properties of the econometric techniques developed in Chapter 5. The reader is referred to that chapter for definitions of the notation.

Let us suppose that we have applied the estimating method to a sample of Western countries and CPEs. One obtains:

$$\hat{B} = Y\hat{Z}'(\hat{Z}\hat{Z}')^{-1}. \tag{D.4}$$

In exactly the same way that the unknown endowments for the CPEs were predicted, one could obtain predicted values for the endowments of the Western countries. The predictions for all countries can be written in the following form:

$$\hat{Z}_{2.} = \begin{bmatrix} \hat{Z}_{21} & \hat{Z}_{22} \end{bmatrix}.$$

Then the predictions are derived using equation (5.7) of Chapter 5:

$$\hat{Z}_{2.} = (\hat{B}_2'\hat{W}^{-1}\hat{B}_2)^{-1}\hat{B}_2'\hat{W}^{-1}(Y - \hat{B}_1 Z_{1.}). \tag{D.5}$$

Now equation (D.4) is just the matrix representation of a set of ordinary least squares regressions. In such regressions, the average of the actual values of the dependent variable (i.e., the trade measures) is equal to the average of the predicted values of that variable, when those predictions are obtained using the actual values of the independent variables and the estimated coefficients. This means that if J is a vector of 1's of appropriate size, then:

$$YJ = [Y_1 \ Y_2]J = \begin{bmatrix} \hat{B}_1 & \hat{B}_2 \end{bmatrix} \cdot \begin{bmatrix} Z_{11} & Z_{12} \\ Z_{21} & \hat{Z}_{22} \end{bmatrix}J. \tag{D.6}$$

Note that the estimated value of Z_{22} is used in the above equation since, because the actual values are unknown, these estimated values are the values used in the regressions to obtain $\hat{B}$. Using the dot notation to rewrite (D.6), one obtains:

$$YJ = [\hat{B}_1 Z_{11} \ \hat{B}_1 Z_{12}]J + [\hat{B}_2 Z_{21} \ \hat{B}_2 \hat{Z}_{22}]J.$$

Hence,

$$(Y - \hat{B}_1 Z_{1.})J = [\hat{B}_2 Z_{21} \ \hat{B}_2 \hat{Z}_{22}]J.$$

Substituting in (D.5), one obtains:

$$\hat{Z}_2 J = (\hat{B}_2'\hat{W}^{-1}\hat{B}_2)^{-1}\hat{B}_2'\hat{W}^{-1}[\hat{B}_2 Z_{21} \ \hat{B}_2\hat{Z}_{22}]J \ .$$

Hence,

$$[\hat{Z}_{21} \ \hat{Z}_{22}]J = \hat{Z}_2 J = [Z_{21} \ \hat{Z}_{22}]J$$

or

$$\hat{Z}_{21}J_1 = Z_{21}J_1 \ .$$

(where J_1 is a vector of 1's, whose dimension is equal to the number of Western countries used to estimate the trade equations). Thus, on average, the techniques cannot produce biased predictions for countries with resource endowments lying in the range of the Western countries' endowments. For such countries the R^2's in Table 6.1 give the correct sense of how accurate the predictions are.

Result 6.3

This and the following result establish reasonable possibilities for the types of biases that can be expected when the mirror statistics of one country omit some trade that is not omitted from the mirror statistics of the countries used to estimate the trade equations. The first case is rather trivial. Suppose the group of countries whose trade reports are missing from the mirror statistics of this one country, say j, are a representative sample of j's trading partners. Then, it is reasonable to assume the following: $\alpha_j X_{ij}^a = X_{ij}^o$ and $\alpha_j M_{ij}^a = M_{ij}^o$, where an a superscript denotes the actual value of j's trade variables, an o superscript represents the observed value of the trade variables, and $0 < \alpha_j < 1$. Then it follows that $\alpha_j W_{ij}^a = W_{ij}^o$. Hence, the observed structure of the trade variable is:

$$\tilde{w}_{ij}^o = \left[\frac{W_{ij}^o}{\displaystyle\sum_{n=1}^{N}(X_{nj}^o + M_{nj}^o)/2}\right] = \left[\frac{\alpha_j W_{ij}^a}{\displaystyle\sum_{n=1}^{N}\alpha_j(X_{nj}^a + M_{nj}^a)/2}\right] \ .$$

Because the α_j's cancel, the observed value of the dependent variable in the trade equation, $\tilde{w}_{ij}$, is equal to the actual value of that variable. There is no effect from the omission of the trade data. Obviously, all this result says is that if the missing data has roughly the same structure as the overall trade of the country of interest, then the omission can make no difference to the structure of trade variables.

Result 6.4

For this result, I make an assumption that is the opposite of the one in the previous result. Thus, in some sense, the combinations of the two results will cover the range of possibilities. I assume that the trade data in the missing trade reports is representative of the trade structure of the nonreporting country, rather than of the trade of the country of interest. Of course, given the whole variety of trading partners that must exist for any one country, one must make a further assumption about the nonreporting country in order to obtain determinate results. (This is even more so because, within the Heckscher-Ohlin model, the absolute levels of trade between any two countries are not determined.) One reasonable assumption, for example, is that the reporting country has a trade structure that is the mirror image of the country of interest, j. This is reasonable because countries obviously buy from trading partners that have a comparative advantage in products in which the importing country has a comparative disadvantage. In the particular case of interest, EE6–Soviet trade, where trade seems to be industrial goods for raw materials, this assumption is particularly reasonable. Thus, assume that $W_{ij}^a W_{i\sigma}^a \leq 0$, for all i, where j is the country of interest and σ is the country whose trade reports are missing from the mirror statistics of j.

Assume that country σ conducts a proportion, β, of its trade with country j. Then, using the notation introduced for the previous result, $W_{ij}^o = W_{ij}^a + \beta W_{i\sigma}^a$. Hence, using the Heckscher-Ohlin relations derived in the text:

$$W_{ij}^o = r_j \left[b_{i0} + \sum_{k=1}^{S} b_{ik} v_{kj} \right] + \beta r_\sigma \left[b_{i0} + \sum_{k=1}^{S} b_{ik} v_{k\sigma} \right]. \qquad (D.7)$$

Now let us examine the observed value of the denominator of the dependent variable in the text's equation that represents the HO model—equation (6.6) of Section 6.1:

$$\left[\sum_{n=1}^{N} \left(X_{nj}^o + M_{nj}^o \right) \right] = \left[\sum_{n=1}^{N} |W_{nj}^o| \right] = \left[\sum_{n=1}^{N} |W_{nj}^a + \beta W_{n\sigma}^a| \right].$$

Let N_+ be the set of goods indexes (n) for which $X_{nj}^a > 0$. Then:

$$\left[\sum_{n=1}^{N} \left(X_{nj}^o + M_{nj}^o \right) \right]$$

$$= \left[\sum_{n \in N_+} |X_{nj}^a - \beta M_{n\sigma}^a| \right] + \left[\sum_{n \notin N_+} |M_{nj}^a - \beta X_{n\sigma}^a| \right]$$

$$= \sum_{n \in N_+} \left| r_j \left[b_{n0} + \sum_{k=1}^{S} b_{nk} v_{kj} \right] + \beta r_\sigma \left[b_{n0} + \sum_{k=1}^{S} b_{nk} v_{k\sigma} \right] \right|$$

$$
+ \sum_{n \notin N_+} \left| -r_j \left[b_{n0} + \sum_{k=1}^{S} b_{nk} v_{kj} \right] - \beta r_\sigma \left[b_{n0} + \sum_{k=1}^{S} b_{nk} v_{k\sigma} \right] \right|
$$

$$
= \sum_{n=1}^{N} \left| r_j \left[b_{n0} + \sum_{k=1}^{S} b_{nk} v_{kj} \right] + \beta r_\sigma \left[b_{n0} + \sum_{k=1}^{S} b_{nk} v_{k\sigma} \right] \right| . \quad (D.8)
$$

Now divide equations (D.7) and (D.8) by $(r_j + \beta r_\sigma)$ and let $\theta = r_j/(r_j + \beta r_\sigma)$. Then divide the resultant equations into each other. One obtains:

$$
\left[\frac{W_{ij}^o}{\sum_{n=1}^{N} (X_{nj}^o + M_{nj}^o)/2} \right]
$$

$$
= \frac{\left[b_{i0} + \sum_{k=1}^{S} b_{ik} \left(\theta v_{kj} + \{1 - \theta\} v_{k\sigma} \right) \right]}{\sum_{n=1}^{N} \left| \left[b_{n0} + \sum_{k=1}^{S} b_{nk} \left(\theta v_{kj} + \{1 - \theta\} v_{k\sigma} \right) \right] \right| /2} . \quad (D.9)
$$

Equation (D.9) is obviously identical in structure to the representation of the HO model in the text (equation (6.6) of section 6.1). However, the resource endowments entered into (D.9) are a linear combination of country j's and country σ's—that is, $(\theta v_{kj} + \{1 - \theta\} v_{k\sigma})$. Because the coefficients in (D.9) are identical to those of (6.6) of Section 6.1, the estimate of j's endowments will actually be an estimate of that linear combination of j's and σ's endowments.

References

Abouchar, Alan J. 1985. "Western Project: Investment Theory and Soviet Investment Rules." *Journal of Comparative Economics*, 9(4), pp. 345–62.

Akhmedvev, A. 1980. "The Quality of Output and the Improvement of Prices." *Problems of Economics*, 23(7), pp. 61–74.

Amann, Ronald. 1977. "Some Approaches to the Comparative Assessment of Soviet Technology: Its Level and Rate of Development." In Ronald Amann, Julian Cooper, and R. W. Davies, eds, *The Technological Level of Soviet Industry*. New Haven: Yale University Press.

Amann, Ronald. 1982. "Industrial Innovation in the Soviet Union: Methodological Perspectives and Conclusions." In Ronald Amann, and Julian Cooper, eds., *Industrial Innovation in the Soviet Union*. New Haven: Yale University Press.

Amann, Ronald, and Julian Cooper, eds. 1982. *Industrial Innovation in the Soviet Union*. New Haven: Yale University Press.

Amann, Ronald, Julian Cooper, and R. W. Davies. 1977. *The Technological Level of Soviet Industry*. New Haven: Yale University Press.

Anderson, James E. 1987. "A Review of *Sources of International Comparative Advantage: Theory and Evidence* by Edward E. Leamer." *Journal of Economic Literature*, 25(1), pp. 146–47.

Arrow, Kenneth J. 1974. *The Limits of Organization*. New York: Norton.

Arrow, Kenneth J. 1987. "Rationality of Self and Others in an Economic System." In Robin M. Hogarth, and Melvin W. Reder, eds., Rational Choice: The Contrast between Economics and Psychology. Chicago: University of Chicago Press.

Balassa, Bela. 1965. "Tariff Protection in Industrial Countries: An Evaluation." *Journal of Political Economy*, 73(6), pp. 573–94.

Balassa, Bela. 1967. *Trade Liberalization among Industrial Countries: Objectives and Alternatives*, New York: McGraw-Hill.

Balassa, Bela. 1977. "'Revealed' Comparative Advantage Revisited: An Analysis of Relative Export Shares of the Industrial Countries, 1953–1971." *Manchester School of Economic and Social Studies*, 45(4), pp. 327–44.

Balassa, Bela. 1978. "The Economic Reform in Hungary: Ten Years After." *European Economic Review*, 11(3), pp. 245–68.

Balassa, Bela, and Luc Bauwens. 1984. "Intra-Industry Specialization in a Multi-Industry Framework." World Bank, December.

Baldwin, William L., and John T. Scott. 1987. *Market Structure and Technological Change*. Chur: Harwood Academic Publishers.

Batra, Raveendra N. 1976. "The Theory of International Trade with an International Cartel or a Centrally Planned Economy." *Southern Economic Journal*, 42(3), pp. 364–76.

Beardsley, George, and Edwin Mansfield. 1987. "A Note on the Accuracy of Industrial

Forecasts of the Profitability of New Products and Processes.'' *Journal of Business*, *5*(1), pp. 127–35.

Bergson, Abram. 1971. ''Comparative Productivity and Efficiency in the USA and the USSR.'' In Alexander Eckstein, ed., *Comparison of Economic Systems: Theoretical and Methodological Approaches*. Berkeley: University of California Press.

Bergson, Abram. 1978. *Productivity and the Social System: The USSR and the West*. Cambridge, Mass.: Harvard University Press.

Bergson, Abram. 1987. ''Comparative Productivity: The USSR, Eastern Europe, and the West.'' *American Economic Review*, 77(3), pp. 342–57.

Berliner, Joseph S. 1957. *Factory and Manager in the USSR*. Cambridge, Mass.: Harvard University Press.

Berliner, Joseph S. 1976. *Innovation Decision in Soviet Industry*. Cambridge, Mass.: MIT Press.

Bhagwati, Jagdish N., and T. N. Srinivasan. 1983. *Lectures on International Trade*. Cambridge, Mass.: MIT Press.

Birman, I. 1978. ''From the Achieved Level.'' *Soviet Studies*, 30(2), pp. 153–72.

Blomstrom, Magnus, Irving B. Kravis, and Robert E. Lipsey. 1988. ''Multinational Firms and Manufactured Exports from Developing Countries.'' Working paper of the National Bureau of Economic Research.

Boltho, Andrea. 1971. *Foreign Trade Criteria in Socialist Economies*. Cambridge: Cambridge University Press.

Bornstein, Morris. 1977. ''Economic Reform in Eastern Europe.'' In *East European Economies Post-Helsinki*. Washington, D.C.: Government Printing Office, August 25.

Bowen, Harry P. 1983. ''On the Theoretical Interpretation of Indices of Trade Intensity and Revealed Comparative Advantage.'' *Weltwirtschaftliches Archiv*, *119*, pp. 464–72.

Brada, Josef C. 1973. ''The Allocative Efficiency of Centrally Planned Foreign Trade: A Programming Approach to the Czech Case.'' *European Economic Review*, *4*(4), pp. 329–46.

Brada, Josef C. 1973. ''The Microallocative Impact of the Hungarian Economic Reform of 1968: Some Evidence from the Export Sector.'' *Economics of Planning*, *13*(1–2), pp. 1–14.

Brada, Josef C. 1974. ''Allocative Efficiency and the System of Economic Management in Some Socialist Countries.'' *Kyklos*, *27*(2), pp.270–85.

Brada, Josef C. 1980. ''Industry Structure and East-West Technology Transfer: A Case Study of the Pharmaceutical Industry,'' *ACES Bulletin*, *22*(1), pp. 31–59.

Brada, Josef C. 1981. ''Technology Transfer by Means of Industrial Cooperation: A Theoretical Appraisal.'' In Paul Marer and Eugeniusz Tabaczynski, *Polish-U.S. Industrial Cooperation in the 1980s*. Bloomington: Indiana University Press.

Brada, Josef C. 1985. ''Soviet Subsidization of Eastern Europe: The Primacy of Economics over Politics?'' *Journal of Comparative Economics*, 9(1), pp.80–92.

Brada, Josef C., and Larry J. Wipf. 1976. ''Romanian Exports to Western Markets.'' In Josef C. Brada, ed., *Quantitative and Analytical Studies in East-West Economic Relations*. Bloomington: Indiana University Press.

Brown, Alan A. 1961. ''Centrally-Planned Foreign Trade and Economic Efficiency.'' *American Economist*, 5(2), pp. 11–28.

Brown, Alan A. 1968. "Towards a Theory of Centrally Planned Foreign Trade." In Alan A. Brown and Egon Neuberger, eds., *International Trade and Central Planning*. Berkeley: University of California Press.

Brubaker, Earl R. 1972. A Sectoral Analysis of Efficiency under Market and Plan." *Soviet Studies*, *23*(3), pp. 435–49.

Collier, Irwin J. 1986. "Effective Purchasing Power in a Quantity Constrained Economy: An Estimate for the German Democratic Republic." *Review of Economics and Statistics*, *68*(1), pp. 24–32.

Comanor, William S., and Thomas A. Wilson. 1974. *Advertising and Market Power*. Cambridge, Mass.: Harvard University Press.

Cook, Edward C. 1987. "Soviet Food Markets: Will the Situation Improve under Gorbachev?" *Comparative Economic Studies*, *29*(1), pp. 1–36.

Coughlin, Cletus C. 1983. "The Relationship Between Foreign Ownership and Technology Transfer." *Journal of Comparative Economics*, *7*(4), pp. 400–414.

Cowling, Keith, and Dennis C. Mueller. 1978. "The Social Costs of Monopoly Power." *Economic Journal*, *88*, pp. 727–48.

Csikos-Nagy, Bela. 1972. "Macrostructural and Microstructural Performance of the Economy". *Soviet Studies*, *23*(3), pp. 474–83.

Davies, R. W. 1977. "The Technological Level of Soviet Industry: An Overview." In Ronald Amann, Julian Cooper, and R. W. Davies, eds., *The Technological Level of Soviet Industry*. New Haven: Yale University Press.

Deardorff, Alan V. 1985. "Testing Trade Theories and Predicting Trade Flows." *Handbook of International Economics, Volume 1: International Trade Theory*. Amsterdam: North-Holland.

Debreu, Gerard. 1951. "The Coefficient of Resource Utilization." *Econometrica*, *19*, pp. 273–92.

Denison, Edward F. 1967. *Why Growth Rates Differ*. Washington, D.C.: Brookings Institution.

Desai, Padma, and R. Martin. 1983. "Efficiency Loss from Resource Misallocation in Soviet Industry." *Quarterly Journal of Economics*, *98*(3), pp. 441–56.

Dezsenyi-Gueulette, Agota. 1983. "The Utilization and Assimilation in Hungary of Advanced Technology Imported from the West." *Soviet Studies*, *35*(2), pp. 196–207.

Dhrymes, Phoebus J. 1978. *Introductory Econometrics*. New York: Springer-Verlag.

Dixit, Avinash K., and Joseph E. Stiglitz. 1977. "Monopolistic Competition and Optimum Product Diversity." *American Economic Review*, *67*(3), pp. 297–308.

Domar, Evsey. 1971. "On the Measurement of Comparative Efficiency." In Alexander Eckstein, ed., *Comparison of Economic Systems: Theoretical and Methodological Approaches*. Berkeley: University of California Press.

Drabek, Zdenek. 1983. "The Impact of Technological Differences on East-West Trade." *Weltwirtschaftliches Archiv*, *119*, pp. 630–48.

Drabek, Zdenek. 1981. "Efficiency in Natural Resource Usage: A Comparison of Market Central Planning Policies." *Journal of Policy Modeling*, *3*(1), pp. 19–35.

Dunning, J. H. 1983. "Market Power of the Firm and International Transfer of Technology: A Historical Excursion." *International Journal of Industrial Organization*, *1*(4) pp. 333–51.

Dyker, David A. 1983. *Process of Investment in the Soviet Union*. Cambridge: Cambridge University Press.

Edwards, Imogene, Margaret Hughes, and James Noren. 1979. "U.S. and USSR: Comparisons of GNP." In *Soviet Economy in a Time of Change Volume 1*, Washington, D.C.: Government Printing Office, October 10.

Ehrlich, Eva 1985. "The Size Structure of Manufacturing Establishments and Enterprises: An International Comparison." *Journal of Comparative Economics*, 9(3), pp. 267–95.

Estrin, Saul. 1983. *Self-Management: Economic Theory and Yugoslav Practice*. Cambridge: Cambridge University Press.

Ethier, Wilfred J. 1984. "Higher Dimensional Issues in Trade Theory." In Ronald W. Jones and Peter B. Kenen, eds., *Handbook of International Economics, Vol. 1*. Amsterdam: North-Holland.

Ethier, Wilfred J. 1985. "The Multinational Firm."University of Pennsylvania, September. Mimeographed.

Feshbach, Murray. 1983. "Population and Labor Force." In Abram Bergson, and Herbert S. Levine, eds., *The Soviet Economy: Toward the Year 2000*. London: Allen and Unwin.

Food and Agriculture Organization. 1975. *Yearbook of Food and Agriculture Statistics*. Rome: FAO of the United Nations.

Freeman, Christopher. 1982. *Economics of Industrial Innovation*. Cambridge, Mass.: MIT Press.

Gardner, Stephen H. 1983. *Soviet Foreign Trade*. Boston: Kluwer-Nijhoff.

Goldman, Marshall I. 1970. "Convergence of Environmental Disruption." *Science*, *170* pp. 37–40.

Goldman, Marshall I. 1972. *Spoils of Progress: Environmental Pollution in the Soviet Union*. Cambridge, Mass.: MIT Press.

Gorizontov, B., and V. Prokudin. 1978. "Environmental Protection in Comecon Member Nations" *Problems of Economics*, *21*(8), pp. 24–40.

Gort, M., and S. Klepper. 1982. "Time Paths in the Diffusion of Product Innovations." *Economic Journal*, *92*(367) pp. 630–53.

Gort, M., and A. Konakayama. 1982. "A Model of Diffusion in the Production of an Innovation." *American Economic Review*, *72*(5), pp. 1111–20.

Granick, David. 1975. *Enterprise Guidance in Eastern Europe*. Princeton: Princeton University Press.

Granick, David. 1980. "The Ministry as the Maximizing Unit in Soviet Industry." *Journal of Comparative Economics*, 4(3), pp. 255–73.

Granick, David. 1987. *Job Rights in the Soviet Union: Their Consequences*. Cambridge: Cambridge University Press.

Gregory, Paul R., and Robert C. Stuart. 1986. *Soviet Economic Structure and Performance*. New York: Harper and Rowe.

Grossman, Sanford, and Joseph E. Stiglitz. 1976. "Information and Competitive Price Systems." *American Economic Review*, 66(2), pp. 246–53.

Grubel, Herbert G., and P. J. Lloyd. 1975. *Intra-Industry Trade: The Theory and Measurement of International Trade in Differentiated Products*. New York: Wiley.

Gruber, William H., and Raymond Vernon. 1970. "The Technology Factor in a World Trade Matrix." In Raymond Vernon, ed., *The Technology Factor in International Trade*. New York: Columbia University Press.

Gruber, William, Dileep Mehta, and Raymond Vernon. 1967. "The R & D Factor in International Trade and International Investment of United States Industries." *Journal of Political Economy*, 75(1), pp. 20–37.

Gruzinov, V. P. 1979. *The USSR's Management of Foreign Trade*. White Plains, N.Y.: M. E. Sharpe.

Hanson, Philip. 1974. *Advertising and Socialism; The Nature and Extent of Consumer Advertising in the Soviet Union, Poland, Hungary, and Yugoslavia*. London: Macmillan.

Hanson, Philip. 1982. "The Soviet System as a Recipient of Foreign Technology." In Ronald Amann and Julian Cooper, eds., *Industrial Innovation in the Soviet Union*. New Haven: Yale University Press.

Hare Paul. 1987. "Economic Reform in Eastern Europe." *Journal of Economic Surveys*, *1*(1), pp. 25–58.

Harmon, Harry H. 1976. *Modern Factor Analysis*. Third edition. Chicago: University of Chicago Press.

Helpman, Elhanan. 1981. "International Trade in the Presence of Product Differentiation, Economies of Scale, and Monopolistic Competition." *Journal of International Economics*, *11*(3), pp. 305–40.

Helpman, Elhanan. 1984a. "Increasing Returns, Imperfect Markets, and Trade Theory." In Ronald W. Jones and Peter B. Kenen, eds., *Handbook of International Economics, vol. 1*, Amsterdam: North-Holland.

Helpman, Elhanan. 1984b. "A Simple Theory of International Trade with Multinational Corporations." *Journal of Political Economy*, 92(3), pp. 451–71.

Helpman, Elhanan, and Paul R. Krugman. 1985. *Market Structure and Foreign Trade: Increasing Returns, Imperfect Competition, and the International Economy*. Cambridge, Mass.: MIT Press.

Hewett, Ed A. 1980. "Foreign Trade Outcomes in Eastern and Western Economies." In Paul Marer and John M. Montias, eds., *Eastern European Integration and East-West Trade*. Bloomington: Indiana University Press.

Hewett, Ed A. 1984. *Energy, Economics, and Foreign Policy in the Soviet Union*. Washington, D.C.: Brookings Institution.

Hewett, Ed A. 1988. *Reforming the Soviet Economy: Equality versus Efficiency*. Washington, D.C.: Brookings Insititution.

Hicks, John R. 1971. *Social Framework: An Introduction to Economics*. Fourth edition. Oxford: Clarendon Press.

Hill, Malcolm R., and Richard McKay. 1988. *Soviet Product Quality*. New York: St. Martin's Press.

Hillman, Arye. 1980. "Observations on the Relation between 'Revealed Comparative Advantage' and Comparative Advantage as Indicated by Pre-Trade Relative Prices." *Weltwirtschaftliches Archiv 116*(2), pp. 315–21.

Hirshleifer, J., and John G. Riley. 1979. "The Analytics of Uncertainty and Information: An Expository Survey." *Journal of Economic Literature*, *17*(4), pp. 1375–1421.

Holmstrom, Bengt. 1985. "Differential Information and the Market: Comment." In Kenneth J. Arrow and Seppo Honkapohja, eds., *Frontiers of Economics*. Oxford: Basil Blackwell.

Holzman, Franklyn D. 1968. "Soviet Foreign Trade Policies, 1929–1961." *American Economic Review*, *58*(4), pp. 801–25.

Holzman, Franklyn D. 1976. *International Trade under Communism*. New York: Basic Books.

Holzman, Franklyn D. 1979. "Some Theories of the Hard Currency Shortages of Centrally Planned Economies." In *Soviet Economy in a Time of Change, Vol. 2*. Washington, D.C.: Government Printing Office, October 10.

Hufbauer, G. C. 1970. "The Impact of National Characteristics and Technology on the Commodity Composition of Trade in Manufactured Goods." In Raymond Vernon, ed., *The Technology Factor in International Trade*. New York: Columbia University Press.

Hufbauer, Gary C., and John G. Chilas. 1974. "Specialization among Industrial Countries: Extent and Consequences." In Herbert Giersch, ed., *International Division of Labour Problems and Perspectives*. Tübingen: Mohr.

International Monetary Fund. (Annual.) *Government Finance Statistics Yearbook*. Washington, D.C.: International Monetary Fund.

International Monetary Fund. (Annual.) *International Financial Statistics Yearbook*. Washington, D.C.: International Monetary Fund.

Ishii, Yasunori. 1986. "On the Theory of International Trade between Capitalist and Labour-Managed Countries." *Economics Letters*, *21*(2), pp. 195–202.

Johnson, Harry G. 1968. "Notes on Some Theoretical Problems Posed by the Foreign Trade of Centrally Planned Economies." In Alan A. Brown and Egon Neuberger, eds., *International Trade and Central Planning*. Berkeley: University of California Press.

Johnson, Harry G. 1969. "Foreward," In Josef Wilczynski's, *The Economics and Politics of East West Trade*. New York: Praeger.

Jorgenson, D. W., and M. Nishimizu. 1978. "U.S. and Japanese Economic Growth, 1952–1974: An International Comparison." *Economic Journal*, 88(352), pp. 707–26.

Kadar, B. 1977. "The Commodity Pattern of East-West Trade." *Acta Oeconomica*, *18*(2), pp. 153–65.

Kaplinsky, R. 1983. "Firm Size and Technical Change in a Dynamic Context." *Journal of Industrial Economics*, *32*(1), pp. 39–59.

Kaser, Michael. 1977. "Trade and Aid in the Albanian Economy." In *East European Economies Post-Helsinki*. Washington, D.C.: Government Printing Office, August 25.

Kelly, Michael G. 1982. "World Trade and Output." *Review of Income and Wealth*, *28*(2), pp. 243–49.

Kennelly, Brendan, and Peter Murrell. 1988. "Industry Characteristics and Collective Action: An Empirical Study." University of Maryland, September. Mimeographed.

Kornai, Janos. 1959. *Overcentralization in Economic Administration*. Oxford: Oxford University Press.

Kornai, Janos. 1980. *Economics of Shortage*. New York: North-Holland.

Kornai, Janos. 1986. "The Hungarian Reform Process." *Journal of Economic Literature*, *24*(4), pp. 1687–1737.

Kornai, Janos. 1987. "The Dual Dependence of the State-Owned Firm in Hungary." In Gene Tidrick and Chen Jiyuan, eds., *China's Industrial Reform*. New York: Oxford University Press.

Koves, Andras. 1985. *The CMEA Countries in the World Economy: Turning Inwards or Turning Outwards*. Budapest: Akademiai Kiado.

Kravis, Irving B., Alan Heston, and Robert Summers. 1982. *World Product and Income: International Comparisons of Real Gross Product*. Baltimore: Johns Hopkins University Press.

Krugman, Paul. 1979. "A Model of Innovation, Technology Transfer, and the World Distribution of Income." *Journal of Political Economy*, *87*(2), pp. 253–66.

Krugman, Paul. 1980. "Scale Economies, Product Differentiation, and the Pattern of Trade." *American Economic Review*, *70*(5), pp. 950–59.

Lacko, Maria. 1984. "Behavioral Rules in the Distribution of Sectoral Investments in Hungary, 1951–1980." *Journal of Comparative Economics*, *8*(3), pp. 290–300.

Lakos, I. 1982. "Hungarian Export Performance in Western Countries." *Acta Oeconomica*, *28*(1–2), pp. 163–78.

Lange, Oskar. 1938. *On the Economic Theory of Socialism*. New York: McGraw-Hill.

Lawley, D. N., and A. E. Maxwell. 1971. *Factor Analysis as a Statistical Method*. Second Edition. London: Butterworths.

Lazarcik, Gregor. 1981. "Comparative Growth, Structure, and Levels of Agricultural Output, Inputs, and Productivity in Eastern Europe, 1965–1979." In *East European Economic Assessment, Part 2: Regional Assessments*, Washington, D.C.: Government Printing Office, July 10.

Leamer, Edward. 1984. *Sources of International Comparative Advantage: Theory and Evidence*. Cambridge, Mass.: MIT Press.

Leamer, Edward. 1988. "The Sensitivity of International Comparisons of Capital Stock Measures to Different "Real" Exchange Rates." *American Economic Review*, *78*(2), pp. 479–83.

Leontief, Wassily. 1953. "Domestic Production and Foreign Trade: The American Capital Position Re-examined." *Proceedings of the American Philosophical Society*, *97*(4), pp. 332–44.

Leontief, Wassily. 1956. "Factor Proportions and the Structure of American Trade: Further Theoretical and Empirical Analysis." *Review of Economics and Statistics*, *38*(4), pp. 386–407.

Levine, H. 1959. "The Centralized Planning of Supply in Soviet Industry." In Joint Economic Committee, *Comparisons of United States and Soviet Union Economies*, Washington, D.C.: Government Printing Office.

Lydall, Harold. 1986. *Yugoslav Socialism Theory: and Practice*. Oxford: Clarendon Press.

Manove, M. 1971. "A Model of Soviet-Type Economic Planning." *American Economic Review*, June.

Mansfield, E. 1968a. *Industrial Research and Technological Innovation: An Econometric Analysis*. New York: Norton.

Mansfield, E. 1968b. *The Economics of Technical Change*. New York: Norton.

Mansfield, E., J. Rapoport, A. Romero, E. Villani, S. Wagner, and F. Husic. 1977. *The Production and Application of New Industrial Technologies*. New York: Norton.

Mansfield, E., J. Rapoport, J. Schnee, S. Wagner, and M. Hamburger. 1971. *Research and Innovation in the Modern Corporation*, New York: Norton.

Mansfield, E., A. Romeo, M. Schwartz, D. Teece, S. Wagner, and P. Brach. 1982. *Technology Transfer, Productivity, and Economic Policy*. New York: Norton.

Marer, Paul 1985. *Dollar GNPs of the USSR and Eastern Europe*. Baltimore: Johns Hopkins University Press.

Marer, Paul. 1978. "Toward a Solution of the Mirror Statistics Puzzle in East-West Commerce." In F. Levcik, ed., *International Economics: Comparisons and Interdependences*. Vienna: Springer-Verlag.

Markusen James R. 1986. "Explaining the Volume of Trade: An Eclectic Approach." *American Economic Review*, 76(5), pp. 1002–11.

Marrese, Michael, and Jan Vanous. 1983. *Soviet Subsidization of Trade with Eastern Europe: a Soviet Perspective*. Berkeley: Institute of International Studies, University of California.

Martens, John A. 1986. "Quantification of Western Exports of High-Technology Products to Communist Countries." In *East European Economies: Slow Growth in the 1980s, Vol. 2*. Washington, D.C.: Government Printing Office, March 28.

Marvel, Howard P. 1980. "Foreign Trade and Domestic Competition." *Economic Inquiry*, 18(1), pp. 103–22.

Marx, Karl, and Friedrick Engels. 1848. *Communist Manifesto*.

McIntyre, Robert J., and James R. Thornton. 1987. "On the Environmental Efficiency of Economic Systems." *Soviet Studies*, 30(2), pp. 173–92.

McNulty, Paul J. 1968. "Economic Theory and the Meaning of Competition." *Quarterly Journal of Economics*, 82(4), pp. 639–56.

Miller, Jeffrey, and Peter Murrell. 1981. "Limitations on the Use of Information Revealing Incentive Schemes in Economic Organizations." *Journal of Comparative Economics*, 5(3), pp. 251–70.

Mises, Lidwig von. 1932. *Socialism*. New York: Macmillan.

Mishan, Ezra J. 1981. *Introduction to Normative Economics*. Oxford: Oxford University Press.

Montias, John M. 1976. *The Structure of Economic Systems*. New Haven: Yale University Press.

Montias, John M. 1977. "Romania's Foreign Trade: An Overview." In *East European Economies Post-Helsinki*,Washington, D.C.: Government Printing Office, August 25.

Moorsteen, Richard H., and Raymond P. Powell. 1966. *The Soviet Capital Stock*, 1928–62. Homewood, Ill.: Irwin.

Morita, Akio. 1986. *Made in Japan: Akio Morita and Sony*. New York: Dutton.

Morrisson, Christian. 1984. "Income Distribution in East European and Western Countries." *Journal of Comparative Economics*, 8(2), pp. 121–38.

Mote, Victor. 1976. "The Geography of Air Pollution in the Soviet Union." In Fred Singleton ed., *Environmental Misuse in the Soviet Union*. New York: Praeger.

Mueller, Dennis C. 1986. *Profits in the Long Run*. Cambridge:Cambridge University Press.

Mueller, Dennis C., and Peter Murrell. 1986. "Interest Groups and the Size of Government." *Public Choice*, *48*(2), pp. 125–45.

Murrell, Peter. 1981. "An Evaluation of the Success of the Hungarian Economic Reform: An Analysis Using International-Trade Data." *Journal of Comparative Economics*, *5*(4), pp. 352–66.

Murrell, Peter. 1982. "Product Quality, Market Signaling, and the Development of East-West Trade." *Economic Inquiry*, *20*(4), pp. 589–603.

Murrell, Peter. 1983. "Did the Theory of Market Socialism Answer the Challenge of Ludwig von Mises? A Reinterpretation of the Socialist Controversy." *History of Political Economy*, *15*(1), pp. 92–105.

Murrell, Peter. 1984. "An Examination of the Factors Affecting the Formation of Interest Groups in OECD countries." *Public Choice*, *43*(2) pp. 151–71.

Murrell, Peter. 1986. "A Framework for Analysis of Bilateral Trade and Countertrade: The Case of the CMEA Countries." CPD Discussion Paper No. 1986–16, World Bank, March.

Nelson,Phillip. 1970. "Information and Consumer Behavior." *Journal of Political Economy*, *78*(2), pp. 311–37.

Nelson, Phillip. 1974. "Advertising as Information." *Journal of Political Economy*, *82*(4), pp. 729–54.

Nelson, Richard R. 1981. "Research on Productivity Growth and Differences." *Journal of Economic Literature*, *19*(3), pp. 1029–64.

Nelson, Richard R., and Sidney G. Winter. 1982. *An Evolutionary Theory of Economic Change*. Cambridge, Mass.: Harvard University Press.

Nie, Norman H. 1975. *SPSS: Statistical Package for the Social Sciences*, Second edition. New York: McGraw-Hill.

Nolting, Louvan E., and Murry Feshbach. 1979. "R & D Employment in the USSR: Definition, Statistics and Comparisons." In *Soviet Economy in a Time of Change, Vol. 1*. Washington, D.C.: Government Printing Office, October 10.

Nove, Alec. 1980. *The Soviet Economic System*. London: Allen and Unwin.

Novshek, William, and Hugo Sonnenschein. 1987. "General Equilibrium with Free Entry: A Synthetic Approach." *Journal of Economic Literature*, *25*(3), pp. 1281–1306.

Oblath, G., and P. Pete. 1985. "Trade with the Soviet Union: The Finnish Case." *Acta Oeconomica*, *35*(1–2), pp. 165–94.

Ofer, Gur. 1973. *The Service Sector in Soviet Economic Growth: A Comparative Study*. Cambridge, Mass.: Harvard University Press.

Olson, Mancur. 1965. *The Logic of Collective Action*. Cambridge, Mass.: Harvard University Press.

Olson, Mancur. 1982. *The Rise and Decline of Nations*. New Haven: Yale University Press.

Panagariya, Arvind. 1981. "Variable Returns to Scale in Production and Patterns of Specialization," *American Economic Review*, *71*(1), pp. 221–30.

Phlips, Louis. 1971. *Effects of Industrial Concentration: A Cross-Section Analysis for the Common Market*. Amsterdam: North-Holland.

PlanEcon Report. 1986. March 31, *2*(12–13).

Popa, Ioan. 1986. "Correlation of Prices and the Measurement of Efficiency in the Foreign Trade of the Socialist Countries." *Soviet and Eastern European Foreign Trade*, *22*(2), pp. 52–66.

Porter, Michael E. 1974. "Consumer Behavior, Retailer Power, and Market Performance in Consumer Goods Industries." *Review of Economics and Statistics*, 56(4), pp. 419–36.

Portes, Richard. 1972. "The Strategy and Tactics of Economic Decentralization." *Soviet Studies*, 23(4), pp. 629–58.

Portes, Richard, and David Winter. 1980. "Disequilibrium Estimates for Consumption Goods Markets in Centrally Planned Economies," *Review of Economic Studies*, 47(2), pp. 137–59.

Pryor, Frederic L. 1963. *Communist Foreign Trade System*. Cambridge, Mass.: MIT Press.

Pryor, Frederic L. 1973. *Property and Industrial Organization in Communist and Capitalist Nations*. Bloomington: Indiana University Press.

Pryor, Frederic L. 1985. *Guidebook to the Comparative Study of Economic Systems*. Englewood Cliffs, N.J.: Prentice-Hall.

Rapacki, Ryszard. 1982. "Factors Determining the Demand for Foreign Technology in a Socialist Economy." *Eastern European Economics*, 21(1), pp. 56–72.

Robison, David. 1983. *Three Applications of Input-Output Modeling*. Ph.D dissertation, University of Maryland.

Rosefielde, Steven. 1973. *Soviet International Trade in Heckscher-Ohlin Perspective: An Input-Output Study*. Lexington, Mass.: Lexington Books.

Rosefielde, Steven. 1981. "Comparative Advantage and the Evolving Pattern of Soviet International Commodity Specialization, 1950–1973." In Steven Rosefielde, ed., *Economic Welfare and the Economics of Soviet Socialism: Essays in Honor of Abram Bergson*. New York: Cambridge University Press.

Scherer, Frederic M. 1980. *Industrial Market Structure and Economic Performance*. Boston: Houghton Mifflin.

Scherer, Frederic M. 1984. "Using Linked Patent and R & D Data to Measure Interindustry Technology Flows." In Zvi Griliches, ed., *R & D, Patents, and Productivity*. Chicago: University of Chicago Press.

Schroeder, Gertrude E. 1983. "Consumption." In Abram Bergson, and Herbert S. Levine, eds., *The Soviet Economy: Toward the Year 2000*. London: Allen and Unwin.

Schumpeter, Joseph A. 1936. *The Theory of Economic Development*. Cambridge, Mass. Harvard University Press.

Schumpeter, Joseph A. 1950. *Capitalism, Socialism, and Democracy*. New York: Harper.

Shapiro, Carl. 1983. "Premiums for High Quality Products as Returns to Reputations." *Quarterly Journal of Economics*, 98(4), pp. 659–79.

Simon, Herbert A. 1977. *Models of Discovery*. Dordrecht: D. Reidel.

Skurski, Roger. 1983. *Soviet Marketing and Economic Development*. New York: St. Martin's Press.

Slama, Jiri. 1986. "An International Comparison of Sulphur Dioxide Emissions." *Journal of Comparative Economics*. 10(3), pp. 277–92.

Stahnke, Arthur A. 1981. "The Economic Dimensions and Political Context of FRG-GDR Trade." In *East European Economic Assessment, Part 1: Country Studies 1980*. Washington, D.C.: Government Printing Office, February 27.

Stiglitz, Joseph E. 1987. "The Causes and Consequences of the Dependence of Quality on Price." *Journal of Economic Literature*, 25(1), pp. 1–48.

Stollar, Andrew J., and G. Rodney Thompson. 1987. "Sectoral Employment Shares: A Comparative Systems Context." *Journal of Comparative Economics*, *11*(1), pp. 62–80.

Sturm, Peter H. 1977. "The System Component in Differences in Per Capita Output between East and West Germany." *Journal of Comparative Economics*, March *1*(1), pp. 5–24.

Summers, Robert, and Alan Heston. 1984. "Improved International Comparisons of Real Product and Its Composition, 1950–1980." *Review of Income and Wealth*, *30*(2), pp. 207–60.

Sveikauskas, Leo. 1983. "Science and Technology in United States Foreign Trade." *Economic Journal*, *93*(371), pp. 542–54.

Tardos, M. 1975. "Impacts of the World Economic Changes on the Hungarian Economy." *Acta Oeconomica*, *15*(3–4), pp. 277–91.

Tardos, M. 1976. "Commodity Pattern of Hungarian Foreign Trade." *Acta Oeconomica*, *17*(3–4), pp. 285–300.

Taylor, Charles L., and David A. Jodice. 1983. *A World Handbook of Political and Social Indicators*. Third edition. New Haven: Yale University Press.

Thornton, Judith. 1971. "Differential Capital Changes and Resource Allocation in Soviet Industry." *Journal of Political Economy*, *79*(3), pp. 545–61.

Treml, Vladimir G. 1981. "The Inferior Quality of Soviet Machinery as Reflected in Export Prices." *Journal of Comparative Economics*, *5*(2), pp. 200–221.

TSP International. 1986. *Time Series Processor*. Palo Alto, Calif.: TSP International.

U.N., Statistical Office. 1961. *Standard International Trade Classification, Revised*. New York: United Nations.

U.N., Statistical Office. 1975. *Yearbook of International Trade Statistics*. New York: United Nations.

UNESCO. 1986. *Statistical Yearbook*. New York: United Nations.

U.S. Department of Commerce. 1982. *Census of Manufactures*.

U.S. Tariff Commission. 1973. *Implications of Multinational Firms for World Trade and Investment and for U.S. Trade and Labor*. Washington, D.C.: Government Printing Office.

Utterback, J. M. 1979. "The Dynamics of Product and Process Innovation." In C. T. Hill and J. M. Utterback, eds., *Technological Innovation for a Dynamic Economy*. New York: Pergamon Press.

Vanous, Jan. 1981a. "Soviet and Eastern European Foreign Trade in the 1970s: A Quantitative Assessment." In *East European Economic Assessment, Part 2: Regional Assessments*. Washington, D.C.: Government Printing Office, July 10.

Vanous, Jan. 1981b. "Eastern European and Soviet Fuel Trade, 1970–1985." In *East European Economic Assessment, Part 2: Regional Assessments*. Washington, D.C.: Government Printing Office, July 10.

Varian, Hal R. 1984. *Microeconomic Analysis*. New York: Norton.

Vernon, Raymond. 1966. "International Investment and Interational Trade in the Product Cycle." *Quarterly Journal of Economics*, *80*(2) pp. 190–207.

Vernon, Raymond. 1966. "International Investment and International Trade in the Product Cycle." *Quarterly Journal of Economics*, *80*(2) pp. 190–207.

Vernon, Raymond. 1979. "The Product Cycle Hypothesis in a New International Environment." *Oxford Bulletin of Economics and Statistics*, *41*(4) pp. 255–67.

Vernon, Raymond. 1980. "The Multinationalization of U.S. Business: Some Basic

Policy Implications." In *Special Study on Economic Change, Volume 9: The International Economy, U.S. Role in a World Market*. Washington, D.C.: Government Printing Office, December 17.

Watson Robin A. 1981. "The Linkage between Energy and Growth Prospects in Eastern Europe," In *East European Economic Assessment, Part 2: Regional Assessments*. Washington, D.C.: Government Printing Office, July 10.

Whitesell, Robert S. 1987. "Comparing Allocative Inefficiency in Four Countries: U.S., USSR, Hungary, and West Germany." Paper presented at the Third Annual Workshop on Soviet and East European Economics, Georgetown University, July.

Wiedeman, P. 1984. "Socio-economic Development in the EEC and the CMEA." *Cambridge Journal of Economics 8*(9), pp. 311–30.

Wilczynski, J. 1965. "The Theory of Comparative Costs and Centrally Planned Economies." *The Economic Journal, 75*(297).

Wilczynski, J. 1974. *Technology in Comecon: Acceleration of Technological Progress Through Economic Planning and the Market*. New York: Praeger.

Wilczynski, Jozef. 1975. "Developmental Strategies and the Quality of Production under Socialist Economic Planning." *Bangladesh Development Studies. 3*(2), pp. 127–52.

Wiles, Peter J. D. 1968. *Communist International Economics*. New York: Praeger.

Wiles, Peter J. D. 1977. *Economic Institutions Compared*. New York: Wiley.

Williamson, Oliver E. 1975. *Markets and Hierarchies, Analysis and Antitrust Implications; A Study in the Economics of Internal Organization*. New York: Free Press.

Winiecki, Jan. 1986. "Are Soviet-Type Economies Entering an Era of Long-Term Decline?" *Soviet Studies. 38*(3), pp. 325–48.

Wolf, Thomas. 1982. "Optimal Foreign Trade for the Price-Insensitive Soviet-Type Economy." *Journal of Comparative Economics, 6*(3), pp. 37–54.

Zaleski, Eugene. 1971. *Planning for Economic Growth in the Soviet Union, 1918–1932*. Chapel Hill: University of North Carolina Press.

Zaleski, Eugene, and Helgard Wienert. 1980. *Technology Transfer between East and West*. Paris: OECD.

ZumBrunnen, Craig. 1976. "Water Pollution in the Black and Azov Seas." In Fred Singleton, ed., *Environmental Misuse in the Soviet Union*. New York: Praeger.

Index